T0178210

Lecture Notes in Computer Science 13030

More information about this subseries at http://www.springer.com/series/7407

Ernst-Rüdiger Olderog ·
Bernhard Steffen · Wang Yi (Eds.)

Model Checking, Synthesis, and Learning

Essays Dedicated to Bengt Jonsson on The Occasion of His 60th Birthday

Editors
Ernst-Rüdiger Olderog
Universität Oldenburg
Oldenburg, Germany

Bernhard Steffen
TU Dortmund University
Dortmund, Germany

Wang Yi
Uppsala University
Uppsala, Sweden

ISSN 0302-9743 ISSN 1611-3349 (electronic)
Lecture Notes in Computer Science
ISBN 978-3-030-91383-0 ISBN 978-3-030-91384-7 (eBook)
https://doi.org/10.1007/978-3-030-91384-7

LNCS Sublibrary: SL1 – Theoretical Computer Science and General Issues

Cover illustration: Essays Dedicated to Bengt Jonsson on the Occasion of his 60th Birthday

This Springer imprint is published by the registered company Springer Nature Switzerland AG
The registered company address is: Gewerbestrasse 11, 6330 Cham, Switzerland

Preface

The traditional measure of quality assurance is testing. Verification, or even the synthesis of programs were considered the "higher art" of achieving system reliability, accomplished via so-called formal methods. Practice has shown, however, that there are no ways around test-based quality assurance: the verification problems are typically undecidable, and even if they were decidable, they would only cover a certain level of abstraction and not the entire system as it runs in its productive environment.

This Festschrift, dedicated to Bengt Jonsson on the occasion of his 60th birthday, indicates such a return to the basics. While the beginning of Bengt's career was clearly devoted to verfication, later he became interested in test-based methods, which of course he approached in a truly formal methods-based fashion. And always with the goal to reach the stars, or, more technically expressed, to do battle with the limits of decidability. The nine invited contributions and the corresponding wealth of references to Bengt's work provided in this Festschrift illustrate the style and influence of his trendsetting efforts.

Ernst-Rüdiger Olderog
Bernhard Steffen
Wang Yi

Organization

Editors

Ernst-Rüdiger Olderog	University of Oldenburg, Germany
Bernhard Steffen	TU Dortmund, Germany
Wang Yi	Uppsala University, Sweden

Contents

Model Checking, Synthesis, and Learning

Ernst-Rüdiger Olderog[1], Bernhard Steffen[2(✉)], and Wang Yi[3]

[1] Department of Computer Science, University of Oldenburg, Oldenburg, Germany
Olderog@Informatik.Uni-Oldenburg.DE

[2] Chair for Programming Systems, TU Dortmund University, Dortmund, Germany
steffen@cs.tu-dortmund.de

[3] Department of Information Technology, Uppsala University, Uppsala, Sweden
wang.yi@it.uu.se

Abstract. Reliability is a central concern of software system development. It can be approached in three ways, in a post-mortem fashion via verification of an unknown artefact, by construction applying correctness preserving steps, and via testing of the final product. In this paper, we introduce the nine contributions to the Festschrift dedicated to Bengt Jonsson on the occasion of his 60th birthday. Verification is addressed here from the model checking perspective, correctness by construction via synthesis, and testing as both a means and a as by-product of active automata learning while reflecting on the impact Bengt had on these developments.

Keywords: Linear-time temporal logic · Büchi automata · Verification · (Regular) Model checking · Petri-nets · Petri games · Model synthesis · Timed systems · Probabilistic systems · Markov chains · Automata learning · Register automata

1 Bengt Jonsson: A Multi-talent

In the 1980s, we met Bengt and were amazed by his many talents. The first meeting took place during an *Advanced Course on Logics and Models for Verification and Specification of Concurrent Systems* organized by Krzysztof Apt in the beautiful La Colle-sur-Loup, France, in October 1984. I, Ernst-Rüdiger, was among the 17 lecturers and Bengt was in the audience. I was lecturing on what I called *Specification-oriented Programming in TCSP*, a topic that grew out of my research on communicating processes that started during a postdoctoral stay at the Programming Research Group in Oxford led by Tony Hoare. Bengt had returned to Uppsala, Sweden, from studies at Stanford University. We were both fascinated by the presentation of Jay Misra on his work with Mani Chandy on *Quiescent Properties in Distributed Computations*, which addressed asynchronous communication in networks rather than the synchronous communication that is at the heart of Hoare's CSP. Willem Paul de Roever, also one of the lecturers, suggested to Bengt in his usual style: "You should visit Ernst-Rüdiger in Kiel." This is what happened.

E.-R. Olderog et al. (Eds.): Jonsson Festschrift, LNCS 13030, pp. 1–7, 2021.
https://doi.org/10.1007/978-3-030-91384-7_1

During the period 1984–1987 Bengt visited several times Kiel to discuss semantic issues of quiescent traces in asynchronous networks. Most notable is his first visit to Kiel in December 1984. His arrival coincided with the start of a longer research stay of Dr. Vitaliy Zubenko from Kiev University, Ukraine, in Kiel. Dr. Zubenko was to visit my supervisor Prof. Hans Langmaack, but it turned out that initially he could speak neither German nor English, a difficult start when lot of formal documents need to be filled. At this stage, Bengt admitted that he can speak a little bit of Russian. Well, it turned out that he spoke fluently Russian, at least fluently enough to serve as a perfect interpreter during the first crucial day of Dr. Zubenko in Kiel.

In the evening of that day, the Langmaacks invited the visitors and his assistants, among them Bernhard Steffen, to a dinner in their home. Mrs Annemarie Langmaack is a great violin player and talked to Bengt. He admitted that he can play piano. Then the guests of that evening were fascinated by Bengt playing pieces of Chopin on Langmaack's piano. Also present at the meeting was Maja, a lady from Ukraine. She turned out to be a gifted singer who would present Ukrainian songs. It was a most beautiful closing of a busy day. Bengt had surprised us with his talents for languages and music. Our scientific meetings also progressed well.

Bengt quickly picked up some suggestions and published his very first paper entitled *A Model and Proof System for Asynchronous Networks* at the renowned ACM Symposium on Principles of Distributed Computing in 1985 [28]. Two years later, he defended his PhD thesis on Compositional Verification of Distributed Systems at Uppsala University.

Scientifically, Bengt Jonsson has made major contributions covering a wide range of topics including verification and learning. His works on verification, infinite-state systems, learning, testing, probabilistic systems, timed systems, and distributed systems reflect both the diversity and the depth of his research. This is witnessed also by his receiving the CAV Award 2017:

> "Parosh Abdulla, Alain Finkel, Bengt Johnsson, and Philippe Schnoebelen receive the CAV Award 2017 for the development of general mathematical structures leading to general decidability results for the verification of infinite-state transition systems."

Besides being an excellent scientist, Bengt is also a leader who has greatly influenced the careers of his students and his colleagues. In the remainder of this paper, we will sketch central elements of Bengt's work along nine invited contributions.

2 Model Checking, Synthesis, and Learning

Scientifically, Bengt's work started with verification [28,29]. The first contribution to this Festschrift refers to a later paper [34]. In *From Linear Temporal Logics to Büchi Automata: The Early and Simple Principle*, Moshe Vardi and Yih-Kuen Tsay reflect on the key principle of linear-time model checking, the translation into Büchi automata, while, in particular, considering the extension to past-time operators [36].

Considering time seems like a natural extension to systematic system analysis. The second contribution to the volume, *Cause-Effect Reaction Latency In Real-Time Systems* [1] by Wang Yi and Jakaria Abdulla, relates to [22,23]. It considers the impact of latency constraints, i.e., of the maximum time an input is allowed to impact a corresponding output. In particular, it provides an algorithm for the safe estimation of the worst-case cause-effect latency for systems following a protocol for non-blocking communication.

Dealing with uncertainty is another natural extension of the scope of verification. The third contribution, *Quantitative Analysis of Interval Markov Chains* [9] by Kim Larsen, Giovanni Bacci, Benoit Delahaye, and Anders Mariegaard bases on [30] where Interval Markov chains (IMCs) were introduced. The paper extends IMC with rewards and compares three corresponding semantics in the context of model checking, shows their equivalence in a reward-bounded setting, and provides corresponding model checking algorithms.

The step moving from regular systems to systems whose state space can be described in a regular fashion generalizes model checking to a verification discipline for infinite systems. The fourth contribution, *Regular Model Checking: Evolution and Perspectives*, by Parosh Abdulla sketches the development of regular model checking in a tutorial-like fashion, providing also direktions to future research. The presented development is strongly linked to contributions of Bengt Jonsson [3,5,6,14,33].

Conceptually different is the step from model checking to model synthesis: it is the step from 'post-mortem' verification to correctness by construction. The fifth contribution, *Regular Model Checking Revisited* by Philipp Rümmer and Anthony Lin [35], is also based on seminal work by Bengt Jonsson et al. on regular model checking [2,4,7]. It shows that a reformulation of regular model checking with length-preserving transducers in terms of existential second-order theory over automatic structures enables powerful synthesis techniques that have been extensively studied in the software verification community.

Also the sixth contribution, *High-Level Representation of Benchmark Families for Petri Games* by Ernst-Rüdiger Olderog and Manuel Gieseking [21], addresses synthesis, this time in a game-based fashion based on Petri Nets. Novel is the study of representing benchmark families for the synthesis of distributed systems modeled with Petri games by specifying an entire benchmark family as one parameterized high-level net.

The shift from verification/synthesis to model (automata) learning is radical. Neither correctness nor completeness can be guaranteed. In practice, automata learning rather provides a systematic, and in a sense optimal, continuous improvement process. Bengt was torn into this field from two sides: The connection to model-based testing [10], and the treatment of potentially infinite sets of data [11,12,18,25,26], an aspect discussed in more detail in the eight contribution to the volume from the perspective of expressiveness.

The seventh contribution to this volume, *Towards Engineering Digital Twins by Active Behaviour Mining* by Tiziana Margaria and Alexander Schieweck [8], applies automata learning for deriving a digital twin for a small cyberphysical system. The paper illustrates the approach and draws a connection towards verification via model checking of the learned digital twin and feature-based, incremental requirement specification [31,32].

The eighth contribution, *Never-Stop Context-Free Learning* by Bernhard Steffen and Markus Frohme [20], elaborates on the fact that the continuous improvement cycle of automata learning [13] of realistic systems typically never ends. The approach is unique in that it treats context-free systems, which, in fact, turn out to be well-suited to deal with the enormous length of monitoring-based counter examples.

The final contribution, *A Taxonomy and Reductions for Common Register Automata Formalisms* by Falk Howar and Simon Dierl [24], explores the expressiveness of a number of formalisms for specifying automata models over infinite alphabets [15–17,19,27]. Combining a number of small-step reductions it is shown that all the considered languages for modelling various notions of register automata are equally expressive.

3 Closing Remark

Bengt as an orienteering racer does not fear hurdles and hardly gets lost. When he wants to achieve something nobody would stop him. When I (Bernhard) started to collaborate with him on automata learning, he immediately aimed at looking at data and infinite alphabets. I am used to jogging and hiking, but some of the routes Bengt took were beyond my zone of comfort. Years later we (this time together with Falk Howar) converged again, establishing a very natural notion of register automata for which active automata learning was still effective. Of course, Bengt immediately started to push further towards the regions of undecidability. This is Bengt, restless, and never satisfied with what he has achieved, two properties that guarantee progress and success.

References

1. Abdulla, J., Yi, W.: Cause-effect reaction latency in real-time systems. In: Olderog, E.-R., et al. (eds.) Jonsson Festschrift. LNCS, vol. 13030, pp. 41–56. Springer, Cham (2021)
2. Abdulla, P.A., Bouajjani, A., Jonsson, B., Nilsson, M.: Handling global conditions in parametrized system verification. In: Halbwachs, N., Peled, D. (eds.) CAV 1999. LNCS, vol. 1633, pp. 134–145. Springer, Heidelberg (1999). https://doi.org/10.1007/3-540-48683-6_14
3. Abdulla, P.A., Cerans, K., Jonsson, B., Tsay, Y.: General decidability theorems for infinite-state systems. In: Proceedings of the 11th Annual IEEE Symposium on Logic in Computer Science, New Brunswick, New Jersey, USA, 27–30 July 1996, pp. 313–321. IEEE Computer Society (1996). https://doi.org/10.1109/LICS.1996.561359

4. Abdulla, P.A., Jonsson, B., Mahata, P., d'Orso, J.: Regular tree model checking. In: Brinksma, E., Larsen, K.G. (eds.) CAV 2002. LNCS, vol. 2404, pp. 555–568. Springer, Heidelberg (2002). https://doi.org/10.1007/3-540-45657-0_47
5. Abdulla, P.A., Jonsson, B., Nilsson, M., d'Orso, J.: Regular model checking made simple and effcient*. In: Brim, L., Křetínský, M., Kučera, A., Jančar, P. (eds.) CONCUR 2002. LNCS, vol. 2421, pp. 116–131. Springer, Heidelberg (2002). https://doi.org/10.1007/3-540-45694-5_9
6. Abdulla, P.A., Jonsson, B., Nilsson, M., d'Orso, J.: Algorithmic improvements in regular model checking. In: Hunt, W.A., Somenzi, F. (eds.) CAV 2003. LNCS, vol. 2725, pp. 236–248. Springer, Heidelberg (2003). https://doi.org/10.1007/978-3-540-45069-6_25
7. Abdulla, P.A., Jonsson, B., Nilsson, M., Saksena, M.: A survey of regular model checking. In: Gardner, P., Yoshida, N. (eds.) CONCUR 2004. LNCS, vol. 3170, pp. 35–48. Springer, Heidelberg (2004). https://doi.org/10.1007/978-3-540-28644-8_3
8. Margaria, T., Schieweck, A.: Towards engineering digital twins by active behaviour mining. In: Olderog, E.-R., et al. (eds.) Jonsson Festschrift. LNCS, vol. 13030, pp. 138–163. Springer, Cham (2021)
9. Bacci, G., Delahaye, B., Larsen, K., Mariegaardwhich, A.: Quantitative analysis of interval Markov chains. In: Olderog, E.-R., et al. (eds.) Jonsson Festschrift. LNCS, vol. 13030, pp. 57–77. Springer, Cham (2021)
10. Berg, T., Grinchtein, O., Jonsson, B., Leucker, M., Raffelt, H., Steffen, B.: On the correspondence between conformance testing and regular inference. In: Cerioli, M. (ed.) FASE 2005. LNCS, vol. 3442, pp. 175–189. Springer, Heidelberg (2005). https://doi.org/10.1007/978-3-540-31984-9_14
11. Berg, T., Jonsson, B., Raffelt, H.: Regular inference for state machines with parameters. In: Baresi, L., Heckel, R. (eds.) FASE 2006. LNCS, vol. 3922, pp. 107–121. Springer, Heidelberg (2006). https://doi.org/10.1007/11693017_10
12. Berg, T., Jonsson, B., Raffelt, H.: Regular inference for state machines using domains with equality tests. In: Fiadeiro, J.L., Inverardi, P. (eds.) FASE 2008. LNCS, vol. 4961, pp. 317–331. Springer, Heidelberg (2008). https://doi.org/10.1007/978-3-540-78743-3_24
13. Bertolino, A., Calabrò, A., Merten, M., Steffen, B.: Never-stop learning: continuous validation of learned models for evolving systems through monitoring. ERCIM News **2012**(88) (2012)
14. Bouajjani, A., Jonsson, B., Nilsson, M., Touili, T.: Regular model checking. In: Emerson, E.A., Sistla, A.P. (eds.) CAV 2000. LNCS, vol. 1855, pp. 403–418. Springer, Heidelberg (2000). https://doi.org/10.1007/10722167_31
15. Cassel, S., Howar, F., Jonsson, B., Merten, M., Steffen, B.: A succinct canonical register automaton model. In: Bultan, T., Hsiung, P.-A. (eds.) ATVA 2011. LNCS, vol. 6996, pp. 366–380. Springer, Heidelberg (2011). https://doi.org/10.1007/978-3-642-24372-1_26
16. Cassel, S., Howar, F., Jonsson, B., Steffen, B.: Learning extended finite state machines. In: Giannakopoulou, D., Salaün, G. (eds.) SEFM 2014. LNCS, vol. 8702, pp. 250–264. Springer, Cham (2014). https://doi.org/10.1007/978-3-319-10431-7_18
17. Cassel, S., Howar, F., Jonsson, B., Steffen, B.: Active learning for extended finite state machines. Formal Aspects Comput. **28**(2), 233–263 (2016). https://doi.org/10.1007/s00165-016-0355-5
18. Cassel, S., Howar, F., Jonsson, B., Steffen, B.: Extending automata learning to extended finite state machines. In: Bennaceur, A., Hähnle, R., Meinke, K. (eds.)

Machine Learning for Dynamic Software Analysis: Potentials and Limits. LNCS, vol. 11026, pp. 149–177. Springer, Cham (2018). https://doi.org/10.1007/978-3-319-96562-8_6
19. Cassel, S., Jonsson, B., Howar, F., Steffen, B.: A succinct canonical register automaton model for data domains with binary relations. In: Chakraborty, S., Mukund, M. (eds.) ATVA 2012. LNCS, pp. 57–71. Springer, Heidelberg (2012). https://doi.org/10.1007/978-3-642-33386-6_6
20. Frohme, M., Steffen, B.: Never-stop context-free learning. In: Olderog, E.-R., et al. (eds.) Jonsson Festschrift. LNCS, vol. 13030, pp. 164–185. Springer, Cham (2021)
21. Gieseking, M., Olderog, E.R.: High-level representation of benchmark families for petri games. In: Olderog, E.-R., et al. (eds.) Jonsson Festschrift. LNCS, vol. 13030, pp. 115–137. Springer, Cham (2021)
22. Hansson, H., Jonsson, B.: A framework for reasoning about time and reliability. In: Proceedings of the Real-Time Systems Symposium, Santa Monica, California, USA, December 1989, pp. 102–111. IEEE Computer Society (1989). https://doi.org/10.1109/REAL.1989.63561
23. Hansson, H., Jonsson, B.: A logic for reasoning about time and reliability. Formal Aspects Comput. **6**(5), 512–535 (1994). https://doi.org/10.1007/BF01211866
24. Howar, F., Dierl, S.: A taxonomy and reductions for common register automata formalisms. In: Olderog, E.-R., et al. (eds.) Jonsson Festschrift. LNCS, vol. 13030, pp. 186–218. Springer, Cham (2021)
25. Howar, F., Jonsson, B., Merten, M., Steffen, B., Cassel, S.: On handling data in automata learning. In: Margaria, T., Steffen, B. (eds.) ISoLA 2010. LNCS, vol. 6416, pp. 221–235. Springer, Heidelberg (2010). https://doi.org/10.1007/978-3-642-16561-0_24
26. Howar, F., Jonsson, B., Vaandrager, F.: Combining black-box and white-box techniques for learning register automata. In: Steffen, B., Woeginger, G. (eds.) Computing and Software Science. LNCS, vol. 10000, pp. 563–588. Springer, Cham (2019). https://doi.org/10.1007/978-3-319-91908-9_26
27. Howar, F., Steffen, B., Jonsson, B., Cassel, S.: Inferring canonical register automata. In: Kuncak, V., Rybalchenko, A. (eds.) VMCAI 2012. LNCS, vol. 7148, pp. 251–266. Springer, Heidelberg (2012). https://doi.org/10.1007/978-3-642-27940-9_17
28. Jonsson, B.: A model and proof system for asynchronous networks. In: Malcolm, M.A., Strong, H.R. (eds.) Proceedings of the Fourth Annual ACM Symposium on Principles of Distributed Computing, Minaki, Ontario, Canada, 5–7 August 1985, pp. 49–58. ACM (1985). https://doi.org/10.1145/323596.323601
29. Jonsson, B.: Modular verification of asynchronous networks. In: Schneider, F.B. (ed.) Proceedings of the Sixth Annual ACM Symposium on Principles of Distributed Computing, Vancouver, British Columbia, Canada, 10–12 August 1987, pp. 152–166. ACM (1987). https://doi.org/10.1145/41840.41853
30. Jonsson, B., Larsen, K.G.: Specification and refinement of probabilistic processes. In: Proceedings of the Sixth Annual Symposium on Logic in Computer Science (LICS '91), Amsterdam, The Netherlands, 15–18 July 1991, pp. 266–277. IEEE Computer Society (1991). https://doi.org/10.1109/LICS.1991.151651
31. Jonsson, B., Margaria, T., Naeser, G., Nyström, J., Steffen, B.: Incremental requirement specification for evolving systems. In: Calder, M., Magill, E.H. (eds.) Feature Interactions in Telecommunications and Software Systems VI, Glasgow, Scotland, UK, 17–19 May 2000, pp. 145–162. IOS Press (2000)
32. Jonsson, B., Margaria, T., Naeser, G., Nyström, J., Steffen, B.: Incremental requirement specification for evolving systems. Nord. J. Comput. **8**(1), 65–87 (2001)

33. Jonsson, B., Nilsson, M.: Transitive closures of regular relations for verifying infinite-state systems. In: Graf, S., Schwartzbach, M. (eds.) TACAS 2000. LNCS, vol. 1785, pp. 220–235. Springer, Heidelberg (2000). https://doi.org/10.1007/3-540-46419-0_16
34. Jonsson, B., Tsay, Y.: Assumption/guarantee specifications in linear-time temporal logic. Theor. Comput. Sci. **167**(1 & 2), 47–72 (1996). https://doi.org/10.1016/0304-3975(96)00069-2
35. Lin, A., Rümmer, P.: Regular model checking revisited. In: Olderog, E.-R., et al. (eds.) Jonsson Festschrift. LNCS, vol. 13030, pp. 97–114. Springer, Cham (2021)
36. Tsay, Y., Vardi, M.: From linear temporal logics to büchi automata: the early and simple principle. In: Olderog, E.-R., et al. (eds.) Jonsson Festschrift. LNCS, vol. 13030, pp. 8–40. Springer, Cham (2021)

From Linear Temporal Logics to Büchi Automata: The Early and Simple Principle

Yih-Kuen Tsay[1](✉) and Moshe Y. Vardi[2]

[1] National Taiwan University, Taipei, Taiwan
tsay@ntu.edu.tw
[2] Rice University, Houston, USA

Abstract. The automata-theoretic approach advocates reducing problems in an application domain to those in automata theory. When there are multiple paths for the reduction, leaving the realm of application and entering that of automata as *early* as possible should be preferred, to take full advantages of the abundant algorithmic techniques from the latter, This makes the entire reduction *simpler* for intuitive understanding and easier for correctness proofs. Indeed, for linear-time temporal logic model checking, there are quite a few ways for translating a temporal formula into an equivalent Büchi automaton. They all go through one or more types of automata as intermediaries, with various interspersing formula manipulation and automaton generation along the way. Among them, translations via alternating automata apparently better adhere to the aforementioned "early and simple" principle. When it comes to translating temporal formulae with past operators, algorithms following the principle generalize more easily by using a two-way alternating automaton as the first intermediary.

In this paper, we give a tutorial presentation of two translation algorithms adhering to the early and simple principle, one for formulae with only future operators and the other for formulae with both future and past operators. They are adaptations of existing works, with a substantially different exposition, further improving simplicity for understanding and easiness for proofs. In particular, we have tried wherever possible to avoid using types of automata or notations that are less common. The relevant notion of a very weak automaton is introduced with two equivalent defining conditions, each offering its unique advantage in a suitable context. Finally, we discuss the role of minimization in such an approach to translation of temporal formulae.

Keywords: Alternating automata · Automata-theoretic approach · Büchi automata · Linear temporal logic · LTL · ω-Automata · PTL · Translation · Two-way automata · Very weak automata

1 Introduction

The automata-theoretic approach advocates reducing problems in an application domain to those in automata theory. In the mid 1980's, Vardi and Wolper [33]

E.-R. Olderog et al. (Eds.): Jonsson Festschrift, LNCS 13030, pp. 8–40, 2021.
https://doi.org/10.1007/978-3-030-91384-7_2

proposed such an approach to the automatic verification of concurrent finite-state systems by model checking, where the correctness of a system with respect to a specification is reduced to the emptiness of a product automaton representing the intersection of the system and the negation of the specification. Model-checking algorithms derived from their approach tend to be simpler and cleaner than tableau-based algorithms. An even more important advantage of the approach is generalizability, to different specification languages or systems and even beyond verification to synthesis as conceived by the seminal work of Pnueli and Rosner [24].

When there are multiple paths for the reduction, leaving the realm of application and entering that of automata as *early* as possible should be preferred, to take full advantages of the abundant algorithmic techniques from the latter. This makes the entire reduction *simpler* for intuitive understanding and easier for correctness proofs. Indeed, for linear-time temporal logic model checking, there are quite a few ways for translating a temporal formula into an equivalent Büchi automaton, e.g., [6,8–14,27]. They all go through one or more types of automata as intermediaries, including particularly generalized Büchi automata [4], with various interspersing formula manipulation and automaton generation along the way. Among them, translations via alternating automata apparently better adhere to the aforementioned "early and simple" principle.

Alternating automata extend nondeterministic automata to allow and-branching, which may be used to force simultaneous acceptance from a selected set of states. Boolean combinations in the input temporal formula can therefore be treated directly by alternation, rather than by restructuring automaton-states when only nondeterminism is available. Consequently, why the constructed intermediate automaton is equivalent to the input temporal formula becomes much clearer. When it comes to translating temporal formulae with past operators, algorithms following the early and simple principle generalize more easily by using a two-way alternating automaton as the first intermediary.

In this paper, we give a tutorial presentation of two translation algorithms adhering to the early and simple principle, one for formulae with only future operators, namely LTL formulae, and the other for formulae with both future and past operators, namely PTL formulae. They both use alternating automata as the first intermediary and, for PTL formulae, the additional machinery of a two-way automaton is employed. The extension of the first algorithm to the second for this part is nearly effortless. Although the subsequent conversions of automata are harder when two-way movements of the read head on the input word are involved, we have much to borrow from the algorithmic techniques developed in automata theory.

The algorithms are adaptations of existing works, specifically those of Vardi [31], Gastin and Oddoux [11,12], and De Wulf, Doyen, Maquet, and Raskin [7], with a substantially different exposition, further improving simplicity for intuitive understanding and easiness for correctness proofs. In particular, we have tried wherever possible to avoid using types of automata or notations that are less common. The relevant notion of a very weak automaton is introduced with two equivalent defining conditions, each offering its unique advantage in a suitable context. Finally, we discuss the role of minimization in such an approach to translation of temporal formulae.

Before we embark on the exposition, a few words about past temporal operators are in order. We have considered past operators for their several advantages, as also having been pointed out by many other researchers, e.g., [18,20]. Though expressively equivalent to LTL, PTL is more intuitive. For example, to say "a grant has to be preceded by a request", one may write $\Box(g \rightarrow \ominus \Diamond\!\!\!-\, r)$ instead of $\neg(\neg r\ \mathcal{U}\, g)$; the semantics of temporal operators is given in the preliminaries section. To say "assume $\Box p$, guarantee $\Box q$", one may write $\Box(\circleddash \boxminus p \rightarrow q)$ (or equivalently, $\Box(\circleddash \boxminus p \rightarrow \boxminus q)$) [16] instead of $\neg p\ \mathcal{R}\, q$. (Note: $\Box(\circleddash \boxminus p \rightarrow q) \wedge \Box(\circleddash \boxminus q \rightarrow p)$ implies $\Box p \wedge \Box q$; this is a well-known mutual induction technique in modular reasoning.) Past operators are also instrumental for classification. For example, $\neg p\ \mathcal{W}\, q$ and $\Box(p \rightarrow \Diamond\!\!\!-\, q)$ are equivalent, but the latter is clearly a safety formula judging from its form; $\Box(p \rightarrow \Diamond q)$ (p "leads-to" q) is equivalent to $\Box\Diamond(\neg p\ \mathcal{B}\, q)$, which is a recurrence property [21]. PTL can be exponentially more succinct than LTL [18]. In some cases, however, temporal formulae using past operators may be longer and their translation may result in larger automata.[1]

A Brief History. The remainder of this section is a brief historical account of research on translation of linear temporal formulae into Büchi automata. Such research works predated the proposal of the automata-theoretic approach by Vardi and Wolper. In particular, the work of Wolper [34] on the expressiveness of linear temporal logic contains a tableau-based decision procedure, which may be adapted to obtain a translation algorithm into generalized Büchi automata. The tableau-based algorithm of Lichtenstein and Pnueli [19] for checking that a system satisfies a linear temporal specification may also be adapted for translation. Extension of such algorithms to handle past operators was quite straightforward and one extension was presented in [19] and also in a related work of Lichtenstein, Pnueli, and Zuck [20] that promotes past operators. The problem is that, with the main purpose of proving an upper bound, these algorithms always get the worst-case exponential blow-up on the number of automaton-states. Nevertheless, these early works established very basic techniques in translation: (automaton-)states represent formulae, and a formula with a leading next operator relates two states such that a transition goes from one state for the formula to the other state for the same formula with the next operator removed.

Another related work is by Wolper, Vardi, and Sistla [35] who investigated variants of linear temporal logic with the same expressive power as Büchi automata. To solve the standard decision problems for those logics, they resorted to translation into Büchi automata. In the interest of expressiveness, however,

[1] The equivalence between two temporal formulae can be conveniently checked with, e.g., the GOAL tool [29].

their temporal logics use automaton structures in place of temporal operators. It is not immediately clear how their translation algorithms could be used to treat formulae with real temporal operators.

The simple on-the-fly algorithm of Gerth, Peled, Vardi, and Wolper [13] is probably the most well-known and influential translation algorithm. It uses generalized Büchi automata as an intermediary. Starting with a single node for the input formula, the algorithm proceeds in a depth-first manner, recursively splitting an existing node or generating new nodes as the formula represented by the current node is expanded and processed. The technique may be categorized as an "incremental" tableau construction according to Kesten, Manna, McGuire, and Pnueli [17], who earlier proposed an incremental (but not quite on-the-fly) translation algorithm for formula with past operators. For an incremental construction, past operators posed some difficulty and required multiple passes as opposed to a single pass for future operators. This is in contrast with the "declarative" tableau constructions in [19,20], which are more intuitive, but always suffer from the worst-case exponential blow-up.

Several subsequent works, including Daniele, Giunchiglia, and Vardi [6], Couvreur [5], Somenzi and Bloem [27], Etessami and Holzmann [8], and Giannakopoulou and Lerda [14] use the on-the-fly algorithm of Gerth *et al.* as a basis. Couvreur proposed to compute node expansions symbolically and impose acceptance conditions on transitions. The work of Daniele *et al.* employs a uniform presentation using the notion of a cover, which is essentially a break-down of the alternatives to satisfy a formula. They also investigated contradiction and redundancy detection relying only on the syntax of temporal formulae. Giannakopoulou and Lerda followed the same line, but chose to get closer to the usual convention of labeling input symbols on the transitions for which some simulation relation and hence redundancy is easier to detect; they also chose to impose acceptance conditions on transitions. The improvements by Somenzi and Bloem and by Etessami and Holzmann were mainly about reducing the number of automaton-states using formula rewriting and simulation relations in intermediate automata. Analysis of the acceptance set and the structure of the transition graph was also considered. All these algorithms deal only with future operators and an extension to past operators is not immediately clear, as experienced by Kesten *et al.* in an incremental construction.

Using alternating automata as the first intermediary in translation was proposed by Vardi [31]. Boolean combinations in the input temporal formula were treated directly by alternation in the intermediate automaton, and the equivalence between the constructed automaton and the input temporal formula became much clearer. With the standard construction of Miyano and Hayashi [23] for alternating automata into Büchi automata conversion, the correctness of the entire translation algorithm follows immediately. However, it would take another few years for the notion of a very weak automaton to be discovered by Rohde [25] and later exploited by Gastin and Oddoux [11] to obtain a translation algorithm competitive enough for practical uses. Further improvements using simulations were subsequently proposed by Fritz [9,10]. In another branch of work, De Wulf, Doyen, Maquet, and Raskin [7] proposed to use a symbolic representation of the alternating automaton from a temporal formula, which suffices for setting up fix-point calculations for satisfiability or model checking and avoids the immediate exponential blow-up in an explicit representation of the transitions.

The use of two-way automata to handle past operators was also proposed by Vardi [30,32]. Gastin and Oddoux [12] adopted the idea to generalize their translation algorithm for LTL to one for PTL. Their algorithm takes a PTL formula as input, translates it into a two-way alternating automaton which is very weak, converts the alternating automaton into a generalized Büchi automaton (with acceptance conditions on the transitions), and then to Büchi automaton. The correspondence between the input formula and the first intermediate automaton is clear as expected, though subsequent conversions are a bit involved.

2 Preliminaries

2.1 Symbols, Words, and Languages

A *word* (or string) is a sequence of symbols taken from some finite alphabet and a *language* is just a set of words. An *infinite* word is a word of infinite length, i.e., an infinite sequence of symbols. Inputs to Büchi automata and other ω-automata are infinite words. They also serve as models for interpreting temporal formulae, when one regards the symbols in a word as truth assignments to the propositions in a formula. The words accepted by an automaton form a language and so do those satisfying a temporal formula. An automaton and a temporal formula are *equivalent* when they specify the same language.

For a symbol to represent a truth assignment to the propositions in a temporal formula, in this paper we always take 2^{AP} to be the finite alphabet, where AP is the set of atomic propositions from which temporal formulae are built. If $AP = \{p, q\}$, then the alphabet is $2^{AP} = \{\emptyset, \{p\}, \{q\}, \{p, q\}\}$, where the symbol $\{p\}$ for instance is the truth assignment in which p is *true* and q is *false*. So, a symbol, as an element of 2^{AP}, has some structure in it rather than just a plain letter.

The set $\{\emptyset, \{p\}, \{q\}, \{p, q\}\}$ may also be written as $\{\neg p \neg q, p \neg q, \neg pq, pq\}$, where the absence of a proposition in a subset of $\{p, q\}$ is explicitly spelt out with the use of $\neg$ (negation). This representation is convenient; e.g., when we want to focus on the symbols/assignments where p is true, we may simply write p instead of $\{pq, p\neg q\}$ or $\{\{p\}, \{p, q\}\}$. In the same vein, *true* alone means the whole of 2^{AP}. We use either of the two representations for symbols, whichever is more convenient.

Formally, let Σ, the alphabet, be 2^{AP} for some given finite set AP of atomic propositions; each element in Σ is called a (propositional) *symbol*. An *infinite word* over Σ is a map from $\mathbb{N}$ (the set of natural numbers, including 0) to Σ. Given a word w, we write w_i instead of $w(i)$ and call it the symbol at position i

of w, where $i \geq 0$. Σ^ω denotes the set of all infinite words over Σ. An *ω-language*, or simply *language*, is a subset of Σ^ω.

2.2 Temporal Logics

We define in this section the full Propositional (Linear) Temporal Logic, namely PTL [1,12,22,26]. LTL is just the subset of PTL without the past operators[2]. Despite a recent trend of enforcing negation normal form (NNF) directly in the syntax, we still follow the classic definition of syntax because after all that is the syntax in real use. In a subsequent section, we invoke as a lemma the possibility of converting every PTL formula into an equivalent formula in NNF and then start the translation with an input formula in NNF.

PTL formulae over a set AP of atomic propositions are constructed by applying *Boolean* and *temporal* operators to elements from AP. Temporal operators are classified into future operators and past operators. Future operators include $\bigcirc$ (next), $\Diamond$ (eventually or sometime), $\Box$ (always), $\mathcal{U}$ (until), and $\mathcal{R}$ (release). Past operators include $\ominus$ (previous), $\circleddash$ (before), $\Diamond\!\!\!-$ (once), $\boxminus$ (so-far), $\mathcal{S}$ (since), and $\mathcal{T}$ (toggle, or toggled). The $\circleddash$ operator is a weaker version of $\ominus$, to be explained after the formal semantics is given.

A variant of PTL [21] adopts a weaker version of $\mathcal{U}$, namely $\mathcal{W}$ (wait-for), and a weaker version of $\mathcal{S}$ (since), namely $\mathcal{B}$ (back-to), in place of $\mathcal{R}$ and $\mathcal{T}$ respectively. We consider $\mathcal{R}$ and $\mathcal{T}$, as they are more commonly used in the model checking community. The $\mathcal{W}$ and $\mathcal{B}$ operators may be treated with the same translation techniques that are presented in subsequent sections. We leave them out for brevity.

Definition 1 (Syntax of PTL). *Let AP be a set of atomic propositions.*

- *Every $p \in AP$ is a PTL formula (over AP).*
- *If f and g are PTL formulae, then so are $\neg f$, $f \vee g$, $f \wedge g$, $\bigcirc f$, $\Diamond f$, $\Box f$, $f\, \mathcal{U}\, g$, $f\, \mathcal{R}\, g$, $\ominus f$, $\circleddash f$, $\Diamond\!\!\!- f$, $\boxminus f$, $f\, \mathcal{S}\, g$, and $f\, \mathcal{T}\, g$.*

All operators associate to the right (e.g., "$f\, \mathcal{U}\, g\, \mathcal{U}\, h$" should be parsed as "$f\, \mathcal{U}\, (g\, \mathcal{U}\, h)$") and the unary operators have precedence over the binary ones. Parentheses may be used to override precedence or just to avoid confusion. We also use common abbreviations: $\neg f \vee g$ is written as $f \rightarrow g$ and $(f \rightarrow g) \wedge (g \rightarrow f)$ as $f \leftrightarrow g$.

A PTL formula over AP is interpreted on an infinite word σ over $\Sigma = 2^{AP}$ relative to a position i in σ. The semantics of PTL in terms of $(\sigma, i) \models f$ (read "f holds at position i of σ") is given below. For a pure propositional formula φ that does not contain a temporal operator, we write $\sigma_i \models \varphi$ as usual to mean that the symbol σ_i satisfies φ in the propositional logic sense; recall that a symbol represents a truth assignment as described in the previous subsection.

[2] The name LTL follows the naming convention in model checking [3]. In other contexts, LTL may refer to the temporal logic of Manna and Pnueli [21,22] with past operators, variables of infinite domains, and quantification. On the other hand, the name PTL was used instead of LTL in some early works on propositional linear temporal logics without past operators, e.g., [34].

Definition 2 (Semantics of PTL). *Let σ be an infinite word over $\Sigma = 2^{AP}$ and i a natural number.*

- *For an* atomic proposition $p \in AP$,
  - $(\sigma, i) \models p \iff p \in \sigma_i$ *(also as $\sigma_i \models p$).*
- *For* Boolean *operators,*
  - $(\sigma, i) \models \neg f \iff (\sigma, i) \models f$ *does not hold.*
  - $(\sigma, i) \models f \vee g \iff (\sigma, i) \models f$ *or* $(\sigma, i) \models g$.
  - $(\sigma, i) \models f \wedge g \iff (\sigma, i) \models f$ *and* $(\sigma, i) \models g$.
- *For* future *temporal operators,*
  - $(\sigma, i) \models \bigcirc f \iff (\sigma, i+1) \models f$.
  - $(\sigma, i) \models \Diamond f \iff$ *for some* $j \geq i$, $(\sigma, j) \models f$.
  - $(\sigma, i) \models \Box f \iff$ *for all* $j \geq i$, $(\sigma, j) \models f$.
  - $(\sigma, i) \models f\, \mathcal{U}\, g \iff$ *for some* $j \geq i$, $(\sigma, j) \models g$ *and for all* k, $i \leq k < j$, $(\sigma, k) \models f$.
  - $(\sigma, i) \models f\, \mathcal{R}\, g \iff$ *for all* $j \geq i$, $(\sigma, j) \models g$ *or for some* k, $i \leq k < j$, $(\sigma, k) \models f$. *(Or equivalently, for all* $j \geq i$, *if* $(\sigma, k) \not\models f$ *for all* k, $i \leq k < j$, *then* $(\sigma, j) \models g$. *In words, g must hold if f has been false up to the previous position, i.e., g may become false only after f has become true in the previous position.)*
- *For* past *temporal operators,*
  - $(\sigma, i) \models \ominus f \iff i > 0$ *and* $(\sigma, i-1) \models f$.
  - $(\sigma, i) \models \circleddash\!\!\sim f \iff i = 0$ *or* $(\sigma, i-1) \models f$.
  - $(\sigma, i) \models \diamondminus f \iff$ *for some* j, $0 \leq j \leq i$, $(\sigma, j) \models f$.
  - $(\sigma, i) \models \boxminus f \iff$ *for all* j, $0 \leq j \leq i$, $(\sigma, j) \models f$.
  - $(\sigma, i) \models f\, \mathcal{S}\, g \iff$ *for some* j, $0 \leq j \leq i$, $(\sigma, j) \models g$ *and for all* k, $j < k \leq i$, $(\sigma, k) \models f$. *(So, $f\, \mathcal{S}\, g$ is the past counterpart of $f\, \mathcal{U}\, g$.)*
  - $(\sigma, i) \models f\, \mathcal{T}\, g \iff$ *for all* j, $0 \leq j \leq i$, $(\sigma, j) \models g$ *or for some* k, $j < k \leq i$, $(\sigma, k) \models f$. *(Or equivalently, for all* j, $0 \leq j \leq i$, *if* $(\sigma, k) \not\models f$ *for all* k, $j < k \leq i$, *then* $(\sigma, j) \models g$. *So, $f\, \mathcal{T}\, g$ is the past counterpart of $f\, \mathcal{R}\, g$.)*

Note that, for $i > 0$, $\circleddash\!\!\sim f$ or $\ominus f$ holds at position i if and only if f holds at position $i-1$. The difference between $\circleddash\!\!\sim f$ and $\ominus f$ occurs at position 0: $\circleddash\!\!\sim f$ always holds at position 0, where $\ominus f$ never holds. Below are two example formulae, the first in LTL and the second in PTL.

- $\Box(r \rightarrow \Diamond g)$, which intends to mean "every request is eventually granted".
- $\Box(g \rightarrow \ominus \diamondminus r)$, which intends to mean "a grant is issued only if there has been a request".

We say that an infinite word σ *satisfies* a PTL formula f or σ is a *model* of f, denoted $\sigma \models f$, if $(\sigma, 0) \models f$.

Definition 3 (Language Defined by a PTL Formula). *The set of all models (infinite words) that satisfy a PTL formula f is called the language of f, or the language* specified *by f, denoted $L(f)$.*

Two formulae are said to be *equivalent* if they have the same set of models. Congruence is a stronger notion of equivalence. Two formulae are *congruent* if they have the same set of "relativized" models/words, or words with a relative position $i \geq 0$. That is, f and g are congruent, denoted $f \cong g$, if, for all $\sigma \in \Sigma^\omega$ and all $i \geq 0$, $(\sigma, i) \models f$ if and only if $(\sigma, i) \models g$.

A PTL formula is said to be in *negation normal form* (NNF) if the negation applies only to atomic propositions. Let $\overline{AP}$ denote the set of negated atomic propositions. PTL formulae in NNF over AP are those built from elements in $AP \cup \overline{AP}$, called literals, using disjunction ($\vee$), conjunction ($\wedge$), and the temporal operators. Every PTL formula can be rewritten into an equivalent formula in NNF using De Morgan's laws and the congruences for duality stated below.

Lemma 1 (Congruences for Duality [3,12,22]**).** *For all PTL formulae f and g, the following congruences hold:*

$$
\begin{array}{ll}
\neg \bigcirc f \cong \bigcirc \neg f & \neg \ominus f \cong \circleddash\!\!\!\sim \neg f \\
 & \neg \circleddash\!\!\!\sim f \cong \ominus \neg f \\
\neg \Diamond f \cong \Box \neg f & \neg \diamondminus f \cong \boxminus \neg f \\
\neg \Box f \cong \Diamond \neg f & \neg \boxminus f \cong \diamondminus \neg f \\
\neg (f \,\mathcal{U}\, g) \cong (\neg f)\, \mathcal{R}\, (\neg g) & \neg (f \,\mathcal{S}\, g) \cong (\neg f)\, \mathcal{T}\, (\neg g) \\
\neg (f \,\mathcal{R}\, g) \cong (\neg f)\, \mathcal{U}\, (\neg g) & \neg (f \,\mathcal{T}\, g) \cong (\neg f)\, \mathcal{S}\, (\neg g)
\end{array}
$$

Lemma 2 (Rewriting into NNF [3,12,22]**).** *Every PTL formula has an equivalent formula in NNF.*

2.3 Labeled DAGs

We define in this section infinite *labeled* directed acyclic graphs (DAGs), with one or more source nodes. They are convenient generalizations, which allow node sharing, of labeled trees or forests for describing the computations of an alternating automaton when run on an infinite word.

Given a possibly infinite set D, a D-*labeled* DAG $G = (V, E)$ is a directed graph that does not contain a directed cycle and is augmented with a labeling function $l_G : V \to D$. We consider only DAGs that have one or more, but a finite number of, source nodes that do not have an incoming edge. For a node $u \in V$, let $E(u)$ denote the set of all nodes $v \in V$ such that $(u, v) \in E$, called the *successors* of u. We extend this to let $E(U)$ denote $\bigcup_{u \in U} E(u)$. An infinite path of a DAG is a path from a source node that goes to infinity without reaching an end.

A DAG is said to be *leveled* if $V = \bigcup_{i \geq 0} V_i$, where V_i's are pair-wise disjoint, and $(u, v) \in E$ only when $u \in V_i$ and $v \in V_{i+1}$ for some $i \geq 0$. A node in V_i is said to be *at level* i. In a leveled DAG, the nodes in $E(u)$ are all at the same level for every $u \in V$; same for $E(U)$, if all nodes in $U \subseteq V$ are at the same level. Consequently, all the paths from some source node to a designated node have the same length, which equals the level of the designated node.

2.4 Büchi and Other ω-Automata

Büchi automata and more generally ω-automata have the same structure as classic finite-state automata but operate on infinite words [2,15,28]; automata on infinite trees are not considered here. We define in this section different types of ω-automata in one collective definition, to avoid repetitions of shared features. For alternating automata, we include both an implicit (symbolic) and an explicit representations of the transition function and the initial states, allowing for a finer modular division in the translation procedure. In the symbolic presentation, $\mathcal{B}^+(AP \cup \overline{AP} \cup X)$ denotes the set of all positive Boolean formulae over $AP \cup \overline{AP} \cup X$, where *true* and *false* are also allowed, i.e., all Boolean formulae built from elements in $AP \cup \overline{AP} \cup X \cup \{true, false\}$ using disjunction ($\vee$) and conjunction ($\wedge$). For $Y \subseteq AP \cup X$ and $\theta \in \mathcal{B}^+(AP \cup \overline{AP} \cup X)$, we say that Y satisfies θ or $Y \models \theta$ if, with the truth assignment that assigns *true* to elements in Y and *false* to elements in $(AP \cup X) \setminus Y$, the formula θ evaluates to *true*; similarly for the simpler $\mathcal{B}^+(X)$.

Definition 4 (Syntax of ω-Automata). *An* ω-automaton *is a* 5*-tuple* $\langle \Sigma, Q, \delta, I, Acc \rangle$ *and a* two-way ω-automaton *is a* 6*-tuple* $\langle \Sigma, Q, \delta, I, Q_E, Acc \rangle$*:*

- Σ *is the finite* alphabet. *We assume* Σ *to be* 2^{AP} *for some given finite set* AP *of atomic propositions.*
- Q *is the finite set of* states/locations.
- δ *is the* transition function*:*
  - nondeterministic*:* $\delta : Q \times \Sigma \to 2^Q$.
  - alternating*:* $\delta : Q \times \Sigma \to 2^{2^Q}$.
  - symbolic alternating*:* $\delta : Q \to \mathcal{B}^+(AP \cup \overline{AP} \cup Q)$.
  - two-way alternating*:* $\delta : Q \times \Sigma \to 2^{2^Q \times 2^Q}$.
  - symbolic two-way alternating*:* $\delta : Q \to \mathcal{B}^+(AP \cup \overline{AP} \cup (Q \times \{-, +\}))$.

  The transition function δ *is also seen as a* relation *whose members are called* transitions *(to be elaborated following this definition).*
- $I \subseteq Q$ *is the set of initial states, for nondeterministic automata;* $I \subseteq 2^Q$ *is the set of initial sets of states, for alternating automata; and* $I \in \mathcal{B}^+(Q)$ *is a positive Boolean constraint on the initial sets, for symbolic alternating automata.*
- $Q_E \subseteq Q$ *is either empty or a singleton* $\{q_E\}$*;* q_E *is called the* end state, *which has no outgoing transition, i.e.,* $\delta(q_E, a) = \emptyset$ *for every* $a \in \Sigma$ *or symbolically* $\delta(q_E) = false$.
- *Acc is the* acceptance *condition:*
  - Büchi*: Acc is a set* $F \subseteq Q$*, containing the* accepting *states.*
  - Co-Büchi*: Acc is a set* $F \subseteq Q$*, containing the "bad" states.*
  - Generalized Büchi (transition-based)*: Acc is a set of sets* $\{F_1, F_2, \cdots, F_k\}$*, where every acceptance set* $F_i \subseteq \delta$ *(with* δ *seen as a set of transitions).*

For a nondeterministic automaton, when $q' \in \delta(q, a)$ holds for some $q, q' \in Q$ and $a \in \Sigma$, we also write it as $(q, a, q') \in \delta$ and call the triple (q, a, q') a *transition*. For an (explicit) alternating automaton, when $Q' \in \delta(q, a)$ holds for some $q \in Q$, $a \in \Sigma$, and $Q' \subseteq Q$, we also write it as $(q, a, Q') \in \delta$ and call the triple (q, a, Q') a transition, which is an "and-branching" from q to all states in Q'. For a symbolic alternating automaton, $a \cup Q' \models \delta(q)$ is treated as $Q' \in \delta(q, a)$ in the explicit representation. For a two-way alternating automaton, when $(Q^-, Q^+) \in \delta(q, a)$ holds for some $q \in Q$, $a \in \Sigma$, and $Q^-, Q^+ \subseteq Q$, we also write it as $(q, a, (Q^-, Q^+)) \in \delta$ and call the triple $(q, a, (Q^-, Q^+))$ a transition. For a symbolic two-way alternating automaton, $a \cup (Q^- \times \{-\}) \cup (Q^+ \times \{+\}) \models \delta(q)$ is treated as $(Q^-, Q^+) \in \delta(q, a)$ in the explicit representation.

Given the current state and the next input symbol, an alternating automaton may have zero, one, or more possible and-branching transitions, among which it selects one nondeterministically (which is "or-branching") as the next step. Two special cases, namely $\delta(q, a) = \{\{\}\}$ (or $a \cup \{\} \models \delta(q)$) and $\delta(q, a) = \{\}$ (or $a \cup Q' \not\models \delta(q)$ for any $Q' \subseteq Q$), may be confusing and are worth noting. The first case intuitively means that there is no further requirement on the remainder of the input after symbol a, while the second means that the input word will not be accepted no matter what its remainder is.

Different combinations of transition function and acceptance condition give rise to different types of ω-automata. Following a conventional system of acronyms, the types of ω-automata we need in this paper are:

- NBW: nondeterministic Büchi (word-)automaton (on words, as opposed to that on trees),
- TNGBW: transition-based nondeterministic generalized Büchi automaton,
- ACW: alternating co-Büchi automaton,
- SACW: symbolic ACW,
- 2ACW: two-way ACW,
- S2ACW: symbolic 2ACW, and
- ABW: alternating Büchi automaton (whose conversion into NBW is discussed for motivating the conversion of ACW or 2ACW into TNGBW).

An automaton either accepts or rejects (does not accept) an input word and the set of words that it accepts constitute the language it specifies/recognizes, to be formally defined shortly. In Fig. 1(a) is an NBW that is equivalent to $\Box(r \rightarrow \Diamond g)$ (they specify the same language), while in Fig. 1(b) is another NBW that is equivalent to $\Box(g \rightarrow \ominus\diamondminus r)$. In both diagrams, an initial state is indicated by an incoming arrow without a label, while a state in the acceptance set is double-circled.

An infinite word as input drives an ω-automaton to go in every step from one state to one or several others, producing runs. An automaton accepts an input word if there exists a run of the automaton on the word that follows the repetition patterns prescribed by the acceptance condition.

A word is accepted by an NBW if and only if there exists a run of the NBW on the word that passes through at least one accepting state infinitely often. A word is accepted by a TNGBW if and only if there exists a run of the TNGBW on the word that passes through each acceptance set infinitely often.

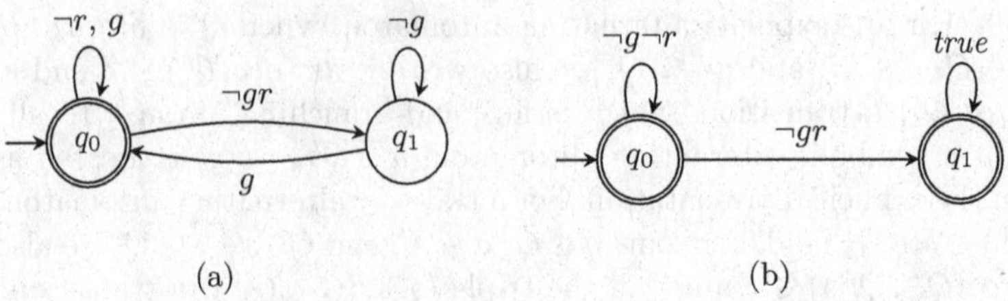

Fig. 1. (a) An NBW equivalent to $\square(r \rightarrow \diamond g)$. The single g as a label on the transition edge from q_0 to itself or from q_1 to q_0 is a shorthand for gr, $g\neg r$, i.e., $\{g, r\}, \{g\}$. So, either edge actually represents two transitions, one labeled with gr (i.e., $\{g, r\}$) and the other with $g\neg r$ (i.e., $\{g\}$); analogously for the $\neg g$-labeled and $\neg r$-labeled edges. (b) An NBW equivalent to $\square(g \rightarrow \ominus \diamondminus r)$. *True* means all possible input symbols, so the *true*-labeled edge actually presents four transitions.

Definition 5 (Semantics of NBW and TNGBW). *For an NBW* $A = \langle \Sigma, Q, \delta, I, F\rangle$, *where* $F \subseteq Q$, *or a TNGBW* $B = \langle \Sigma, Q, \delta, I, F\rangle$, *where* $F = \{F_1, F_2, \cdots, F_k\}$ *with every* $F_i \subseteq \delta$, *a run on an infinite word* $w = w_0w_1w_2 \cdots \in \Sigma^\omega$ *is an infinite sequence of states* $q_0q_1q_2 \cdots \in Q^\omega$ *s.t.* $q_0 \in I$ *and for every* $i \geq 0$, $(q_i, w_i, q_{i+1}) \in \delta$. *Given a run* ρ *on word* w, *let* $\inf(\rho)$ *denote the set of states that appear infinitely many times in* ρ *and* $\inf_\delta(\rho)$ *denote the set of transitions that appear infinitely many times in* ρ, *i.e., all* $(q, a, q') \in \delta$ *that equals* (q_i, w_i, q_{i+1}) *for infinitely many* $i \geq 0$.

For NBW A, *a run* ρ *on a word is* accepting *if* $\inf(\rho) \cap F \neq \emptyset$; *and, for TNGBW* B, *a run* ρ *on a word is* accepting *if, for every* F_i, $\inf_\delta(\rho) \cap F_i \neq \emptyset$.

For an alternating automaton, a run on a given input word is a labeled DAG. Let us first consider one-way automata, for which the set of states Q serves as the set of labels. A transition (q, a, Q') produces for a q-labeled node as many successors as the number of states in Q', each labeled with a distinct state in Q'. The "branches" to the successors are and-branching. For knowing which symbol of the input word the automaton is reading, the DAG is leveled. The level of a node reflects the current position of the read head on the input and also the number of steps/transitions that have been taken so far. An input word typically induces multiple runs, due to the nondeterminism present in the transition function. A run DAG dies if some of its paths cannot continue while complying with the transition function. A run DAG is accepting if every infinite path is accepting with respect to the acceptance condition. An infinite path is accepting for a co-Büchi acceptance condition if it eventually stays outside of F (i.e., inside of $Q \setminus F$) and never returns to F (i.e., remains in $Q \setminus F$).

For an infinite path ρ in a run DAG, let $\inf(\rho)$ be the set of states that appear infinitely many times in ρ.

Definition 6 (Semantics of ACW and SACW). *For an ACW or SACW* $A = \langle \Sigma, Q, \delta, I, F\rangle$, *a run of* A *on an infinite word* $w = w_0w_1w_2 \cdots \in \Sigma^\omega$ *is a leveled* Q*-labeled DAG* $G = (V, E)$, *where*

- *for some $Q' \in I$ or $Q' \models I$, $|Q'|$ equals the number of source nodes in G and for every $q \in Q'$ there is a source node s with $l_G(s) = q$, and*
- *for every node u at level $i \geq 0$, if $l_G(u) = q$, then, for some $Q' \subseteq Q$ s.t. $Q' \in \delta(q, w_i)$ or $w_i \cup Q' \models \delta(q)$, we have $|E(u)| = |Q'|$ and, for every $q' \in Q'$, there is a node $v \in E(u)$ s.t. $l_G(v) = q'$.*

A run on a word is accepting *if every infinite path ρ of the run is accepting, satisfying* $\inf(\rho) \cap F = \emptyset$.

Note that a run of an alternating automaton may contain some finite paths, each ending with a node at some level i and labeled with some state q such that $\{\} \in \delta(q, w_i)$ or $w_i \cup \{\} \models \delta(q)$. Also, every run DAG may be made minimal, by forcing node sharing, i.e., disallowing distinct nodes on the same level to have the same label. When a run DAG is minimal, there can be at most $|Q|$ nodes on a level. In the other extreme, without any sharing, the leveled run DAG becomes a tree or forest. All these variations in node sharing do not affect the existence of an accepting run on the input word.

For a two-way alternating automaton, every node in the run DAG is labeled with a pair of state and position (of the input word, where the automaton's read head is reading the next symbol). Like in a one-way alternating automaton, for a transition $(q, a, (Q^-, Q^+))$, the branches to the states in $Q^- \cup Q^+$ are and-branching. A branch to a state in Q^- is accompanied by a left move of the read head on the input word, and a branch to a state in Q^+ is accompanied by a right (usual) move of the read head. A special end state, if it exists, permits the read head to go left beyond position 0 while entering the end state.

Definition 7 (Semantics of 2ACW and S2ACW). *For a 2ACW or S2ACW $A = \langle \Sigma, Q, \delta, I, Q_E, F \rangle$, a run of A on an infinite word $w = w_0 w_1 w_2 \cdots \in \Sigma^\omega$ is a $Q \times (\mathbb{N} \cup \{-1\})$-labeled DAG $G = (V, E)$ where*

- *for some $Q' \in I$ or $Q' \models I$, $|Q'|$ equals the number of source nodes in G and, for every $q \in Q'$, there is a source node s with $l_G(s) = (q, 0)$, and*
- *for every node $u \in V$, if $l_G(u) = (q, j)$ with $j \geq 0$, then, for some $Q^-, Q^+ \subseteq Q$ s.t. $(Q^-, Q^+) \in \delta(q, w_j)$ or $w_j \cup (Q^- \times \{-\}) \cup (Q^+ \times \{+\}) \models \delta(q)$, we have $|E(u)| = |Q^-| + |Q^+|$ and.*
  - *for every $q \in Q^-$, there is a node $v \in E(u)$ s.t. $l_G(v) = (q, j-1)$, and*
  - *for every $q \in Q^+$, there is a node $v \in E(u)$ s.t. $l_G(v) = (q, j+1)$.*

  The position part of a label may not go below 0, i.e., become -1, except in the case of $(q_E, -1)$, where q_E is the end state designated in Q_E.

A run on a word is accepting *if every infinite path ρ of the run is accepting, satisfying* $\inf(\rho) \cap F = \emptyset$.

Note that a run DAG of a 2ACW or S2ACW is not necessarily leveled. The level of a node is unimportant here, as the current position of the read head is recorded in the label (not the level) of a node, unlike in the case of an ACW. Still, one may choose to have a leveled run DAG such that the level of a node reflects the number of steps that have been taken so far.

Definition 8 (Language Defined by an ω-Automaton). *An input word is accepted by an ω-automaton A if there is an accepting run of A on the word. The set of words accepted by A is called the language of A, or the language* recognized *by A, denoted $L(A)$.*

All these variants of ω-automata, except nondeterministic co-Büchi automata, are expressively equivalent to NBW. For further information, the reader is referred to the book by Grädel, Thomas, and Wilke [15].

2.5 Very Weak Automata

The first intermediate automaton that we construct for a linear temporal formula in the translation has a simpler structure than just an arbitrary automaton. It is called a "very weak" automaton. We give defining properties for such simpler structures.

The *transition graph* of an automaton is a directed graph whose nodes represent states and edges show the one-step reachability relation among the states as dictated by the transition function. In particular, for an alternating automaton, every possible branch in a transition from a state to another counts as a directed edge. This is formalized as follows.

For a nondeterministic automaton, when (q, a, q') is a transition, we call q' a *successor state* of q. For an alternating automaton, when (q, a, Q') is a transition, we call every $q' \in Q'$ a successor state of q; analogously for a symbolic alternating automaton. For a two-way alternating automaton, when $(q, a, (Q^-, Q^+))$ is a transition, we call every $q' \in Q^- \cup Q^+$ a successor state of q; analogously for a symbolic two-way alternating automaton.

Definition 9 (Transition Graph of an ω-Automaton). *The transition graph of an ω-automaton A is a directed graph $G_A = (V, E)$, where V equals the set of states and $(q, q') \in E$ if q' is a successor state of q.*

Very weak automata may be defined using any of several equivalent criteria. Below we give two of them that are used in this paper.

Lemma 3 (Equivalence of Conditions for Very-Weakness). *For every ω-automaton, the following conditions (for very-weakness) are equivalent:*

C1 Every strongly connected component (SCC) of the transition graph contains only one state.

C2 There is a partial order $\preceq$ on the set of states s.t. if q' is a successor state of q, then $q' \preceq q$. (The partial order may be replaced by a total order that is compatible with the partial order.)

Proof. (C1 implies C2): The SCCs of the transition graph, which is directed, form a SCC graph where the SCCs are the nodes and an edge connects one SCC to another if a state in the former SCC has a successor state in the latter. For any directed graph, its SCC graph is a DAG, which induces a partial order on the SCCs. Now that every SCC contains only one state (C1), the induced partial order on the SCCs and hence on the states provides what is needed for C2.

(C2 implies C1): A partial order is antisymmetric, i.e., $q \preceq q'$ and $q' \preceq q$ imply $q = q'$. So, C2 implies that every cycle in the transition graph is a self loop, which is equivalent to C1. □

Definition 10 (Very Weak Automaton). *An ω-automaton is said to be* very weak *if the conditions in Lemma 3 hold for the automaton.*

For very weak automata, Büchi and co-Büchi acceptance conditions are expressively equivalent. This is so, since visiting a state infinitely many times, i.e., self-looping on a state, is the same as staying away from all the other states forever and hence a Büchi condition F is equivalent to a co-Büchi condition $Q \setminus F$ for a very weak automaton. Automata from LTL/PTL formulae are naturally very weak, as shown in subsequent sections. Their simpler structures allow for more efficient constructions of the next intermediate automata. We need four types of ω-automata that are also very weak:

- VWACW: very weak ACW,
- SVWACW: symbolic VWACW,
- VW2ACW: very weak 2ACW, and
- SVW2ACW: symbolic VW2ACW.

3 Preprocessing of the Input Formula for Translation

There are quite a few possible ways to go from an LTL/PTL formula (in NNF) to an equivalent NBW. All existing translation algorithms, including the very early tableau decision procedures, share several basic ideas, requiring fundamental manipulations on the input temporal formula and its subformulae in preparation of a translation. In particular, to convey the semantics of a temporal formula to that of an automaton, the temporal formula is *expanded* to divide the requirements it imposes on the input word into two parts: the requirements on the current position (to be checked by transitions from the current automaton-state) and those on the remainder of the input (left for some next automaton-states to check) and, if a past temporal operator is present, also on the input starting from the previous position (left for some next automaton-states to check, but moving the read head backward by one position). This expansion is carried out iteratively on the subformulae of the input wherever needed.

Before looking into the expansion of a temporal formula, let us first find out what parts of the input temporal formula constitute the automaton-states. With the power of alternation that comes from the targeted intermediate automaton, this becomes rather straightforward. We need the notion of an elementary formula. A PTL formula is said to be an *elementary* formula if it is not a disjunction or conjunction of other formulae, i.e., it is either a literal or a temporal formula with a temporal operator as the outmost operator. The term "elementary" is to signify that these formulae are the "elements" which may be composed by Boolean combinations to enforce non-elementary/composite requirements.

Definition 11 (Elementary Subformula). *Given a PTL formula φ (in NNF) over AP, the set esform(φ) of all elementary subformulae of φ is defined as follows, where f and g are PTL formulae,* $* \in \{\bigcirc, \Diamond, \Box, \ominus, \circleddash, \diamondminus, \boxminus\}$, *and* $\circ \in \{\mathcal{U}, \mathcal{R}, \mathcal{S}, \mathcal{T}\}$*:*

$$esform(\varphi) = \begin{cases} \{\varphi\} & \text{if } \varphi \in AP \cup \overline{AP} \\ esform(f) & \text{if } \varphi = (f) \\ esform(f) \cup esform(g) & \text{if } \varphi = f \vee g \\ esform(f) \cup esform(g) & \text{if } \varphi = f \wedge g \\ \{\varphi\} \cup esform(f) & \text{if } \varphi = *f \\ \{\varphi\} \cup esform(f) \cup esform(g) & \text{if } \varphi = f \circ g \end{cases}$$

So, the definition of *esform* excludes subformulae that are a mere disjunction or conjunction of others, i.e., not elementary, perhaps even φ itself. An elementary subformula is said to be *maximal* if it is not a subformula of another longer elementary subformula. In the alternating automaton that is to be constructed for a temporal formula, only the elementary subformulae get represented by a distinct state. Boolean combinations contained in the input formula or resulted from expansion of the formula are handled by alternation.

Next, let us return to the issue of how a temporal formula is expanded to convey its semantics to that of an automaton. We start by examining how each temporal operator as the outmost operator of a formula is expanded.

Lemma 4 (Congruences for Expansion [12,22]**).** *For all PTL formulae f and g, the following congruences hold:*

$$\begin{array}{rlrl} \Diamond f & \cong f \vee \bigcirc\Diamond f & \diamondminus f & \cong f \vee \ominus\diamondminus f \\ \Box f & \cong f \wedge \bigcirc\Box f & \boxminus f & \cong f \wedge \circleddash\boxminus f \\ f\,\mathcal{U}\,g & \cong g \vee (f \wedge \bigcirc(f\,\mathcal{U}\,g)) & f\,\mathcal{S}\,g & \cong g \vee (f \wedge \ominus(f\,\mathcal{S}\,g)) \\ f\,\mathcal{R}\,g & \cong g \wedge (f \vee \bigcirc(f\,\mathcal{R}\,g)) & f\,\mathcal{T}\,g & \cong g \wedge (f \vee \circleddash(f\,\mathcal{T}\,g)) \end{array}$$

The formula on the right hand side of a congruence is called the *expansion formula* for that particular temporal operator. These expansion formulae are essential building blocks in obtaining the transition function of the target automaton in the translation of a PTL formula. Take $\Diamond p \cong p \vee \bigcirc\Diamond p$ as an example. The formula $\Diamond p$ requires that either p holds right at the current position of the input word (the first disjunct) or the entire requirement be postponed till the next position (the second disjunct); an additional acceptance condition should be imposed to forbid postponing indefinitely. There are also congruences for simplification, which is important but not the main concern of this paper.

We now may apply the primitive expansions in Lemma 4 for the temporal operators to an arbitrary PTL formula, as below. This "one-step" expansion separates the requirements of the formula into those on the current position and those on the rest of the input word and, if a past temporal operator is present, also on the input relative to the previous position.

Definition 12 (One-Step Expansion). *Given a PTL formula φ (in NNF) over AP, its one-step expansion $exp(\varphi)$ is defined as follows:*

$$exp(\varphi) = \begin{cases} \varphi & \textit{if } \varphi \in AP \cup \overline{AP} \\ (exp(f)) & \textit{if } \varphi = (f) \\ exp(f) \vee exp(g) & \textit{if } \varphi = f \vee g \\ exp(f) \wedge exp(g) & \textit{if } \varphi = f \wedge g \\ distr(\varphi) & \textit{if } \varphi = \bigcirc f \\ exp(f) \vee \bigcirc\Diamond f & \textit{if } \varphi = \Diamond f \\ exp(f) \wedge \bigcirc\Box f & \textit{if } \varphi = \Box f \\ exp(g) \vee (exp(f) \wedge \bigcirc(f\, \mathcal{U}\, g)) & \textit{if } \varphi = f\, \mathcal{U}\, g \\ exp(g) \wedge (exp(f) \vee \bigcirc(f\, \mathcal{R}\, g)) & \textit{if } \varphi = f\, \mathcal{R}\, g \\ distr(\varphi) & \textit{if } \varphi = \ominus f \textit{ or } \tilde{\ominus} f \\ exp(f) \vee \ominus \diamondminus f & \textit{if } \varphi = \diamondminus f \\ exp(f) \wedge \tilde{\ominus} \boxminus f & \textit{if varphi} = \boxminus f \\ exp(g) \vee (exp(f) \wedge \ominus(f\, \mathcal{S}\, g)) & \textit{if } \varphi = f\, \mathcal{S}\, g \\ exp(g) \wedge (exp(f) \vee \tilde{\ominus}(f\, \mathcal{T}\, g)) & \textit{if } \varphi = f\, \mathcal{T}\, g \end{cases}$$

$$distr(\varphi) = \begin{cases} (distr(\bigcirc f) \vee distr(\bigcirc g)) & \textit{if } \varphi = \bigcirc(f \vee g) \\ (distr(\bigcirc f) \wedge distr(\bigcirc g)) & \textit{if } \varphi = \bigcirc(f \wedge g) \\ (distr(\ominus f) \vee distr(\ominus g)) & \textit{if } \varphi = \ominus(f \vee g) \\ (distr(\ominus f) \wedge distr(\ominus g)) & \textit{if } \varphi = \ominus(f \wedge g) \\ (distr(\tilde{\ominus} f) \vee distr(\tilde{\ominus} g)) & \textit{if } \varphi = \tilde{\ominus}(f \vee g) \\ (distr(\tilde{\ominus} f) \wedge distr(\tilde{\ominus} g)) & \textit{if } \varphi = \tilde{\ominus}(f \wedge g) \\ \varphi & \textit{otherwise} \end{cases}$$

Note that $\bigcirc, \ominus, \tilde{\ominus}$ are distributed over a disjunction or conjunction wherever possible so that these three "one-step" operators may only precede an elementary subformula (which corresponds to an automaton-state) in the expanded formula.

Lemma 5 (Formula and Its One-Step Expansion (cf. [6,12])). *If φ is a PTL formula (in NNF) and $exp(\varphi)$ is the one-step expansion of φ as defined in Definition 12, then $exp(\varphi)$ is congruent to φ.*

Proof. The lemma can be proven by structural induction on φ, using simpler congruences such as those in Lemma 4 for individual temporal operators and those for distributivity of $\bigcirc$, $\ominus$, $\tilde{\ominus}$ over disjunction and conjunction. $\square$

Now, having done all the needed manipulations on PTL formulae, we conclude this section by envisioning an "expanded-subformulae collection" of the input formula: for each elementary subformula ψ of the input formula, the collection contains the one-step expansion $exp(\psi)$ of ψ. These expanded-subformulae correspond to "covers" as in a tableau-based translation and are the formulae needed for the construction of the first intermediate automaton.

4 From Temporal Formulae to Alternating Automata

With the expanded-subformulae collection of the input formula ready, we show how it is translated into an alternating automaton, which is very weak.

4.1 LTL to VWACW

Given an LTL formula (in NNF) preprocessed, we construct first a symbolic alternating automaton and then covert it into an explicit alternating automaton; both are very weak. Symbolic alternating automata suffice for setting up fix-point calculations for satisfiability or model checking [7]. They are adopted as intermediary automata here mainly to show that the immediate exponential blow-up in the explicit representation of transitions can be avoided if it is not needed.

LTL to SVWACW. In the symbolic representation of the transition function of an SACW, a literal may occur as a constraint on the input symbol or the name of a next state. To distinguish the two different occurrences, we introduce the *quote* function that puts a formula inside a pair of double quotes, when the formula is intended as an automaton-state, and extend it for a set of formulae.

Construction 1 (From LTL to SACW). *Given an LTL formula φ (in NNF) over AP, an SACW $A_\varphi = \langle \Sigma, Q, \delta, I, F\rangle$ is defined as follows:*

1. *$\Sigma = 2^{AP}$. (This can be represented by listing the elements in AP.)*
2. *$Q = quote(esform(\varphi))$. (This is the set of elementary subformulae of φ, each put inside a pair of double quotes; a state that is neither an initial state nor the target of any transition may be removed.)*
3. *$\delta : Q \to \mathcal{B}^+(AP \cup \overline{AP} \cup Q)$, where, for every $quote(f) \in Q$, let $\delta(quote(f))$ be $strans(exp(f))$, which is $exp(f)$ with every maximal elementary subformula of the form $\bigcirc g$ replaced by $quote(g)$, as formalized below.*

$$strans(\psi) = \begin{cases} \psi & \text{if } \psi \in AP \cup \overline{AP} \\ (strans(g)) & \text{if } \psi = (g) \\ strans(g_1) \vee strans(g_2) & \text{if } \psi = g_1 \vee g_2 \\ strans(g_1) \wedge strans(g_2) & \text{if } \psi = g_1 \wedge g_2 \\ quote(g) & \text{if } \psi = \bigcirc g \end{cases}$$

4. *$I = \varphi$ with every maximal elementary subformula quoted.*
5. *F contains exactly $quote(f)$ of every $f \in esform(\varphi)$ that has $\Diamond$ or $\mathcal{U}$ as the outmost operator.*

Note that, by definition, $esform(\varphi)$ does not contain φ if the input φ is a disjunction or conjunction, i.e., it is not elementary. I is defined such that it is a positive Boolean combination of the states corresponding to the maximal elementary subformulae of φ, in exactly the same way as φ is a positive Boolean combination of its maximal elementary subformulae. An elementary subformula that is neither a maximal elementary subformula of the input (an initial state) nor preceded by $\bigcirc$ in some expansion (the target of a transition) is not useful as a state; such elementary subformulae are always just literals and can be enforced by putting appropriate symbols on the relevant transitions.

To understand Construction 1 better, let us work out a simple case of translating the LTL formula $\Box\Diamond p$, where p is an atomic proposition, into an SACW. The input formula $\Box\Diamond p$ has three elementary subformulae: $\Box\Diamond p$ itself, $\Diamond p$, and p. We expand them as follows; literal p needs no expansion.

$$\begin{aligned} exp(\Box\Diamond p) &= exp(\Diamond p) \wedge \bigcirc\Box\Diamond p \\ &= (p \vee \bigcirc\Diamond p) \wedge \bigcirc\Box\Diamond p \\ exp(\Diamond p) &= p \vee \bigcirc\Diamond p \end{aligned}$$

With the expanded-subformulae, the components of the symbolic alternating automaton for $\Box\Diamond p$ can now be defined as follows.

1. $\Sigma = 2^{\{p\}} = \{\{\}, \{p\}\}$.
2. $Q = \{\text{“}\Box\Diamond p\text{”}, \text{“}\Diamond p\text{”}\}$. (The state “$p$” is neither an initial state nor the target of a transition, so it has been removed.)
3. $\delta : Q \to \mathcal{B}^+(\{p\} \cup \{\neg p\} \cup Q)$, where

$$\begin{cases} \delta(\text{“}\Box\Diamond p\text{”}) = (p \vee \text{“}\Diamond p\text{”}) \wedge \text{“}\Box\Diamond p\text{”} \\ \delta(\text{“}\Diamond p\text{”}) \quad = p \vee \text{“}\Diamond p\text{”} \end{cases}$$

4. $I = \text{“}\Box\Diamond p\text{”}$.
5. $F = \{\text{“}\Diamond p\text{”}\}$.

State “$\Diamond p$” is included in the acceptance set, as a bad state, for co-Büchi acceptance condition, because the corresponding formula $\Diamond p$ has $\Diamond$ as the outmost operator.

Why are SACWs from LTL very weak? From the symbolic transition function obtained from expanded-subformulae, we observe the following:

- Every transition/branch from a state for some formula φ either
  1. is a self-loop back to the same state for φ or
  2. goes to another state representing an elementary subformula of φ, or to nothing (meaning that no further requirement needs to be met).
- The “is-an-elementary-subformula-of” relation as induced by *esform* is a partial order, which is the needed partial order on states for very-weakness.

Lemma 6 (Very-Weakness of Automata from LTL [7,11]**).** *For every LTL formula φ (in NNF), the SACW A_φ obtained from Construction 1 is very weak.*

Theorem 1 (Correctness and Complexity of Construction 1 [7,11]**).** *If φ is the LTL formula (in NNF) given as input to Construction 1 and $A_\varphi = \langle \Sigma, Q, \delta, I, F\rangle$ is the SACW obtained, then $L(A_\varphi) = L(\varphi)$, $|Q| \le |esform(\varphi)|$, $|\delta| = O(|esform(\varphi)||\varphi|)$, and $|F| = k$, where k is the number of formulae in $esform(\varphi)$ that have $\Diamond$ or $\mathcal{U}$ as the outmost operator.*

SVWACW to VWACW. The symbolic representation in an SACW can be easily translated into an explicit representation, and the fact that the number of transitions may be exponential in the number of atomic propositions becomes apparent.

Before looking into the detailed conversion, let us make the SACW for $\Box\Diamond p$ explicit as an exercise. From state "$\Box\Diamond p$", with p *true*, there are two transitions:

- ("$\Box\Diamond p$", $\{p\}$, $\{$"$\Box\Diamond p$"$\}$), as $\{p\} \cup \{$"$\Box\Diamond p$"$\} \models \delta($"$\Box\Diamond p$"$) = (p \vee$ "$\Diamond p$"$) \wedge$ "$\Box\Diamond p$", which is equivalent to $(p \wedge$ "$\Box\Diamond p$"$) \vee ($"$\Diamond p$" $\wedge$ "$\Box\Diamond p$"$)$, and
- ("$\Box\Diamond p$",{p},$\{$"$\Diamond p$", "$\Box\Diamond p$"$\}$) (and-branching), as $\{p\} \cup \{$"$\Diamond p$", "$\Box\Diamond p$"$\} \models \delta($"$\Box\Diamond p$"$)$;

and, with p *false*, one transition ("$\Box\Diamond p$", $\{\}$, $\{$"$\Diamond p$", "$\Box\Diamond p$"$\}$) (and-branching), as $\{\} \cup \{$"$\Diamond p$", "$\Box\Diamond p$"$\} \models \delta($"$\Box\Diamond p$"$)$. Note again that the symbol $\{p\}$ is also written as p and $\{\}$ as $\neg p$.

From state "$\Diamond p$", with p *true*, there are two transitions:

- ("$\Diamond p$", $\{p\}$, $\{\}$), as $\{p\} \cup \{\} \models \delta($"$\Diamond p$"$) = (p \vee$ "$\Diamond p$"$)$, and
- ("$\Diamond p$", $\{p\}$, $\{$"$\Diamond p$"$\}$), as $\{p\} \cup \{$"$\Diamond p$"$\} \models \delta($"$\Diamond p$"$)$

and, with p *false*, one transition ("$\Diamond p$", $\{\}$, $\{$"$\Diamond p$"$\}$), as $\{\} \cup \{$"$\Diamond p$"$\} \models \delta($"$\Diamond p$"$)$. The set of initial states equals $\{\{$"$\Box\Diamond p$"$\}\}$, as $\{$"$\Box\Diamond p$"$\} \models$ "$\Box\Diamond p$". The explicit automaton is depicted in Fig. 2, where a box-shaped connector is used to represent and-branching.

Construction 2 (From SACW to ACW). *Given an SACW* $A = \langle \Sigma, Q, \delta, I, F \rangle$, *an ACW* $B = \langle \Sigma, Q', \delta', I', F' \rangle$ *is defined as follows.*

1. $Q' = Q$.
2. $\delta' : Q' \times \Sigma \to 2^{2^{Q'}}$, *where* $Q'' \in \delta'(q, a)$ *iff* $a \cup Q'' \models \delta(q)$, *for every* $q \in Q'$ *and* $a \in \Sigma$.
   (If $Q_1, Q_2 \in \delta'(q, a)$ *and* $Q_1 \subseteq Q_2$, *then* Q_2 *may be removed.)*
3. I' *contains exactly every* $Q' \subseteq Q$ *s.t.* $Q' \models I$.
   (If $Q_1, Q_2 \in I$ *and* $Q_1 \subseteq Q_2$, *then* Q_2 *may be removed.)*
4. $F' = F$.

The construction of the explicit transition function may be carried out by rewriting the symbolic constraint in DNF and accounting for each conjunctive clause separately, as we have hinted when making the SACW for $\Box\Diamond p$ explicit, where $(p \vee$ "$\Diamond p$"$) \wedge$ "$\Box\Diamond p$" is rewritten as $(p \wedge$ "$\Box\Diamond p$"$) \vee ($"$\Diamond p$" $\wedge$ "$\Box\Diamond p$"$)$.

Lemma 7 (Preservation of Very-Weakness by Construction 2). *If the SACW given as input to Construction 2 is very weak, then the ACW obtained is also very weak.*

Proof. By Construction 2, in particular $Q'' \in \delta'(q, a)$ iff $a \cup Q'' \models \delta(q)$, the transition graph of the ACW obtained is identical to that of the input SACW. If the SACW is very weak, then so is the ACW. $\Box$

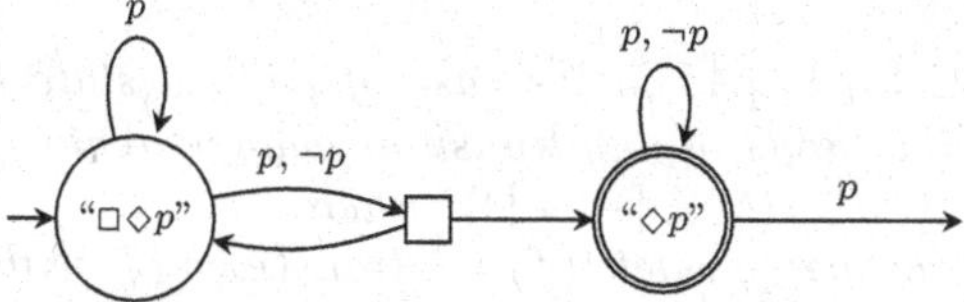

Fig. 2. An ACW for $\Box\Diamond p$. The and-branching of transition ("$\Box\Diamond p$", p, {"$\Box\Diamond p$", "$\Diamond p$"}) is represented by an arrow from state "$\Box\Diamond p$" to a box-shaped connector and then to the two states "$\Box\Diamond p$" and "$\Diamond p$" respectively; analogously for transition ("$\Box\Diamond p$", $\neg p$, {"$\Box\Diamond p$", "$\Diamond p$"}). State "$\Diamond p$" belongs to the acceptance set and is enclosed in a double circle.

Theorem 2 (Correctness and Complexity of Construction 2). *If $A = \langle \Sigma, Q, \delta, I, F\rangle$ is the SACW given as input to Construction 2 and $B = \langle \Sigma, Q', \delta', I', F'\rangle$ is the ACW obtained, then $L(B) = L(A)$, $|Q'| = |Q|$, and $|F'| = |F|$.*

Proof. For every word $w \in \Sigma^\omega$, if A has an accepting run on w, then B also has an accepting run on w, and vice versa, according to Definition 6 and Construction 2, in particular $Q'' \in \delta'(q, a)$ iff $a \cup Q'' \models \delta(q)$. So, $L(B) = L(A)$. $|Q'| = |Q|$ and $|F'| = |F|$ are obvious. □

4.2 PTL to VW2ACW

We next turn to dealing with the past temporal operators. With the machinery of a two-way automaton that we target, past temporal operators do not pose particular technical difficulty. Best of all, they do not bring new acceptance conditions. We just need to specify for them that the read head should move to the left on the input word. For $\circleddash$, we allow the alternative to transit to the special end state q_E; if the transition is taken right at position 0 of the input word during a run, then the corresponding path in the run is finite.

Like in the case of LTL, we obtain first a symbolic two-way alternating automaton and then covert it into an explicit two-way alternating automaton; both are very weak.

PTL to SVW2ACW. For an S2ACW, the next state in a constraint of the transition function always appears in the form of $(q, +)$ or $(q, -)$ and there is no confusion of a literal occurring as a constraint on the input symbol or the name of a next state. So, the *quote* function is not needed, unlike in the translation of LTL into SACW. Below are the details of the construction, followed by an illustrative example.

Construction 3 (From PTL to S2ACW) *Given a PTL formula φ (in NNF) over AP, an S2ACW $A_\varphi = \langle \Sigma, Q, \delta, I, Q_E, F\rangle$ is defined as follows:*

1. $\Sigma = 2^{AP}$.
2. $Q = esform(\varphi) \cup \{q_E\}$. *(As in the case of LTL, a state that is neither an initial state nor the target of any transition may be removed.)*
3. $\delta : Q \to \mathcal{B}^+(AP \cup \overline{AP} \cup (Q \times \{-,+\}))$, *where*
   - *for every* $f \in esform(\varphi)$, *let* $\delta(f)$ *be* $strans(exp(f))$ *with strans as defined below.*

$$strans(\psi) = \begin{cases} \psi & \text{if } \psi \in AP \cup \overline{AP} \\ (strans(g)) & \text{if } \psi = (g) \\ strans(g_1) \vee strans(g_2) & \text{if } \psi = g_1 \vee g_2 \\ strans(g_1) \wedge strans(g_2) & \text{if } \psi = g_1 \wedge g_2 \\ (g,+) & \text{if } \psi = \bigcirc g \\ (g,-) & \text{if } \psi = \ominus g \\ ((g,-) \vee (q_E,-)) & \text{if } \psi = \widetilde{\ominus} g \end{cases}$$

   - $\delta(q_E) = false$.
4. $I = \varphi$.
5. $Q_E = \{q_E\}$. *(If* $\widetilde{\ominus}$ *never occurs in the one-step expansion of any elementary subformula of the input, then the end state* q_E *is not reachable and may be removed from* Q_E *as well as* Q.*)*
6. F *contains exactly every* $f \in esform(\varphi)$ *that has* $\Diamond$ *or* $\mathcal{U}$ *as the outmost operator.*

An elementary subformula that is neither a maximal elementary subformula of the input (an initial state) nor preceded by $\bigcirc$, $\ominus$, or $\widetilde{\ominus}$ in some expansion (the target of a transition) is not useful as a state. In the construction of δ, for the case of $\widetilde{\ominus} g$ in the definition of *strans*, $(q_E, -)$ is introduced to reflect that $\widetilde{\ominus} g$ is a weaker version of $\ominus g$. A formula of the form $\widetilde{\ominus} g$ should evaluate to *true* at position 0 of the input word, no matter what g is. The constraint $(q_E, -)$ serves exactly that purpose. It prescribes a transition/branch that can be correctly taken only at position 0 of the input word, after which the corresponding finite path in the run is completed, according to the semantics of a (symbolic) two-way alternating automaton (Definition 7). Going into state q_E at any position other than 0 will cause the run to be killed, as $\delta(q_E) = false$.

Let us follow Construction 3 to work out the case for $\Box \diamondminus p$. The input formula $\Box \diamondminus p$ has three elementary subformulae: $\Box \diamondminus p$ itself, $\diamondminus p$, and p. We expand them as follows; literal p needs no expansion.

$$\begin{aligned} exp(\Box \diamondminus p) &= exp(\diamondminus p) \wedge \bigcirc \Box \diamondminus p \\ &= (p \vee \ominus \diamondminus p) \wedge \bigcirc \Box \diamondminus p \\ exp(\diamondminus p) &= p \vee \ominus \diamondminus p \end{aligned}$$

With the expanded-subformulae, the components of the symbolic two-way alternating automaton for $\Box \diamondminus p$ can be defined as follows.

1. $\Sigma = 2^{\{p\}} = \{\{\}, \{p\}\}$.
2. $Q = \{\Box \diamondminus p, \diamondminus p\}$. (The elementary subformula p is neither an initial state nor the target of a transition, so it has been removed; q_E has also been removed, as $\widetilde{\ominus}$ does not occur in any expanded-subformula.)

3. $\delta : Q \rightarrow \mathcal{B}^+(\{p\} \cup \{\neg p\} \cup (Q \times \{-,+\}))$, where

$$\begin{cases} \delta(\Box \ominus\!\!\!\!\diamond p) = (p \vee (\ominus\!\!\!\!\diamond p, -)) \wedge (\Box \ominus\!\!\!\!\diamond p, +) \\ \delta(\ominus\!\!\!\!\diamond p) \quad = p \vee (\ominus\!\!\!\!\diamond p, -) \end{cases}$$

4. $I = \Box \ominus\!\!\!\!\diamond p$.
5. $Q_E = \{\}$. (The end state q_E has been removed, as explained above.)
6. $F = \{\}$. (The acceptance set is empty, as no elementary subformula has either $\diamond$ or $\mathcal{U}$ as the outmost operator.)

Very-weakness of the constructed S2ACW is clear to see, by defining a partial order on the states in the same way as in the case of SACW from LTL except with the additional special end state q_E taken as the least element. So, every SCC of the transition graph of the S2ACW has only one node/state. In addition, the self-loops of a state move the read head either forward (right) or backward (left), but never both. This is so, because self-loops are produced by expansion of an elementary formula and every temporal operator is either future or past, but never both.

When in state q with a "forward self-loop" and about to read at position i, the automaton either

- stays in q, moving the read head forward to position $i + 1$, or
- goes to another state and will never return to q.

Analogous scenarios can be argued for a "backward self-loop". So, an SVW2ACW from PTL enjoys two additional properties, which are equivalent for SVW2ACW and useful for the construction of the next intermediate automaton [12]:

- *loop-free* (w.r.t. state-position pairs): a pair of state and read head position never repeats along a path of a run, and
- *progressing*: the read head advances towards infinity in every infinite path of a run.
  (Moving backward beyond position 0, i.e., to position -1, will kill a run unless it is accompanied by a transition to the special end state q_E, which completes a finite path in the run.)

Lemma 8 (Properties of Two-Way Automata from PTL [12]**).** *For every PTL formula φ (in NNF), the S2ACW A_φ obtained from Construction 3 is very weak and progressing.*

Theorem 3 (Correctness and Complexity of Construction 3 [12]**).** *If φ is the PTL formula (in NNF) given as input to Construction 3 and $A_\varphi = \langle \Sigma, Q, \delta, I, Q_E, F \rangle$ is the S2ACW obtained, then $L(A_\varphi) = L(\varphi)$, $|Q| \leq |esform(\varphi)| + 1$, $|\delta| = O(|esform(\varphi)||\varphi|)$, and $|F| = k$, where k is the number of formulae in $esform(\varphi)$ that have $\diamond$ or $\mathcal{U}$ as the outmost operator.*

SVW2ACW to VW2ACW. The symbolic representation in an S2ACW, like in the case of SACW, can be easily translated into an explicit representation. Before looking into the detailed construction, let us try to make the S2ACW for $\Box \diamondminus p$ explicit.

From state $\Box \diamondminus p$, with p *true*, there are two transitions:

- $(\Box \diamondminus p, \{p\}, (\{\}, \{\Box \diamondminus p\}))$, as $\{p\} \cup \{(\Box \diamondminus p, +)\} \models \delta(\Box \diamondminus p) = (p \vee (\diamondminus p, -)) \wedge (\Box \diamondminus p, +))$, which is equivalent to $(p \wedge (\Box \diamondminus p, +)) \vee ((\diamondminus p, -) \wedge (\Box \diamondminus p, +))$, and
- $(\Box \diamondminus p, \{p\}, (\{\diamondminus p\}, \{\Box \diamondminus p\}))$, as $\{p\} \cup \{(\diamondminus p, -), (\Box \diamondminus p, +)\} \models \delta(\Box \diamondminus p)$,

and, with p *false*, one transition $(\Box \diamondminus p, \{\}, (\{\diamondminus p\}, \{\Box \diamondminus p\}))$, as $\{\} \cup \{(\diamondminus p, -), (\Box \diamondminus p, +)\} \models \delta(\Box \diamondminus p)$.

From state $\diamondminus p$, with p *true*, there are two transitions:

- $(\diamondminus p, \{p\}, (\{\}, \{\}))$, as $\{p\} \cup \{\} \models \delta(\diamondminus p) = p \vee (\diamondminus p, -)$, and
- $(\diamondminus p, \{p\}, (\{\diamondminus p\}, \{\}))$, as $\{p\} \cup \{(\diamondminus p, -)\} \models \delta(\diamondminus p)$,

and, with p *false*, one transition $(\diamondminus p, \{\}, (\{\diamondminus p\}, \{\}))$, as $\{\} \cup \{(\diamondminus p, -)\} \models \delta(\diamondminus p)$. Figure 3 depicts the automaton.

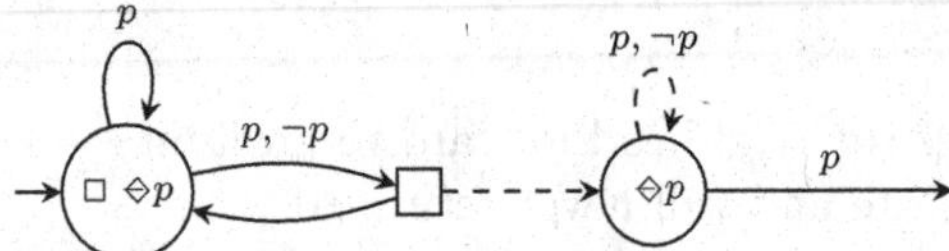

Fig. 3. A 2ACW for $\Box \diamondminus p$. The read head moves to the left when a dashed transition/branch is taken.

Construction 4 (From S2ACW to 2ACW). *Given an S2ACW* $A = \langle \Sigma, Q, \delta, I, Q_E, F \rangle$, *a 2ACW* $B = \langle \Sigma, Q', \delta', I', Q'_E, F' \rangle$ *is defined as follows.*

1. $Q' = Q$.
2. $\delta' : Q' \times \Sigma \to 2^{2^{Q'} \times 2^{Q'}}$, *where* $(Q^-, Q^+) \in \delta'(q, a)$ *iff* $a \cup (Q^- \times \{-\}) \cup (Q^+ \times \{+\}) \models \delta(q)$, *for every* $q \in Q'$ *and* $a \in \Sigma$.
(If $(Q_1^-, Q_1^+), (Q_2^-, Q_2^+) \in \delta'(q, a)$, $Q_1^- \subseteq Q_2^-$, *and* $Q_1^+ \subseteq Q_2^+$, *then* (Q_2^-, Q_2^+) *may be removed.)*
3. I' *contains exactly every* $Q' \subseteq Q$ *s.t.* $Q' \models I$.
(If $Q_1, Q_2 \in I$ *and* $Q_1 \subseteq Q_2$, *then* Q_2 *may be removed.)*
4. $Q'_E = Q_E$.
5. $F' = F$.

So, Construction 4 is almost identical to Construction 2, except the slight adaptation for the new type of transition function.

Lemma 9 (Preservation of Properties by Construction 4). *If the S2ACW given as input to Construction 4 is very weak and progressing, then the 2ACW obtained is also very weak and progressing.*

Proof. By Construction 4, in particular $(Q^-, Q^+) \in \delta'(q, a)$ iff $a \cup (Q^- \times \{-\}) \cup (Q^+ \times \{+\}) \models \delta(q)$, the transition graph of the 2ACW is identical to that of the S2ACW. Also, the read head movement of every self-loop in the transition graph of the 2ACW is the same as that of the corresponding self-loop in the transition graph of the S2ACW. Therefore, if the S2ACW is very weak and progressing, then so is the 2ACW. □

Theorem 4 (Correctness and Complexity of Construction 4). *If* $A = \langle \Sigma, Q, \delta, I, Q_E, F \rangle$ *is the S2ACW given as input to Construction 4 and* $B = \langle \Sigma, Q', \delta', I', Q'_E, F' \rangle$ *is the 2ACW obtained, then* $L(B) = L(A)$, $|Q'| = |Q|$, *and* $|F'| = |F|$.

Proof. For every word $w \in \Sigma^\omega$, if A has an accepting run on w, then B also has an accepting run on w, and vice versa, according to Definition 7 and Construction 4, in particular $(Q^-, Q^+) \in \delta'(q, a)$ iff $a \cup (Q^- \times \{-\}) \cup (Q^+ \times \{+\}) \models \delta(q)$. So, $L(B) = L(A)$. $|Q'| = |Q|$ and $|F'| = |F|$ are obvious. □

5 From Alternating Automata to Büchi Automata

We first review the construction of Miyano and Hayashi [23] for the conversion of an ABW into an NBW, to get the basic ideas for simulating the and-branching in a transition and enforcing the acceptance condition on every infinite path of a run. We then exploit very-weakness to produce simpler and smaller automata. Note that their construction assumes a Büchi acceptance condition, which is expressively equivalent to co-Büchi acceptance condition for very weak automata as we have explained earlier.

A state of the target NBW includes (among other things) a subset of states of the ABW, representing an entire level of a run DAG (with node sharing). Nondeterminism of the NBW provides the power of guessing the "right" run DAG to follow. Below are the main steps in the conversion of an ABW into an NBW:

- The NBW maintains a pair (U, V) of subsets of states of the ABW such that $U \cup V$ represents the current level of the guessed run DAG.
- U records the set of states yet to visit an accepting state since last reset, which is a state with U empty. That is, when a state in U transits via and-branching to several other states, the accepting ones are moved to V, while the non-accepting ones are kept in U.
- The accepting set contains exactly every possible reset.

In an accepting run DAG of the ABW, different paths may visit an accepting state at different times. Requiring that there are infinitely many levels with all accepting states would be too strong as an acceptance condition. This is illustrated in an example subsequently but in the setting of co-Büchi acceptance condition. The additional set U of states is needed in the conversion to keep track of the progresses of the different paths that visit an accepting state at different times.

5.1 VWACW to TNGBW

For a VWACW, once a path in a run leaves a state (good or bad), it never returns. Thanks to this very-weakness, the conversion of a VWACW into a TNGBW can be simpler. Below are the basic ideas:

- The TNGBW maintains just a subset of states of the VWACW, representing the current level of the guessed run DAG.
- For each bad state in the VWACW, define an acceptance set in the TNGBW containing every possible transition that stays away or "subsumes" an escape from the bad state.

Let us elaborate with an example. In Fig. 4 is a run DAG (which happens to be a tree) of the ACW in Fig. 2 on input word $p, p, p, \cdots$ (or $\{p\}, \{p\}, \{p\}, \cdots$). There is only one infinite path in the run DAG, which always stays in q_0 and never enters the bad state q_1; all the other paths from the source node are finite, each eventually escaping from q_1 upon reading symbol $\{p\}$ as the final step. The run DAG thus is accepting, and yet every level from level 1 onward contains the bad state q_1. So, a simple acceptance condition based on the states of a level would not work. This also explains why, without very-weakness, a pair of states is needed in the construction of Miyano and Hayashi.

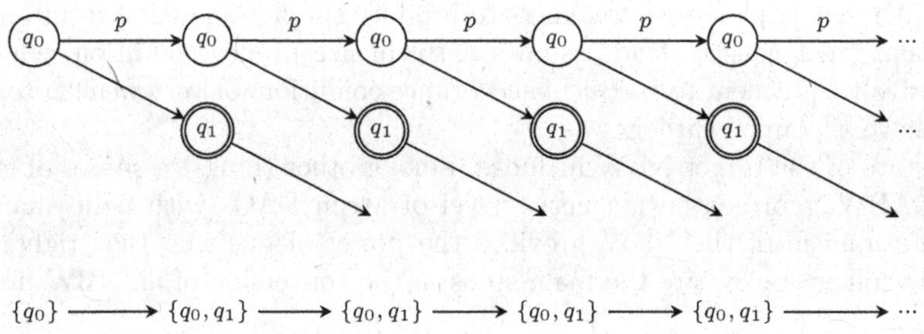

Fig. 4. A run DAG of the ACW in Fig. 2 on input word $p, p, p, \cdots$ (or $\{p\}, \{p\}, \{p\}, \cdots$), along with a simulating run sequence of the target TNGBW. States q_0 and q_1 represent "$\Box\Diamond p$" and "$\Diamond p$" respectively.

However, we observe that the occurrence of q_1 in each level from level 1 onward is spawned by the and-branching transition from q_0 rather than the q_1 in the previous level. A newly spawned q_1 disappears thanks to the escaping transition $(q_1, \{p\}, \{\})$ which can be taken upon reading symbol $\{p\}$. If we account for the infinitely many escapes from state q_1, then we can conclude, thanks to very-weakness, that every path eventually stays away from the only bad state q_1 (and never returns to q_1) and thus the run is accepting. In general, a run (made minimal with forced node sharing) of a VWACW is not accepting only if one or more infinite paths get stuck at a bad state. So, if for each bad state we see infinitely many stay-away or escape-subsuming transitions in the simulating run of the target TNGBW, then the simulated run of the VWACW is accepting.

The escape $(q_1, \{p\}, \{\})$ from q_1 of the original VWACW is considered to be "subsumed" by $(\{q_0, q_1\}, \{p\}, \{q_0, q_1\})$ in the TNGBW, because the input symbol $\{p\}$ enabling the former transition also enables the latter transition and $q_1 \notin \{\} \subseteq \{q_0, q_1\}$. When the transition $(\{q_0, q_1\}, \{p\}, \{q_0, q_1\})$ is taken, the current occurrence of q_1 in the original run DAG disappears and a new occurrence of q_1 is spawned on a different path, though this is not directly observable in the simulating run sequence of the TNGBW underneath the run DAG.

To facilitate the conversion and its presentation, we define a basic product operation (which is associative and commutative) on sets of subsets of states. For $R_1, R_2 \subseteq 2^Q$, let $R_1 \otimes R_2 = \{Q_1 \cup Q_2 \mid Q_1 \in R_1 \text{ and } Q_2 \in R_2\}$. So, the product produces another set of subsets of states, including every subset of states that is the union of a subset from R_1 and another subset from R_2.

Construction 5 (From VWACW to TNGBW). *Given a VWACW* $A = \langle \Sigma, Q, \delta, I, F \rangle$, *a TNGBW* $B = \langle \Sigma, Q', \delta', I', F' \rangle$ *is defined as follows:*

- $Q' = 2^Q$.
- $\delta' : Q' \times \Sigma \to 2^{Q'}$, *where* $\delta'(U, a) = \bigotimes_{q \in U} \delta(q, a)$ *for* $U \in Q'$ *and* $a \in \Sigma$.
  (If $V, V' \in \delta'(U, a)$ *and* $V \subseteq V'$, *then* V' *may be removed.)*
- $I' = I$. *(Every set* $U \subseteq Q$ *in* I *is a state in* I'.*)*
- F' *contains, for every* $q_i \in F$, *a set* F_i *that contains exactly all of the following transitions:*
  - $(U, a, V) \in \delta'$ *s.t.* $q_i \notin V$ *and*
  - $(U, a, V) \in \delta'$ *s.t.* $q_i \in U$ *and, for some* $V' \in \delta(q_i, a)$, $q_i \notin V'$ *and* $V' \subseteq V$.

Note that a state of the VWACW may have several possible successor-sets of states (cf. DNF), one of which is picked and joined with the selection of every other state on the same level (in a run DAG). So, when $V \in \delta'(U, a)$, V is one of the possible next levels that may occur following U after reading symbol a. In the construction of F', the first type of transitions are those staying away from the bad state q_i, while the second type of transitions are those subsuming an escape from q_i. The subsumption of an escape ensures that the occurrence of q_i in U disappears and a new occurrence of q_i, if any, in V is spawned by some other state than q_i in U.

Theorem 5 (Correctness and Complexity of Construction 5 [11]**).** *If* $A = \langle \Sigma, Q, \delta, I, F \rangle$ *is the VWACW given as input to Construction 5 and* $B = \langle \Sigma, Q', \delta', I', F' \rangle$ *is the TNGBW obtained, then* $L(B) = L(A)$, $|Q'| = 2^{|Q|}$, *and* $|F'| = |F|$.

5.2 VW2ACW to TNGBW

The case of converting a VW2ACW into a TNGBW is a bit more involved, while the treatment of the acceptance condition remains analogous to that for

VWACW. Fortunately, a VW2ACW from PTL is loop-free and progressing, as we have shown earlier. Thanks to loop-freedom (w.r.t. state-position pairs), a leveled run DAG of a progressing VW2ACW may be condensed as a run DAG where nodes labeled with the same position value are aligned without introducing loops. In Fig. 5 is a leveled run DAG (which is also a tree) of the progressing VW2ACW for $\Box \ominus p$ in Fig. 3 over the input word $p, \neg p, \neg p, \neg p, \cdots$ (or $\{p\}, \{\}, \{\}, \{\}, \cdots$). The leveled run DAG is condensed as a run DAG as shown in Fig. 6.

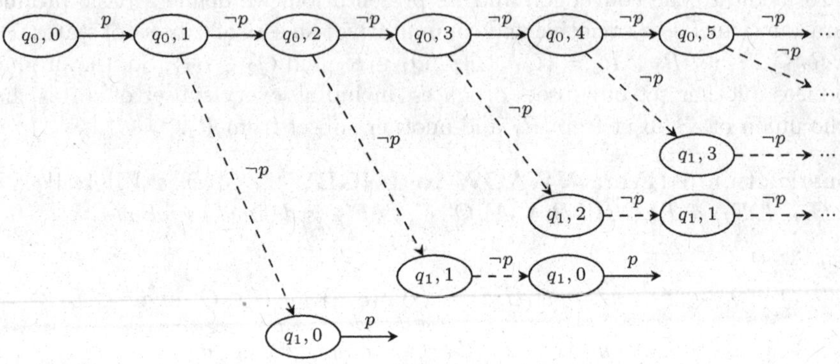

Fig. 5. A leveled run DAG of the VW2ACW for $\Box \ominus p$ in Fig. 3 over the input word $p, \neg p, \neg p, \neg p, \cdots$ (or $\{p\}, \{\}, \{\}, \{\}, \cdots$). States q_0 and q_1 represent $\Box \ominus p$ and $\ominus p$ respectively.

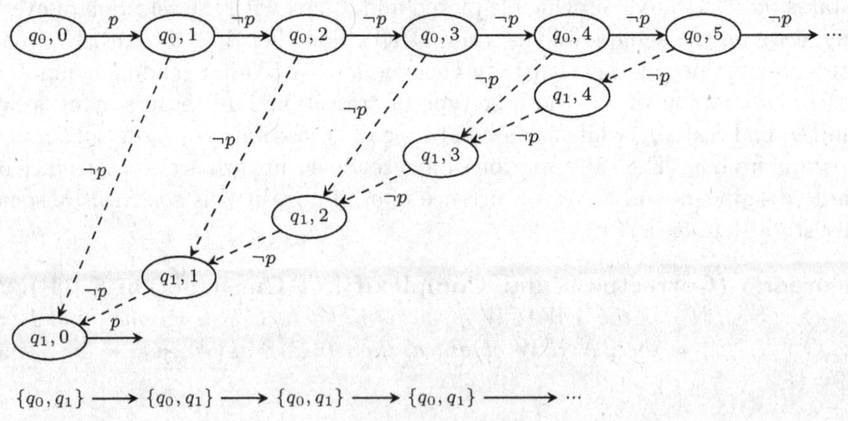

Fig. 6. A run DAG condensed from the leveled run DAG in Fig. 5, along with a "run sequence" it induces.

The condensed run DAG is not leveled, as a node may be reached from the source node by multiple paths with different lengths. However, the graph is drawn in such a way that two pairs of state and position are aligned if they have the same position value. The states at the same aligned level are exactly those states that the VW2ACW will be in (for this run) when reading the input word at the corresponding position. So, the run DAG can be seen as inducing a run sequence $Q_0, Q_1, Q_2, \ldots$ of sets of states, where Q_i is the set of all possible states when the read head position is at i, $i \geq 0$. The target TNGBW tries to produce that run, but in a slightly indirect way.

So, the main ideas for converting a VW2ACW into a TNGBW are as follows:

- To produce the run sequence $Q_0, Q_1, Q_2, \ldots$, the TNGBW tries to anticipate/guess all possible combinations of states for the Q_i, $i \geq 0$, on the fly.
- To check inducibility of the run sequence from some run DAG of the VW2ACW, the TNGBW keeps track of the *previous* and the *current* levels of the guessed run DAG that has been condensed and aligned according to the read head position. For example, if starting with $(\{q_E\}, Q_0)$, the actual run produced is
$$(\{q_E\}, Q_0), (Q_0, Q_1), (Q_1, Q_2), \ldots.$$
- A pair (Q_i, Q_{i+1}) legally follows (Q_{i-1}, Q_i) if Q_{i-1} includes one possible set of successor states of Q_i that are accompanied with a left move of the read head and Q_{i+1} includes the corresponding set of successor states of Q_i that are accompanied with a right move of the read head.

To facilitate the conversion and its presentation, we extend the basic product operation, defined for the case of VWACW to TNGBW, to a product operation on binary relations on the set of subsets of states. For $R_1, R_2 \subseteq 2^Q \times 2^Q$, let $R_1 \otimes R_2 = \{(Q_1^- \cup Q_2^-, Q_1^+ \cup Q_2^+) \mid (Q_1^-, Q_1^+) \in R_1 \text{ and } (Q_2^-, Q_2^+) \in R_2\}$. So, the product produces from R_1 and R_2 another binary relation, where a pair of subsets of states are related if the first (resp. second) subset is the union of the first (resp. second) subset of a pair from R_1 and the first (resp. second) subset of another pair from R_2.

Construction 6 (From Progressing VW2ACW to TNGBW). *Given a progressing VW2ACW $A = \langle \Sigma, Q, \delta, I, Q_E, F\rangle$, a TNGBW $B = \langle \Sigma, Q', \delta', I', F'\rangle$ is defined as follows:*

- $Q' = 2^Q \times 2^Q$.
- $\delta' : Q' \times \Sigma \to 2^{Q'}$, *where* $(V_1, V_2) \in \delta'((U_1, U_2), a)$ *if* $V_1 = U_2$ *and, for some* $(Q^-, Q^+) \in \bigotimes_{q \in U_2} \delta(q, a)$, $Q^- \subseteq U_1$ *and* $Q^+ \subseteq V_2$.
- $I' = \{(Q_{-1}, Q_0) \mid Q_{-1} \subseteq Q_E$ *and* $U_0 \subseteq Q_0$ *for some* $U_0 \in I\}$. *(Recall that* $I \subseteq 2^Q$ *and* $I' \subseteq Q' = 2^Q \times 2^Q$.*)*
- F' *contains, for every* $q_i \in F$, *a set* F_i *that contains exactly all of the following transitions:*
  - $((U_1, U_2), a, (V_1, V_2)) \in \delta'$ *s.t.* $q_i \notin V_2$ *and*
  - $((U_1, U_2), a, (V_1, V_2)) \in \delta'$ *s.t.* $q_i \in U_2$ $(= V_1)$ *and, for some* $(Q^-, Q^+) \in \delta(q_i, a)$, $Q^- \subseteq U_1$, $q_i \notin Q^+$, *and* $Q^+ \subseteq V_2$.

In the construction of δ', the condition $V_1 = U_2$ says that the current level U_2 should become the previous level V_1 after the transition. The condition $Q^- \subseteq U_1$ says that U_1 has been a sufficient guess as the previous level, as it includes one possible set of successor states accompanied with a left move of the read head from the current level; and the condition $Q^+ \subseteq V_2$ says that the next current level V_2 should include at least the corresponding set of successor states accompanied with a right move of the read head from the current level. Note also that, in the construction of F', an escape from a bad state (designated for some elementary subformula whose outmost operator is $\Diamond$ or $\mathcal{U}$, both of which are future operators) in F is always accompanied with a right move of the read head, which is why only $q_i \notin Q^+$ is needed.

Theorem 6 (Correctness and Complexity of Construction 6 [12]**).** *If $A = \langle \Sigma, Q, \delta, I, Q_E, F\rangle$ is the progressing VW2ACW given as input to Construction 6 and $B = \langle \Sigma, Q', \delta', I', F'\rangle$ is the TNGBW obtained, then $L(B) = L(A)$, $|Q'| = 2^{2|Q|}$, and $|F'| = |F|$.*

We note that Construction 6 may contain a great deal of redundancy. When $(U_2, V_2), (U_2, V_2') \in \delta'((U_1, U_2), a)$ and $V_2 \subseteq V_2'$, either V_2 is insufficiently guessed or V_2' is overly guessed; analogously, when $(Q_{-1}, Q_0), (Q_{-1}, Q_0') \in I'$ and $Q_0 \subseteq Q_0'$. An incremental construction with backtracking, by adapting the saturation procedure in [12], would eliminate insufficiently or overly-guessed states.

5.3 TNGBW to NBW

Finally, we present a construction for converting a TNGBW into an NBW. The main idea is analogous to that of the well-known construction for converting a usual generalized Büchi automaton into an NBW. A state is augmented with an index that keeps track, in a round-robin manner, of the latest acceptance set visited.

Construction 7 (From TNGBW to NBW) *Given a TNGBW $A = \langle \Sigma, Q, \delta, I, F\rangle$, where $F = \{F_1, F_2, \cdots, F_k\}$ with every $F_i \subseteq \delta$, an NBW $B = \langle \Sigma, Q', \delta', I', F'\rangle$ is defined as follows:*

- $Q' = Q \times \{0, 1, 2, \cdots, k\}$
- $\delta' : Q' \times \Sigma \to 2^{Q'}$, *where* $(q', x') \in \delta'((q, x), a)$ *if*
  - $q' \in \delta(q, a)$, $(q, a, q') \notin F_i$, *and* $x = x' = i - 1$,
  - $q' \in \delta(q, a)$, $(q, a, q') \in F_i$, $x = i - 1$, *and* $x' = i$, *or*
  - $q' \in \delta(q, a)$, $x = k$, *and* $x' = 0$.
- $I' = I \times \{0\}$.
- $F' = Q \times \{k\}$.

An improvement may allow the index to increment by more than one, when the transition taken belongs to consecutive acceptance sets, as in [11]. Also, a pair (q, i) is not reachable and may be removed if q cannot be reached via a transition in F_i.

If it is preferred to have just one single initial state for the NBW, an additional state may be created to act as the initial state. It simulates the first move by the initial states of the TNGBW and is never entered again. After the first move, the new NBW behaves according to the construction above.

Lemma 10 (Correctness and Complexity of Contruction 7 [11]**).** *If* $A = \langle \Sigma, Q, \delta, I, F \rangle$ *is the TNGBW given as input to Construction 7 and* $B = \langle \Sigma, Q', \delta', I', F' \rangle$ *is the NBW obtained, then* $L(B) = L(A)$, $|Q'| = (|F|+1)|Q|$, *and* $|F'| = |Q|$.

6 Summary

We now have all the necessary building blocks for translating a linear temporal formula into a Büchi automaton. Below are the chains of constructions constituting two complete translation algorithms, one for LTL and the other for PTL:

1. Preprocessing of the input temporal formula: Lemmas 2 and 5,
2. Translation into alternating automaton:
   - LTL to very weak alternating co-Büchi automaton: Constructions 1 and 2,
   - PTL to progressing very weak two-way alternating co-Büchi automaton: Constructions 3 and 4,
3. Alternating automaton into generalized Büchi automaton:
   - very weak alternating co-Büchi automaton into transition-based generalized Büchi automaton: Construction 5,
   - progressing very weak two-way alternating co-Büchi automaton into transition-based generalized Büchi automaton: Construction 6,
4. Generalized Büchi automaton into Büchi automaton: Construction 7.

To sum up, we have the following two theorems.

Theorem 7 (LTL to NBW). *For every LTL formula* φ *(in NNF), there is an equivalent NBW with at most* $(k+1)2^{|esform(\varphi)|}$ *states and* $2^{|esform(\varphi)|}$ *accepting states, where* k *is the number of formulae in* $esform(\varphi)$ *that have* $\Diamond$ *or* $\mathcal{U}$ *as the outmost operator.*

Theorem 8 (PTL to NBW). *For every PTL formula* φ *(in NNF), there is an equivalent NBW with at most* $(k+1)2^{2(|esform(\varphi)|+1)}$ *states and* $2^{2(|esform(\varphi)|+1)}$ *accepting states, where* k *is the number of formulae in* $esform(\varphi)$ *that have* $\Diamond$ *or* $\mathcal{U}$ *as the outmost operator.*

7 Discussion: Optimization

We have focused on the simplicity of the main chain of translation and hardly addressed the issue of minimization/optimization, except exploiting very-weakness. We note that the numbers of states and transitions in the intermediate and final automata, as having been investigated by many other researchers, may be greatly reduced by:

- formula rewriting, either on the whole or the parts, and
- simplification using simulation relations.

There are also miscellaneous techniques that cannot be easily categorized, e.g., analysis of the acceptance set and the structure of the transition graph. All these techniques may be developed as add-on modules and inserted into wherever appropriate in the main chain of translation.

Acknowledgements. This paper has been written on the occasion of Bengt Jonsson's 60th birthday. The first author Yih-Kuen Tsay worked as a postdoctoral researcher with Bengt at Uppsala University for near two years, from 1993 to 1995. One of their collaborative works [16] shows how the LTL of Manna and Pnueli [22], which includes past temporal operators, can be conveniently used to write and reason about modular specifications in the "assume-guarantee" style.

We thank the anonymous reviewers and our colleagues Ming-Hsien Tsai, Wayne Zeng, Dror Fried, Suguman Bansal, and Kevin Smith for many helpful comments and suggestions on earlier drafts of this work.

References

1. Benedetti, M., Cimatti, A.: Bounded model checking for past LTL. In: Garavel, H., Hatcliff, J. (eds.) Tools and Algorithms for the Construction and Analysis of Systems, TACAS 2003. LNCS, vol. 2619, pp. 18–33. Springer, Heidelberg (2003). https://doi.org/10.1007/3-540-36577-X_3
2. Büchi, J.R.: On a decision method in restricted second-order arithmetic. In: Proceedings of the 1960 International Congress on Logic, Methodology and Philosophy of Science, pp. 1–11. Stanford University Press (1962). https://doi.org/10.1007/978-1-4613-8928-6_23, The doi refers to republication of the paper. In: Mac Lane S., Siefkes D. (eds) The Collected Works of J. Richard Büchi. Springer
3. Clarke, E.M., Grumberg, O., Kroening, D., Peled, D.A., Veith, H.: Model Checking. The MIT Press, Cambridge (2018)
4. Courcoubetis, C.,Vardi, M.Y., Wolper, P., Yannakakis, M.: Memory-efficient algorithms for the verification of temporal properties. Formal Methods Syst. Des. **1**(2/3), 275–288 (1992). https://doi.org/10.1007/BF00121128
5. Couvreur, J.-M.: On-the-fly verification of linear temporal logic. In: Wing, J.M., Woodcock, J., Davies, J. (eds.) FM'99 — Formal Methods, FM 1999. LNCS, vol. 1708, pp. 253–271. Springer, Heidelberg (1999). https://doi.org/10.1007/3-540-48119-2_16
6. Daniele, M., Giunchiglia, F., Vardi, M.Y.: Improved automata generation for linear temporal logic. In: Halbwachs, N., Peled, D. (eds.) Computer Aided Verification, CAV 1999. LNCS, vol. 1633, pp. 249–260. Springer, Heidelberg (1999). https://doi.org/10.1007/3-540-48683-6_23
7. De Wulf, M., Doyen, L., Maquet, N., Raskin, J.-F.: Antichains: alternative algorithms for LTL satisfiability and model-checking. In: Ramakrishnan, C.R., Rehof, J. (eds.) Tools and Algorithms for the Construction and Analysis of Systems, TACAS 2008. LNCS, vol. 4963, pp. 63–77. Springer, Heidelberg (2008). https://doi.org/10.1007/978-3-540-78800-3_6

8. Etessami, K., Holzmann, G.J.: Optimizing Büchi automata. In: Palamidessi, C. (ed.) CONCUR 2000 — Concurrency Theory, CONCUR 2000. LNCS, vol. 1877, pp. 153–168. Springer, Heidelberg (2000). https://doi.org/10.1007/3-540-44618-4_13
9. Fritz, C.: Constructing Büchi automata from linear temporal logic using simulation relations for alternating Büchi automata. In: Ibarra, O.H., Dang, Z. (eds.) Implementation and Application of Automata, CIAA 2003. LNCS, vol. 2759, pp. 35–48. Springer, Heidelberg (2003). https://doi.org/10.1007/3-540-45089-0_5
10. Fritz, C.: Concepts of automata construction from LTL. In: Sutcliffe, G., Voronkov, A. (eds.) Logic for Programming, Artificial Intelligence, and Reasoning, LPAR 2005. LNCS (LNAI), vol. 3835, pp. 728–742. Springer, Heidelberg (2005). https://doi.org/10.1007/11591191_50
11. Gastin, P., Oddoux, Denis: Fast LTL to Büchi automata translation. In: Berry, G., Comon, H., Finkel, A. (eds.) Computer Aided Verification, CAV 2001. LNCS, vol. 2102, pp. 53–65. Springer, Heidelberg (2001). https://doi.org/10.1007/3-540-44585-4_6
12. Gastin, P., Oddoux, D.: LTL with past and two-way very-weak alternating automata. In: Rovan, B., Vojtáš, P. (eds.) Mathematical Foundations of Computer Science 2003, MFCS 2003. LNCS, vol. 2747, pp. 439–448. Springer, Heidelberg (2003). https://doi.org/10.1007/978-3-540-45138-9_38
13. Gerth, R., Peled, D., Vardi, M.Y., Wolper, P.: Simple on-the-fly automatic verification of linear temporal logic. In: Protocol Specification, Testing and Verification XV, PSTV 1995. IAICT, pp. 3–18. Springer, Boston, MA (1996). https://doi.org/10.1007/978-0-387-34892-6_1
14. Giannakopoulou, D., Lerda, F.: From States to Transitions: Improving Translation of LTL Formulae to Büchi Automata. In: Peled, D.A., Vardi, M.Y. (eds.) Formal Techniques for Networked and Distributed Sytems — FORTE 2002, FORTE 2002. LNCS, vol. 2529, pp. 308–326. Springer, Heidelberg (2002). https://doi.org/10.1007/3-540-36135-9_20
15. Grädel, E., Thomas, W., Wilke, T.: Automata Logics, and Infinite Games. LNCS, vol. 2500. Springer, Heidelberg (2002). https://doi.org/10.1007/3-540-36387-4
16. Jonsson, B., Tsay, Y.K.: Assumption/guarantee specifications in linear-time temporal logic. Theoret. Comput. Sci. **167**, 47–72 (1996). https://doi.org/10.1016/0304-3975(96)00069-2
17. Kesten, Y., Manna, Z., McGuire, H., Pnueli, A.: A decision algorithm for full propositional temporal logic. In: Courcoubetis, C. (ed.) Computer Aided Verification, CAV 1993. LNCS, vol. 697, pp. 97–109. Springer, Heidelberg (1993). https://doi.org/10.1007/3-540-56922-7_9
18. Laroussinie, F., Markey, N., Schnoebelen, P.: Temporal logic with forgettable past. In: Proceedings of the 17th IEEE Symposium on Logic in Computer Science (LICS 2002), pp. 383–392. IEEE (2002). https://doi.org/10.1109/LICS.2002.1029846
19. Lichtenstein, O., Pnueli, A.: Checking that finite state concurrent programs satisfy their linear specification. In: Proceedings of the 12th ACM SIGACT-SIGPLAN Symposium on Principles of Programming Languages (POPL 1985), pp. 97–107. ACM (1985). https://doi.org/10.1145/318593.318622
20. Lichtenstein, O., Pnueli, A., Zuck, L.: The glory of the past. In: Parikh, R. (ed.) Logic of Programs 1985. LNCS, vol. 193, pp. 196–218. Springer, Heidelberg (1985). https://doi.org/10.1007/3-540-15648-8_16
21. Manna, Z., Pnueli, A.: The Temporal Logic of Reactive and Concurrent Systems: Specification. Springer, Berlin (1992). https://doi.org/10.1007/978-1-4612-0931-7

22. Manna, Z., Pnueli, A.: Temporal Verification of Reactive Systems: Safety. Springer, Berlin (1995). https://doi.org/10.1007/978-1-4612-4222-2
23. Miyano, S., Hayashi, T.: Alternating finite automata on *omega*-words. Theoret. Comput. Sci. **32**, 321–330 (1984). https://doi.org/10.1016/0304-3975(84)90049-5
24. Pnueli, A., Rosner, R.: On the synthesis of a reactive module. In: Proceedings of the 16th ACM SIGPLAN-SIGACT Symposium on Principles of Programming Languages (POPL 1989), pp. 179–190. ACM (1989). https://doi.org/10.1145/75277.75293
25. Rohde, G.S.: Alternating Automata and the Temporal Logic of Ordinals. Ph.D. thesis, University of Illinois at Urbana-Champaign, Champaign, IL, USA (1997). http://hdl.handle.net/2142/86954
26. Sistla, A.P.: Theoretical Issues in the Design and Verification of Distributed Systems. Ph.D. Thesis, Harvard (1983)
27. Somenzi, F., Bloem, R.: Efficient Büchi automata from LTL formulae. In: Emerson, E.A., Sistla, A.P. (eds.) CAV 2000. LNCS, vol. 1855, pp. 248–263. Springer, Heidelberg (2000). https://doi.org/10.1007/10722167_21
28. Thomas, W.: Automata on infinite objects. In: van Leeuwen, J. (ed.) Handbook of Theoretical Computer Science, Volume B: Formal Models and Semantics, pp. 133–191. MIT Press (1990). https://doi.org/10.1016/B978-0-444-88074-1.50009-3
29. Tsay, Y.-K., Chen, Y.-F., Tsai, M.-H., Chan, W.-C., Luo, C.-J.: GOAL extended: towards a research tool for omega automata and temporal logic. In: Ramakrishnan, C.R., Rehof, J. (eds.) TACAS 2008. LNCS, vol. 4963, pp. 346–350. Springer, Heidelberg (2008). https://doi.org/10.1007/978-3-540-78800-3_26
30. Vardi, M.Y.: A temporal fixpoint calculus. In: Proceedings of the 15th ACM SIGPLAN-SIGACT Symposium on Principles of Programming Languages (POPL 1988), pp. 250–259. ACM (1988). https://doi.org/10.1145/73560.73582
31. Vardi, M.Y.: An automata-theoretic approach to linear temporal logic. In: Moller, F., Birtwistle, G. (eds.) Logics for Concurrency. LNCS, vol. 1043, pp. 238–266. Springer, Heidelberg (1996). https://doi.org/10.1007/3-540-60915-6_6
32. Vardi, M.Y.: Reasoning about the past with two-way automata. In: Larsen, K.G., Skyum, S., Winskel, G. (eds.) Automata, Languages and Programming, ICALP 1998. LNCS, vol. 1443, pp. 628–641. Springer, Heidelberg (1998). https://doi.org/10.1007/BFb0055090
33. Vardi, M.Y., Wolper, P.: An automata-theoretic approach to automatic program verification. In: Proceedings of the 1st Annual IEEE Symposium on Logic in Computer Science (LICS 1986), pp. 332–344. IEEE (1986). http://hdl.handle.net/2268/116609
34. Wolper, P.: Temporal logic can be more expressive. Inf. Comput. **56**(1–2), 72–99 (1983). https://doi.org/10.1016/S0019-9958(83)80051-5
35. Wolper, P., Vardi, M.Y., Sistla, A.P.: Reasoning about infinite computation paths (extended abstract). In: Proceedings of the 24th Annual Symposium on Foundations of Computer Science (FOCS 1983). pp. 185–194. IEEE (1983). https://doi.org/10.1109/SFCS.1983.51

Cause-Effect Reaction Latency in Real-Time Systems

Jakaria Abdullah(✉) and Wang Yi(✉)

Uppsala University, Uppsala, Sweden
{jakaria.abdullah,yi}@it.uu.se

Abstract. In embedded real-time systems, a functionality is often implemented as a dataflow chain over a set of communicating tasks. An important requirement in such systems is to restrict the amount of time an input data requires to impact its corresponding output. Such temporal requirements over dataflow chains also known as the end-to-end latency constraints, are well-studied in the context of lock-based blocking inter-task communication. However, lock-based communication does not preserve the functional semantics and complicates latency calculation due to its reliance on response times of the communicating tasks. We propose to use non-blocking inter-task communications to preserve the functional semantics. Unfortunately a naive method to compute the reaction latency by adding worst-case delays between each write-read pair is unsafe for systems with non-blocking communication. In this paper, we study a non-blocking communication protocol. We present an algorithm to compute the exact worst-case delay in a cause-effect chain, which provides a safe estimation of the worst-case cause-effect latency for systems using this protocol for non-blocking communication.

1 Introduction

A simple use case in real-time embedded applications is a dataflow chain where a sampler task samples an input data, passes the data to a controller task for processing and the processed output is used by an actuator task. The specification of the system often includes temporal constraints on such dataflow chains, also known as the end-to-end timing or latency constraints. More specifically, a latency constraint restricts the amount of time required before the input is taken into account by the corresponding output. Latency constraints are important temporal requirements in real-time systems implemented by multiple communicating tasks with different periods. Proving that the implementation of a system satisfies all such requirements is non-trivial but mandatory for safety-critical reasons.

A widely used practice is to design a system using high-level model-based designer tools such as Simulink [1] and verify all the functional requirements using simulation. System design tools like Simulink commonly use specific functional semantics such as the one for Synchronous-Reactive (SR) programming [3] which assumes computation and communication time as zero. When such a

E.-R. Olderog et al. (Eds.): Jonsson Festschrift, LNCS 13030, pp. 41–56, 2021.
https://doi.org/10.1007/978-3-030-91384-7_3

design is implemented on a real platform using preemptive scheduling, the following problems related to inter-task communication arise in preserving any functional semantics [4]:

- Data consistency: If preemption occurs in the middle of an input-output operation, data can get corrupted.
- Deterministic data transfer: Input-output operations of a task may occur at different time points in different jobs depending on the point in the program where preemption takes place. Similarly, non-determinism in execution times creates variation in the timing of the data transfer operations.

The most widely used solution for inter-task communication is lock-based communication. Lock-based communication in a complex embedded system such as the Engine Management System (EMS) [5] makes the design inflexible to change as the computation of end-to-end timing constraints depends on the execution times of all communicating tasks. Besides, lock-based protocols are not designed to preserve any functional semantics [4]. It has been reported that existing state-of-the-art tools for end-to-end timing constraint analysis (in the automotive domain) ignore functional semantics preservation and model transformations are required to ensure data consistency [6].

In a recent work [7], we have shown that non-blocking communication preserving functional semantics is critical for the design of dynamically updatable systems. In this context, we propose to use a wait-free inter-task communication protocol called the DBP [4] in system implementation. DBP preserves functional semantics similar to SR and its correctness does not depend on the execution times of the tasks. This protocol is widely used for designing control systems in the context of synchronous programming. In this work, we study the problem of end-to-end latency computation under this protocol. Specifically, our interest is in computing the reaction latency [8] of an input in a multi-rate dataflow chain either initiated by a periodic or a sporadic task. Here the main challenge lies in the multi-rate nature of the communication where a writer can write at a higher or a lower rate compared to its reader. As a result, input data may not propagate to output or may propagate multiple times.

We show that for tasks using DBP, a worst-case reaction latency computation algorithm that only considers the worst-case delay between releases of each writer-reader pair in a chain provides an unsafe estimation. We also show that the unsafeness of this naive approach originates from the effect of oversampling-undersampling of data in the presence of read-write pairs with non-harmonic periods. We give a safe worst-case reaction latency computation algorithm for the input data that propagates to the output of the chain. This algorithm provides the exact worst-case delay between releases of the first job and the last job in a cause-effect chain.

The rest of the paper is organized as follows. First, in Sect. 2, we review the previous related work on end-to-end timing analysis in the context of multi-rate systems and non-blocking communication. Next in Sect. 3, we give details of the problem and the system model considered in this work. Our proposed latency analysis method is described in Sect. 4 and evaluated in Sect. 5. Finally, we conclude the paper with a summary together with future works in Sect. 6.

2 Related Work

The analysis of latency constraints in multi-rate systems using asynchronous (non-blocking) communication was first studied in the context of synthesizing task parameters [9]. A renewed interest in such analysis stems from an industrial publication [10] where the authors propose a framework to calculate end-to-end latencies in automotive systems supporting the asynchronous communication model. Existing state-of-the-art tools for latency computation such as Symta-S [11] are applicable at the implementation level and mostly based on the availability of lock-based communication. Until recently, state-of-the-art latency analysis techniques such as [12] did not consider the preservation of any functional semantics. Recent research from Bosch [6] emphasized the preservation of model-level functional semantics in end-to-end latency estimation. Similarly, the industrial trend to replace traditional distributed embedded systems with fewer multicore chips increases the potential of semantic preserving non-blocking communication which is difficult to implement in distributed architecture [13].

Non-blocking asynchronous communication for real-time systems is first considered in [14] to meet the freshest value semantics, assuming the data validity time as the worst-case response time of a reader. In [15], an asynchronous protocol that guarantees data consistency with the freshest-value semantics between a writer and multiple readers is presented. This protocol needs hardware-dependent compare and swap operations. This idea of data validity is also used in [16] and [17] to optimize memory use while preserving the freshest value and the SR semantics respectively. These protocols compute a maximum buffer size by upper bounding the number of times the writer can produce new data while a given data is considered valid by at least one reader.

In [18], a double buffer mechanism for one-to-one communication with SR semantics is presented. In the case of uniprocessor systems, given that the code that updates the buffer index variables are executed inside the kernel at task release time, there is no need for a hardware mechanism to ensure atomicity when swapping buffer pointers or comparing state variables. In [4], the Dynamic Buffering Protocol (DBP) is defined for single-writer multiple-reader systems with unit communication delay links, under the assumption that each job finishes before its next release. In [19], the communication scenario presented in [4] is further generalized to handle arbitrary multi-unit communication delays and multiple jobs of a task active at the same time. In [20], multi-task implementation is formulated as an MILP (Mixed Integer Linear Programming) optimization problem which tries to minimize buffer places or total read-write delays in the system to improve control performance. Commercial system design software Simulink [1] provides a wait-free access control mechanism called the Rate Transition (RT) similar to DBP. In the case of communicating tasks with identical phase and harmonic periods, the RT mechanism guarantees data consistency and functional semantics preservation. However, all the above-mentioned works do not consider the computation of latency values in multi-rate dataflow chains.

An alternative non-blocking communication concept called the logical execution time (LET) [21] assumes I/O as time-triggered zero execution time activity which is performed at the release time (read) and the deadline (write) of the task. Although LET preserves time-triggered functional semantics independent of scheduling methods, it increases the delay in data reading as a task can finish computation of data long before the deadline of the current job which affects the end-to-end latency [22].

Prelude [23] is an architecture language intended for the design of multi-rate dependent control systems preserving functional semantics in communication. It supports rate-transition operations similar to Simulink for the needs of multi-rate real-time systems. The communication model assumed in Prelude is causal where a reader is not allowed to start before the completion of its writer. Such causal communication is considered as job-level dependencies where the constraint specifies which job of a writer task needs to finish its execution before a job of the reader task can start. Job-level dependency is used in [24,25] for computing latency constraints at the model-level.

3 Problem Formulation

In this section, we introduce the details of the end-to-end latency problem that we solve and the system model that we use for it. Our considered model is based on automotive software architecture AUTOSAR [8] and end-to-end latencies of complex automotive software like EMS [5].

3.1 Execution Model

An automotive software system consists of multiple software components. The software components that can not be decomposed further are called atomic software components or runnables. In an implementation, a runnable can be implemented as a function that is called whenever required, within the body of an operating system (OS) task. Usually, there are many more runnables in a system than the maximum number of tasks allowed by automotive operating systems. So runnables having the same functional period according to control dynamics are mapped into an OS task with the same period. In the simplest case, one functionality is realized by a single runnable. However, complex functionalities are typically implemented using several communicating runnables which can be distributed on different OS tasks.

We assume runnables of a system S is implemented by a set of n periodic or sporadic real-time tasks $\Gamma = \{\tau_1, \tau_2, ..., \tau_n\}$. We denote a periodic task τ_i by a tuple (C_i, T_i, D_i) where WCET $C_i = \sum C_i^j$, T_i is the period and D_i is the relative deadline. Interrupt service routines that are triggered by hardware events are usually modeled as sporadic tasks in the system. In the case of a sporadic task, T_i denotes the minimum inter-arrival time between consecutive jobs. In automotive operating systems only one job of a recurring task can be active at a time. This restriction implies all periodic or sporadic tasks to have deadlines less than or equal to their respective periods.

Tasks are scheduled by the operating system based on the assigned (fixed) priorities. The scheduling policy may be either preemptive or cooperative. Preemptive tasks may always preempt lower priority tasks, while cooperative tasks may preempt a lower priority one only at runnable boundaries. Preemptive tasks are assumed to have a higher priority than any cooperative task.

3.2 Communication Model

Communication between tasks is based on shared memory locations also known as *labels*. A label can be a shared variable allocated in the memory or a register. We assume tasks execute like read-execute-write, where the task reads all the required data at the beginning of execution and writes at the end of its execution.

For accessing a label, AUTOSAR allows two different mechanisms. In explicit or direct access, a runnable directly reads or writes memory location. As a result, data may be overwritten before the reader finishes its reading resulting in data inconsistency. In a more frequently used communication mechanism called implicit access, a task-local copy for data access is created. The copying is performed at the beginning of the job execution and the modified data is written back at the job's termination. Using this mechanism the value of a used label does not change during the runtime of a job and all runnables operate on consistent data. This mechanism is a form of non-blocking communication but does preserve any functional semantics.

In this paper, we use a different non-blocking communication protocol that preserves functional semantics [4] similar to synchronous programming. The principle of synchronous programming is based on the idea of zero time computation and communication. As a result, a data writer task computes and writes its data at the same time when it is released. Then the data reader task can always read the freshest data available at its release time. Here the release time is the time when the job of a task becomes ready for execution.

Let t_i^k represents the release time of the k-th job of task τ_i where $t_i^k \in \mathbb{R}_{\geq 0}$. Now job release times of the task τ_i forms a set $R_i = \{t_i^1, t_i^2, \cdots\}$ where $t_i^k < t_i^{k+1}$. Given time $t \geq 0$, we define $n_i(t)$ to be the maximum index of any job from τ_i that has released before or at t. By definition, $n_i(t) = \sup_k\{k | t_i^k \leq t\}$. We denote x_i^k and y_i^k to be the data that the k-th job of τ_i reads and writes respectively. Now for inter-task communication between writer task τ_i and its reader task τ_j, synchronous semantics assumes:

$$x_j^k = y_i^m, \text{where } m = n_i(t_j^k). \tag{1}$$

As for the case when τ_i has not occurred yet, $m = 0$ and the reader task should read a default value.

In a real execution, tasks do not have zero execution time. In the case of preemptive scheduling, it may be the case that τ_j preempts τ_i before completion. As a result, the τ_i outputs may not be available for τ_j computations. To overcome this problem, a high priority task should read the data written by the job immediately before the latest released writer job as:

$$x_j^k = y_i^m, \text{where } m = max\{0, n_i(t_j^k) - 1\}. \quad (2)$$

For systems where all tasks execute with the same period, synchronous semantics is preserved when the tasks are executed according to their data dependency order. In the case of multi-rate or multi-periodic systems, data may be needed to be communicated between two tasks with different execution rates or periods. The Dynamic Buffering Protocol (DBP) [4] is designed to preserve synchronous semantics in multi-rate multi-task implementation.

We now briefly introduce the DBP protocol in the context of fixed-priority real-time scheduling. The correctness of the protocol is dependent on the following assumptions:

1. The taskset that executes functions communicating using synchronous semantics is schedulable.
2. There is no cyclic communication between tasks without delayed data propagation.
3. All the tasks in the taskset have their relative deadlines constrained by their periods or minimum inter-arrival times.
4. Each pair of communicating tasks should have different fixed priority. In general, the protocol works for any priority assignment policy which assigns a fixed priority to a job during its release time.

To ensure deterministic communication between a writer and its reader tasks, the DBP protocol uses the following rules:

1. A low priority reader job reads the data written by the latest job of its high priority writer released before or with it.
2. A high priority reader job reads the data written by the predecessor job of the latest job of its low priority writer that is released before or with the reader.

The protocol manages the buffer that is written by a writer task and later read by a reader task. Whenever a job is released the kernel or runtime system modifies the pointer to variables which the released task will use for reading and writing. Similarly, when a reader finishes, the runtime marks the used buffer as free. If a reader and a writer are released simultaneously then the pointer fixing function for the writer should execute before the ones for the reader. The code for the original software remains unchanged.

It has been shown that a writer with N readers requires maximum $(N + 2)$ buffer places using the DBP protocol [4]. This bound is intuitive as in the worst-case situation, all the N readers may be still using the different data written by the previous writer jobs when a new writer job is released, thus N buffer places can be in use. The additional two buffer places are to keep the latest and the one-before-latest data to be used by any future arrival of high and low priority readers. Note that here the future release of any reader job means their previous job is finished and one of the previously occupied N buffers is no longer in use.

Automotive software systems sometimes use co-operative scheduling. A low priority co-operative task can block a high priority co-operative task if it starts executing before the release of the second one. However, as long as the tasks are schedulable the DBP protocol does not fail as it is not dependent on the finishing time of the jobs and the protocol ensures a reader job never reads from a writer job that is released after it (Fig. 1).

3.3 Latency Requirements

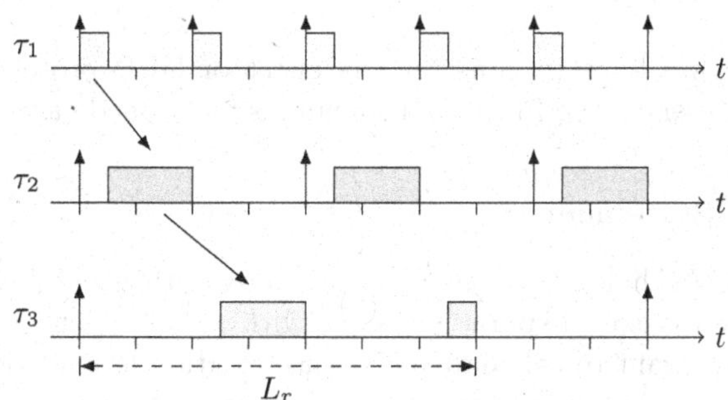

Fig. 1. Reaction latency in a cause-effect chain $\tau_1 \rightarrow \tau_2 \rightarrow \tau_3$ comprising three periodic tasks. The arrows indicate flow of data from one task to another one.

In automotive software, a complex functional requirement is often implemented by a chain of runnables where each of these except the first one reads the data written by its predecessor and writes data for its successor. The first runnable in the chain is either released by an event (sporadic) or a periodic polling function. These type of chains are called event chains or cause-effect chains [8]. The runnable that initiates an event chain is called its stimulus and the final runnable in the chain is called its response. A simple example of an event chain is wherein data is sensed by runnable for sensing, passed on to control runnables to compute and finally output of the control runnable is used by the runnables for actuation. A cause-effect chain does not contain any cyclic data dependency [5].

Each of these cause-effect chains is associated with an end-to-end latency requirement. In this work, we are concerned with end-to-end latency from the perspective of a stimulus also known as reaction latency. A reaction latency constraint of L time units to a particular stimulus implies that the first response should occur no later than L time units after that input. As each runnable is mapped into a task and tasks execute in a read-execute-write pattern, we can express reaction latency as the duration between the release time of the task with the first runnable and the completion time of the task with the final runnable.

A cause-effect chain may consists of tasks executing at different rates or periods. Such multi-rate dataflow chains thus often suffer from the effects of undersampling or oversampling of data. Undersampling happens when a slow reader reads from a fast writer and not all data will be read. Oversampling occurs when a fast reader reads from a slow writer and an input data propagates to the output multiple times. With these effects, it is challenging to calculate the reaction latency of multi-rate cause-effect chains due to the following reasons:

- If the chain contains any undersampling effect then the reaction latency calculation should only consider the input data that reaches the output.
- If the chain contains any oversampling effect then the reaction latency calculation should only consider the delay of the first reader job (out of multiple readers that reads the same data) which can propagate data to the next segment of the chain.

Additionally, we have to consider the effect of DBP protocol in reaction latency which preserves the functional semantics mentioned earlier.

3.4 Problem Statement

Given a cause-effect chain $C = \tau_1 \rightarrow \tau_2 \rightarrow \ldots \rightarrow \tau_N$ with either N synchronously released periodic tasks or a sporadic task τ_1 with $N-1$ synchronously released periodic tasks, we want to calculate worst-case reaction latency of any stimulus of C in uniprocessor where tasks use fixed-priority preemptive scheduling and non-blocking DBP communication protocol.

4 Reaction Latency Estimation

In this section, we present how to compute the worst-case reaction latency of a cause-effect chain in a uniprocessor where tasks are communicating using the non-blocking DBP protocol and scheduled using fixed priority scheduling. As the definition of the worst-case reaction latency, we consider the maximum time that an input data requires to reach the output for the first time by traversing a cause-effect chain. Such an interval starts with the release time of the first job in the chain and finishes with the finishing time of the last job that generates the final output.

4.1 Reaction Latency in Non-blocking Communication

There are two cases of data flow between tasks with different priorities where DBP uses different operations. According to DBP protocol, written data is valid for high priority readers from the release time of the next writer job until the moment before the release of a writer job after that. In the case of low priority readers, the written data is only valid during the interval starting from the writer job release until the moment before its next release. In both cases, the readers released during the defined interval will read the data.

The above cases do not assume anything about periods of the communicating tasks. If the tasks have fixed periods then the oversampling or undersampling effects determine the latency of the propagated data. Note that, the use of a non-blocking communication protocol ensures that the delay of data propagation from a writer to a reader does not depend on the response time of the writer job. Instead, the time distance between the release times of a writer job and its corresponding reader job determines how late the data reaches its final output task. The only response times required to calculate reaction latency are the response times of the jobs of the final task in the chain. So, first we consider a naive way to calculate the worst-case reaction latency of a cause-effect chain $\tau_1 \rightarrow \tau_2 \rightarrow \ldots \rightarrow \tau_N$ as

$$L_{1N} = \sum_{i=1}^{N-1} \Delta_{i \rightarrow i+1} + R_N \tag{3}$$

where $\Delta_{i \rightarrow i+1}$ is the worst-case data propagation delay between tasks τ_i and τ_{i+1}, and R_N is the worst-case response time (WCRT) [26] of the last reader task τ_N. Here the data propagation delay means the time distance between release times of a writer job and its corresponding reader job. R_N can be calculated by the smallest value of R_N that satisfies the recursive equation

$$R_{N_i} = C_r + \sum_{j \in hp(i)} \left\lceil \frac{R_{N_i}}{T_j} \right\rceil \cdot C_j. \tag{4}$$

Note that due to the effect of undersampling a data may not reach the output of the chain. Similarly, due to the effect of oversampling, the job that propagates the data may not be the first job that reads this data. As a result, *Algorithm 1* may not give a safe overapproximation of the worst-case reaction latency of the input data that reaches the output.

To show the problem of adding local worst-cases in delay computation, we use a simple cause-effect chain $\tau_1 \rightarrow \tau_2 \rightarrow \tau_3$ with three periodic tasks as shown in Fig. 3. We assume $prior(\tau_3) < prio(\tau_1) < prio(\tau_2)$. As we see from the Figure, due to the combination of low to high (oversampling) and high to low (undersampling) data propagation, the first job of τ_2 that reads data from τ_1 is not propagating data to the next reader task τ_3. Note that such an effect can only happen when the writer and its reader task have non-harmonic periods. This makes *Algorithm 1* unsafe as it assumes that the first reader of any data is always propagating it (Fig. 2).

We observe that if a cause-effect chain contains data exchange between a fast writer and a slow reader then many of the writer jobs will not be able to propagate data to its reader task. In the simplest case, we consider the cause-effect chain consists of only two tasks executing at different rates or periods. In a two task event chain, we have a writer task $\tau_w = (C_w, T_w, D_w)$ and a reader task $\tau_r = (C_r, T_r, D_r)$. According to DBP protocol, a reader job only reads data from two types of writer jobs released before or with it. The first type used in high to low priority communication is the latest writer job that is released before or with the release of the reader. If the reader job is released at time t then the maximum index of a writer job released in the interval $[0, t]$ is $\lfloor \frac{t}{T_w} \rfloor$. In case of low to high priority communication, the relevant job is the one released immediately before the latest writer job. The index of such a job is $\lfloor \frac{t}{T_w} \rfloor - 1$.

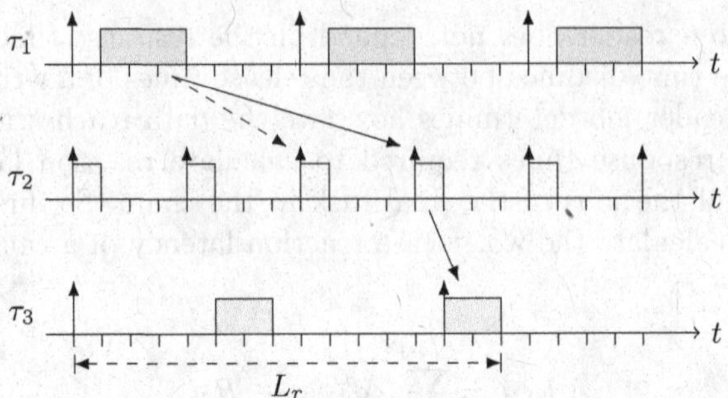

Fig. 2. The effect of oversampling in reaction latency of a cause-effect chain. The arrows indicate dataflow between tasks. The dashed arrow shows the first read that is not propagated.

Based on the observations regarding data misses in a cause-effect chain, we have an algorithm to compute delays of all data that reach from input to output. The algorithm shown in Fig. 3 starts from the jobs of the final task in the chain and computes indexes of the writer jobs that are propagating each of the data. All possible job release combinations of a synchronous periodic taskset are present in the hyperperiod of the taskset which is equal to the Least Common Multiple (LCM) of all the periods in it. As DBP protocol also requires reading data from the previous period of the writer, our algorithm needs to check job release propagation in an interval of at least twice the length of the hyperperiod. This requirement is necessary because the first two tasks in a chain can have low to high priority communication. The algorithm works like this, we use a two-dimensional matrix M where each row represents a task in the chain and each column represents a data propagation path. Starting from the last row with job indexes of the output task, we calculate the indexes of the writer jobs using $\lfloor \frac{t}{T_w} \rfloor - 1$ or $\lfloor \frac{t}{T_w} \rfloor$ based on priorities of the reader and writer tasks where t is the release time of the reader job. A special case happens when the calculated index becomes negative. The origin of this negative value is low to high communication in DBP. In it, the initial reader jobs are reading a default value due to the absence of propagated data. We mark these indexes with -1 in the matrix. In the computed matrix, a non-negative value in the item $M[i][j]$ indicates the job index of the job of task τ_{i-1} that propagates data to $(j-1)$-th job of the final output task in the chain.

The output matrix of the algorithm in Fig. 3 captures information of all the jobs that are included in any data propagation path of a cause-effect chain that reaches the output. To get the maximum delay in any such path from M, we use the algorithm in Fig. 4. This algorithm checks for each non-negative job index of the input task τ_0, the corresponding release distance of its reader job from the output task τ_{N-1}. As we are only concerned with the first output of data, the algorithm skips the input data that are read multiple times. The maximum value among these distances is the maximum delay a data suffers reaching from

C: chain $\{\tau_0, \tau_1, \ldots, \tau_{N-1}\}$ of N tasks
M: $N \times (2 \cdot P + 1)$ zero matrix where $P = \frac{LCM(C)}{T_N}$
procedure END-TO-END(T, M)
    $c_i \leftarrow 0$
    for $j = 0$ to $2 \cdot P$ **do**
        $M[N-1][j] \leftarrow c_i$
        $c_i \leftarrow c_i + 1$
    for $i = N - 1$ to 1 **do**
        for $j = 0$ to $2 \cdot P$ **do**
            $t \leftarrow M[i][j] \cdot T_i$
            if $prio(\tau_i) > prio(\tau_{i-1})$ **then**
                $w \leftarrow \lfloor \frac{t}{T_{i-1}} \rfloor - 1$
            else
                $w \leftarrow \lfloor \frac{t}{T_{i-1}} \rfloor$
            if $(w \cdot T_{i-1} \geq 0)$ **then**
                $M[i-1][j] \leftarrow w$
            else
                $M[i-1][j] \leftarrow -1$
    return M

Fig. 3. Algorithm for computing delays in all cause-effect chains where data reaches the output

C: chain $\{\tau_0, \tau_1, \ldots, \tau_{N-1}\}$ of N tasks
M: $N \times (P + 1)$ matrix from algorithm in Figure 3.
procedure FIND-MAX-CHAIN(T, M)
    $Max \leftarrow 0$
    $V \leftarrow 0$
    $Prev \leftarrow -1$
    for $j = 0$ to $2 \cdot P$ **do**
        if $(M[0][j] \geq 0) \wedge (M[0][j] \neq Prev)$ **then**
            $V \leftarrow M[[N-1][j] \cdot T_{N-1} - M[0][j] \cdot T_0$
            $Prev \leftarrow M[0][j]$
            if $V > Max$ **then**
                $Max \leftarrow V$
    return Max

Fig. 4. Algorithm for finding maximum delay in cause-effect chains.

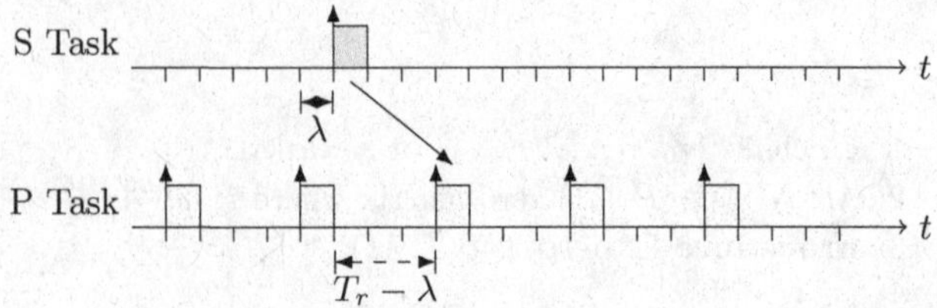

Fig. 5. Worst-case situation in communication between a high priority sporadic writer task and its periodic reader. The sporadic task is released $\lambda > 0$ time units after the previous reader job.

the input to the output. Finally, a safe upper bound of the worst-case latency can be calculated by adding the WCRT of the final task with the calculated delay. We denote this latency computation method as *Algorithm 2*.

Note that the complexity of *Algorithm 2* is linear in the size of the resulting matrix M. This means our algorithm has a time-complexity linear in the size of the hyperperiod of the tasks in a cause-effect chain. The hyperperiod is in the worst-case exponential with respect to the number of tasks of the chain. However, this worst-case happens when all the communicating tasks have co-prime periods which is a rare case in practice.

4.2 Data Propagation Delay Between Sporadic Input and Synchronous Periodic Output Tasks

Now we consider a special type of cause effect chain where the first task in the chain is released sporadically with a minimum inter-arrival time. Similar to the analysis of periodic tasks, we first consider the simple case of a sporadic writer τ_w and a periodic reader task τ_r. As τ_w is sporadic, T_w is the minimum inter-arrival time between two writer jobs. We assume a sporadic writer task is always assigned higher priority than its reader task. This is reasonable considering the fact that sporadic tasks are event-triggered for capturing input events (Fig. 5).

For $T_w > T_r$, the reader task will always read the latest data written by the writer. Note that for $T_w \leq T_r$, multiple sporadic writer jobs can release between releases of two consecutive reader jobs. As the sporadic writer job with new data can arrive indefinitely later after T_w, even the slowest periodic reader task will oversample in the absence of new writer jobs. In that case, the delay suffered by the first reader job determines the reaction latency of the sporadic writer. In the worst-case, the latest sporadic writer releases immediately after the release of a reader job to maximize the delay for the next release of the reader job that will read the data for the first time. Hence the maximum delay between releases of the periodic reader and sporadic writer is

$$S_{hl}(\tau_w, \tau_r) = T_r - \lambda \tag{5}$$

where $\lambda > 0$ is the smallest granularity of time by which an operating system can separate two consecutive job release events.

Suppose we have a cause-effect chain $\tau_1 \rightarrow \tau_2 \rightarrow \ldots \rightarrow \tau_N$ where τ_1 is sporadic and rest of the tasks are periodic. We calculate the maximum delay D_{2N} for the periodic part of the chain (τ_2 to τ_N) using either *Algorithm 1* or *Algorithm 2*. If $prio(\tau_1) > prio(\tau_2)$, then using Eq. 5 we can calculate a safe upper bound on worst-case reaction latency as

$$L_{1N}^S = T_2 - \lambda + D_{2N} + R_N. \tag{6}$$

5 Evaluation

For evaluation, we implemented the algorithms described in Sect. 4 using Python programming language. We consider cause-effect chains from the Bosch case study of an EMS [5]. The case study is for a multi-core platform with a global memory and local scratchpads. Interestingly, each core can access all the scratchpads via a crossbar connection. Although the chains in the case study allow placing tasks in different cores, we consider all the tasks of a chain to execute in the same processor. This is reasonable as we ignore memory access overhead and the only effect of placing tasks in different core in our analysis is the change of WCRT values of the final output task. In the case study, all the periodic tasks have periods in milliseconds (ms) such as $1, 2, 10, 20, 50, 100, 200, 500$ and 1000. Sporadic tasks have their inter-arrival times specified in microseconds. All the tasks in the case study are assigned unique priorities using rate-monotonic policy [27]. These priorities are positive integers where a large value means a high priority.

In the evaluation, we used *Algorithm 1* and *Algorithm 2*. We want to highlight the unsafeness of *Algorithm 1* and use the following result from [28]:

$$\Delta_{i \rightarrow i+1} = \begin{cases} T_i + \min(T_i, T_{i+1}) - gcd(T_i, T_{i+1}), & \text{if } \pi_i < \pi_{i+1} \\ \min(T_i, T_{i+1}) - gcd(T_i, T_{i+1}), & \text{if } \pi_i > \pi_{i+1} \end{cases} \tag{7}$$

where π_i represents priority of τ_i.

Figure 6 shows reaction latency computation of three chains with periodic tasks. Here the first chain is from the case study [5]. Note that, as each pair of tasks in the considered chains has harmonic periods, both of our algorithms computed the same latency values. For the third chain, the reaction latency is the WCRT of the output task because all the write-read pairs have high-to-low data transfer.

Next, we compute reaction latency of cause-effect chain with sporadic stimulus where we consider λ is $1\,\mu$s. We use two such chains where minimum inter-arrival times of sporadic input tasks are specified in microseconds. For calculation, we convert periods of the periodic tasks into microseconds. Figure 7 shows the latency of two such chains where both of our algorithms give identical latency due to the harmonic periods of the periodic tasks. Here the first sporadic chain

Chain Periods	Priority	Latency Alg1	Latency Alg2
$100 \rightarrow 10 \rightarrow 2$	$[1, 2, 3]$	$110 + R_2$	$110 + R_2$
$20 \rightarrow 10 \rightarrow 100$	$[2, 3, 1]$	$20 + R_{100}$	$20 + R_{100}$
$10 \rightarrow 20 \rightarrow 50$	$[3, 2, 1]$	R_{50}	R_{50}

Fig. 6. Reaction latency computations using Algorithm 1 and 2 where R_i is the WCRT of task with period i.

Chain Periods	Priority	Latency
$800 \rightarrow 2000 \rightarrow 50000$	$[3, 2, 1]$	$1999 + R_{50000}$
$6660 \rightarrow 10000 \rightarrow 20000$	$[3, 2, 1]$	$9999 + R_{20000}$

Fig. 7. Reaction latency computations for chain with sporadic task where R_i is the WCRT of task with period i.

Chain Periods	Priority	Latency Alg1	Latency Alg2
$10 \rightarrow 35 \rightarrow 50$	$[3, 2, 1]$	$35 + R_{50}$	$30 + R_{50}$
$7 \rightarrow 1 \rightarrow 100$	$[2, 3, 1]$	$7 + R_{100}$	$13 + R_{100}$
$100 \rightarrow 3 \rightarrow 8$	$[1, 3, 2]$	$104 + R_8$	$108 + R_8$

Fig. 8. Reaction latency computations with non-harmonic periods using Algorithm 1 and 2 where R_i is the WCRT of task with period i.

is from [5] and the second chain assumes an angle-synchronous task as sporadic input.

Finally, Fig. 8 shows how reaction latencies computed by both algorithms differ in the presence of non-harmonic periods between communicating tasks. We used three chains each consisting of three periodic tasks where all write-read pairs do not have harmonic periods. We see for the second and the third chain of Fig. 8, *Algorithm 1* computes unsafe lower delays compared to *Algorithm 2*. As the differences in calculated delays are not so large, it is intuitive that the usefulness of *Algorithm 2* will be more evident in longer chains with more non-harmonic read-write pairs. However, the maximum number of tasks in multi-rate cause-effect chains is three in the case study [5].

6 Conclusion

In this paper, we have studied the problem of estimating the worst-case reaction latency of a cause-effect chain in the multi-rate real-time system that uses non-blocking inter-task communication. We have shown that any naive estimation algorithm that combines the worst-case data propagation delays of each write-read pair is unsafe. We provide an algorithm to compute the exact worst-case data propagation delay between releases of a stimulus and its response in cause-effect chains. Our algorithm does not depend on the response times of the data writer jobs and only assumes the system to be schedulable. An evaluation based on a realistic system [5] shows that our algorithm is able to remove the unsafeness of the naive approach.

As future work, we want to provide a more efficient algorithm for reaction latency computation that can construct the global worst-case situation without enumerating paths of all reachable data. We will extend this work for multi-core platforms and will evaluate the overheads of the considered non-blocking communication protocol. Another interesting direction in latency computation is to consider age latencies [8]. Age latencies are important for control performance but these are more relevant in the system which can tolerate deadline misses.

Finally, we would like to thank authors Bengt Jonsson and Hans Hansson for their seminal work [2] on temporal logic to check timing properties in probabilistic chains. To the best of our knowledge, their work is one of the earliest known contributions to check properties similar to the reaction latency. The problem is still relevant in different settings and their pioneering work continues to inspire us.

References

1. Simulink user's guide: the MathWorks. Natick, MA, USA (2016)
2. Hansson, H., Jonsson, B.: A logic for reasoning about time and reliability. Form. Asp. Comput. **6**(5), 512–535 (1994)
3. Edwards, S.A., Lee, E.A.: The semantics and execution of a synchronous block-diagram language. Sci. Comput. Program. **48**(1), 21–42 (2003)
4. Caspi, P., Scaife, N., Sofronis, C., Tripakis, S.: Semantics-preserving multitask implmentation of synchronous programs. ACM Trans. Embed. Comput. Syst. **7**(2), 15:1–15:40 (2008)
5. Kramer, S., Ziegenbein, D., Hamann, A.: Real world automotive benchmark for free. In: 6th International Workshop on Tools and Methodologies for Embedded and Real-time Systems at ECRTS 15, July 2015
6. Hamann, A., Dasari, D., Kramer, S., Pressler, M., Wurst, F.: Communication centric design in complex automotive embedded systems. In: 29th Euromicro Conference on Real-Time Systems (ECRTS 2017), ser. Leibniz International Proceedings in Informatics (LIPIcs), vol. 76, pp. 10:1–10:20 (2017)
7. Yi, W.: Towards customizable cps: composability, efficiency and predictability. In: Duan, Z., Ong, L. (eds.) ICFEM 2017. LNCS, vol. 10610, pp. 3–15. Springer, Cham (2017). https://doi.org/10.1007/978-3-319-68690-5_1
8. Specification of timing extensions, autosar.org. https://www.autosar.org
9. Gerber, R., Hong, S., Saksena, M.: Guaranteeing end-to-end timing constraints by calibrating intermediate processes. In: Proceedings of Real-Time Systems Symposium, pp. 192–203 (1994)
10. Feiertag, N., Richter, K., Nordlander, J., Jonsson, J.: A compositional framework for end-to-end path delay calculation of automotive systems under different path semantics. In: Workshop on Compositional Theory and Technology for Real-Time Embedded Systems (co-located with RTSS 2008) (2008)
11. Henia, R., Hamann, A., Jersak, M., Racu, R., Richter, K., Ernst, R.: System level performance analysis - the symta/s approach. IEE Proc. Comput. Digit. Tech. **152**(2), 148–166 (2005)

12. Schlatow, J., Ernst, R.: Response-time analysis for task chains in communicating threads. In: IEEE Real-Time and Embedded Technology and Applications Symposium (RTAS), pp. 1–10 (2016)
13. Tripakis, S., Pinello, C., Benveniste, A., Sangiovanni-Vincent, A., Caspi, P., Natale, M.D.: Implementing synchronous models on loosely time triggered architectures. IEEE Trans. Comput. **57**(10), 1300–1314 (2008)
14. Kopetz, H., Reisinger, J.: The non-blocking write protocol NBW: a solution to a real-time synchronization problem. In: Proceedings Real-Time Systems Symposium, pp. 131–137 (1993)
15. Chen, J., Burns, A.: A three-slot asynchronous reader/writer mechanism for multiprocessor real-time systems. York University, Technical report (1997)
16. Huang, H., Pillai, P., Shin, K.G.: Improving wait-free algorithms for interprocess communication in embedded real-time systems. In: Proceedings of the Annual Conference on USENIX Annual Technical Conference, pp. 303–316 (2002)
17. Baleani, M., Ferrari, A., Mangeruca, L., Sangiovanni-Vincentelli, A.: Efficient embedded software design with synchronous models. In: Proceedings of the 5th ACM International Conference on Embedded Software, pp. 187–190 (2005)
18. Scaife, N., Caspi, P.: Integrating model-based design and preemptive scheduling in mixed time- and event-triggered systems. In: Proceedings of the 16th Euromicro Conference on Real-Time Systems, pp. 119–126 (2004)
19. Di Natale, M., Wang, G., Vincentelli, A.S.: Optimizing the implementation of communication in synchronous reactive models. In: IEEE Real-Time and Embedded Technology and Applications Symposium, pp. 169–179 (2008)
20. Natale, M.D., Guo, L., Zeng, H., Sangiovanni-Vincentelli, A.: Synthesis of multitask implementations of simulink models with minimum delays. IEEE Trans. Ind. Inf. **6**(4), 637–651 (2010)
21. Kirsch, C.M., Sokolova, A.: The logical execution time paradigm. In: Chakraborty, S., Eberspächer, J. (eds.) Advances in Real-Time Systems. Springer, Berlin, Heidelberg (2012). https://doi.org/10.1007/978-3-642-24349-3_5
22. Matic, S., Henzinger, T.A.: Trading end-to-end latency for composability. In: 26th IEEE International Real-Time Systems Symposium (RTSS 2005), pp. 12–110 (2005)
23. Pagetti, C., Forget, J., Boniol, F., Cordovilla, M., Lesens, D.: Multi-task implementation of multi-periodic synchronous programs. Discret. Event Dyn. Syst. **21**(3), 307–338 (2011)
24. Becker, M., Dasari, D., Mubeen, S., Behnam, M., Nolte, T.: End-to-end timing analysis of cause-effect chains in automotive embedded systems. J. Syst. Archit. **80**, 104–113 (2017)
25. Forget, J., Boniol, F., Pagetti, C.: Verifying end-to-end real-time constraints on multi-periodic models. In: 22nd IEEE International Conference on Emerging Technologies and Factory Automation, pp. 1–8 (2017)
26. Joseph, M., Pandya, P.: Finding response times in a real-time system. Comput. J. **29**(5), 390–395 (1986)
27. Liu, C.L., Layland, J.W.: Scheduling algorithms for multiprogramming in a hard-real-time environment. J. ACM **20**(1), 46–61 (1973)
28. Abdullah, J., Dai, G., Yi, W.: Worst-case cause-effect reaction latency in systems with non-blocking communication. In: DATE, pp. 1625–1630 (2019)

Quantitative Analysis of Interval Markov Chains

Giovanni Bacci[1], Benoît Delahaye[2], Kim G. Larsen[1], and Anders Mariegaard[1](✉)

[1] Department of Computer Science, Aalborg University, Aalborg, Denmark
{giovbacci,kgl,am}@cs.aau.dk

[2] Université de Nantes/LS2N UMR CNRS, 6004 Nantes, France
benoit.delahaye@univ-nantes.fr

Abstract. Interval Markov chains (IMCs), as first introduced by Larsen and Jonsson in 1991 are succinct specifications for probabilistic systems that generalise Markov chains (MCs) by allowing state transition probabilities to lie within an interval. In this work, we address the study of IMCs in a quantitative setting by extending the notion of IMCs by associating with each state a reward that is gained when leaving the state. Specifically, we compare three different semantic interpretations proposed in the literature (once-and-for-all, interval Markov decision process and at-every-step) in the context of model-checking rPCTL, an extension of PCTL where each path-formula is equipped with the specification of a bound on the accumulated reward. We prove that for the full logic, the three semantics are not equivalent, but for the fragment of reward-bounded reachability properties, the interval Markov decision process semantics and the at-every-step semantics are equivalent. Finally, we discuss model-checking algorithms for the three semantics by reduction to the model-checking problem for parametric Markov chains.

1 Introduction

The early work of Bengt Jonsson contains several contributions to the verification of distributed systems [20]. This still very active research direction [7] has been dominated by two schools: the North American school stressing automata and temporal logics, and the European school with focus on process algebra and behavioural equivalences. Both directions have their pros and cons with respect to compositionality and refinement: in the process algebraic approach compositional reasoning was guaranteed by congruence properties of the considered equivalences. However, specifications are typically very explicit being single equivalence classes leaving no room for a stepwise refinement process. In contrast, in the temporal logic approach logical implication between specifications provides the basis for stepwise refinement. However, it is notoriously hard to derive logical properties of composite systems from properties of their components, see [2,30]. Within the process algebraic approach, the introduction of Modal Transition Systems [27] (MTS) may be seen as a step towards support of a true stepwise refinement process. In MTS the transitions of a labelled

E.-R. Olderog et al. (Eds.): Jonsson Festschrift, LNCS 13030, pp. 57–77, 2021.
https://doi.org/10.1007/978-3-030-91384-7_4

transition system are classified as either mandatory (must) of optional (may) leading to a modal refinement precongruence generalizing the strict behavioural equivalences.

At the same time, probabilistic extensions of process algebra were introduced, e.g. [15], including the introduction of probabilistic bisimulation [25,26]. In collaboration with the last author of this paper (during a nice sabbatical at SICS in 1990), Bengt Jonsson quickly followed up with a probabilistic extension of MTS [22], originally termed Probabilistic Specifications, but by now better known as Interval Markov Chains (IMC). It is fair to say that IMC has inspired much subsequent research (including this paper).

On the temporal logical side, the introduction of PCTL in the seminal paper [17,21] by Bengt Jonsson and Hans Hansson is by now considered a prime logic for specifying properties of probabilistic systems. Since its introduction significant effort has been made towards efficient model checking algorithms for PCTL. However, there are still open problems foremost the question of decidability of satisfiability. One research direction that we will pursue in this paper is that of model checking PCTL with respect to IMC.

Our Contribution. We consider interval Markov reward models (IMRMs), a class of models that extend interval Markov chains by assigning a (positive) reward to each state. For regular IMCs, three distinct semantics have been proposed in the literature: the once-and-for-all semantics [5], the interval Markov decision process (IMDP) semantics [5,8,29] and the at-every-step semantics [22]. We provide a natural extension of the three semantics to IMRMs and investigate the differences between the three semantics in the context of model-checking. For this we consider the logic Probabilistic CTL (PCTL) [18] with reward-bounded path-formulae (rPCTL). For a given fragment of the logic, we say that two semantics are *equivalent* if for some IMRM specification and rPCTL formula, whenever there exists a satisfying model of one semantics, there exists a satisfying model of the other semantics.

Our contribution is twofold. The first part of the paper concerns the comparison of the above mentioned semantics:

(i) we prove that the three semantics are not equivalent with respect to the full fragment of rPCTL;
(ii) if one restricts the attention to probabilistic bounded reachability queries (a) we show that the once-and-for-all semantics and the IMDP-semantics are not equivalent, whereas (b) the IMDP-semantics and at-every-step semantics are.

The result in (i) can be seen as a generalisation of a similar result by Bart et al. [5] for IMCs against PCTL properties. In contrast to [5], where three IMCs semantics where shown to be equivalent with respect to reachability queries, we show that such an equivalence does not generalise to IMRMs.

In the second part of the paper we present algorithms for model-checking IMRMs for the three semantics. For the full logic and the once-and-for-all semantics, we present a reduction to the (existential) model-checking problem for parametric Markov reward models [1] with interval-constraints on the parameters. As for the IMDP semantics, we devise a reduction to the model-checking problem of IMRMs using the once-and-for-all semantics.

Notably, thanks to the semantic equivalence result relative to reachability queries mentioned earlier, such a reduction solves also the model checking problem against reachability queries when one interprets IMRMs using the at-every-step semantics. However, model checking generic rPCTL properties with respect to the at-every-step semantics still remains an open problem.

Related Work. Since their introduction by Jonsson and Larsen [22], IMCs have been investigated from different perspectives. In particular, [12,13] tackles the computational complexity of several decision problems, such as deciding whether or not an IMC has an implementation (the *consistency* problem) and whether the set of implementations of one IMC is entailed by the set of implementation by another IMC (thorough refinement). For model-checking, [6] considers LTL model-checking w.r.t IMCs with the once-and-for-all semantics, while [8,29] presents algorithms for verifying PCTL properties for both the once-and-for-all semantics as well as the IMDP semantics. The work in [8] also considers general ω-regular properties. From a computational complexity perspective, Chen et al. [9] proved that the two variants of the PCTL model-checking problem w.r.t. the once-and-for-all semantics and the IMDP semantics are both P-complete.

Another body of research is the work on *parametric* IMCs (PIMCs) [5,11, 14,28] where, instead of an interval, one can instead place a parameter. All the problems for IMCs can then be re-cast in two variants for PIMCs, depending on the quantification over the parameters (existential or universal). Closest to our work is [5], in which the equivalence between the three different semantics is investigated for IMCs. In the same paper, verifying a probabilistic reachability property for a given PIMCs is reduced to solving a constraint satisfaction problem.

2 Preliminaries and Notation

We denote by $\mathbb{R}$, $\mathbb{Q}$, and $\mathbb{N}$ respectively the set of real, rational, and natural numbers. Given a binary relation $R \subseteq X \times Y$ and $x \in X$, we define the projection of R on x as $R(x) = \{y \in Y \mid (x, y) \in R\}$, and we denote by R^{-1} the inverse of R, i.e., $R^{-1} = \{(y, x) \mid (x, y) \in R\}$.

For a finite nonempty set X, $\mu \colon X \to [0, 1]$ is a probability distribution on X if $\sum_{x \in X} \mu(x) = 1$. Moreover μ is extended to sets $Y \subseteq X$ as $\mu(Y) = \sum_{y \in Y} \mu(y)$. We write $\mathcal{D}(X)$ for the set of probability distributions on X. For $\mu \in \mathcal{D}(X)$ we define the support of μ as $\mathtt{support}(\mu) = \{x \in X \mid \mu(x) > 0\}$.

3 Markov Reward Models

In this section we recall the definitions of Markov reward model (MRM), probabilistic reward bisimulation, and Reward-Bounded Probabilistic CTL (rPCTL).

For the rest of the paper, we fix a countable set of atomic propositions A.

Definition 1 (Markov Reward Model). *A* Markov reward model *is a tuple* $\mathcal{M} = (S, s_0, \pi, \rho, \ell)$ *consisting of a finite set of states* S*, an initial state* $s_0 \in S$*, a transition probability function* $\pi \colon S \to \mathcal{D}(S)$*, a state-reward function* $\rho \colon S \to \mathbb{N}_{>0}$ *assigning to each state a positive reward*[1] *and a labelling function* $\ell \colon S \to 2^A$ *mapping states to atomic propositions.*

Intuitively, if $\mathcal{M}$ is in state s it moves to state s' with probability $\pi(s)(s')$, thereby receiving the reward $\rho(s)$. In this sense $\mathcal{M}$ can be seen as a state-machine that generates paths of states starting from the initial state s_0.

We denote by $G_\mathcal{M} = (S, \to)$ the *underlying labelled graph of* $\mathcal{M}$, where $s, s' \in S$ are connected by a labelled directed edge $s \xrightarrow{p,r} s'$ if and only if $p = \pi(s)(s') > 0$ and $r = \rho(s)$. We will assume without loss of generality that all states of $\mathcal{M}$ are reachable from the initial state s_0 in its underlying graph. For $s \in S$ we define the set of *successors* of s as $\texttt{succ}(s) = \texttt{support}(\pi(s))$.

Example 1. Figures 1b–d depicts three MRMs. Consider the MRM $\mathcal{M}_o = (T_o, t_0, \pi_o, \rho_o, \ell^{\mathcal{M}_o})$ in Fig. 1b. States $T_o = \{t_i \mid 0 \leq i \leq 4\}$ are visualised by a circle split in two, with the name of a state t_i at the top and the reward $\rho_o(t_i)$ at the bottom. The initial state t_0 is identified by a double-stroke border. State labels $\ell^{\mathcal{M}_o}(t_i)$ are visualised next to the state t_i unless the set is empty, in which case the set is omitted. From the underlying graph $G_{\mathcal{M}_o}$ we have $\texttt{succ}(t_0) = \{t_1, t_2\}$, $t_0 \xrightarrow{0.3,1} t_1$ and $t_0 \xrightarrow{0.7,1} t_2$.

A *path* is an infinite sequence of states $\sigma = s_0, s_1, \ldots \in S^\omega$; for $j \in \mathbb{N}$, we denote by $\sigma[j]$ the $(j+1)$-th state of σ, i.e., $\sigma[j] = s_j$ and by $\mathcal{W}(\sigma)(j) = \sum_{i=0}^{j-1} \rho(s_i)$ the accumulated reward of σ after j transitions. For a finite path $\sigma = s_0, \ldots, s_j \in S^*$ we define the length of σ as $|\sigma| = j$.

To associate probabilities to measurable events, we adopt the classical cylinder set construction from [4, Chapter 10]. For $w \in S^*$, the cylinder set of w is the set of all paths having prefix w, i.e., $cyl(w) = wS^\omega$. Given an *initial probability distribution* $\iota \in \mathcal{D}(S)$, we define the probability space $(S^\omega, \Sigma_\mathcal{M}, \mathbb{P}^\mathcal{M}_\iota)$, where $\Sigma_\mathcal{M}$ is the smallest σ-algebra that contains all the cylinder sets, and $\mathbb{P}^\mathcal{M}_\iota$ is the unique probability measure such that, for all $w = s_0 \cdots s_n \in S^*$,

$$\mathbb{P}^\mathcal{M}_\iota(cyl(w)) = \iota(s_0) \cdot \textstyle\prod_{0 \leq i < n} \pi(s_i)(s_{i+1}) \,.$$

When ι is the Dirac distribution pointed at s, i.e. $\iota(s) = 1$, we write $\mathbb{P}^\mathcal{M}_s$, or just $\mathbb{P}_s$ when $\mathcal{M}$ is clear from the context. Similarly, we may write $\mathbb{P}^\mathcal{M}$ as a shorthand for $\mathbb{P}^\mathcal{M}_{s_0}$ when s_0 is the initial state of $\mathcal{M}$.

Definition 2 (Bisimulation). *Let* $\mathcal{M} = (S, s_0, \pi, \rho, \ell)$ *be an MRM. An equivalence relation* $\mathcal{R} \subseteq S \times S$ *is a* probabilistic reward bisimulation *for* $\mathcal{M}$ *if whenever* $(s, t) \in \mathcal{R}$*, then (i)* $\rho(s) = \rho(t)$*, (ii)* $\ell(s) = \ell(t)$*, and (iii)* $\pi(s)(C) = \pi(t)(C)$ *for all* $C \in S_{/\mathcal{R}}$*.*

[1] All results presented in this paper can be generalized to MRMs having positive rational state rewards by multiplying the vector of rewards by a suitably large scaling factor.

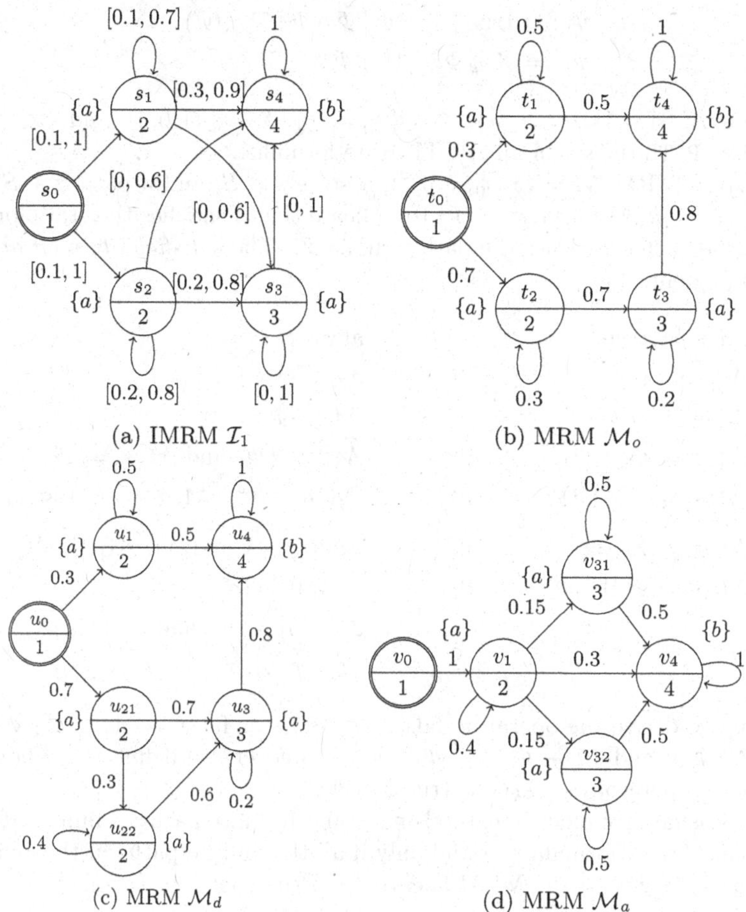

Fig. 1. IMRM $\mathcal{I}_1$ and implementations $\mathcal{M}_o \in [\![\mathcal{I}_1]\!]_o$, $\mathcal{M}_d \in [\![\mathcal{I}_1]\!]_d$ and $\mathcal{M}_a \in [\![\mathcal{I}_1]\!]_a$.

Two states $s, s' \in S$ are probabilistic bisimilar, written $s \sim s'$, if they are related by some probabilistic bisimulation. By abuse of notation we may write $\mathcal{M} \sim \mathcal{M}'$ to indicate that the initial states of the MRMs $\mathcal{M}$ and $\mathcal{M}'$ are bisimilar w.r.t. their disjoint union.

We now present an extension of probabilistic CTL (PCTL) [18], namely reward-bounded PCTL (rPCTL), where the next and the until operators are equipped with the specification of a finite bound on the accumulated reward. As any CTL-based logic, rPCTL allows for state formulae describing properties about states in an MRM and path formulae describing properties about paths in an MRM. State formulae Φ and path formulae Ψ are formed according to the following abstract syntax:

$$\Phi ::= \text{true} \mid a \mid \neg\Phi \mid \Phi \wedge \Phi \mid \mathcal{P}_{\bowtie\lambda}(\Psi)$$
$$\Psi ::= \mathsf{X}_{\trianglelefteq k}\,\Phi \mid \Phi\,\mathsf{U}_{\trianglelefteq k}\,\Phi$$

where $a \in A$, $\bowtie = \{<, \leq, \geq, >\}$, $\trianglelefteq = \{\leq, =, \geq\}$, $\lambda \in \mathbb{Q} \cap [0, 1]$, and $k \in \mathbb{N}$. We denote by $\mathtt{rPCTL}$ the set of all rPCTL state-formulae.

Given an MRM $\mathcal{M} = (S, s_0, \pi, \rho, \ell)$, a state $s \in S$, and a path $\sigma \in S^\omega$, we write $\mathcal{M}, s \models \Phi$ (resp. $\mathcal{M}, \sigma \models \Psi$) to indicate that s satisfies the state formula Φ (resp. the path σ satisfies the path formula Ψ). The *satisfiability relation* $\models$ is inductively defined as:

$$\begin{array}{lll}
\mathcal{M}, s \models \text{true} & & \text{always} \\
\mathcal{M}, s \models a & \text{iff} & a \in \ell(s) \\
\mathcal{M}, s \models \neg\Phi & \text{iff} & \mathcal{M} \not\models \Phi \\
\mathcal{M}, s \models \Phi_1 \wedge \Phi_2 & \text{iff} & \mathcal{M}, s \models \Phi_1 \text{ and } \mathcal{M}, s \models \Phi_2 \\
\mathcal{M}, s \models \mathcal{P}_{\bowtie\lambda}(\Psi) & \text{iff} & \mathbb{P}_s(\{\sigma \in S^\omega \mid \mathcal{M}, \sigma \models \Psi\}) \bowtie \lambda \\
\mathcal{M}, \sigma \models \mathsf{X}_{\trianglelefteq k}\Phi & \text{iff} & \rho(\sigma[0]) \trianglelefteq k \text{ and } \mathcal{M}, \sigma[1] \models \Phi \\
\mathcal{M}, \sigma \models \Phi_1 \mathsf{U}_{\trianglelefteq k}\Phi_2 & \text{iff} & \exists j \geq 0.\, \mathcal{W}(\sigma)(j) \trianglelefteq k, \\
& & \mathcal{M}, \sigma[j] \models \Phi_2 \text{ and} \\
& & \forall i < j.\, \mathcal{M}, \sigma[i] \models \Phi_1.
\end{array}$$

As usual, we derive the operators false, $\vee$, and $\rightarrow$ as false $:= \neg$true, $\Phi_1 \vee \Phi_2 := \neg(\neg\Phi_1 \wedge \neg\Phi_2)$, and $\Phi_1 \rightarrow \Phi_2 := \neg\Phi_1 \vee \Phi_2$. Moreover, we define the k-bounded reachability operator as $\Diamond_{\trianglelefteq k}\Phi := \text{true}\,\mathsf{U}_{\trianglelefteq k}\,\Phi$.

The satisfiability relation extends naturally to finite paths: a finite path $\sigma \in S^*$ satisfies a path-formula Ψ if and only if all the infinite paths in the cylinder-set $cyl(\sigma)$ satisfy Ψ. If the MRM is clear from the context, we sometimes write $s \models \Phi$ instead of $\mathcal{M}, s \models \Phi$. We may also write $\mathcal{M} \models \Phi$ as a shorthand for $\mathcal{M}, s_0 \models \Phi$ and $\mathbb{P}^{\mathcal{M}}(\Psi)$ as a shorthand for $\mathbb{P}^{\mathcal{M}}_{s_0}(\{\sigma \in S^\omega \mid \mathcal{M}, \sigma \models \Psi\})$, where s_0 is the initial state of $\mathcal{M}$.

Example 2. Consider the three MRMs $\mathcal{M}_o, \mathcal{M}_d$ and $\mathcal{M}_a$ depicted in Figs. 1b–d and let $\Phi = \mathcal{P}_{\geq 0.15}(\Diamond_{\leq 3}\, b)$. By rPCTL semantics we have $\mathcal{M}_o \models \Phi$, witnessed by the path t_0, t_1, t_4 and similarly, $\mathcal{M}_d \models \Phi$ and $\mathcal{M}_a \models \Phi$. If the probability threshold is increased from 0.15 to 0.3, $\mathcal{M}_o$ and $\mathcal{M}_d$ no longer satisfy the formula, i.e. for formula $\Phi' = \mathcal{P}_{\geq 0.3}(\Diamond_{\leq 3}\, b)$, we have $\mathcal{M}_o \not\models \Phi'$, $\mathcal{M}_d \not\models \Phi'$ but $\mathcal{M}_a \models \Phi'$.

For $s, s' \in S$, we say that s and s' are logically equivalent w.r.t. rPCTL, written $s \cong_{\mathtt{rPCTL}} s'$, if

$$\forall \Phi \in \mathtt{rPCTL}.\, \mathcal{M}, s \models \Phi \iff \mathcal{M}, s' \models \Phi.$$

The following theorem states that probabilistic bisimilarity equals logical equivalence w.r.t rPCTL.

Theorem 1. *Let $\mathcal{M} = (S, s_0, \pi, \rho, \ell)$ be an MRM and $s, s' \in S$. Then, $s \sim s' \iff s \cong_{\mathtt{rPCTL}} s'$.*

4 Interval Markov Reward Models

In this section we introduce the notion of interval Markov reward model (IMRM) and present three distinct semantic interpretations of IMRMs, comparing their expressivity with respect to rPCTL.

Before defining IMRMs, it is convenient to introduce some notation. We write $\mathbb{I}$ for the set of all non-empty closed interval subsets of $[0,1]$, and $\mathcal{D}_{\mathbb{I}}(X) = \{f \mid f \colon X \to \mathbb{I}\}$ denotes the set of *interval specifications* on a finite set X. An interval specification $f \in \mathcal{D}_{\mathbb{I}}(X)$ describes a family of probability distributions on X that satisfy the specification i.e., $[\![f]\!] = \{\pi \in \mathcal{D}(X) \mid \forall x \in X. \pi(x) \in f(x)\}$.

Definition 3 (Interval Markov Reward Model). *An* interval Markov reward model *(IMRM) is a tuple $\mathcal{I} = (S, s_0, \Pi, R, \ell)$ where*

- *S is a finite nonempty set of states,*
- *$s_0 \in S$ is the initial state,*
- *$\Pi \colon S \to \mathcal{D}_{\mathbb{I}}(S)$ is the interval transition function,*
- *$R \colon S \to \mathbb{N}_{>0}$ is the state-reward function, and*
- *$\ell \colon S \to 2^A$ is the state-labeling function.*

Given an IMRM $\mathcal{I} = (S, s_0, \Pi, R, \ell)$ and state $s \in S$, $\Pi(s) = I_s$ is the interval-specification for state s, defining for each state $s' \in S$ a probability interval $I_s(s')$, within which s moves to s'. By abuse of notation we may refer to MRMs as particular cases of IMRMs having singleton intervals specifications. Hence, an IMRM $\mathcal{I}$ is a succinct specification for a family of MRMs where the transition function satisfies boundary conditions dictated by the interval transition function Π. Hereafter, we will assume that all IMRMs we will be working with have non-empty interval specifications, i.e., $[\![\Pi(s)]\!] \neq \emptyset$ for all $s \in S$. In literature this condition is known as (local) *consistency* [13]. The definition of paths, finite paths and accumulated weight are defined similarly as for MRMs.

Example 3. Consider the IMRM $\mathcal{I}_1 = (S, s_0, \Pi, R, \ell^{\mathcal{I}})$ depicted in Fig. 1a. For any state $s_i \in \{s_0, s_1, s_2, s_3, s_4\}$, the interval specification $\Pi(s_i)$ is depicted by edges connecting s_i to states in $\mathtt{succ}(s_i)$. These edges are labelled by the interval assigned by $\Pi(s_i)(s_j)$. Singleton intervals $[p, p]$ are simply represented by p.

In the literature [5,8,22,29], there have been proposed three different semantic interpretations of IMRMs, namely, the *once-and-for-all semantics*, the *interval Markov decision process semantics* (IMDP), and the *at-every-step semantics.* We now present the three distinct semantics for IMRMs and some basic results showing the relationship among the different semantics. To ease the presentation, we fix an MRM $\mathcal{M} = (T, t_0, \pi, \rho, \ell^{\mathcal{M}})$ and an IMRM $\mathcal{I} = (S, s_0, \Pi, R, \ell^{\mathcal{I}})$ and we will implicitly refer to their components in the remainder of this section.

The *once-and-for-all* semantics [5], also called the Uncertain Markov Chain semantics [29] is the simplest among the three semantics. It requires to choose for each state of the IMRM a probability distribution satisfying the corresponding interval specification.

Definition 4 (Once-and-for-all semantics). *An arbitrary MRM* $\mathcal{M}$ *satisfies the IMRM* $\mathcal{I}$ *w.r.t. the once-and-for-all semantics, written* $\mathcal{M} \models_o \mathcal{I}$, *if and only if* $T \subseteq S$, $t_0 = s_0$, *and for all* $t \in T$, $\rho(t) = R(t)$, $\ell^{\mathcal{M}}(t) = \ell^{\mathcal{I}}(t)$, *and* $\pi(t) \in [\![\Pi(t)]\!]$.

Example 4. Consider again the IMRM $\mathcal{I}_1$ in Fig. 1a. Figure 1b depicts an MRM $\mathcal{M}_o$ that satisfies $\mathcal{I}_1$ with the once-and-for-all semantics.

In contrast to the once-and-for-all semantics, in the *interval Markov decision process semantics* (IMDP semantics) [5,8,29], the choice of the transition probability distribution for a state $s \in S$ is performed each time a state is visited.

Definition 5 (IMDP semantics). *An MRM* $\mathcal{M}$ *satisfies the IMRM* $\mathcal{I}$ *w.r.t. the IMDP semantics, written* $\mathcal{M} \models_d \mathcal{I}$, *if and only if there exists a mapping* $\tau \colon T \to S$ *such that* $\tau(t_0) = s_0$, *and for all* $t \in T$, $\ell^{\mathcal{M}}(t) = \ell^{\mathcal{I}}(\tau(t))$, $\rho(t) = R(\tau(t))$, *and there exists* $\delta_t \in [\![\Pi(\tau(t))]\!]$ *such that for all* $t' \in T$, $t' \in \mathtt{succ}(t)$ *implies that* $\pi(t)(t') = \delta_t(\tau(t'))$.

As its name suggests, the IMDP semantics is reminiscent of the way one resolves nondeterminism in a Markov decision process (MDP) by means of a deterministic memory-dependent scheduler (*cf.* [4, Ch10]). With respect to similar semantic interpretations given for interval Markov chains [5,8,29], Definition 5 is more similar in spirit to that given in [5] for the fact that the MRM $\mathcal{M}$ needs to be finite.

Example 5. The MRM in Fig. 1c satisfies the IMRM $\mathcal{I}_1$ in Fig. 1a w.r.t. the IMDP semantics. To see this, consider the mapping $\tau(u_0) = s_0, \tau(u_1) = s_1, \tau(u_{21}) = \tau(u_{22}) = s_2, \tau(u_3) = s_3$ and $\tau(u_4) = s_4$. Note that u_{21} and u_{22} are two different implementations of the IMRM state s_2.

Remark 1. Notice that $\mathcal{M} \models_o \mathcal{I}$ implies $\mathcal{M} \models_d \mathcal{I}$ and the mapping $\tau \colon T \to S$ witnessing this fact is the identity function, i.e., $\tau(t) = t$ for all $t \in T$.

The last semantic interpretation for IMRMs is the so-called *at-every-step semantics*. Its definition is a simple extension of the original semantics given for interval Markov chains by Jonsson and Larsen [22]. Its main feature consists in generalizing the mapping $\tau \colon T \to S$ from the IMDP semantics to a relation $\mathcal{R} \subseteq T \times S$. This allows one to "aggregate" compatible states of the IMRM into a single state of the MRM implementation, as well as "redistributing" the successors of a state of the IMRM into multiple states.

Definition 6 (At-every-step semantics). *An MRM* $\mathcal{M}$ *satisfies the IMRM* $\mathcal{I}$ *w.r.t. the at-every-step semantics, written* $\mathcal{M} \models_a \mathcal{I}$ *if and only if there exists a relation* $\mathcal{R} \subseteq T \times S$ *such that* $(t_0, s_0) \in \mathcal{R}$ *and for all pairs* $(t, s) \in \mathcal{R}$ *we have that* $\ell^{\mathcal{M}}(t) = \ell^{\mathcal{I}}(s)$, $\rho(t) = R(s)$, *and there exists a correspondence function* $\delta_{(t,s)} \colon T \to (S \to [0,1])$ *such that*

1. *for all* $t' \in \mathtt{succ}(t)$, $\delta_{(t,s)}(t') \in \mathcal{D}(S)$.
2. *for all* $s' \in S$,

$$\left(\sum_{t' \in T} \pi(t)(t') \cdot \delta_{(t,s)}(t')(s')\right) \in \Pi(s)(s').$$

3. *for all* $(t', s') \in T \times S$, *if* $\delta_{(t,s)}(t')(s') > 0$ *then* $(t', s') \in \mathcal{R}$.

Example 6. The MRM $\mathcal{M}_a$ depicted in Fig. 1d is one possible at-every-step implementation of the IMRM $\mathcal{I}_1$ of Fig. 1a. This is witnessed by the relation

$$\mathcal{R} = \{(v_0, s_0), (v_1, s_1), (v_1, s_2), (v_{31}, s_3), (v_{32}, s_3), (v_4, s_4)\}$$

and the following correspondence functions:

$$\delta_{(v_0,s_0)}(v_1)(s_1) = \delta_{(v_0,s_0)}(v_1)(s_2) = \tfrac{1}{2}, \quad \delta_{(v_1,s_1)}(v_{31})(s_3) = \delta_{(v_1,s_1)}(v_{32})(s_3) = 1.$$

Note that the state v_1 in $\mathcal{M}_a$ implements both s_1 and s_2, while the state s_3 is "redistributed" into v_{31} and v_{32}. The example illustrates that one is allowed to aggregate and split states under the at-every-step semantics.

As shown in Example 6, the at-every-step semantics allows one MRM state to implement multiple IMRM states by aggregation. Next, we show that for any MRM with such aggregated states, there exists an at-every-step implementation with no aggregated states, which is probabilistic bisimilar to the MRM with aggregated states. The result follows immediately from a similar result for IMCs as presented in [5, Proposition 5]. To formalize the result, we borrow the notion of *degree of satisfaction* from [5].

Definition 7. *Let* $n \in \mathbb{N}$. *The MRM* $\mathcal{M}$ *satisfies the IMRM* $\mathcal{I}$ *w.r.t. the at-every-step semantics with degree of satisfaction* n, *written* $\mathcal{M} \models^n_a \mathcal{I}$, *if there exists a relation* $\mathcal{R} \subseteq T \times S$ *witnessing* $\mathcal{M} \models_a \mathcal{I}$ *such that* $|\mathcal{R}(t)| \leq n$ *for all states* $t \in T$.

Note that if an MRM $\mathcal{M}$ satisfies IMRM $\mathcal{I}$ with degree 1, all correspondence functions $\delta_{(t,s)}$ are Dirac distributions i.e. $\delta_{(t,s)}(t')(s') > 0 \implies \delta_{(t,s)}(t')(s') = 1$.

The following Lemma states that for any at-every-step implementation $\mathcal{M}$ of the IMRM $\mathcal{I}$, there exists an at-every-step implementation $\mathcal{M}'$ of $\mathcal{I}$ with degree 1 that is probabilistic bisimilar to $\mathcal{M}$.

Lemma 1. *Let* $\mathcal{M} \models^n_a \mathcal{I}$ *for some* $n \in \mathbb{N}$. *Then, there exists an MRM* $\mathcal{M}'$ *such that* $\mathcal{M} \sim \mathcal{M}'$ *and* $\mathcal{M}' \models^1_a \mathcal{I}$.

Remark 2. Note that $\mathcal{M} \models_d \mathcal{I}$ implies $\mathcal{M} \models^1_a \mathcal{I}$, since the mapping $\tau \colon T \to S$ witnessing $\mathcal{M} \models_d \mathcal{I}$ induces a functional relation $\mathcal{R} = \{(t, \tau(t)) \mid t \in T\}$ which can be easily verified to be a witness for $\mathcal{M} \models^1_a \mathcal{I}$.

The following result identifies the properties that a relation $\mathcal{R}$ witnessing $\mathcal{M} \models_a \mathcal{I}$ has when the MRM $\mathcal{M}$ satisfies also $\mathcal{M} \models_d \mathcal{I}$.

Proposition 1. *Let $\mathcal{R} \subseteq T \times S$ be a relation witnessing $\mathcal{M} \models_a^1 \mathcal{I}$. Then, $\mathcal{M} \models_d \mathcal{I}$ iff for all $(t, s) \in \mathcal{R}$ there exists no $s' \in \mathtt{succ}(s)$ such that $|\mathcal{R}^{-1}(s') \cap \mathtt{succ}(t)| > 1$.*

We are now ready to establish some basic relationship between the three semantics in terms of their expressivity. For any semantics $x \in \{o, d, a\}$, we denote by $[\![\mathcal{I}]\!]_x = \{\mathcal{M} \mid \mathcal{M} \models_x \mathcal{I}\}$ the family of MRMs that satisfy the IMRM $\mathcal{I}$ with respect to the semantic x.

The following result states that the three semantics presented in this section have different expressivity, with the at-every-step semantics being the most expressive semantics, followed by the IMDP semantics which in turn is more expressive than the once-and-for-all semantics.

Proposition 2. *For any IMRM $\mathcal{I}$, $[\![\mathcal{I}]\!]_o \subseteq [\![\mathcal{I}]\!]_d \subseteq [\![\mathcal{I}]\!]_a$ and for some IMRM $\mathcal{I}'$ these inclusions are strict, i.e., $[\![\mathcal{I}']\!]_o \subset [\![\mathcal{I}']\!]_d \subset [\![\mathcal{I}']\!]_a$.*

Proof. $[\![\mathcal{I}]\!]_o \subseteq [\![\mathcal{I}]\!]_d$ and $[\![\mathcal{I}]\!]_d \subseteq [\![\mathcal{I}]\!]_a$ follow for the arguments sketched respectively in Remarks 1 and 2. For the IMRM $\mathcal{I}_1$ in Fig. 1 in particular it holds that $\mathcal{M}_d \in [\![\mathcal{I}_1]\!]_d \setminus [\![\mathcal{I}_1]\!]_o$ and $\mathcal{M}_a \in [\![\mathcal{I}_1]\!]_a \setminus [\![\mathcal{I}_1]\!]_d$. □

5 Comparing Semantics Against rPCTL

In this section we investigate the IMRM semantics presented in Sect. 4 in the context of rPCTL model-checking. The rPCTL satisfiability relation naturally extends to IMRMs by requiring that an rPCTL formula is satisfied by some MRM implementation.

Definition 8. *We say that an IMRM $\mathcal{I}$ (existentially) satisfies the formula $\Phi \in$ $\mathtt{rPCTL}$ with respect to the semantics $x \in \{o, d, a\}$, written $\mathcal{I} \models_x \Phi$, iff there exists $\mathcal{M} \in [\![\mathcal{I}]\!]_x$ such that $\mathcal{M} \models \Phi$.*

The above definition is implicitly given in terms of the initial state s_0 of $\mathcal{I}$, but can be generalized to arbitrary states $s \in S$, as $\mathcal{I}, s \models \Phi$ by replacing s_0 with s.

In the following, we compare the three different semantics with respect to different classes of rPCTL formulae. To this end introduce a notion of semantic equivalence.

Definition 9 (Semantic equivalence). *For a fragment of rPCTL, $\mathcal{L} \subseteq$ $\mathtt{rPCTL}$ and two IMRM semantics $x, y \in \{o, d, a\}$, we say that the semantics x and y are* equivalent *w.r.t. $\mathcal{L}$ if for any IMRM $\mathcal{I}$ and state formula $\Phi \in \mathcal{L}$, $\mathcal{I} \models_x \Phi \iff \mathcal{I} \models_y \Phi$.*

The next result states that the at-every-step semantics is not equivalent to the IMDP semantics w.r.t. the full logic.

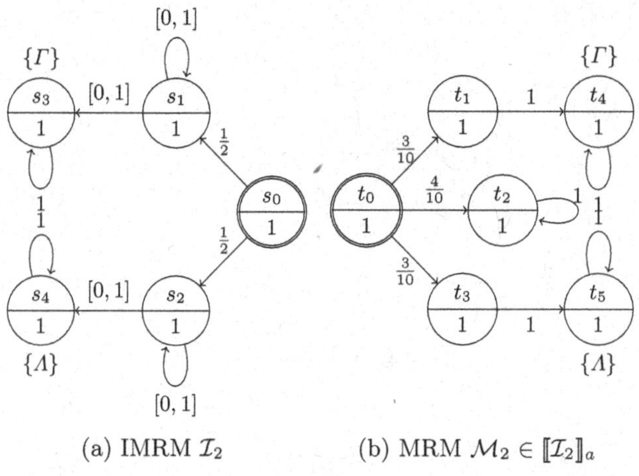

Fig. 2. IMRM $\mathcal{I}_2$ with at-every-step MRM implementation $\mathcal{M}_2$

Proposition 3. *The at-every-step semantics is not semantically equivalent to the IMDP semantics with respect to* rPCTL.

Proof. Consider the IMRM $\mathcal{I}_2$ and MRM $\mathcal{M}_2$ depicted in Fig. 2. One can verify that $\mathcal{M}_2 \models_a \mathcal{I}_2$. Let Φ be the following rPCTL formula

$$\Phi = \mathcal{P}_{>0}(\mathsf{X}_{\leq 1}\Phi_1) \wedge \mathcal{P}_{>0}(\mathsf{X}_{\leq 1}\Phi_2) \wedge \mathcal{P}_{>0}(\mathsf{X}_{\leq 1}\Phi_3),$$

where

$$\Phi_1 = \mathcal{P}_{\geq 1}(\mathsf{X}_{\leq 1}(\neg\Gamma \wedge \neg\Lambda)),\ \Phi_2 = \mathcal{P}_{\geq 1}(\mathsf{X}_{\leq 1}\Gamma) \text{ and } \Phi_3 = \mathcal{P}_{\geq 1}(\mathsf{X}_{\leq 1}\Lambda).$$

Clearly $\mathcal{M}_2 \models \Phi$ as the three outgoing transitions serve to satisfy each of the sub-formulae Φ_i ($i \in \{1, 2, 3\}$).

Consider an MRM $\mathcal{M}' \in [\![\mathcal{I}_2]\!]_d$. By IMDP semantics, $\mathcal{M}'$ must have an initial state with exactly two successors, say t'_1 and t'_2. Therefore there exists $i \in \{1, 2, 3\}$ such that $\mathcal{M}', t_j \not\models \Phi_i$ for any $j = 1, 2$ as no single successor can satisfy each Φ_i simultaneously. Hence, $\mathcal{I}_2 \not\models_d \Phi$. □

The above result is analogous to [5, Section 4.1], where it was proven that for internal Markov chains the at-every-step semantics and the IMDP semantics are not equivalent with respect to PCTL.

Reachability Queries. In the rest of the section we focus our attention on a semantic comparison relative to reachability queries, namely, formulae of the form $\mathcal{P}_{\bowtie\lambda}(\Diamond_{\trianglelefteq k}\Gamma)$, for arbitrary $\Gamma \in AP$, $k \in \mathbb{N}_{>0}$, $\lambda \in [0, 1]$, $\bowtie \in \{<, \leq, \geq, >\}$, and $\trianglelefteq \in \{\leq, \geq\}$. We denote by $\mathcal{L}_{\mathtt{reach}}$ the set of reachability queries and we write $\mathcal{L}^{\leq}_{\mathtt{reach}}$ (resp. $\mathcal{L}^{\geq}_{\mathtt{reach}}$) when we fix $\trianglelefteq = \leq$ (resp. $\trianglelefteq = \geq$).

Reachability properties are one of the fundamental questions for the quantitative analysis of systems. The atomic proposition Γ may represent a set of

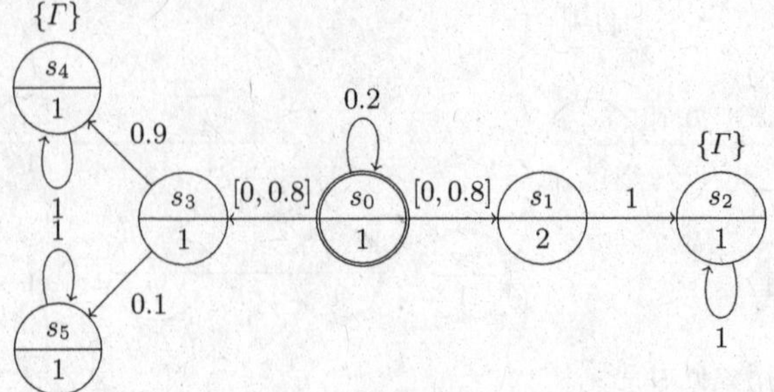

Fig. 3. IMRM $\mathcal{I}_3$

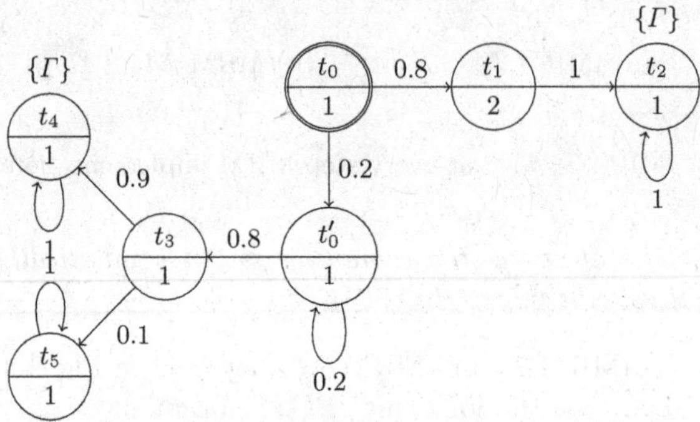

Fig. 4. MRM $\mathcal{M}_3$ such that $\mathcal{M}_3 \models \mathcal{P}_{>0.8}(\Diamond_{\leq 3}\Gamma)$

certain *bad* states which should be unlikely to be visited, or dually, a set of *good* states which should rather be visited with high probability. In the context of interval Markov chains, Bart et al. [5] have shown that the three semantic interpretations are equivalent with respect to reachability queries.

In contrast, the ability to express bounds on the reward accumulated until reaching a some goal state makes the IMPD semantics and the at-every-step semantics, more expressive than the once-and-for-all semantics relative to reachability queries.

Proposition 4. *The once-and-for-all semantics is not equivalent to the IMDP semantics w.r.t.* $\mathcal{L}_{\mathsf{reach}}$.

Proof. Consider the IMRM $\mathcal{I}_3$ in Fig. 3 and the formula $\mathcal{P}_{>0.8}(\Diamond_{\leq 3}\Gamma)$. Figure 4 shows $\mathcal{M}_3 \in [\![\mathcal{I}]\!]_d$ witnessed by the mapping $\tau(t_0) = \tau(t'_0) = s_0$ and $\tau(t_i) = s_i$ for $1 \leq i \leq 5$. Clearly $\mathcal{M}_3 \models \mathcal{P}_{>0.8}(\Diamond_{\leq 3}\Gamma)$.

Figure 5 shows the once-and-for-all MRM implementation of $\mathcal{I}_3$, $\mathcal{M}_4$, that maximizes the probability of reaching Γ without exceeding the weight budget of 3. One can see that $\mathcal{M}_4 \not\models \mathcal{P}_{>0.8}(\Diamond_{\leq 3}\Gamma)$. □

It remains to compare the at-every-step semantics and IMDP semantics w.r.t. reachability queries. To this end we first present two technical lemmas.

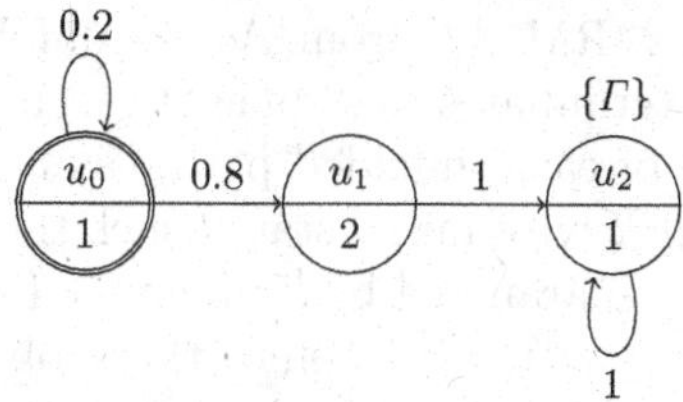

Fig. 5. MRM $\mathcal{M}_4$ such that $\mathcal{M}_4 \not\models \mathcal{P}_{>0.8}(\Diamond_{\leq 3}\Gamma)$

Lemma 2. *Let $\mathcal{I}$ be an IMRM, $\mathcal{M} \in [\![\mathcal{I}]\!]_a$, $\Gamma \in AP$, and $k \in \mathbb{N}$. Then, there exist $\mathcal{M}_{\leq}, \mathcal{M}_{\geq} \in [\![\mathcal{I}]\!]_d$ such that $\mathbb{P}^{\mathcal{M}_{\leq}}(\Diamond_{\leq k}\Gamma) \leq \mathbb{P}^{\mathcal{M}}(\Diamond_{\leq k}\Gamma) \leq \mathbb{P}^{\mathcal{M}_{\geq}}(\Diamond_{\leq k}\Gamma)$.*

Proof (sketch). By Lemma 1 and Theorem 1 we can assume w.l.o.g. that $\mathcal{M} \models_a^1 \mathcal{I}$. To construct $\mathcal{M}_{\leq}$ and $\mathcal{M}_{\geq}$ we proceed in two steps. We present the construction of $\mathcal{M}_{\leq}$ and then explain how to adapt it for $\mathcal{M}_{\geq}$.

(Step 1) We build an MRM $\mathcal{M}'$ from $\mathcal{M}$ by unfolding its structure. The unfolding of each path terminates when its accumulated weight exceeds k or when a state satisfying Γ is reached. Then, the last state of each unfolded path, say t, is replaced with an arbitrary once-and-for-all model of $\mathcal{I}$ with initial state t.
Note that $\mathbb{P}^{\mathcal{M}}(\Diamond_{\leq k}\Gamma) = \mathbb{P}^{\mathcal{M}'}(\Diamond_{\leq k}\Gamma)$ since the probability value is obtained as the sum over all the cylinders obtained from paths constructed in the unfolding. Moreover, $\mathcal{M}' \models_a^1 \mathcal{I}$ because $\mathcal{M} \models_a^1 \mathcal{I}$ and the unfolding does not introduce any aggregation.
(Step 2) From $\mathcal{M}'$ we construct $\mathcal{M}_{\leq}$. Let $\mathcal{R}$ be the relation witnessing $\mathcal{M}' \models_a^1 \mathcal{I}$. If $\mathcal{R}$ satisfies the conditions of Proposition 1 we choose $\mathcal{M}' = \mathcal{M}_{\leq}$. Otherwise, for each state t of $\mathcal{M}$ such that $(t, s) \in \mathcal{R}$ and $|\mathcal{R}^{-1}(s') \cap \mathsf{succ}(t)| > 1$ for some $s' \in \mathsf{succ}(s)$ we proceed as follows. Let $t' \in \mathcal{R}^{-1}(s') \cap \mathsf{succ}(t)$ be the successor of t that minimizes the probability of reaching Γ within the reward bound up to t', i.e., $\mathbb{P}_{t'}^{\mathcal{M}'}(\Diamond_{\leq k'}\Gamma)$ where $k' = k - \mathcal{W}(\sigma)(|\sigma|)$ and σ is the finite path from the initial state of $\mathcal{M}'$ to t'. Then we redirect all the probability mass that was from t to $\mathcal{R}^{-1}(s') \cap \mathsf{succ}(t)$ to the single state t', "disconnecting" the set of states $(\mathcal{R}^{-1}(s') \cap \mathsf{succ}(t)) \setminus \{t'\}$ from t.
Let $\mathcal{M}_{\leq}$ be the MRM obtained from the above procedure. Note that $\mathcal{M}_{\leq}$ satisfies the conditions of Proposition 1 and $\mathbb{P}^{\mathcal{M}_{\leq}}(\Diamond_{\leq k}\Gamma) \leq \mathbb{P}^{\mathcal{M}'}(\Diamond_{\leq k}\Gamma)$.

As for the construction of $\mathcal{M}_{\geq}$, (Step 1) is done in the same way while in (Step 2) t' is chosen as the one that maximizes $\mathbb{P}_{t'}^{\mathcal{M}'}(\Diamond_{\leq k'}\Gamma)$. □

Lemma 3. *Let $\mathcal{I}$ be IMRM, $\mathcal{M} \in [\![\mathcal{I}]\!]_a$, $\Gamma \in AP$, and $k \in \mathbb{N}$. Then, there exist $\mathcal{M}_{\leq}, \mathcal{M}_{\geq} \in [\![\mathcal{I}]\!]_d$ such that $\mathbb{P}^{\mathcal{M}_{\leq}}(\Diamond_{\geq k}\Gamma) \leq \mathbb{P}^{\mathcal{M}}(\Diamond_{\geq k}\Gamma) \leq \mathbb{P}^{\mathcal{M}_{\geq}}(\Diamond_{\leq k}\Gamma)$.*

Proof (sketch). The proof proceeds in two steps analogously as for Lemma 2.
By Lemma 1 and Theorem 1 we can assume w.l.o.g. that $\mathcal{M} \models_a^1 \mathcal{I}$. We present the construction of $\mathcal{M}_{\leq}$ and then explain how to adapt it for $\mathcal{M}_{\geq}$.

(Step 1) We build an MRM $\mathcal{M}'$ from $\mathcal{M}$ by unfolding its structure. The unfolding of each path terminates as soon as its accumulated weight exceeded k. Then, the last state of each unfolded path, say t, is replaced with a once-and-for-all model $\mathcal{M}''$ of $\mathcal{I}$ with initial state t such that $\mathbb{P}_t^{\mathcal{M}''}(\Diamond\Gamma) \le \mathbb{P}_t^{\mathcal{M}}(\Diamond\Gamma)$. The existence of $\mathcal{M}''$ is guaranteed by [5, Lemma 4].
Note that $\mathbb{P}^{\mathcal{M}'}(\Diamond_{\ge k}\Gamma) \le \mathbb{P}^{\mathcal{M}}(\Diamond_{\ge k}\Gamma)$ since the probability value is obtained as the sum over all the cylinders obtained from paths constructed in the unfolding. Moreover, $\mathcal{M}' \models_a^1 \mathcal{I}$ because $\mathcal{M} \models_a^1 \mathcal{I}$ and the unfolding does not introduce any aggregation.
(Step 2) From $\mathcal{M}'$ we construct $\mathcal{M}_{\le}$ following the same procedure used for (Step 2) in the proof of Lemma 2.

As for the construction of $\mathcal{M}_{\ge}$, in (Step 1) we need to choose $\mathcal{M}''$ such that $\mathbb{P}_t^{\mathcal{M}''}(\Diamond\Gamma) \ge \mathbb{P}_t^{\mathcal{M}}(\Diamond\Gamma)$ and (Step 2) is modified as done for Lemma 2. □

Theorem 2. *The IMDP semantics and the at-every-step semantics are equivalent w.r.t.* $\mathcal{L}_{\mathtt{reach}}$.

Proof. Let $\mathcal{I}$ be an IMRM, $\Phi = \mathcal{P}_{\bowtie\lambda}(\Diamond_{\trianglelefteq k}\Gamma) \in \mathcal{L}_{\mathtt{reach}}$ and $\mathcal{M} \in [\![\mathcal{I}]\!]_a$ such that $\mathcal{M} \models \Phi$. We proceed by cases.

If $\trianglelefteq = \le$, we consider two sub-cases. If $\bowtie \in \{<, \le\}$ then by Lemma 2 there exists $\mathcal{M}_{\le} \in [\![\mathcal{I}]\!]_d$ such that $\mathbb{P}^{\mathcal{M}_{\le}}(\Diamond_{\le k}\Gamma) \le \mathbb{P}^{\mathcal{M}}(\Diamond_{\le k}\Gamma)$. Therefore $\mathcal{I} \models_d \Phi$. If $\bowtie \in \{\ge, >\}$ then by Lemma 2 there exists $\mathcal{M}_{\ge} \in [\![\mathcal{I}]\!]_d$ such that $\mathbb{P}^{\mathcal{M}_{\ge}}(\Diamond_{\le k}\Gamma) \ge \mathbb{P}^{\mathcal{M}}(\Diamond_{\le k}\Gamma)$. Hence $\mathcal{I} \models_d \Phi$.

If $\trianglelefteq = \ge$ we use the same arguments as before by using Lemma 3 in place of Lemma 2. □

6 Model-Checking Algorithms

In this section we turn our attention to model-checking different fragments of rPCTL. By the results of the previous section, each IMRM semantics requires its own treatment for the full logic rPCTL. For the important fragment of reachability queries in $\mathcal{L}_{\mathtt{reach}}$, we need two algorithms, one for the once-and-for-all semantics and one for the IMDP semantics. In the following, we restrict ourselves to formulae with only upper bounds on path-formulae and similar to $\mathcal{L}_{\mathtt{reach}}^{\le}$, we denote by $\mathtt{rPCTL}^{\le}$ the set of all rPCTL formulae with only upper bounds on the path formulae.

For the once-and-for-all semantics we reduce the model-checking problem w.r.t $\mathtt{rPCTL}^{\le}$ to the (existential) model-checking problem for parametric Markov reward models (PMRMs) [1] with interval constraints on the parameters. Efficient procedures for model-checking PMRMs against various logics have received a lot of attention in recent years and are now supported by modern tools such as PRISM [24], PARAM [16] and PROPHESY [10]. For the IMDP semantics we exploit the fact that all rewards are strictly positive to devise a reduction to the model-checking problem for the once-and-for-all semantics. For the at-every-step semantics we leave the model-checking problem for fragments containing $\mathcal{L}_{\mathtt{reach}}^{\le}$ open. We proceed by treating each semantics in turn.

6.1 Once-and-for-all Semantics

For the fragment rPCTL$^{\leq}$ we present a reduction to the (existential) model-checking problem for PMRMs with interval constraints on the parameters. We first recall the definition of PRMMs and then present the reduction. PMRMs extend MRMs by allowing the transition probabilities to take values in a finite nonempty set P of *parameters*. Thus, for any finite nonempty set X, the function $\mu_P\colon X \to [0,1] \cup P$ is a parametric distribution. The set $\mathcal{D}_P(X)$ is then the set of all parametric distributions.

Definition 10 (Parametric MRM). *A* parametric *Markov Reward Model (PMRM) is defined as a tuple $\mathcal{M}_P = (S, s_0, \rho, \pi_P, \ell^{\mathcal{M}})$ where S, s_0, ρ and $\ell^{\mathcal{M}}$ are defined as for MRMs and for each $s \in S$, $\pi_P \in \mathcal{D}_P(S)$ is the* parametric *probability transition function.*

A given PMRM gives rise to a set of MRMs by interpreting the parameters as rational values and making sure that the resulting distribution are probability distributions (i.e. sum up to 1). Formally, a valuation function $\kappa\colon \mathbb{Q}_{>0} \cup P \to [0,1]$ is a function such that for all $r \in \mathbb{Q}_{>0}$, $\kappa(r) = r$, for all $p \in P$, $\kappa(p) > 0$ and for all states $s \in S$, $\sum_{s' \in S} \kappa(\pi_P(s)(s'))) = 1$. We abuse notation and for any PMRM $\mathcal{M}_P$ write $\kappa(\mathcal{M}_P)$ for the MRM induced by κ.

Existential Model-Checking. We consider the following decision problem for PMRMs: given a PMRM $\mathcal{M}_P$ and formula $\Phi \in$ rPCTL$^{\leq}$, does there exist a valuation function κ such that $\kappa(\mathcal{M}_P) \models \Phi$?

The problem is extended with interval-constraints on the parameters as follows: for all $(s, s') \in S \times S$ let $I_{s,s'} = [l_{s,s'}, u_{s,s'}] \in \mathbb{I}$ be some interval. The parameter valuation function κ must then also satisfy the following constraints:

$$\bigwedge_{(s,s') \in S \times S} \kappa(\pi_P(s)(s')) \in I_{s,s'}.$$

The Reduction. Let $\mathcal{I} = (S, s_0, \Pi, R, \ell^{\mathcal{I}})$ be an IMRM and $\Phi \in$ rPCTL$^{\leq}$ an arbitrary formula. We now construct a PMRM $\mathcal{M}_P$ and a set of interval constraints such that if there exists a valuation function κ where $\kappa(\mathcal{M}_P) \models \Phi$, while κ satisfies the given interval constraints, then $\mathcal{I} \models_o \Phi$.

Let $\mathcal{M}_P$ be the PMRM identical to $\mathcal{I}$ except that each interval $\Pi(s)(s')$ is replaced by a parameter $p_{s,s'}$. For each $p_{s,s'}$, the interval constraint that κ must satisfy, is given by $\Pi(s)(s')$ i.e. any parameter valuation function κ must satisfy the following interval constraints:

$$\bigwedge_{(s,s') \in S \times S} \kappa(p_{s,s'}) \in \Pi(s)(s').$$

Assume that there exists a valuation function κ such that $\kappa(\mathcal{M}_P) \models \Phi$ in addition to satisfying the above interval constraints. Without loss of generality, we assume that all states in $\kappa(\mathcal{M}_P)$ are reachable as all states of any MRM have to be reachable. If that is not the case, one can simply remove all unreachable states as they do not influence satisfiability. By construction, it is clear that $\kappa(\mathcal{M}_P) \in [\![\mathcal{I}]\!]_o$ as κ induces a probability distribution for each state s that satisfies the interval-specifications $\Pi(s)$ given by $\mathcal{I}$, while preserving rewards and labels of each state.

Interpreting $\mathtt{rPCTL}^{\leq}$ *on PMRMs.* In literature, papers on PCTL model-checking for PMRMs only consider step-bounded or unbounded until-formulae, in contrast to the reward-bounded until formulae in $\mathtt{rPCTL}^{\leq}$. This is not a restriction since any PMRM that contains a state s with a reward greater than 1 can be replaced by a sequence of states with reward 1. Hence, any upper bound on the formula can be interpreted as a step-bound in this (larger) model. In the same way, it is possible to "unroll" the model to reduce (step)-bounded reachability to unbounded reachability [23, Remark 4]. Thus, any technique for model-checking PCTL where the until is step-bounded or unbounded on PMRMs can be used for $\mathtt{rPCTL}^{\leq}$ [3,10,16,23,24]. In the case of unbounded until, the model-checking problem for PMRMs is in PSPACE [19].

6.2 IMDP Semantics

Our approach for verifying properties with the IMDP semantics is based on the fact that the IMDP semantics is a simple extension of the once-and-for-all semantics, where one is allowed to choose a different probability distribution each time a state is visited. Recall that every reward in the model is strictly positive and we have concrete upper bounds on all path-formulae. Hence, even if one is allowed to choose a different distribution each time a state is visited, for the purpose of verifying Φ, we can bound the number of times a different probability distribution needs to be chosen for any IMDP implementation that satisfies Φ. Hence, one can do a bounded unfolding of the IMRM that preserves interval specifications, to encode all possible implementations that may satisfy Φ. The unfolding itself is an IMRM, where the set of states is the set of all non-empty finite paths, S^+, bounded by a given depth k. Interval-preservation is ensured by letting the transitioning between any two such states be defined by the transitioning between their two last states in the original IMRM.

Definition 11 (IMRM k-unfolding). *For any IMRM* $\mathcal{I} = (S, s_0, \Pi, R, \ell^{\mathcal{I}})$ *and* $k \in \mathbb{N}$, *let* $\mathcal{I}{\downarrow_k} = (S_k, s_0, \Pi_k, R_k, \ell^{\mathcal{I}\downarrow_k})$ *be the* interval specification preserving *k-unfolding of $\mathcal{I}$, defined as follows*[2]*:*

- $S_k = \{\sigma \in S^+ \mid \mathcal{W}(\sigma)(|\sigma|) \leq k,$
  $\forall_{0 \leq i < |\sigma|}.\Pi(\sigma[i], \sigma[i+1]) \neq [0,0]\}.$
- *For all* $\sigma \in S_k \cup \{\epsilon\}$[3] *and* $s, s_1 \in S$, $\Pi_k(\sigma s, \sigma s s_1) = \Pi(s, s_1)$.
- *For any path* $\sigma = s_1, \ldots, s_n$ *in* S_k, $R_k(\sigma) = R(s_n)$ *and* $\ell^{\mathcal{I}\downarrow_k}(\sigma) = \ell^{\mathcal{I}}(s_n)$.

[2] Technically, self-loops must be added for states that represent maximal paths w.r.t. k in order for the unfolding to be a proper IMRM.
[3] Where ϵ is the empty string.

As any MRM $\mathcal{M}$ can be seen as an IMRM with singleton intervals, we abuse notation and write $\mathcal{M}{\downarrow_k}$ for the k-unfolding of the MRM $\mathcal{M}$.

The following two lemmas prove two key properties of our unfolding definition. The first lemma states that for an IMRM $\mathcal{I}$ with initial state s_0, if any successor s_0s' of s_0 in the k-unfolding of $\mathcal{I}$ satisfies a given formula Φ, then this can be verified by changing the initial state to s' and performing a $(k - R(s_0))$-unfolding of $\mathcal{I}$ where $R(s_0)$ is the reward assigned by $\mathcal{I}$ to s_0. The second lemma states that whenever an MRM is an IMDP implementation of an IMRM $\mathcal{I}$ then the k-unfolding of $\mathcal{M}$ is an once-and-for-all implementation of the k-unfolding of $\mathcal{I}$. This implies that if from any formula $\Phi \in \texttt{rPCTL}^{\leq}$ we can define a $k \in \mathbb{N}$ such that the k-unfolding of $\mathcal{I}$ includes all the paths needed for verifying Φ, we can reduce the model-checking problem using the IMDP semantics to model-checking using the once-and-for-all semantics on the k-unfolding of $\mathcal{I}$, $\mathcal{I}{\downarrow_k}$.

Lemma 4. *For any two IMRMs defined as* $\mathcal{I}^{s_0} = (S, s_0, \Pi, R, \ell^{\mathcal{I}})$ *and* $\mathcal{I}^{s'} = (S, s', \Pi, R, \ell^{\mathcal{I}})$ *with* $s' \in \texttt{succ}(s_0)$, $k \geq R(s_0)$, $\Phi \in \texttt{rPCTL}^{\leq}$ *and semantics* $x \in \{o, d, a\}$, *it holds that*

$$\mathcal{I}^{s_0}{\downarrow_k}, s_0s' \models_x \Phi \implies \mathcal{I}^{s'}{\downarrow_{k-R(s_0)}}, s' \models_x \Phi.$$

Proof. The lemma follows easily from the definition of unfolding and rPCTL semantics. The condition $k \geq R(s_0)$ ensures that s_0s' is a state in $\mathcal{I}^{s_0}$.

Lemma 5. *For any IMRM* $\mathcal{I}$, *MRM* $\mathcal{M}$ *and* $k \in \mathbb{N}$, *if* $\mathcal{M} \in [\![\mathcal{I}]\!]_d$ *then* $\mathcal{M}{\downarrow_k} \in [\![\mathcal{I}{\downarrow_k}]\!]_o$.

Remark 3. Strictly speaking, Lemma 5 only holds up to isomorphism as $\mathcal{M}$ by the IMDP semantics may contain states not in $\mathcal{I}$. In this case, the states of $\mathcal{M}{\downarrow_k}$ is not a subset of the states of $\mathcal{I}{\downarrow_k}$ as required by the once-and-for-all semantics.

For any formula $\Phi \in \texttt{rPCTL}^{\leq}$ we define the reward-depth denoted by $K(\Phi) \in \mathbb{N}$, on the structure of Φ. For a probabilistic reward-bounded reachability objective of the form $\Phi = \mathcal{P}_{\bowtie\lambda}(\Diamond_{\leq k}\Gamma)$, $K(\Phi) = k$ implies that only paths with an accumulated reward of at most k is of interest. Hence, a k-unfolding of $\mathcal{I}$ is sufficient for the purpose of verifying Φ.

Definition 12 (Reward-depth). *For every property* $\Phi \in \texttt{rPCTL}^{\leq}$*, the* reward-depth, $K(\Phi) \in \mathbb{N}$ *is defined inductively on the structure of* Φ*:*

$$\begin{aligned}
&K(true) = 0\\
&K(a) = 0\\
&K(\neg\Phi) = K(\Phi)\\
&K(\Phi_1 \wedge \Phi_2) = \max\{K(\Phi_1), K(\Phi_2)\}\\
&K(\mathcal{P}_{\bowtie\lambda}(X_{\leq k}\Phi)) = k + K(\Phi)\\
&K(\mathcal{P}_{\bowtie\lambda}(\Phi_1 U_{\leq k}\Phi_2)) = k + \max\{K(\Phi_1), K(\Phi_2)\}
\end{aligned}$$

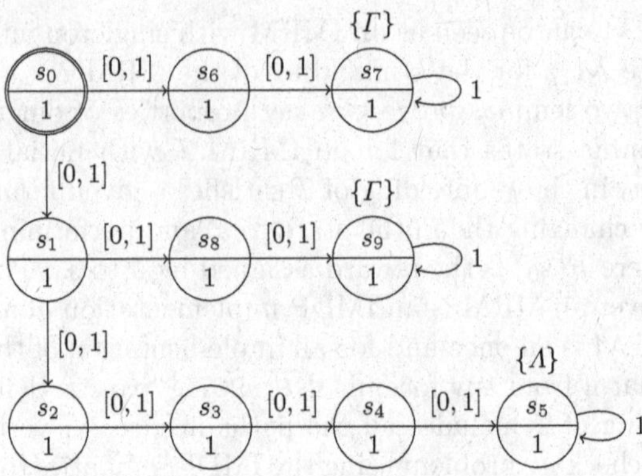

Fig. 6. IMRM $\mathcal{I}_4$

Example 7. Consider the IMRM $\mathcal{I}_3$ in Fig. 3 and formula $\Phi = \mathcal{P}_{>0.8}(\Diamond_{\leq 3}\Gamma)$. By definition, $K(\Phi) = 3 + \max\{K(\text{true}), K(\Gamma)\} = 3$. Notice that $\mathcal{I}_3 \models_d \Phi$ if and only if $k \geq 3$, with the witnessing implementation being the MRM in Fig. 4. Consider now the IMRM $\mathcal{I}_4$ in Fig. 6 and the property $\Phi' = \mathcal{P}_{\geq \lambda_1}(\Phi_1 \, U_{\leq 2} \, \Phi_2)$ where $\Phi_1 = \mathcal{P}_{\geq \lambda_2}(\Diamond_{\leq 2} \Gamma)$, $\Phi_2 = \mathcal{P}_{\geq \lambda_3}(\Diamond_{\leq 3} \Lambda)$ and $\lambda_1, \lambda_2, \lambda_3 \in [0, 1]$. For any semantics $x \in \{o, d, a\}$ it is clear that $\mathcal{I}_4{\downarrow_k} \not\models_x \Phi'$ if $k < 5$, irrespective of the concrete values for λ_1, λ_2 and λ_3, as the path $s_0, s_1, s_2, s_3, s_4, s_5$ must be preserved. By definition, $K(\Phi') = 5$ i.e. if one performs an unfolding of $\mathcal{I}$ with a reward-depth less than $K(\Phi')$, one cannot hope to find any implementation satisfying any concrete instantiation of Φ'.

As indicated by Example 7, $K(\Phi)$ is the reward-depth required for the verification of Φ. Hence, unfolding to a reward-depth greater than $K(\Phi)$ should not influence the satisfaction of Φ. The following lemma proves this monotonicity property.

Lemma 6 (Monotonicity). *For any MRM $\mathcal{M}$, formula $\Phi \in$ rPCTL$^{\leq}$, $k \geq K(\Phi)$ and $\varepsilon > 0$,*

$$\mathcal{M}{\downarrow_k} \models \Phi \implies \mathcal{M}{\downarrow_{k+\varepsilon}} \models \Phi.$$

The next lemma states that if an MRM $\mathcal{M}$ satisfies Φ, then the $K(\Phi)$-unfolded model $\mathcal{M}{\downarrow_{K(\Phi)}}$ also satisfies Φ i.e. unfolding to a reward-depth of at least $K(\Phi)$ is sufficient to verify Φ.

Lemma 7. *For any MRM $\mathcal{M} \in [\![I]\!]_d$ and formula $\Phi \in$ rPCTL$^{\leq}$,*

$$\mathcal{M} \models \Phi \implies \mathcal{M}{\downarrow_{K(\Phi)}} \models \Phi.$$

We now present the main theorem of this section, stating that rPCTL model-checking for IMRMs with the IMDP semantics can be reduced to model-checking using the once-and-for-all semantics on an IMRM constructed by unfolding to the reward-depth required by the given formula of interest.

Theorem 3. *For IMRM $\mathcal{I}$ and formula $\Phi \in \mathtt{rPCTL}^{\leq}$,*

$$\mathcal{I} \models_d \Phi \implies \mathcal{I}{\downarrow}_{K(\Phi)} \models_o \Phi.$$

Proof. We assume $\mathcal{I} \models_d \Phi$, hence $\exists \mathcal{M} \in [\![I]\!]_d . \mathcal{M} \models \Phi$. By Lemma 7, $\mathcal{M} \models \Phi \implies \mathcal{M}{\downarrow}_{K(\Phi)} \models \Phi$ and by Lemma 5 we get $\mathcal{M} \in [\![I]\!]_d \implies \mathcal{M}{\downarrow}_{K(\Phi)} \in [\![I{\downarrow}_{K(\Phi)}]\!]_o$. Hence, $\mathcal{I}{\downarrow}_{K(\Phi)} \models_o \Phi$ as required. □

Complexity. For any IMRM $\mathcal{I} = (S, s_0, \Pi, R, \ell^{\mathcal{I}})$ let $R_{\min} = \min_{s \in S} R(s)$ be the smallest reward present in $\mathcal{I}$. The unfolded model, $\mathcal{I}{\downarrow}_{K(\Phi)}$ is then a model of size $\mathcal{O}\left(|S|^{\lfloor \frac{K(\Phi)}{R_{\min}} \rfloor}\right)$, as each state of $\mathcal{I}{\downarrow}_{K(\Phi)}$ is a leaf of the underlying $K(\Phi)$-bounded unfolding of $\mathcal{I}$ which is a tree with branching factor $\mathcal{O}(|S|)$ and height $\mathcal{O}\left(\lfloor \frac{K(\Phi)}{R_{\min}} \rfloor\right)$.

Remark 4. By Theorem 2, for any $\Phi \in \mathcal{L}^{\leq}_{\mathtt{reach}}$ the approach presented in Sect. 6.2 is valid also for model checking Φ w.r.t. the at-every-step semantics.

7 Conclusion and Future Work

We investigated model-checking questions relative to IMRMs specifications interpreted according to three semantics: once-and-for-all, interval Markov decision process, and at-every-step. This work builds on the results of [5] on interval Markov chains by introducing an additional ingredient: rewards. We showed that by introducing rewards the one-at-for-all semantics is no longer expressive enough to answer (existential) reachability queries with respect to the other two semantics. Nevertheless, the IMDP semantics and the at-every-step semantics are still logically equivalent with respect to the reward-bounded reachability fragment of rPCTL.

We then presented how to algorithmically solve the model-checking problem for IMRMs by proposing different reductions to the model-checking problem for parametric Markov reward models (PMRMs). First, we presented a reduction to the model-checking problem of PMRMs for model checking IMRMs interpreted over the once-and-for-all semantics. Then, for the IMDP semantics, we presented a reduction to the model-checking problem for the once-and-for-all semantics, via a finite unfolding of the model. Crucial for our reduction is that the state rewards are positive. Notably, this reduction can also be used also to answer reward-bounded reachability queries for IMRMs interpreted according to the at-every-step semantics.

As future work, we plan to further investigate the model-checking problem with respect to the at-every-step semantic interpretations of IMRMs.

References

1. Alur, R., Henzinger, T.A., Vardi, M.Y.: Parametric real-time reasoning. In: Proceedings of the Twenty-Fifth Annual ACM Symposium on Theory of Computing, San Diego, CA, USA, 16–18 May 1993, pp. 592–601 (1993). https://doi.org/10.1145/167088.167242

2. Andersen, H.R., Stirling, C., Winskel, G.: A compositional proof system for the modal mu-calculus. In: Proceedings of the Ninth Annual Symposium on Logic in Computer Science (LICS '94), Paris, France, 4–7 July 1994, pp. 144–153 (1994). https://doi.org/10.1109/LICS.1994.316076
3. Bacci, G., Hansen, M., Larsen, K.G.: Model checking constrained Markov reward models with uncertainties. In: Parker, D., Wolf, V. (eds.) QEST 2019. LNCS, vol. 11785, pp. 37–51. Springer, Cham (2019). https://doi.org/10.1007/978-3-030-30281-8_3
4. Baier, C., Katoen, J.: Principles of Model Checking. MIT Press, Cambridge (2008)
5. Bart, A., Delahaye, B., Fournier, P., Lime, D., Monfroy, E., Truchet, C.: Reachability in parametric interval Markov chains using constraints. Theor. Comput. Sci. **747**, 48–74 (2018). https://doi.org/10.1016/j.tcs.2018.06.016
6. Benedikt, M., Lenhardt, R., Worrell, J.: LTL model checking of interval Markov chains. In: Piterman, N., Smolka, S.A. (eds.) TACAS 2013. LNCS, vol. 7795, pp. 32–46. Springer, Heidelberg (2013). https://doi.org/10.1007/978-3-642-36742-7_3
7. Benveniste, A., et al.: Contracts for system design. Found. Trends Electron. Design Autom. **12**(2–3), 124–400 (2018). https://doi.org/10.1561/1000000053
8. Chatterjee, K., Sen, K., Henzinger, T.A.: Model-checking ω-regular properties of interval Markov chains. In: Amadio, R. (ed.) FoSSaCS 2008. LNCS, vol. 4962, pp. 302–317. Springer, Heidelberg (2008). https://doi.org/10.1007/978-3-540-78499-9_22
9. Chen, T., Han, T., Kwiatkowska, M.Z.: On the complexity of model checking interval-valued discrete time Markov chains. Inf. Process. Lett. **113**(7), 210–216 (2013). https://doi.org/10.1016/j.ipl.2013.01.004
10. Dehnert, C.: PROPhESY: A PRObabilistic ParamEter SYnthesis tool. In: Kroening, D., Păsăreanu, C.S. (eds.) CAV 2015. LNCS, vol. 9206, pp. 214–231. Springer, Cham (2015). https://doi.org/10.1007/978-3-319-21690-4_13
11. Delahaye, B.: Consistency for parametric interval Markov chains. In: 2nd International Workshop on Synthesis of Complex Parameters, SynCoP 2015, London, United Kingdom, 11 April 2015, pp. 17–32 (2015). https://doi.org/10.4230/OASIcs.SynCoP.2015.17
12. Delahaye, B., Larsen, K.G., Legay, A., Pedersen, M.L., Wąsowski, A.: Decision problems for interval Markov chains. In: Dediu, A.-H., Inenaga, S., Martín-Vide, C. (eds.) LATA 2011. LNCS, vol. 6638, pp. 274–285. Springer, Heidelberg (2011). https://doi.org/10.1007/978-3-642-21254-3_21
13. Delahaye, B., Larsen, K.G., Legay, A., Pedersen, M.L., Wasowski, A.: Consistency and refinement for interval Markov chains. J. Log. Algebr. Program. **81**(3), 209–226 (2012). https://doi.org/10.1016/j.jlap.2011.10.003
14. Delahaye, B., Lime, D., Petrucci, L.: Parameter synthesis for parametric interval Markov chains. In: Jobstmann, B., Leino, K.R.M. (eds.) VMCAI 2016. LNCS, vol. 9583, pp. 372–390. Springer, Heidelberg (2016). https://doi.org/10.1007/978-3-662-49122-5_18
15. van Glabbeek, R.J., Smolka, S.A., Steffen, B., Tofts, C.M.N.: Reactive, generative, and stratified models of probabilistic processes. In: Proceedings of the Fifth Annual Symposium on Logic in Computer Science (LICS '90), Philadelphia, Pennsylvania, USA, 4–7 June 1990, pp. 130–141 (1990). https://doi.org/10.1109/LICS.1990.113740
16. Hahn, E.M., Hermanns, H., Wachter, B., Zhang, L.: PARAM: a model checker for parametric Markov models. In: Touili, T., Cook, B., Jackson, P. (eds.) CAV 2010. LNCS, vol. 6174, pp. 660–664. Springer, Heidelberg (2010). https://doi.org/10.1007/978-3-642-14295-6_56

17. Hansson, H., Jonsson, B.: A framework for reasoning about time and reliability. In: Proceedings of the Real-Time Systems Symposium - 1989, Santa Monica, California, USA, December 1989, pp. 102–111. IEEE Computer Society (1989). https://doi.org/10.1109/REAL.1989.63561. https://ieeexplore.ieee.org/xpl/conhome/268/proceeding
18. Hansson, H., Jonsson, B.: A logic for reasoning about time and reliability. Formal Asp. Comput. **6**(5), 512–535 (1994). https://doi.org/10.1007/BF01211866
19. Hutschenreiter, L., Baier, C., Klein, J.: Parametric Markov chains: PCTL complexity and fraction-free gaussian elimination. In: Proceedings Eighth International Symposium on Games, Automata, Logics and Formal Verification, GandALF 2017, Roma, Italy, 20–22 September 2017, pp. 16–30 (2017). https://doi.org/10.4204/EPTCS.256.2
20. Jonsson, B.: Modular verification of asynchronous networks. In: Proceedings of the Sixth Annual ACM Symposium on Principles of Distributed Computing, Vancouver, British Columbia, Canada, 10–12 August 1987, pp. 152–166 (1987). https://doi.org/10.1145/41840.41853
21. Jonsson, B.: A fully abstract trace model for dataflow and asynchronous networks. Distrib. Comput. **7**(4), 197–212 (1994). https://doi.org/10.1007/BF02280834
22. Jonsson, B., Larsen, K.G.: Specification and refinement of probabilistic processes. In: Proceedings of the Sixth Annual Symposium on Logic in Computer Science (LICS '91), Amsterdam, The Netherlands, 15–18 July 1991, pp. 266–277 (1991). https://doi.org/10.1109/LICS.1991.151651
23. Junges, S., et al.: Parameter synthesis for Markov models. CoRR abs/1903.07993 (2019). http://arxiv.org/abs/1903.07993
24. Kwiatkowska, M., Norman, G., Parker, D.: PRISM 4.0: verification of probabilistic real-time systems. In: Gopalakrishnan, G., Qadeer, S. (eds.) CAV 2011. LNCS, vol. 6806, pp. 585–591. Springer, Heidelberg (2011). https://doi.org/10.1007/978-3-642-22110-1_47
25. Larsen, K.G., Skou, A.: Bisimulation through probabilistic testing. In: Conference Record of the Sixteenth Annual ACM Symposium on Principles of Programming Languages, Austin, Texas, USA, 11–13 January 1989, pp. 344–352 (1989). https://doi.org/10.1145/75277.75307
26. Larsen, K.G., Skou, A.: Bisimulation through probabilistic testing. Inf. Comput. **94**(1), 1–28 (1991). https://doi.org/10.1016/0890-5401(91)90030-6
27. Larsen, K.G., Thomsen, B.: A modal process logic. In: Proceedings of the Third Annual Symposium on Logic in Computer Science (LICS '88), Edinburgh, Scotland, UK, 5–8 July 1988, pp. 203–210. IEEE Computer Society (1988). https://doi.org/10.1109/LICS.1988.5119. https://ieeexplore.ieee.org/xpl/conhome/203/proceeding
28. Petrucci, L., van de Pol, J.: Parameter synthesis algorithms for parametric interval Markov chains. In: Baier, C., Caires, L. (eds.) FORTE 2018. LNCS, vol. 10854, pp. 121–140. Springer, Cham (2018). https://doi.org/10.1007/978-3-319-92612-4_7
29. Sen, K., Viswanathan, M., Agha, G.: Model-checking Markov chains in the presence of uncertainties. In: Hermanns, H., Palsberg, J. (eds.) TACAS 2006. LNCS, vol. 3920, pp. 394–410. Springer, Heidelberg (2006). https://doi.org/10.1007/11691372_26
30. Winskel, G.: A complete proof system for SCCS with modal assertions. In: Maheshwari, S.N. (ed.) FSTTCS 1985. LNCS, vol. 206, pp. 392–410. Springer, Heidelberg (1985). https://doi.org/10.1007/3-540-16042-6_22

Regular Model Checking: Evolution and Perspectives

Parosh Aziz Abdulla(✉)

Uppsala University, Uppsala, Sweden
parosh@it.uu.se

Abstract. We describe the main ideas behind the framework of regular model checking in a tutorial-like manner. First, we recall the original framework, and then describe an over-approximation scheme that we have designed to make the method more scalable. Finally, we point to some directions for future work.

1 Introduction

During the last two decades, a vast research effort has been devoted to extending the applicability of algorithmic verification to infinite-state systems, using approaches based on abstraction, deductive techniques, decision procedures, etc. One primary approach has been to extend the paradigm of symbolic model checking [21] to new classes of models such as timed automata, push-down systems, systems with unbounded communication channels, Petri nets, and systems that operate on integers and reals (e.g., [13,18,22,23]).

Regular Model Checking (RMC) is one such an extension. In RMC, regular sets represent sets of states and regular transducers represent transition relations. Such sets and relations are typically defined over finite or infinite words or tree structures. Most initial works considered models whose configurations can be represented as finite words of arbitrary length over a finite alphabet. Such models include parameterized systems consisting of an arbitrary number of homogeneous finite-state processes connected in a linear or ring-formed topology, as well as systems that operate on queues, stacks, integers, and other linear data structures. Regular model checking was first advocated by Kesten et al. [33] and by Boigelot and Wolper [35], as a uniform framework for analyzing several classes of parameterized and infinite-state systems. The idea was that regular sets would provide an efficient representation of infinite-state spaces, and play a role similar to the role that Binary Decision Diagrams (BDDs) used to play for symbolic model checking of finite-state systems. We can then exploit automata-theoretic algorithms for manipulating regular sets. Such algorithms have been successfully implemented, e.g., in the Mona [31] system.

A generic task in symbolic model checking is to verify safety or liveness properties by computing properties of the set of reachable states. For finite-state systems, this is typically done by state-space exploration (which is guaranteed to

E.-R. Olderog et al. (Eds.): Jonsson Festschrift, LNCS 13030, pp. 78–96, 2021.
https://doi.org/10.1007/978-3-030-91384-7_5

terminate). For infinite-state systems, the procedure terminates only if there is a bound on the distance (in number of transitions) from the initial configurations to any reachable configuration. An analogous observation holds if we perform reachability analysis backwards, by iteration-based methods [25,34] from a set of target configurations. A parameterized or infinite-state system does not have such a bound, and the model checking problem for such systems can even be undecidable. In contrast to the deductive application of systems like Mona [14], the goal in regular model checking is to verify system properties algorithmically (automatically). One way to accomplish that is devising so-called *acceleration techniques* that calculate the effect of an arbitrarily long sequence of transitions. This problem has been addressed in regular model checking [11,20,32]. In general, the effect of acceleration is not computable. However, computability have been obtained for certain classes [32]. Analogous techniques for computing accelerations have successfully been developed for several classes of parameterized and infinite-state systems, e.g., systems with unbounded FIFO channels [2,15,16,19], systems with stacks [18,24,28,30], and systems with counters [17,26].

While RMC, in its pure form, is an elegant and theoretically interesting framework, it became eventually clear that the applicability of the method was limited. The main bottleneck was the automata representation which would not scale beyond small examples. A main research direction has been to find over-approximations that allow more light-weight symbolic representations than the full class of regular languages, while still being sufficiently precise to successfully carry out the verification of non-trivial examples.

In this tutorial, I will use two running examples to explain the main ideas behind the two approaches.

2 Framework

We describe the framework of RMC, using a running example, namely a simple token passing protocol.

2.1 Regular Model Checking

In its simplest form, the RMC framework represents a transition system in the following manner.

- A *configuration* (state) of the system is a word over a finite alphabet Σ.
- Sets of configurations are represented by regular sets over Σ. In particular, this applies to the set of *initial configurations.*
- The *transition relation* is a regular and length-preserving relation on Σ^*. We represent the relation by a finite-state transducer $\mathcal{T}$ over $(\Sigma \times \Sigma)$. The transducer $\mathcal{T}$ accepts all words $(a_1, a'_1) \cdots (a_n, a'_n)$ (of pairs of elements) such that $(a_1 \cdots a_n \ a'_1 \cdots a'_n)$ is in the transition relation. Sometimes, the transition relation is given as a union of a finite number of relations, each of which is called an *action.*

In this paper, we often abuse notation and identify the transducer $\mathcal{T}$ with the relation defined by $\mathcal{T}$. We will apply the transducer relation on (regular) sets of configurations. For a set $\mathcal{C}$ of configurations and a binary relation R on configurations, let $\mathcal{C} \circ R$ denote the set of configurations w such that $w' \, R \, w$ for some $w' \in \mathcal{C}$. Let R^+ denote the transitive closure of R and R^* denote the reflexive transitive closure of R.

The simple instance of RMC, introduced in the previous paragraphs, is already powerful and can model several interesting classes of systems. On example is *parameterized systems* which consist of arbitrary numbers of linear or ring-shaped collections of processes. We can do this by letting each position in the word represent one process in the system. It is also possible to model programs that operate on linear unbounded data structures such as queues, stacks, integers, etc. For instance, a stack can be modeled by letting each position in the word represent the corresponding position in the stack.

For reachability properties, the requirement of the transducer to be length-preserving is not a restriction. For instance, in the case of parameterized systems, the length-preserving condition implies that we cannot dynamically create new processes. However, the system can initially contain an arbitrary but bounded number of processes which are "statically allocated". We can then faithfully model all finite computations of the system, by initially allocating sufficiently many processes in their configurations. Thus, the restriction to length-preserving transducers introduces no limitations for analyzing safety properties, but may incur restrictions on the ability to specify and verify liveness properties of systems with dynamically allocated data structures. The latter follows from the fact that liveness properties quantify over the set of infinite computations. Therefore, restricting the lengths of the configurations makes it impossible to faithfully model all infinite computations of the system.

2.2 Examples

In Fig. 1 we consider a *token passing protocol*: a simple parameterized system consisting of an arbitrary (but finite) number of processes organized in a linear fashion. Initially, the left-most process has the token. In each step, the process currently having the token passes it to the right. A configuration of the system is a word over the alphabet $\{t, n\}$, where t represents that the process has the token, and n represents not having it. For instance, the word $nntnn$ represents a configuration of a system with five processes where the third process has the token. The set of initial configurations is given by the regular expression tn^* (Fig. 1(a)), i.e., in an initial configuration, the left-most process, and only the left-most process, has the token. The transition relation is represented by the transducer in (Fig. 1(b)). For instance, the transducer accepts the word $(n,n)(n,n)(t,n)(n,t)(n,n)$, representing the pair $(nntnn,\ nnntn)$ of configurations where the token is passed from the third to the fourth process.

As a second example, we consider a system consisting of a finite-state process operating on one unbounded FIFO channel. Let Q be the set of control states of the process, and let M be the (finite) set of messages which can reside inside the

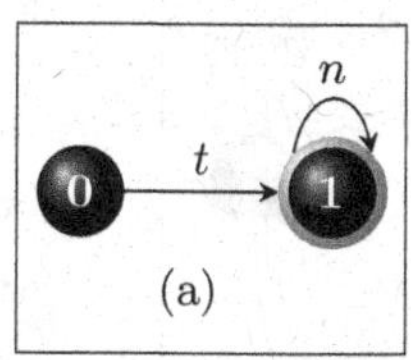

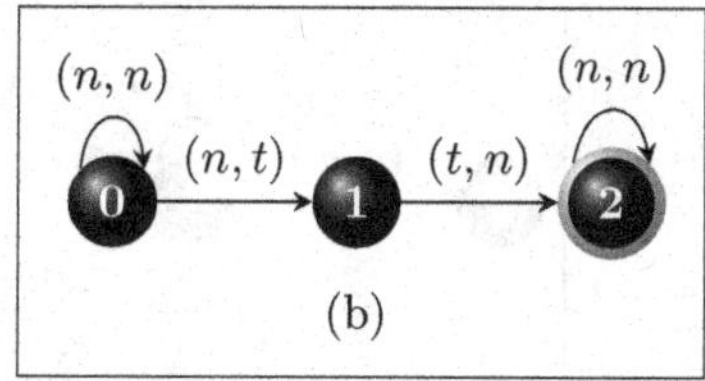

Fig. 1. The token passing protocol: (a) the set of initial configurations, (b) the transducer describing the transition relation.

channel. A configuration of the system is a word over the alphabet $Q \cup M \cup \{\bot\}$, where the *padding symbol* $\bot$ represents an empty position in the channel. For instance the word $q_1 \bot m_3 m_1 \bot\bot$ corresponds to a configuration where the process is in state q_1 and the channel (of length four) contains the messages m_3 and m_1 in this order. The set of configurations of the system can thus be described by the regular expression $Q\bot^* M^* \bot^*$.

By allowing arbitrarily many padding symbols $\bot$, one can model channels of arbitrary but bounded length. As an example, assume that the stack alphabet is the set $\{a, b\}$. Then, the action where the process sends the message m to the channel and changes state from q to q' is modeled by the transducer in Fig. 2.

2.3 Verification Problems

We will consider two types of verification problems in this paper.

The first problem is verification of *safety properties.* A safety property is typically of form "bad things do not happen during system execution". A safety property can be verified by solving a *reachability* problem. Formulated in the regular model checking framework, the corresponding problem is the following: given a set of initial configurations I, a regular set of *bad configurations* B, and a transition relation specified by a transducer T, does there exist a path from I to B through the transition relation T? This amounts to checking whether $(I \circ T^*) \cap B = \emptyset$. The problem can be solved by computing the set $Inv = I \circ T^*$ and checking whether it intersects B.

The second problem is verification of *liveness properties.* A liveness property is of form "a good thing happens during system execution". Often, liveness properties are verified using fairness requirements on the model, which can state that certain actions must infinitely often be either disabled or executed. Since, by the restriction to length-preserving transducers, any infinite system execution can only visit a finite set of configurations, the verification of a liveness property can be reduced to a *repeated reachability* problem. The repeated reachability problem asks, given a set of initial configurations I, a set of *accepting configurations* F, and a transition relation T, whether there exists an infinite computation from I through T that visits F infinitely often. By letting F be the configurations where the fairness requirement is satisfied, and by excluding states where the

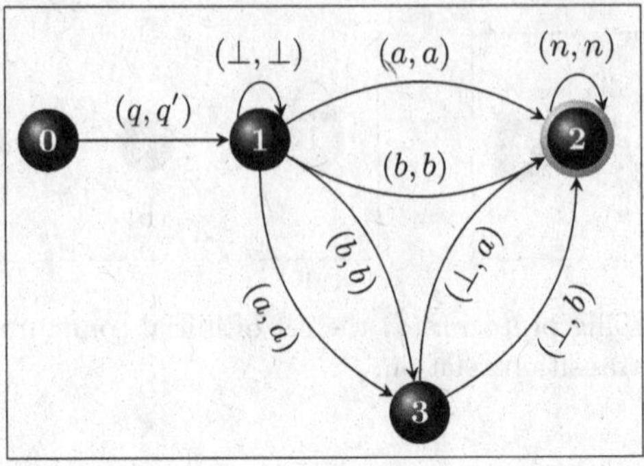

Fig. 2. The push operation in a stack.

"good thing" happens from T, the liveness property is satisfied if and only if the repeated reachability problem is answered negatively.

Since the transition relation is length-preserving, and hence each execution can visit only a finite set of configurations, the repeated reachability problem can be solved by checking whether there exists a reachable loop containing some configuration from F. This can be checked by computing $(\mathit{Inv} \cap F)^2 \cap \mathit{Id}$ and checking whether this relation intersects T^+. Here Id is the identity relation on the set of configurations, and $\mathit{Inv} = I \circ T^*$ as before.

Sets like $I \circ T^*$ and relations like T^+ are in general not regular or even computable (note that T could model the computation steps of a Turing machine). Even if they are regular, they are sometimes not effectively computable. In these cases, the above verification problems cannot be solved by the proposed techniques. Therefore, a main challenge in regular model checking is to design semi-algorithms which successfully compute such sets and relations for as many examples as possible. We will look at this aspect in the next section.

3 Transducers

In Sect. 2, we mentioned that we can carry out verification by computing a representation of $I \circ T^*$ (or T^+) for some transition relation T and some set of configurations I. Given a set of *bad* configurations B, we want to check whether $I \circ T^* \cap B \neq \emptyset$. Algorithms for regular model checking are usually based on starting from I and repeatedly applying T. As a running illustration, we will consider the problem of computing the transitive closure T^+ for the transducer in Fig. 1. A first attempt is to compute T^n, i.e., to compute the composition of T with itself n times for $n = 1, 2, 3, \cdots$. For example, T^3 is the transition relation where the token gets passed three positions to the right. Its transducer is given in Fig. 4.

A transducer for T^+ is one whose relation represents that the token gets passed an arbitrary number of times. There (infinitely) many transducers characterizing this relation. One such a transducer is depicted in Fig. 3.

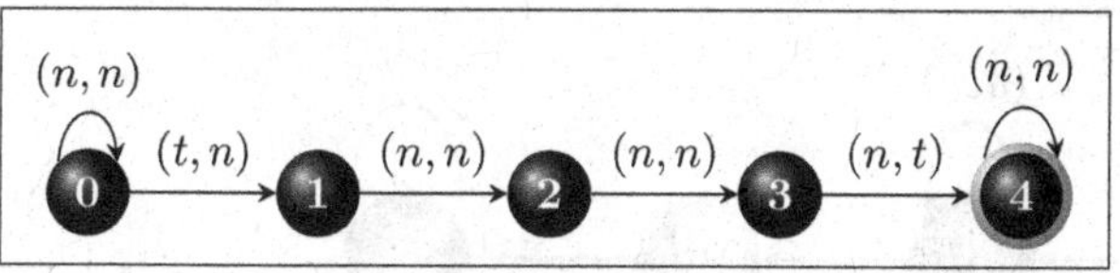

Fig. 3. Applying the token passing transducer relation three times.

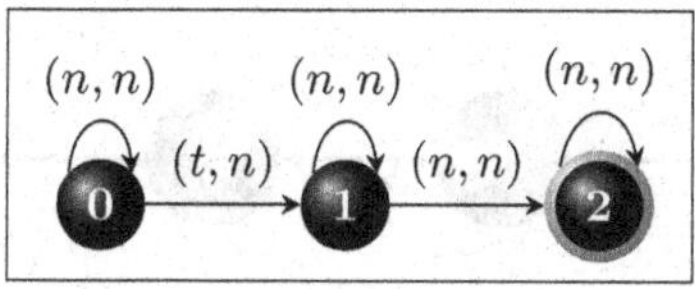

Fig. 4. A transducer characterizing the transitive closure of the token passing transducer.

The challenge is to derive (one of) these transducers *algorithmically*. Obviously, we cannot do this naively by simply computing the approximations T^n for $n = 1, 2, 3, \cdots$, since such a procedure would not converge. We can solve the problem by applying *acceleration* or *widening* techniques that can compute a representation of T^+. Below, we present a technique based on acceleration to illustrate the idea.

Acceleration techniques are usually based on *quotienting* of transducers that represent approximations of T^n for some value(s) of n. This involves finding an *equivalence relation* $\simeq$ on the states of approximations, and to merge equivalent states, obtaining a quotient transducer. For instance, in the transducer that represents T^3 above, we can define the states 1, 2, and 3 to be equivalent. By merging them, we obtain the transducer $T^3/\simeq$ which in this example happens to be equivalent to T^+.

One problem is that quotienting in general increases the language accepted by a transducer: $L(T^n) \subseteq L(T^n/\simeq)$, usually with strict inclusion. This problem was resolved in [10,11,20,27] by characterizing equivalence relations $\simeq$ such that T^+ is equivalent to $(T/\simeq)^+$ for any transducer T, i.e., the quotienting does not increase the transitive closure of the transducer. To explain the idea, let us first build explicitly a transducer for T^+ as the union of transducers T^n for $n = 1, 2, 3, \cdots$. Each state of T^n is labeled with a sequence of states from T, resulting from the product construction using n copies of T. The result is called the *history transducer*. The history transducer corresponding to the token passing protocol is shown in Fig. 5. Recall minimization algorithms for automata. They are based on building a *forward* bisimulation $\simeq_F$ on the states, and then carry out minimization by quotienting. For instance, in the history transducer of Fig. 5, all states with names of form 2^i1 for any $i \geq 0$ are forward bisimilar. Analogously, we can find a backward bisimulation $\simeq_B$. For instance, all states with names of form 10^i, $i \geq 0$, are backward bisimilar. Dams et al. [27] showed how to combine a forward $\simeq_F$ and a backward bisimulation $\simeq_B$ into an equivalence relation $\simeq$

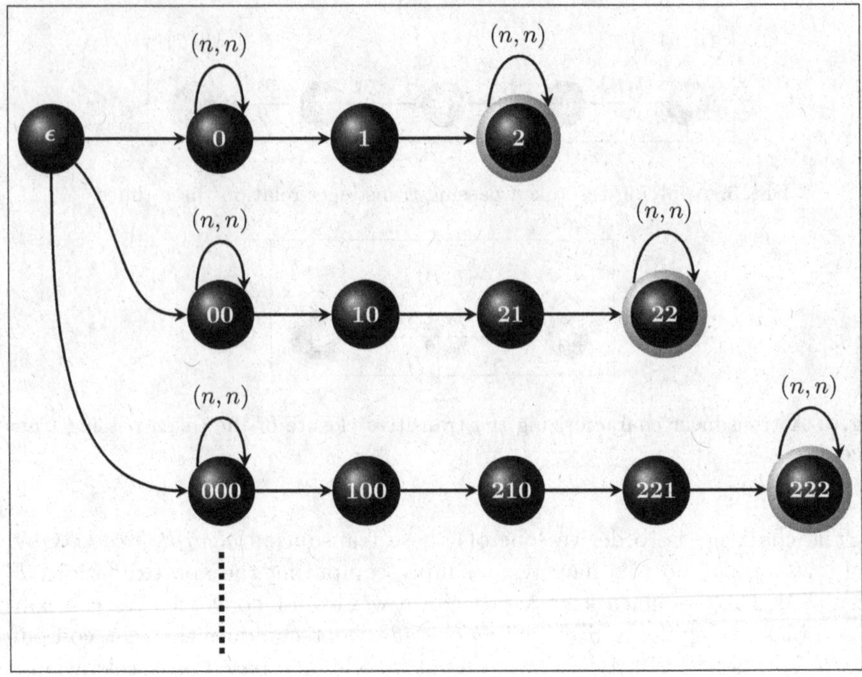

Fig. 5. The history transducer for the token passing protocol.

which preserves the transitive closure of the transducer. In [12], this result was generalized to consider *simulations* instead of bisimulations. The simulations can be obtained by computing properties of the original automaton T (as in [11,12]), or on successive approximations of T^n (as in [27]).

From the results in [12] it follows for the history transducer that the states with names in 2^i1 can be merged for $i \geq 1$, and the same holds for 10^i. The equivalence classes for that transducer would be 2^+, 0^+, 10^+, 2^+1 and 2^+10^+. Hence, it can be quotiented to the transducer depicted in Fig. 6, which, in turn, can be minimized to the three-state representation shown in Fig. 4.

4 Monotonic Abstraction

In this section, we present an approach that avoids using the full power of regular languages and transducers. Instead, we compute an over-approximation of the set of reachable configurations through a particular technique which we call *monotonic abstraction.* We will instantiate the framework to a special class of parameterized systems. In this section, a *parameterized system* consists of an arbitrary number of identical processes each of which is a finite-state process. The processes are organized as a linear array. In each step in the execution of the system, one process, called the *active process*, changes state. The rest of

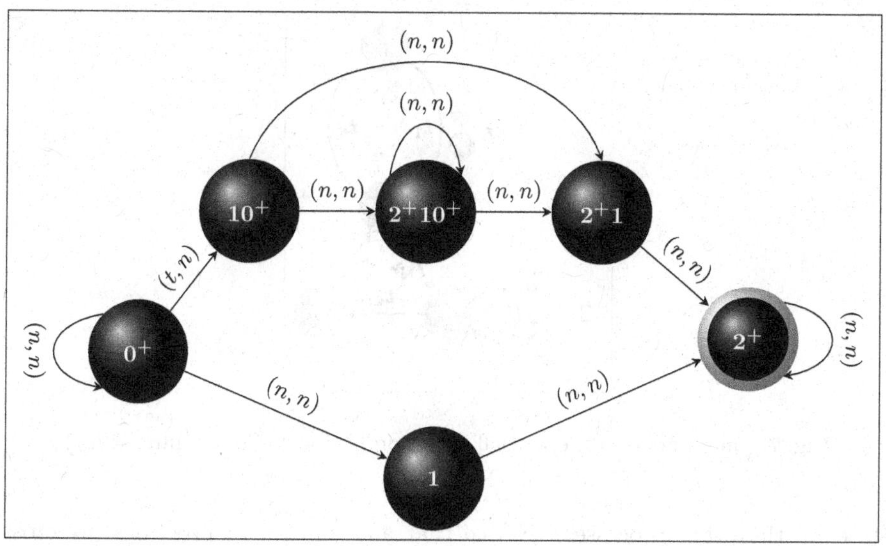

Fig. 6. The history transducer for the token passing protocol.

the processes, called the *passive processes*, do not change states. We call the passive processes to the left of the active process the *left context* of the active process. The *right context* is defined analogously. The active process may perform a *local transition* in which it changes its state independently of the states of the passive processes. The active process may also perform a global transition in which it checks the states of the passive processes. A global transition is either *universally* or *existentially* quantified. An example of a universal condition is that *all* processes in the left context of the active process should be in certain states. In an existential transition we require that *some* (rather than all) processes should be in certain states.

We use a running example of a mutual exclusion protocol, among an array of processes, where each process is of the form depicted in Fig. 7. The process has four local states, namely the green, black, blue, and red states. We represent these states by colored balls ●, ●, ●, and ●. Sometimes, when no confusion arises, we refer to a process in a configuration by its state, so we say e.g. "the red process" rather than "the process in its red state".

Initially, all the processes are green (they are idle). When a process becomes interested in accessing the critical section (which corresponds to the red state), it declares its interest by moving to the black state. This is described by the global universal transition rule t_1 in which the move is allowed only if all the other processes are in their green or black states. The universal quantifier labeling t_1 encodes the condition that all other processes (whether in the left or the right context – hence the index LR of the quantifier) of the active process should be green or black. In the black state, the process may move to the blue state through the local transition t_2 (in which the process does not need to check the

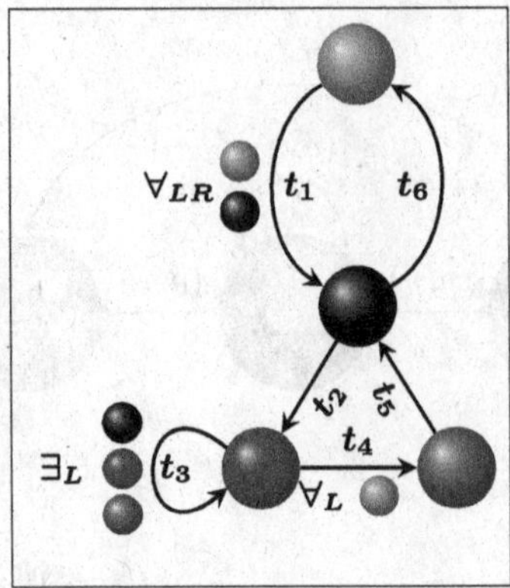

Fig. 7. One process in the mutual exclusion protocol (Color figure online)

states of the other processes). Notice that any number of processes my cross from the initial (green) state to the black state. However, once the first process has crossed to the blue state, it "closes the door" on the processes which are still in their green states. These processes will no longer be able to leave their green states until the door is opened again (when no process is blue or red). From the set of processes which have declared interest in accessing the critical section (those which have left their green states and are now black or blue) the leftmost process has the highest priority. This is encoded by the global universal transition t_4 where a process may move from its blue state to its red state only subject to the universal condition that all processes in its left context are green (the index L of the quantifier stands for "Left"). If the process finds out, through the existential global condition, that there are other processes that are black, blue, or red, then it loops back to the blue state through the existential transition t_3. Once the process leaves the critical section, it will return back to the black state through the local transition t_5. In the black state, the process chooses either to try to reach the critical section again, or to become idle (through the local transition t_6).

Formally, we represent a parameterized systems P by a pair $\langle Q, T \rangle$, where Q is the set of the local states of the processes, and T is the set of transition rules which define the behaviour of each process. In the above example, the set Q consists of four states (green, black, blue, and red), while the set T consists of six rules, namely three local rules (t_2, t_5, and t_6), two universal rules (t_1 and t_4), and one existential rule (t_3).

4.1 Transition System

A parameterized system $P = \langle Q, T \rangle$ induces a transition systems $T = \langle \mathcal{C}, \longrightarrow \rangle$, where $\mathcal{C}$ is the set of configurations and $\longrightarrow$ is a transition relation on $\mathcal{C}$. A configuration is a word in Q^*, where each element of the word represents the local state of one process.

Let us consider the example of Fig. 7. The word represents a configuration in an instance of the system with five processes that are in their green, blue, red, blue, and black states, in that order. Since there is no bound on the configuration sizes, the set of configurations is infinite. We define the transition relation $\longrightarrow := \cup_{t \in T} \xrightarrow{t}$, where $\xrightarrow{t}$ is a relation on configurations that captures the effect of the transition rule t. The definition of $\longrightarrow$ depends on the type of t (whether it is local, existential, or universal). We will consider three transition rules from Fig. 7 to illustrate the idea.

The local rule t_2 induces transitions of the form

$$\xrightarrow{t_2}$$

Here, the active process changes its local state from black to blue.

The existential rule t_3 induces transitions of the form

$$\xrightarrow{t_3}$$

The blue process can perform the transition since there is a black process in its left context. However, the transition is not enabled from the configuration , since there are no red, blue, or black processes in the left context of the process trying to perform the transition.

The universal rule t_4 induces transitions of the form t_4

$$\xrightarrow{t_4}$$

The active process can perform the transition since all the processes in its left con- text are green. On the other hand, neither of the blue processes can perform the transition form the configuration since, for each one of them, there is at least one process in its left context which is not green. As usual, we use $\xrightarrow{*}$ to denote the reflexive transitive closure of $\longrightarrow$. For sets C_1 and C_2 of configurations, we use $C_1 \xrightarrow{*} C_2$ to denote that there are configurations $c_1 \in C_1$ and $c_2 \in C_2$ such that $c_1 \xrightarrow{*} c_2$.

An initial configuration is one in which all processes are in their initial (green) states. In this section, we use *Init* to denote the set of initial configurations. Examples of initial configurations are and corresponding to instances of the system with two and four processes respectively. Notice that there is an infinite set of initial configurations, namely one for each size of the system.

As mentioned above, the protocol is intended to observe mutual exclusion. In other words, we are interested in verifying a safety property. To do this we characterize the set *Bad* of configurations: all configurations which contain at least two red processes. Examples of configurations in *Bad* are , and . Showing the safety property amounts to proving that the protocol, starting from an initial configuration, will never reach a bad configuration. In other words, we want to answer the question whether $Init \xrightarrow{*} Bad$.

4.2 Ordering

We define an ordering on configurations, which we use to define bad sets of configurations, and hence also to formulate the class of safety properties which we consider. For configurations c_1 and c_2, we use $c_1 \preceq c_2$ to denote that c_1 is a (not necessarily contiguous) subword of c_2. For instance, we have ●● $\preceq$ ●●●●●. A set U of configurations is said to be *upward-closed*, if whenever $c \in U$ and $c \preceq c'$ then $c' \in U$. For a configuration c, we use $\widehat{c}$ denote the upward-closed set $U := \{c' \mid c \preceq c'\}$, i.e., $\widehat{c}$ contains all configurations which are larger than c w.r.t. the ordering $\preceq$. In such a case, we call c the generator of U.

We are interested in upward-closed sets for two reasons. First, all sets of bad configurations which we work with are upward-closed. For instance, in the above example, the set *Bad* of configurations violating mutual exclusion are those which contain at least two red processes. The set is upward-closed since whenever a configuration contains two red processes then any larger configuration will also contain (at least) two red processes. The second reason why we are interested in upward-closed sets is that they have an efficient symbolic representation. In fact, it can be shown that each upward-closed set can be characterized by a finite set of generators. More precisely, for an upward-closed set U, there are configurations $c_1, \ldots, c_n$ with $U = \widehat{c_1} \cup \cdots \cup \widehat{c_n}$. For instance, the set *Bad* above has a single generator, namely ●●. Thus, operations which manipulate upward-closed sets can be translated into operations which manipulate words. In this manner we avoid using the full power of regular languages, when performing reachability analysis. This makes monotonic abstraction more efficient in practice compared to the automata-based methods such as the one we described in Sect. 3.

We will check safety properties using backward reachability analysis. For a set C of configurations, we define $Pre\,(C) := \{c \mid \exists c' \in C.\, c \longrightarrow c'\}$. In other words, the set contains exactly all configurations from which a configuration in C can be reached through a single application of the transition relation.

To solve the safety problem, we present a scheme for backward reachability analysis. The scheme is an instantiation of the framework of *well-structured systems* [3,29]. We start with the set *Bad* of bad configurations which is upward-closed. Then, we apply the function *Pre* repeatedly generating a sequence $U_0, U_1, U_2, \ldots$ of sets of configurations, where $U_0 = Bad$, and $U_{i+1} = U_i \cup Pre\,(U_i)$, for $i \geq 0$. We observe that the set U_i characterizes the set of configurations from which the set *Bad* is reachable within i steps. We would like the sets U_i to be upward-closed (so that we can represent them by their finite sets of generators). In order to achieve that, we introduce a sufficient condition, namely that of *monotonicity*. Monotonicity implies that $Pre\,(U)$ is upward-closed whenever U itself is upward-closed. Since U_0 is upward-closed by definition, monotonicity would imply that all the sets U_i are upward-closed.

A transition system is said to be *monotone* if $\preceq$ forms a simulation on the set $\mathcal{C}$ of configurations. In other words, for all configurations c_1, c_2, c_3, whenever $c_1 \longrightarrow c_2$ and $c_1 \preceq c_3$ then $c_2 \longrightarrow c_4$ for some c_4 with $c_3 \preceq c_4$.

Monotonicity implies that upward-closedness is preserved through the application of *Pre*. The reasoning goes as follows. Consider an upward-closed set

U. Let $c_1 \in \mathit{Pre}(U)$ and let $c_2 \succeq c_1$. We will show that $c_2 \in \mathit{Pre}(U)$. Since $c_1 \in \mathit{Pre}(U)$, we know by definition that there is a $c_3 \in U$ such that $c_1 \longrightarrow c_3$. By monotonicity it follows that there is a c_4 such that $c_3 \preceq c_4$ and $c_2 \longrightarrow c_4$. From $c_3 \in U$ and $c_3 \preceq c_4$ it follows that $c_4 \in U$. This means that we have found a configuration $c_4 \in U$ such that $c_2 \preceq c_4$, which implies that $c_2 \in \mathit{Pre}(U)$.

4.3 Abstraction

We define an abstraction that generates an over-approximation of the transition system. The abstract transition system is monotone, thus allowing to work with upward-closed sets. We first show that local and existential transitions are monotone, and hence need not be approximated. Therefore, we only provide an over-approximation for universal transitions. Consider the transition

$$c_1 = \quad \xrightarrow{t_2} \quad = c_3$$

in which a process changes state from black to blue. Consider the configuration $c_2 =$ that is larger than c_1. Clearly, c_2 can perform the local transition

$$c_2 = \quad \xrightarrow{t_2}_A \quad = c_4 \succeq c_3$$

In general, local transitions are monotone, since the active process in the small configuration (the black process in c_1) also exists in the larger configuration (i.e., c_2). A local transition does not check or change the states of the passive processes; and hence the larger configuration c_2 is also able to perform the transition, while maintaining the ordering $c_3 \preceq c_4$.

Consider the existential transition

$$c_1 = \quad \xrightarrow{t_3}_A \quad = c_3$$

We can divide the configuration c_1 to three parts: the *active process* , the *left context* , and the *right context* . Furthermore, the left context contains a *witness* which enables the transition. Consider the configuration $c_2 =$ that is larger than c_1. Also, the configuration c_2 comprises three parts: the active process , the left context , and the right context . The left context of c_2 is larger than the left context of c_1, and hence the former will also contain the witness , which means c_2 can perform the same transition

$$c_2 = \quad \xrightarrow{t_3}_A \quad = c_4 \succeq c_2$$

While local and existential transitions are monotone, universal transitions are *not*. To see the reason, we consider the transition

$$c_1 = \quad \xrightarrow{t_4} \quad = c_3$$

The transition is enabled since all processes in the left context of the active process satisfy the condition of the transition (they are green). Consider the configuration $c_2 =$. Although $c_1 \preceq c_2$, the transition t_4 is not enabled from c_2 since the left context of the active process contains processes that violate the condition of the transition. This means that universal transitions are not monotone.

In order to deal with non-monotonicity of universal transitions, we will work with an abstract transition relation $\longrightarrow_A$ that is an over-approximation of the concrete transition relation $\longrightarrow$. We call $\longrightarrow_A$ the *monotonic abstraction* of $\longrightarrow$. We let $\xrightarrow{t}_A$ coincide $\xrightarrow{t}$ when t is a local or an existential transition. The reason is that, in these two cases, the relation is monotone and hence no over-approximation is needed. For the case when t is universal, we let $c_1 \xrightarrow{t}_A c_2$ if there is a $c_1' \preceq c_1$ with $c_1' \xrightarrow{t}_A c_2$. In other words, we allow c_1 to first "transform" to a smaller configuration from which it can perform the transition. For instance

$$\xrightarrow{t_4}$$

since

$$\preceq \xrightarrow{t_4}$$

The abstract transition relation $\longrightarrow_A$ is monotone also w.r.t. universal transitions, since for configurations c_1, c_2, c_3, and a transition t, if $c_1 \preceq c_2$ and $c_1 \xrightarrow{t}_A c_3$ then, by definition $c_2 \xrightarrow{t}_A c_3$. Notice that the over-approximation essentially deletes those processes in the configuration that violate the condition of the universal transition. Since $\longrightarrow_A$ is an over-approximation of the original transition relation $\longrightarrow$, it follows that if a safety property holds in the abstract model, then it will also hold in the original model.

4.4 Backward Reachability

We present a backward algorithm for approximated reachability analysis. Here, we compute the function *Pre* w.r.t. the abstract relation $\longrightarrow_A$ rather than the concrete relation $\longrightarrow$. This means that we can work with upward-closed sets in the scheme for backward reachability analysis that we presented earlier. Recall that we generate a sequence $U_0, U_1, U_2, \ldots$ of sets of configurations where $U_0 = Bad$, and $U_{i+1} = U_i \cup Pre\,(U_i)$, for $i \geq 0$. Since U_0 is upward-closed by definition, and $\longrightarrow_A$ is monotone, all the sets U_i are upward-closed.

Recall that each set can be represented by its finite set of generators. Given a configuration c, we show below how to compute the set of generators for the set $Pre\,(\widehat{c})$. This means that we only need to work with generators (configurations) as a symbolic representation of the sets which arise in the algorithm.

Now, we show that the algorithm is guaranteed to terminate. Suppose that the algorithm, during its execution, produces two generators c_1, c_2 such that $c_1 \preceq c_2$. Since $\widehat{c_2} \subseteq \widehat{c_1}$, we can safely discard c_2 from the analysis without the loss of precision. In such a case, we say that c_2 is *subsumed* by c_1. Discarding configurations in this manner makes it possible to apply the well-structured framework [3, 29]. According to the framework, termination of the algorithm is guaranteed since $\preceq$ is a *well quasi-ordering*. That $\preceq$ is a well quasi-ordering means that for any infinite sequence $c_0, c_1, c_2, \ldots$ of configurations, there are $i < j$ such that $c_i \preceq c_j$.

It remains to show that we can compute the generators of $Pre\,(\widehat{c})$ for any configuration c. We define $Pre\,(\widehat{c}) := \cup_{t \in T} Pre_t\,(\widehat{c})$ where $Pre_t\,(\widehat{c})$ gives the generators of the set of configurations from which we can reach $\widehat{c}$ through one application of the transition rule t. The definition of Pre_t depends on the type of t (whether it is local, existential, or universal). We will consider the different transition rules in Fig. 7 to illustrate how to compute Pre_t. For the local rule t_5, we have

$$Pre_{t_5}\left(\widehat{\quad}\right) := \{\quad\}$$

In other words, the predecessor set is characterized by one generator, namely . Strictly speaking, the set contains also a number of other configurations such as . However such configurations are subsumed by the original configuration, and therefore we will not include them in the set.

For existential transitions, there are two cases depending on whether a witness exists or not in the configuration. Consider the existential rule t_3 in Fig. 7. We have

$$Pre_{t_3}\left(\widehat{\quad}\right) = \{\quad\}$$

In this case, there is a witness, namely, in the left context of the active process . On the other hand, we have

$$Pre_{t_3}\left(\widehat{\quad}\right) := \left\{ \quad , \quad , \quad , \quad , \quad , \quad \right\}$$

In this case there is no witness available in the left context of the active process. Therefore, we add a witness explicitly in each possible state (, , or), and each possible place in the left context of the active process. Notice that the sizes of the new generators (four processes) is larger than the size of the original configuration (three processes). This means that the sizes of the configurations generated by the backward algorithm may increase, and hence there is a priori no bound on the sizes of the configurations. However, termination is still guaranteed due to the well quasi-ordering of $\preceq$. For universal conditions, let us consider the universal rule t_4 in Fig. 7. We have

$$Pre_{t_4}\left(\widehat{\quad}\right) = \emptyset$$

since there is a black process in the left context of the potential active process (which is in state). On the other hand

$$Pre_{t_4}\left(\widehat{\quad}\right) = $$

since all processes in the left context of the active process are in their green states.

4.5 Example

We show how the backward reachability algorithm runs on our example. We start by the generator

$$g_0 =$$

of the set of bad configuration. The only transition which can be enabled backwards from a red state, is the one induced by the rule t_4. From the two red processes in g_0, only the left one can perform t_4 backwards (the right process cannot perform t_4 backwards since its left context contains a process not satisfying the condition of the quantifier):

$$Pre_{t_4}(g_0) = \{g_1 = \}$$

From g_1, two rules are enabled backwards (both from the blue process): the local rule t_2

$$Pre_{t_2}(g_1) = \{g_2 = \}$$

and the existential rule t_3

$$Pre_{t_3}(g_1) = \{ \, , \, , \, \}$$

Since a witness is missing in the left context, we add it explicitly. All the three generators in $Pre_{t_3}(g_1)$ are subsumed by g_1. One rule is enabled backwards from g_2, namely the local rule t_5 from the black process

$$Pre_{t_5}(g_1) = \{g_0 = \}$$

Notice that the universal transition t_1 is not enabled from the black process, since there is another process (the red process) in the configuration that violates the condition of the quantifier. At this point, the algorithm terminates, since it is not possible to provide any new generators which are not subsumed by the existing ones.

Since there is no initial configuration (with only green processes) in $\widehat{g_0} \cup \widehat{g_1} \cup \widehat{g_2}$, the set of bad configurations is not reachable from the set of initial configurations in the abstract semantics. Therefore, we can conclude that the set of bad configurations is not reachable from the set of initial configurations in the concrete semantics, either.

5 Perspective and Future Work

Since its introduction [33,35], RMC has played an important role in the development of verification techniques for infinite-state systems.

In addition to the basic techniques we describe in this tutorial, the framework has been developed in many directions [4]. We mention some of these extensions in this paragraph. A *broadcast* transition is initiated by a process, called the *initiator*. Together with the initiator, an arbitrary number of processes change state simultaneously. In *binary* communication two processes perform a rendezvous changing state simultaneously.

We have also considered parameterized systems where the individual processes operate on numerical variables over the natural numbers [5]. The conditions on the numerical variables are stated as *gap-order constraints*: a logical formalism which can express simple relations such as lower and upper bounds on the values of individual variables; and equality, and gaps (minimal differences) between values of pairs of variables.

Furthermore, we have studied abstraction techniques that approximate the set of *forward-reachable* configurations [7] (rather than the set of backward-reachable configurations as was the case with monotonic abstraction). The framework is based on establishing a *cut-off theorem*. More precisely, it needs to inspect only a small number of processes in order to show correctness of the whole system. It relies on an abstraction function that views the system from the perspective of a fixed number of processes. The abstraction is used during the verification procedure in order to dynamically detect cut-off points beyond which the search of the state space need not continue.

Interesting directions for future work include:

- Parameterized timed systems [6].
- Applying symbolic partial order techniques [9] to increase efficiency.
- Applying RMC to concurrent programs that operate on weak consistency models such as the release-acquire semantics [1].
- Refining the granularity of quantified transitions [8]

Acknowledgement. Bengt Jonsson introduced me to the world of research in computer science. Since those early days, he has been my colleague, friend, and mentor. He was a leader and influential in developing the frameworks of regular model checking and well-structured systems. Many thanks, Bengt, for your support and for being an inspiration throughout the years.

References

1. Abdulla, P.A., Arora, J., Atig, M.F., Krishna, S.N.: Verification of programs under the release-acquire semantics. In: McKinley, K.S., Fisher, K. (Eds.) Proceedings of the 40th ACM SIGPLAN Conference on Programming Language Design and Implementation, PLDI 2019, Phoenix, AZ, USA, 22–26 June 2019, pp. 1117–1132. ACM (2019)
2. Abdulla, P.A., Bouajjani, A., Jonsson, B.: On-the-fly analysis of systems with unbounded, lossy FIFO channels. In: Hu, A.J., Vardi, M.Y. (eds.) Computer Aided Verification, CAV 1998. LNCS, vol. 1427, pp. 305–318. Springer, Heidelberg (1998). https://doi.org/10.1007/BFb0028754
3. Abdulla, P.A., Čerāns, K., Jonsson, B., Tsay, Y.-K.: General decidability theorems for infinite-state systems. In: Proceedings of the LICS 1996 11th IEEE International Symposium on Logic in Computer Science, pp. 313–321 (1996)

4. Abdulla, P.A., Delzanno, G., Henda, N.B., Rezine, A.: Regular model checking without transducers (on efficient verification of parameterized systems). In: Grumberg, O., Huth, M. (eds.) Tools and Algorithms for the Construction and Analysis of Systems, TACAS 2007. LNCS, vol. 4424, pp. 721–736. Springer, Heidelberg (2007). https://doi.org/10.1007/978-3-540-71209-1_56
5. Abdulla, P.A., Delzanno, G., Rezine, A.: Parameterized verification of infinite-state processes with global conditions. In: Damm, W., Hermanns, H. (eds.) Computer Aided Verification, CAV 2007. LNCS, vol. 4590, pp. 145–157. Springer, Heidelberg (2007). https://doi.org/10.1007/978-3-540-73368-3_17
6. Abdulla, P.A., Deneux, J., Mahata, P.: Multi-clock timed networks. In: 19th IEEE Symposium on Logic in Computer Science (LICS 2004), 14–17 July 2004, Turku, Finland, Proceedings, pp. 345–354. IEEE Computer Society (2004)
7. Abdulla, P.A., Haziza, F., Holík, L.: Parameterized verification through view abstraction. Int. J. Softw. Tools Technol. Transfer **18**(5), 495–516 (2015). https://doi.org/10.1007/s10009-015-0406-x
8. Abdulla, P.A., Ben Henda, N., Delzanno, G., Rezine, A.: Handling parameterized systems with non-atomic global conditions. In: Logozzo, F., Peled, D.A., Zuck, L.D. (eds.) Verification, Model Checking, and Abstract Interpretation, VMCAI 2008. LNCS, vol. 4905, pp. 22–36. Springer, Heidelberg (2008). https://doi.org/10.1007/978-3-540-78163-9_7
9. Abdulla, P.A., Jonsson, B., Kindahl, M., Peled, D.: A general approach to partial order reductions in symbolic verification. In: Hu, A.J., Vardi, M.Y. (eds.) Computer Aided Verification, CAV 1998. LNCS, vol. 1427, pp. 379–390. Springer, Heidelberg (1998). https://doi.org/10.1007/BFb0028760
10. Abdulla, P.A., Jonsson, B., Mahata, P., d'Orso, J.: Regular tree model checking. In: Brinksma, Ed., Larsen, K.G. (eds.) Computer Aided Verification, CAV 2002. LNCS, vol. 2404, pp. 555–568. Springer, Heidelberg (2002). https://doi.org/10.1007/3-540-45657-0_47
11. Abdulla, P.A., Jonsson, B., Nilsson, M., d'Orso, J.: Regular model checking made simple and effcient*. In: Brim, L., Křetínský, M., Kučera, A., Jančar, P. (eds.) CONCUR 2002—Concurrency Theory, CONCUR 2002. LNCS, vol. 2421, pp. 116–131. Springer, Heidelberg (2002). https://doi.org/10.1007/3-540-45694-5_9
12. Abdulla, P.A., Jonsson, B., Nilsson, M., d'Orso, J.: Algorithmic improvements in regular model checking. In: Hunt, W.A., Somenzi, F. (eds.) Computer Aided Verification, CAV 2003. LNCS, vol. 2725, pp. 236–248. Springer, Heidelberg (2003). https://doi.org/10.1007/978-3-540-45069-6_25
13. Alur, R., Courcoubetis, C., Dill, D.L.: Model-checking for real-time systems. In: Proceedings of the Fifth Annual Symposium on Logic in Computer Science (LICS 1990), Philadelphia, Pennsylvania, USA, 4–7 June 1990, pp. 414–425. IEEE Computer Society (1990)
14. Basin, D.A., Klarlund, N.: Automata based symbolic reasoning in hardware verification. Formal Methods Syst. Des. **13**(3), 255–288 (1998)
15. Boigelot, B., Godefroid, P.: Symbolic verification of communication protocols with infinite state spaces using QDDs. In: Alur, R., Henzinger, T.A. (eds.) Computer Aided Verification, CAV 1996. LNCS, vol. 1102, pp. 1–12. Springer, Heidelberg (1996). https://doi.org/10.1007/3-540-61474-5_53
16. Boigelot, B., Godefroid, P., Willems, B., Wolper, P.: The power of QDDs (extended abstract). In: Van Hentenryck, P. (ed.) Static Analysis, SAS 1997. LNCS, vol. 1302, pp. 172–186. Springer, Heidelberg (1997). https://doi.org/10.1007/BFb0032741

17. Boigelot, B., Wolper, P.: Symbolic verification with periodic sets. In: Dill, D.L. (ed.) Computer Aided Verification, CAV 1994. LNCS, vol. 818, pp. 55–67. Springer, Heidelberg (1994). https://doi.org/10.1007/3-540-58179-0_43
18. Bouajjani, A., Esparza, J., Maler, O.: Reachability analysis of pushdown automata: application to model checking. In: Proceedings of the International Conference on Concurrency Theory (CONCUR 1997). LNCS 1243 (1997)
19. Bouajjani, A., Habermehl, P.: Symbolic reachability analysis of FIFO-channel systems with nonregular sets of configurations. In: Degano, P., Gorrieri, R., Marchetti-Spaccamela, A. (eds.) Automata, Languages and Programming, ICALP 1997. LNCS, vol. 1256, pp. 560–570. Springer, Heidelberg (1997). https://doi.org/10.1007/3-540-63165-8_211
20. Bouajjani, A., Jonsson, B., Nilsson, M., Touili, T.: Regular model checking. In: Emerson, E.A., Sistla, A.P. (eds.) Computer Aided Verification, CAV 2000. LNCS, vol. 1855, pp. 403–418. Springer, Heidelberg (2000). https://doi.org/10.1007/10722167_31
21. Burch, J.R., Clarke, E.M., McMillan, K.L., Dill, D.L.: Symbolic model checking: 10^{20} states and beyond. Inf. Comput. **98**, 142–170 (1992)
22. Burkart, O., Steffen, B.: Model checking for context-free processes. In: Cleaveland, W.R. (ed.) CONCUR 1992, CONCUR 1992. LNCS, vol. 630, pp. 123–137. Springer, Heidelberg (1992). https://doi.org/10.1007/BFb0084787
23. Burkart, O., Steffen, B.: Model checking the full modal mu-calculus for infinite sequential processes. Theor. Comput. Sci. **221**(1–2), 251–270 (1999)
24. Caucal, D.: On the regular structure of prefix rewriting. Theoret. Comput. Sci. **106**(1), 61–86 (1992)
25. Clarke, E.M., Emerson, E.A., Sistla, A.P.: Automatic verification of finite-state concurrent systems using temporal logic specification. ACM Trans. Program. Lang. Syst. **8**(2), 244–263 (1986)
26. Comon, H., Jurski, Y.: Multiple counters automata, safety analysis and presburger arithmetic. In: Hu, A.J., Vardi, M.Y. (eds.) Computer Aided Verification, CAV 1998. LNCS, vol. 1427, pp. 268–279. Springer, Heidelberg (1998). https://doi.org/10.1007/BFb0028751
27. Dams, D., Lakhnech, Y., Steffen, M.: Iterating transducers. In: Berry, G., Comon, H., Finkel, A. (eds.) Computer Aided Verification, vol. 2102. Lecture Notes in Computer Science (2001)
28. Esparza, J., Schwoon, S.: A BDD-based model checker for recursive programs. In: Berry, G., Comon, H., Finkel, A. (eds.) Computer Aided Verification, CAV 2001. LNCS, vol. 2102, pp. 324–336. Springer, Heidelberg (2001). https://doi.org/10.1007/3-540-44585-4_30
29. Finkel, A., Schnoebelen, P.: Well-structured transition systems everywhere. Tech. Rep. LSV-98-4, Ecole Normale Supérieure de Cachan (1998)
30. Finkel, A., Willems, B., Wolper, P.: A direct symbolic approach to model checking pushdown systems (extended abstract). In: Proceedings of the Infinity 1997, Electronic Notes in Theoretical Computer Science, Bologna, August 1997
31. Henriksen, J.G., Jensen, J., Jørgensen, M., Klarlund, N., Paige, B., Rauhe, T., Sandholm, A.: Mona: Monadic second-order logic in practice. In: Proceedings of the TACAS 1995, 1th International Confererence on Tools and Algorithms for the Construction and Analysis of Systems, vol. 1019, Lecture Notes in Computer Science (1996)

32. Jonsson, B., Nilsson, M.: Transitive closures of regular relations for verifying infinite-state systems. In: Graf, S., Schwartzbach, M. (eds.) Proceedings of the TACAS 1900, 6th International Conference on Tools and Algorithms for the Construction and Analysis of Systems, vol. 1785, Lecture Notes in Computer Science (2000)
33. Kesten, Y., Maler, O., Marcus, M., Pnueli, A., Shahar, E.: Symbolic model checking with rich assertional languages. Theoret. Comput. Sci. **256**, 93–112 (2001)
34. Queille, J.P., Sifakis, J.: Specification and verification of concurrent systems in CESAR. In: Dezani-Ciancaglini, M., Montanari, U. (eds.) International Symposium on Programming, Programming 1982. LNCS, vol. 137, pp. 337–351. Springer, Heidelberg (1982). https://doi.org/10.1007/3-540-11494-7_22
35. Wolper, P., Boigelot, B.: Verifying systems with infinite but regular state spaces. In: Hu, A.J., Vardi, M.Y. (eds.) Computer Aided Verification, CAV 1998. LNCS, vol. 1427, pp. 88–97. Springer, Heidelberg (1998). https://doi.org/10.1007/BFb0028736

Regular Model Checking Revisited

Anthony W. Lin[1(✉)] and Philipp Rümmer[2(✉)]

[1] TU Kaiserslautern and MPI-SWS, Kaiserslautern, Germany
lin@cs.uni-kl.de

[2] Uppsala University, Uppsala, Sweden
philipp.ruemmer@it.uu.se

Abstract. In this contribution we revisit regular model checking, a powerful framework—pioneered by Bengt Jonsson *et al.*—that has been successfully applied for the verification of infinite-state systems, especially parameterized systems (concurrent systems with an arbitrary number of processes). We provide a reformulation of regular model checking with length-preserving transducers in terms of existential second-order theory over automatic structures. We argue that this is a natural formulation that enables us to tap into powerful synthesis techniques that have been extensively studied in the software verification community. More precisely, in this formulation the first-order part represents the verification conditions for the desired correctness property (for which we have complete solvers), whereas the existentially quantified second-order variables represent the relations to be synthesized. We show that many interesting correctness properties can be formulated in this way, examples being safety, liveness, bisimilarity, and games. More importantly, we show that this new formulation allows new interesting benchmarks (and old regular model checking benchmarks that were previously believed to be difficult), especially in the domain of parameterized system verification, to be solved.

1 Introduction

Verification of infinite-state systems has been an important area of research in the past few decades. This is one of the (many) areas to which Bengt Jonsson has made significant research contributions. In the late 1990s and early 2000s, an important stride advancing the verification of infinite-state systems was made when Jonsson *et al.* spearheaded the development of an elegant, simple, but powerful framework for modelling and verifying infinite-state systems, which they dubbed *regular model checking*, e.g., [1–3,12,25].

Regular model checking, broadly construed, is the idea of reasoning about infinite-state systems using regular languages as symbolic representations. This means that configurations of the infinite systems are encoded as finite words over some finite alphabet Σ, while other important infinite sets (e.g. of initial and final configurations) will be represented as regular languages over Σ. The transition relation $\Delta \subseteq \Sigma^* \times \Sigma^*$ of the system is, then, represented as a finite-state transducer of some sort.

E.-R. Olderog et al. (Eds.): Jonsson Festschrift, LNCS 13030, pp. 97–114, 2021.
https://doi.org/10.1007/978-3-030-91384-7_6

Example 1. As a simple illustration, we have a unidirectional token passing protocol with n processes $p_1, \ldots, p_n$ arranged in a linear array. Here n is a parameter, regardless of whose value (so long as it is a positive integer) the correctness property has to hold. This is also one reason why such systems are referred to as *parameterized systems.* Multiple tokens might exist at any given time, but at most one is held by a process. At each point in time, a process holding a token can pass it to the process to its right. If a process holding a token receives a token from its left neighbor, then it discards one of the two tokens. Each configuration of the system can be encoded as a word $w_1 \cdots w_n$ over $\Sigma = \{\top, \bot\}$, where $w_i = \top$ (resp. $w_i = \bot$) denotes that process p_i holds (resp. does not hold) a token. The set of all configurations is, therefore, Σ^*, i.e., a regular language. Various correctness properties can be mentioned for this system. An example of a safety property is that if the system starts with a configuration in $\top\bot^*$ (i.e. with only one token), then it will never visit a configuration in $\Sigma^*\top\Sigma^*\top\Sigma^*$ (i.e. with at least two tokens). An example of a liveness property is that it always terminates with configurations in the regular set $\bot^*(\bot + \top)$. □

This basic idea of regular model checking was already present in the work of Pnueli *et al.* [27] and Boigelot and Wolper [47]. However, a lot of the major development of regular model checking—the term which Jonsson *et al.* coined in [12]—was spearheaded by Jonsson *et al.* These include fundamental contributions to acceleration techniques (including the first [12,25]) for reachability sets and reachability relations, which could successfully verify interesting examples from parameterized systems. His works have made the works of subsequent researchers in regular model checking (including the authors of the present paper) possible. A lot of the initial work in regular model checking focussed on developing scalable algorithms (mostly via acceleration and widening) for verifying safety, while unfortunately going beyond safety (e.g. to liveness) posed a significant challenge; see [3,45]. It is now 20 years since the publication of Jonsson's seminal paper [12] on regular model checking. The area of computer-aided verification has undergone some paradigm shifts including the rise of SAT-solvers and SMT-solvers (e.g. see the textbooks [13,28]), as well as synthesis algorithms [5]. In the meantime, regular model checking was also affected by this in some fashion. In 2013 Neider and Jansen [37] proposed an automata synthesis algorithm for verifying safety in regular model checking using SAT-solvers to guide the search of an inductive invariant. This new way of looking at regular model checking has inspired a new class of regular model checking algorithms, which could solve old regular model checking benchmarks that could not be solved automatically by any known automatic techniques (e.g. liveness, even for probabilistic distributed protocols [30,34]), as well as new correctness properties (e.g. safety games [38] and probabilistic bisimulation with applications to proving anonymity [24]). Despite these recent successes, these techniques are rather *ad-hoc*, and often difficult to adapt to new correctness properties.

Contributions. We provide a new and clean reformulation of regular model checking inspired by deductive verification. More precisely, we show how to express RMC as *satisfaction of existential second-order logic (ESO) over automatic structures.* Among others, this new framework puts virtually all interesting correctness properties (e.g. safety, liveness, safety games, bisimulation, etc.) in regular model checking under one broad umbrella. We provide new automata synthesis algorithms for solving any regular model checking problem that is expressible in this framework.

In deductive verification, we encode correctness properties of a program as formulas in some (first-order) logic, commonly called *verification conditions,* and then check the conditions using a theorem prover. This approach provides a clean separation of concerns between generating and checking "correctness proofs," and underlies several verification methodologies and systems, for instance in deductive verification (with systems like Dafny [29] or KeY [4]) or termination checkers (e.g., AProVE [21] or T2 [14]). For practical reasons, the most attractive case is of course the one where all verification conditions can be kept within decidable theories. We propose to use *first-order logic over universal automatic structures* [8–10,15] for the decidable theories expressing the verification conditions. Furthermore, we show that the correctness properties can be shown as satisfactions of ESO formulas over automatic structures, where the second-order variables express the existence of proofs such that the verification conditions are satisfied. Finally, we show that restricting to *regular proofs* (i.e. proofs that can be expressed by finite automata) is sufficient in practice, and allows us to have powerful verification algorithms that unify the recent successful automata synthesis algorithms [24,30,34,37] for safety, liveness, reachability games, and other interesting correctness properties.

Organization. Section 2 contains preliminaries. We provide our reformulation of regular model checking in terms of existential second-order logic (ESO) over automatic structures in Sect. 3. We provide a synthesis algorithm for solving formulas in ESO over automatic structures in Sect. 4. We conclude in Sect. 5 with research challenges.

2 Preliminaries

2.1 Automata

We assume basic familiarity with finite automata (e.g. see [41]). We use Σ to denote a finite alphabet. In this paper, we exclusively deal with automata over finite words, but the framework and techniques extend to other classes of structures (e.g. trees) and finite automata (e.g. finite tree automata). An *automaton* over Σ is a tuple $\mathcal{A} = (Q, \Delta, q_0, F)$, where Q is a finite set of states, $\Delta \subseteq Q \times Q$ is the transition relation, $q_0 \in Q$ is the initial state, and $F \subseteq Q$ is the set of final states. In this way, our automata are by default assumed to be non-deterministic. The notion of *runs* of $\mathcal{A}$ on an input word $w \in \Sigma^*$ is standard (i.e., a function $\pi : \{0, \ldots, |w|\} \to Q$ so that $\pi(0) = q_0$, $\pi(|w|) \in F$, and the transition relation Δ is respected. We use $\mathcal{L}(\mathcal{A})$ to denote the language (i.e. subset of Σ^*) accepted by $\mathcal{A}$.

2.2 Regular Model Checking

Regular Model Checking (RMC) is a generic symbolic framework for modelling and verifying infinite-state systems pioneered and advanced by Jonsson et al. [3,12,25]. The basic principle behind the framework is to use finite automata to represent an infinite-state system, and witnesses for a correctness property. For example, an infinite set of states can be represented as a regular language over Σ^*. How do we represent a transition relation $\rightarrow \subseteq \Sigma^* \times \Sigma^*$? In the basic setting (as described in the seminal papers [12,25] of Jonsson), we can use *length-preserving transducers* for representing $\rightarrow$. A length-preserving transducer $\mathcal{A}$ is simply an automaton over the alphabet $\Sigma \times \Sigma$. Given an input tuple $t = (u_1 \cdots u_n, v_1 \cdots v_n) \in \Sigma^n \times \Sigma^n$, an acceptance of t by $\mathcal{A}$ is defined to be the acceptance of the "product" word $(u_1, v_1) \cdots (u_n, v_n) \in (\Sigma \times \Sigma)^n$ by the automaton $\mathcal{A}$. In this way, a transition relation $\rightarrow$ can now be represented by an automaton.

In this paper, we will deal mostly with systems whose transition relations can be represented by length-preserving transducers. This is not a problem in practice because this is already applicable for a lot of applications, including reasoning about distributed algorithms (arguably the most important class of applications of RMC), where the number of processes is typically fixed at runtime. That said, we will show how to easily extend the definition to non-length-preserving relations (called automatic relations [8–10,15]) since they are needed in our decidable logic. This is done by the standard trick of padding the shorter strings with a special padding symbol. More precisely, given two words $v = v_1 \cdots v_n$ and $w = w_1 \cdots w_m$, we define the *convolution* $v \otimes w$ to be the word $u = (u_1, u_1') \cdots (u_k, u_k') \in (\Sigma_\perp \times \Sigma_\perp)^*$ (where $\Sigma_\perp := \Sigma \cup \{\perp\}$ and $\perp \notin \Sigma$) such that $k = \max(n, m)$, $u_i = v_i$ for all $i \leq |v|$ (for $i > |v|$, $u_i := \perp$), and $u_i' = w_i$ for all $i \leq |w|$ (for all $i > |w|$, $u_i' = \perp$). For example, $ab \otimes abba$ is the word $(a, a)(b, b)(\perp, b)(\perp, a)$. Whether (v, w) is accepted by $\mathcal{A}$ now is synonymous with acceptance of $v \otimes w$ by $\mathcal{A}$. In this way, transition relations that relate words of different lengths can still be represented using finite automata.

2.3 Weakly-Finite Systems

In this paper, we will restrict ourselves to transition systems whose domain is a regular subset of Σ^*, and whose transition relations can be described by length-preserving transducers. That is, since Σ is finite, from any given configuration $w \in \Sigma^*$ of the system there is a finite number of configurations that are reachable from w (in fact, there is at most $|\Sigma|^{|w|}$ reachable configurations). Such transition systems (which can be infinite, but where the number of reachable configurations from any given configuration is finite) are typically referred to as *weakly-finite systems* [19]. As we previously mentioned, this restriction is not a big problem in practice since many practical examples (including those from distributed algorithms) can be captured. The restriction is, however, useful when developing a *clean* framework that is unencumbered by a lot of extra assumptions, and at the same time captures a lot of interesting correctness properties.

2.4 Existential Second-Order Logic

In this paper, we will use Existential Second-Order Logic (ESO) to reformulate RMC. Second-order Logic (e.g. see [31]) is an extension of first-order logic by quantifications over relations. Let σ be a vocabulary consisting of relations (i.e. relational vocabulary). A *relational variable* will be denoted by capital letters R, X, Y, etc. Each relational variable R has an arity $\mathtt{ar}(R) \in \mathbb{Z}_{>0}$. ESO over σ is simply the fragment of second-order logic over σ consisting of formulas of the form

$$\psi = \exists R_1, \ldots, R_n. \varphi$$

where φ is a first-order logic over the vocabulary $\sigma' = \sigma \cup \{R_i\}_{i=1}^n$, where R_i is a relation symbol of arity $\mathtt{ar}(R_i)$. Given a structure $\mathfrak{S}$ over σ and an ESO formula ψ (as above), checking whether $\mathfrak{S} \models \psi$ amounts to finding relations $R_1, \ldots, R_n$ over the domain of $\mathfrak{S}$ such that φ is satisfied (with the standard definition of first-order logic); in other words, extending $\mathfrak{S}$ to a structure $\mathfrak{S}'$ over σ' such that $\mathfrak{S}' \models \varphi$.

3 RMC as ESO Satisfaction over Automatic Structures

As we previously described, our new reformulation of RMC is inspired by deductive verification, which provides a separation between generating and checking correctness proofs. The verification conditions should be describable in decidable logical theories. As a concrete example, suppose we want to prove a safety property for a program P. Then, a correctness proof would be a finitely-representable inductive invariant *Inv* that contains all initial states of P, and is disjoint from the set of all bad states of P. The termination of a program can similarly be proven by finding a well-founded relation *Rank* that subsumes the transition relation of a program. In both cases, a correctness proof corresponds to a solution for *existentially quantified second-order variables* that encode the desired correctness property; in the spirit of Sect. 2.4, the correctness of a proof can be verified by evaluating just the first-order part φ of a formula. The generation of the candidate proofs will then be taken care of separately, which we will talk about in the next section. Suffice to say for now that the counterexample guided inductive synthesis (CEGIS) framework [5] would be appropriate for the proof generation. In this section, we provide a reformulation of RMC in the aforementioned framework for software verification.

3.1 Automatic Structures

What is the right decidable theory to capture regular model checking? We venture that the answer is the first-order theory of an automatic structure [8–10,15]. An *automatic structure* over the vocabulary consisting of relations $R_1, \ldots, R_n$ with arities $r_1, \ldots, r_n$ is a structure $\mathfrak{S}$ whose universe is the set Σ^* of all strings over some finite alphabet Σ, and where each relation $R_i \subseteq (\Sigma^*)^{r_i}$ is *regular*, i.e., the set $\{w_1 \otimes \cdots \otimes w_{r_i} : (w_1, \ldots, w_r) \in R_i\}$ is regular. The following well-known closure and algorithmic property is what makes the theory of automatic structures appealing.

Theorem 2. *There is an algorithm which, given a first-order formula $\varphi(\bar{x})$ and an automatic structure $\mathfrak{S}$ over the vocabulary σ, computes a finite automaton for $[\![\varphi]\!]$ consisting of tuples $\bar{w}$ of words, such that $\mathfrak{S} \models \varphi(\bar{w})$.*

The algorithm is a standard automata construction (e.g. see [42] for details), which is indeed similar to the standard automata construction from the weak second-order theory of one successor [22]. [In fact, first-order logic over automatic structures can be encoded (and vice versa) to weak second-order theory of one successor via the so-called *finite set interpretations* [18], which would allow us to use tools like MONA to check first-order formulas over automatic structures.]

Automatic structures are extremely powerful. We can encode the linear integer arithmetic theory $\langle \mathbb{N}; + \rangle$ as an automatic structure [15]. In fact, we can even add the predicate $x|_2 y$ (where $a|_2 b$ iff a divides b and $a = 2^n$ for some natural number n) to $\langle \mathbb{N}; + \rangle$, while still preserving decidability. This essentially implies that ESO over automatic structures is undecidable; in fact, this is the case even when formulas are restricted to monadic predicates.

We are now ready to describe our framework for RMC in ESO over automatic structures:

(i) **Specification:**
Express the verification problem as a formula

$$\psi := \exists R_1, \ldots, R_n . \varphi$$

in ESO over automatic structures.

(ii) **Specification Checking:**
Search for *regular* witnesses for $R_1, \ldots, R_n$ that satisfy φ.

Note that while the specification (Item (i)) would provide a complete and faithful encoding of the verification problem, our method for checking the specification (Item (ii)) restricts to regular proofs. It is expected that this is an incomplete proof rule, i.e., for ψ to be satisfied, it is not sufficient in general to restrict to regular relations. Therefore, two important questions arise. Firstly, how expressive is the framework of regular proofs? Numerous results suggest that the answer is that it is very expressive. On the practical side, many benchmarks (especially from parameterized systems) have indicated this to be the case, e.g., see [3,17,24,30,33,34,37–39,45]. On the theoretical side, this framework is in fact complete for important properties like safety and liveness for many classes of infinite-state systems that can be captured by regular model checking, including pushdown systems, reversal-bounded counter systems, two-dimensional vector addition systems, communication-free Petri nets, and tree-rewrite systems (for the extension to trees), among others, e.g., see [7,23,32,35,42,43]. In addition, the restriction to regular proofs is also attractive since it gives rise to a simple method to enumerate all regular proofs that check φ. This naive method would not work in practice, but *smart enumeration techniques of regular proofs* (e.g., using automata learning and CEGIS) are available, which we will discuss in Sect. 4.

3.2 Safety

We start with the most straightforward example: safety. We assume that our transition system is represented by a length-preserving system with domain $Dom \subseteq \Sigma^*$ and a transition relation $\Delta \subseteq Dom \times Dom$ given by a length-preserving transducer. Furthermore, we assume that the system contains two regular languages $Init, Bad \subseteq Dom$, representing the set of initial and bad states. As we mentioned earlier in this section, safety amounts to checking the existence of an invariant $Inv \subseteq Dom$ that contains $Init$ but is disjoint from Bad. That is, the safety property holds iff there exists a set $Inv \subseteq Dom$ such that:

- $Init \subseteq Inv$
- $Inv \cap Bad = \emptyset$
- Inv is inductive, i.e., for every configuration $s \in Inv$, if $(s, s') \in \Delta$, then $s' \in Inv$.

The above formulation immediately leads to a first-order formula φ over the vocabulary of $\langle \Delta, Init, Bad, Inv \rangle$. Therefore, the desired ESO formula over the original vocabulary (i.e. $\langle \Delta, Init, Bad \rangle$) is

$$\exists Inv.\, \varphi,$$

where φ is a conjunction of the three properties above.

Example 3. Fix $\Sigma = \{0, 1\}$. Consider the transition relation $\Delta \subseteq \Sigma^* \times \Sigma^*$ generated by the regular expression $((0,0) + (1,1))^*(1,0)(0,1)((0,0) + (1,1))^*$. Intuitively, Δ nondeterministically picks a substring 10 in an input word w and rewrites it to 01. Let $Init = 0\Sigma^*1$ and $Bad = 1^*0^*$. Observe that there is a regular proof Inv for this safety property: $Inv = Init$. Note that this is despite the fact that $post^*(Init)$ in general is not a regular set.

3.3 Liveness

A second class of properties are *liveness properties,* for instance checking whether a program is guaranteed to terminate, guaranteed to answer requests eventually, or guaranteed to visit certain states infinitely often. In the context of RMC, liveness has been studied a lot less than safety, and methods successful for proving safety usually do not lend themselves to an easy generalisation to liveness.

For simplicity, the special case of program termination is consider, which can be generalized to full liveness. As before, we assume that a transition system is defined by a domain $Dom \subseteq \Sigma^*$, a transition relation $\Delta \subseteq Dom \times Dom$, and a set $Init \subseteq Dom$ of initial states. Proving termination amounts to showing that no infinite runs starting from a state in $Init$ exist; to this end, we can search for a pair $\langle Inv, Rank \rangle$ consisting of an inductive invariant and a well-founded ranking relation:

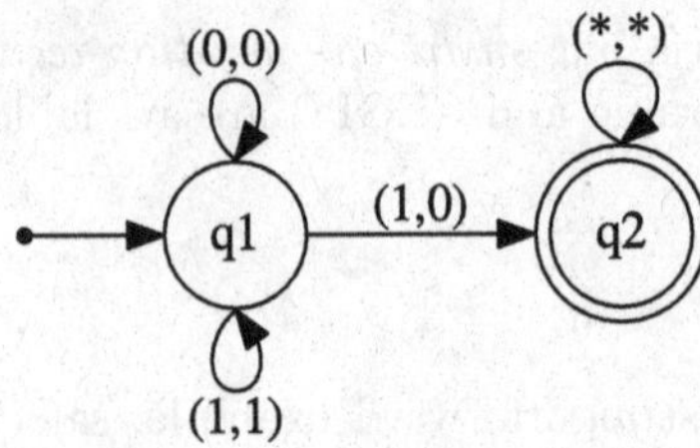

Fig. 1. Lexicographic ranking relation for Example 4

- *Init* $\subseteq$ *Inv*;
- *Inv* is inductive (as in Sect. 3.2);
- the relation *Rank* covers the reachable transitions: $\Delta \cap (\mathit{Inv} \times \mathit{Inv}) \subseteq \mathit{Rank}$;
- *Rank* is transitive: $(s, s') \in \mathit{Rank}$ and $(s', s'') \in \mathit{Rank}$ imply $(s, s'') \in \mathit{Rank}$;
- *Rank* is irreflexive: $(s, s) \notin \mathit{Rank}$ for every $s \in \mathit{Dom}$.

The last two conditions ensure that *Rank* is a strict partial order, and therefore is even well-founded on fixed-length subsets $\mathit{Dom} \cap \Sigma^n$ of the domain. All five conditions can easily be expressed by a first-order formula φ over the relations $\langle \Delta, \mathit{Init}, \mathit{Inv}, \mathit{Rank} \rangle$. Now, for length-preserving relations R, expressing in first-order logic that a transitive relation is well-founded is simple: it is not the case that there are words x, y such that $(x, y) \in R$ and $(y, y) \in R$. This "lasso" shape is owing to the fact that in every finite system every infinite path always leads to one state that is visited infinitely often. In summary, termination of a system is therefore captured by the following ESO formula:

$$\exists \mathit{Inv}, \mathit{Rank}.\, \varphi$$

where φ is the first-order part that encodes the aforementioned verification conditions.

Example 4. We consider here the same example as Example 3, but we instead want to prove termination. It is quite easy to see that every configuration will always lead to a configuration of the form 0^*1^*, which is a dead end. Termination of the system can be proven using the trivial inductive invariant $\mathit{Inv} = \mathit{Dom}$, and a lexicographic ranking relation *Rank*, represented as a transducer with two states and shown in Fig. 1. Using the algorithms proposed in Sect. 4, this ranking relation can be computed fully automatically in a few milliseconds.

3.4 Winning Strategies for Two-Player Games on Infinite Graphs

We only need to slightly modify the ESO formula for program termination, given in the previous section, to reason about the existence of winning strategies in a reachability game. Instead of a single transition relation Δ, for a two-player game we assume that two relations $\Delta_1, \Delta_2 \subseteq \mathit{Dom} \times \mathit{Dom}$ are given, encoding the possible moves of Player 1 and Player 2, respectively. A reachability game starts in any configuration in the set $Init \subseteq Dom$. The players move in alternation, with Player 2 winning if the game eventually reaches a configuration in $Final \subseteq Dom$, whereas Player 1 wins if the game never enters *Final*. The first move in a game is always done by Player 1.

As in the previous section, we formulate the existence of a winning strategy for Player 2 (for any initial configuration in *Init*) in terms of a pair $\langle Inv, Rank \rangle$ of relations. The set *Inv* now represents the possible configurations that Player 1 visits during games, whereas the ranking relation *Rank* expresses progress made by Player 2 towards the region *Final*.

- $Init \subseteq Inv$;
- *Rank* is transitive and irreflexive (as in Sect. 3.3);
- Player 2 can force the game to progress: for every $s \in Inv \setminus Final$, and every move $(s, s') \in \Delta_1$ of Player 1 with $s' \notin Final$, there is a move $(s', s'') \in \Delta_2$ of Player 2 such that $s'' \in Inv$ and $(s, s'') \in Rank$.

It is again easy to see that all conditions can be expressed by a first-order formula over the relations $\langle \Delta_1, \Delta_2, Init, Final, Inv, Rank \rangle$, and the existence of a winning strategy as an ESO formula:

$$\exists Inv, Rank. \varphi.$$

A similar encoding has been used in previous work of the authors to reason about almost-sure termination of parameterised probabilistic systems [30,34]. In this setting, the two players characterise non-determinism (demonic choice, e.g., the scheduler) and probabilistic choice (angelic choice, e.g., randomisation).

Example 5. We consider a classical take-away game [20] with two players. In the beginning of the game, there are n chips on the table. In alternating moves, with Player 1 starting, each player can take 1, 2, or 3 chips from the table. The first player who has no more chips to take loses. It can be observed that Player 2 has a winning strategy whenever the initial number n is a multiple of 4.

Configurations of this game can be modelled as words $(p_1 + p_2)1^*0^*$, in which the first letter (p_1 or p_2) indicates the next player to make a move, and the number of 1*s* represents the number of chips left. To prove that Player 2 can win whenever $n = 4k$, we choose $Init = p_1(1111)^*0^*$ as the initial states, and $Final = p_1 0^*$, i.e., we check whether Player 2 can move first to a configuration in which no chips are left. The transitions of the two players are described by the regular expressions

$$\begin{aligned} \Delta_1 &= (p_1, p_2)\,(1,1)^*\,\big((1,0) + (11,00) + (111,000)\big)\,(0,0)^* \\ \Delta_2 &= (p_2, p_1)\,(1,1)^*\,\big((1,0) + (11,00) + (111,000)\big)\,(0,0)^* \end{aligned}$$

The witnesses proving that Player 2 indeed has a winning strategy are shown in Fig. 2 and Fig. 3, respectively. The ranking relation *Rank* in Fig. 3 is similar to the one proving termination in Example 4, and expresses that the number of 1*s* is monotonically decreasing. The invariant *Inv* in Fig. 2 expresses that Player 2

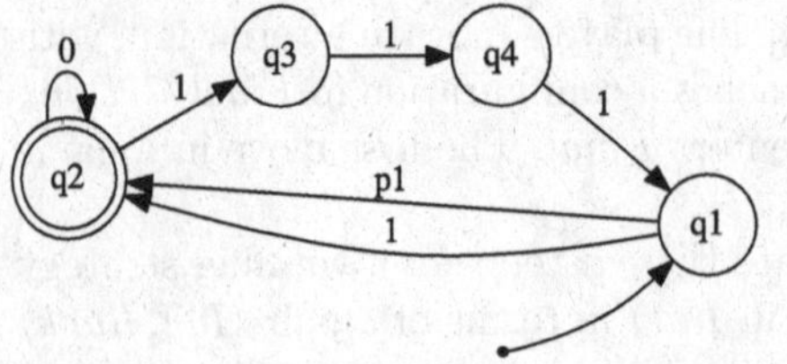

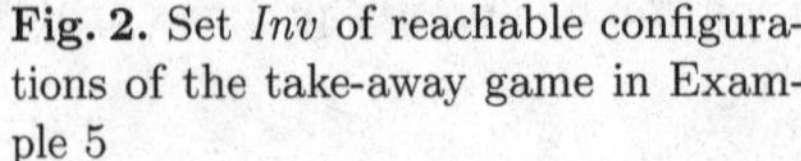
Fig. 2. Set *Inv* of reachable configurations of the take-away game in Example 5

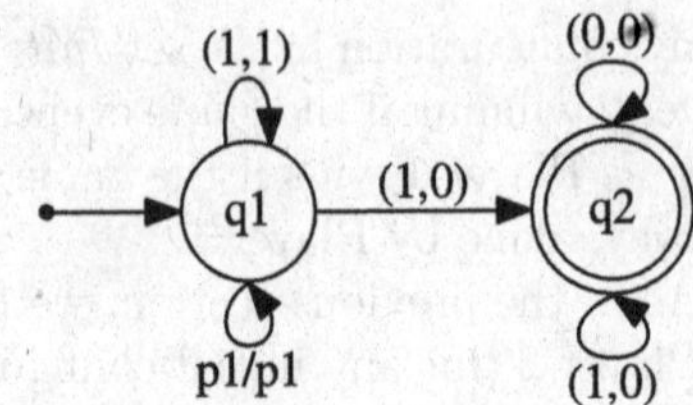

Fig. 3. Relation *Rank* in Example 5

should move in such a way that the number of chips on the table remains divisible by 4; *Rank* and *Inv* in combination encode the strategy that Player 2 should follow to win. The witness relations were found by the tool SLRP, presented in [34], in around 3 s on an Intel Core i5 computer with 3.2 GHz.

3.5 Isomorphism and Bisimulation

We now describe how we can compare the behaviour of two given systems described by length-preserving transducers. There are many natural notions of "similarity", but we target isomorphism, bisimulation, and probabilistic bisimulation (or variants thereof). All of these are important properties since they show *indistinguishability* of two systems, which are applicable to proving *anonymity*, e.g., in the case of the Dining Cryptographer Protocol [16]. Isomorphism can also be used to detect symmetries in systems, which can be used to speed up regular model checking [33]. Here, we only describe how to express isomorphism of two systems. Encoding bisimulation and probabilistic bisimulation for parameterized systems is a bit trickier since we will need infinitely many action labels (i.e. to distinguish the action of the ith process), but this can also be encoded in our framework; see the first-order proof rules over automatic structures in the recent paper [24].

We are given two systems $\mathfrak{S}_1, \mathfrak{S}_2$, whose domains are $Dom_1, Dom_2 \subseteq \Sigma^*$ and whose transition relations R_1 and R_2 are described by transducers. We would like to show that $\mathfrak{S}_1$ and $\mathfrak{S}_2$ are the same up to isomorphism. The desired ESO formula is of the form

$$\exists F. \varphi$$

where φ says that $F \subseteq Dom_1 \times Dom_2$ describes the desired isomorphism between $\mathfrak{S}_1$ and $\mathfrak{S}_2$. To this end, we will first need to say that F is a bijective function. This can easily be described in first-order logic over the vocabulary $\langle Dom_1, Dom_2, R_1, R_2 \rangle$. For example, F is a function can be described as

$$\forall x, y, z. (F(x, y) \wedge F(x, z) \rightarrow y = z).$$

Note that $y = z$ can be described by a simple transducer, so this is a valid first-order formula over automatic structures. We then need to add some more conjuncts in φ saying that F is a homomorphism and its reverse is also a homomorphism. This is also easily described in first-order logic, e.g.,

$$\forall x, x', y, y'. (R_1(x, y) \wedge F(x, x') \wedge F(y, y') \rightarrow R_2(x', y'))$$

says that F is a homomorphism.

Example 6. We describe the Dining Cryptographer example [16], and how to prove this by reasoning about isomorphism. [There is a cleaner way to do this using probabilistic bisimulation [24].] In this protocol there are n cryptographers sitting at a round table. The cryptographers knew that the dinner was paid by NSA, or *exactly one* of the cryptographers at the table. The protocol aims to determine which one of these without revealing the identity of the cryptographer who pays. The ith cryptographer is in state $c_i = 0$ (resp. $c_i = 1$) if he did not pay for the dinner. Any two neighbouring cryptographers keep a private fair coin (that is only visible to themselves). There is a transition to toss any of the coins (in this case, probability is replaced by non-determinism). Let us use p_i to denote the value of the coin that is shared by the ith and $i + 1 \pmod n$st cryptographers. If the ith cryptographer paid, it will announce $p_{i-1} \oplus p_i$ (here $\oplus$ is the XOR operator); otherwise, it will announce the negation of this. We call the value announced by the ith cryptographer a_i. At the end, we take the XOR of $a_1, \ldots, a_n$, which is 0 iff none of the cryptographers paid.

This example can easily be encoded by a length-preserving transducer R. For example, the domain is a word of the form

$$(c_1 p_1 a_1) \ldots (c_n p_n a_n)$$

where $c_i \in \{0, 1\}$ and $p_i, a_i \in \{?, 0, 1\}$. Here, the symbol '?' is used to denote that the value of p_i is not yet determined. In the case of a_i, the symbol '?' means that it is not yet announced. Although it is a bit cumbersome, it is possible to describe the dynamics of the system by a transducer. The desired property to prove then is whether there is an isomorphism between 0100^m and 0010^m for every $m \in \mathbb{N}$, i.e., that the first cryptographer, who did not pay, cannot distinguish if it were the second or the third cryptographer who paid. There is a transducer R' describing the isomorphism that maps 0100^m to 0010^m, which is done by inverting the value of p_2.

4 How to Satisfy Existential Second-Order Quantifiers

We have given several examples for the **Specification** step in Sect. 3.1, but the question remains how one can solve the **Specification Checking** step and automatically compute witnesses $R_1, \ldots, R_n$ for the existential quantifiers in a formula $\exists R_1, \ldots, R_n. \varphi$ (where the matrix φ is first-order, as introduced in Sect. 2.4). We present two solutions for this problem, two approaches to automata learning whose respective applicability depends on the shape of the matrix φ. Both methods have in previous work proven to be useful for analysing complex parameterised systems. On the one hand, it has been shown that automata learning is competitive with tailor-made algorithms, for instance with Abstract Regular Model Checking (ARMC) [11], for safety proofs [17,44]; on the other hand, automata learning is general and can help to automate the verification of properties for which no bespoke approaches exist, for instance liveness properties or properties of games.

4.1 Active Automata Learning

The more efficient, though also more restricted approach is to use classical automata learning, for instance Angluin's L^* algorithm [6], or one of its variants (e.g., [26,40]), to compute witnesses for $R_1, \ldots, R_n$. In all those algorithms, a *learner* attempts to reconstruct a regular language $\mathcal{L}$ known to the *teacher* by repeatedly asking two kinds of queries: *membership,* i.e., whether a word w should be in $\mathcal{L}$; and *equivalence,* i.e., whether $\mathcal{L}$ coincides with some candidate language $\mathcal{H}$ constructed by the learner. When equivalence fails, the teacher provides a positive or negative counterexample, which is a word in the symmetric difference between $\mathcal{L}$ and $\mathcal{H}$.

This leads to the question how *membership* and *equivalence* can be implemented in the ESO setting, in order to let a learner search for $R_1, \ldots, R_n$. In general, it is clearly not possible to answer membership queries about $R_1, \ldots, R_n$, since there can be many choices of relations satisfying φ, some of which might contain a word, while others do not; in other words, the relations are in general not uniquely determined by φ. We need to make additional assumptions.

As the simplest case, active automata learning can be used if two properties are satisfied: (i) the relations $R_1, \ldots, R_n$ are uniquely defined by φ and the structure $\mathfrak{S}$; and (ii) for any $k \in \mathbb{N}$, the sub-relations $R_i^k = \{w \in R_i \mid |w| \leq k\}$ can be effectively computed from φ and $\mathfrak{S}$. Given those two assumptions, automata learning can be used to approximate the genuine solution $R_1, \ldots, R_n$ up to any length bound k, resulting in a candidate solution $R_1^{\mathcal{H}}, \ldots, R_n^{\mathcal{H}}$. It can also be verified whether $R_1^{\mathcal{H}}, \ldots, R_n^{\mathcal{H}}$ coincide with the genuine solution by evaluating φ, i.e., by checking whether $\mathfrak{S}, R_1^{\mathcal{H}}, \ldots, R_n^{\mathcal{H}} \models \varphi$. If this check succeeds, learning has been successful; if it fails, the bound k can be increased and a better approximation computed. Whenever the unique solution $R_1, \ldots, R_n$ exists and is regular, this algorithm is guaranteed to terminate and produce a correct answer.

In the setting of weakly-finite systems, assumption (ii) is usually satisfied, since only finitely many configurations are reachable for any $k \in \mathbb{N}$. In particular, for the examples in Sect. 3, the sub-relations $R_1^k, \ldots, R_n^k$ can be computed using standard methods such as symbolic model checking [36]. Assumption (i) is less realistic, because witnesses to be computed in verification are often not uniquely defined. For instance, a safe system (Sect. 3.2) will normally have many inductive invariants, each of which is sufficient to demonstrate safety.

What can be done when assumption (i) does not hold, and the relations $R_1, \ldots, R_n$ are not unique? Depending on the shape of φ, a simple trick can be applicable, namely the learning algorithm can be generalised to search for a *unique smallest* or *unique largest* solution (in the set-theoretic sense) of φ, provided those solutions exist. This is the case in particular when φ can be rephrased as a fixed-point equation

$$\langle R_1, \ldots, R_n \rangle = F(R_1, \ldots, R_n)$$

for some monotonic function F; for instance, if φ can be written as a set of Horn clauses. We still require property (ii), however, and need to be able to compute sub-relations $R_i^k = \{w \in R_i \mid |w| \leq k\}$ of the smallest or largest solution to answer membership queries.

In order to check whether a solution candidate $R_1^{\mathcal{H}}, \ldots, R_n^{\mathcal{H}}$ is correct (for equivalence queries), we can as before evaluate φ, and terminate the search if φ is satisfied. In general, however, there is no way to verify that $R_1^{\mathcal{H}}, \ldots, R_n^{\mathcal{H}}$ is indeed the *smallest* solution of φ, which affects termination and completeness in a somewhat subtle way. If the smallest solution of φ exists and is regular, then termination of the overall search is guaranteed, and the produced solution will indeed satisfy φ; but what is found is not necessarily the smallest solution of φ.

This method has been implemented in particular for proving safety [17,44] and probabilistic bisimulations [24] of length-preserving systems, cases in which φ is naturally monotonic, and where active learning methods are able to compute witnesses with hundreds (sometimes thousands) of states within minutes.

4.2 SAT-Based Automata Learning

L^*-style learning is not applicable if the matrix of an ESO formula $\exists R_1, \ldots, R_n. \varphi$ does not have a smallest or largest solution, or if the sub-relations $R_1^k, \ldots, R_n^k$ (for some $k \in \mathbb{N}$) cannot be computed because a system is not weakly finite. An example of such non-monotonic formulas are the formulas characterising winning strategies of reachability games presented in Sect. 3.4; indeed, multiple minimal but incomparable strategies can exist to win a game, so that in general there is no smallest solution. A more general learning strategy to solve ESO formulas in the non-monotonic case is *SAT-based learning,* i.e., using a Boolean encoding of finite-state automata to systematically search for solutions of φ [34,37,46]. SAT-based learning is a more general solution than active automata learning for constructing ESO proofs, although experiments show that it is also a lot slower for simpler analysis tasks like safety proofs [17].

We outline how a SAT solver can be used to construct deterministic finite-state automata (DFAs), following the encoding used in [34]. The encoding assumes that a finite alphabet Σ and the number n of states of the automaton are fixed. The states of the automaton are assumed to be $q_1, \ldots, q_n$, and without loss of generality q_1 is the unique initial state. The Boolean decision variables of the encoding are (i) variables $\{z_i\}$ that determine which of the states are accepting; and (ii) variables $\{x_{i,a,j}\}$ that determine, for any letter $a \in \Sigma$ and states q_i, q_j, whether the automaton has a transition from q_i to q_j with label a.

A number of Boolean constraints are then asserted to ensure that only well-formed DFAs are considered: determinism; reachability of every automaton state from the initial state; reachability of an accepting state from every state; and symmetry-breaking constraints.

Next, the formula φ can be translated to Boolean constraints over the decision variables. This translation can be done eagerly for all conjuncts of φ that can be represented succinctly:

- a positive atom $x \in R$ in which the length of x is bounded can be translated to constraints that assert the existence of a run accepting x;
- a negative atom $x \notin R$ can similarly be encoded as a run ending in a non-accepting state, thanks to the determinism of the automaton;
- for automata representing binary relations $R(x, y)$, several universally quantified formulas can be encoded as a polynomial-size Boolean constraint as well, including:

$$\begin{aligned} \text{Reflexivity:} &\quad \forall x.\, R(x,x) \\ \text{Irreflexivity:} &\quad \forall x.\, \neg R(x,x) \\ \text{Functional consistency:} &\quad \forall x,y,z.\, (R(x,y) \wedge R(x,z) \rightarrow y = z) \\ \text{Transitivity:} &\quad \forall x,y,z.\, (R(x,y) \wedge R(y,z) \rightarrow R(x,z)) \end{aligned}$$

Other conjuncts in φ can be encoded lazily with the help of a refinement loop, resembling the classical CEGAR approach. The SAT solver is first queried to produce a candidate automaton $\mathcal{H}$ that satisfies a partial encoding of φ. It is then checked whether the candidate $\mathcal{H}$ indeed satisfies φ; if this is the case, SAT-based learning has been successful and terminates; otherwise, a blocking constraint is asserted that rules out the candidate $\mathcal{H}$ in subsequent queries.

It should be noted that this approach can in principle be implemented for *any* formula φ, since it is always possible to generate a naïve blocking constraint that blocks exactly the observed assignment of the variables $\{z_i, x_{i,a,j}\}$, i.e., that exactly matches the automaton $\mathcal{H}$. It is well-known in Satisfiability Modulo Theories, however, that good blocking constraints are those which eliminate as many similar candidate solutions as possible, and need to be designed carefully and specifically for a theory (or, in our case, based on the shape of φ).

Several implementations of SAT-based learning have been described in the literature, for instance for computing inductive invariants [37], synthesising state machines satisfying given properties [46], computing symmetries of parameterized systems [33], and for solving various kinds of games [34]. Experiments show that the automata that can be computed using SAT-based learning tend to be several order of magnitudes smaller than with active automata learning methods (typically, at most 10–20 states), but that SAT-based learning can solve a more general class of synthesis problems as well.

4.3 Stratification of ESO Formulas

The two approaches to compute regular languages can sometimes be combined. For instance, in [34] active automata learning is used to approximate the reachable configurations of a two-player game (in the sense of computing an inductive invariant), whereas SAT-based learning is used to compute winning strategies; the results of the two procedures in combination represent a solution of an ESO formula $\exists A, \mathit{Rank}.\, \varphi$ with two second-order quantifiers.

More generally, since the active automata learning approach in Sect. 4.1 is able to compute smallest or greatest solutions of formulas, a combined approach is possible when the matrix φ of an ESO formula $\exists R_1, \ldots, R_n.\, \varphi$ can be stratified. Suppose φ can be decomposed into $\varphi_1[R_1] \wedge \varphi_2[R_1, \ldots, R_n]$ in such a way that (i) φ_1 has a unique smallest solution in R_1, and (ii) φ_2 contains R_1 only in literals $x \in R_1$ in negative positions, i.e., underneath an odd number of negations. In this situation, one can clearly proceed by first computing a smallest relation R_1 satisfying φ_1, using the methods in Sect. 4.1, and then solve the remaining formula $\exists R_2, \ldots, R_n.\, \varphi_2$ given this fixed solution for R_1. The case where φ_1 has a greatest solution, and φ_2 contains R_1 only positively can be handled similarly.

We believe that this combined form of automata learning is promising, and in [34] it turned out to be the most efficient method to solve reachability games as introduced in Sect. 3.4. Further research is needed, however, to evaluate the approach for other verification problems.

5 Conclusions

In this paper, we have proposed existential second-order logic (ESO) over automatic structures as an umbrella covering a large number of regular model checking tasks, continuing a research programme that was initiated by Bengt Jonsson 20 years ago. We have shown that many important correctness properties can be represented elegantly in ESO, and developed unified algorithms that can be applied to any correctness property captured using ESO. Experiments showing the practicality of this approach have been presented in several recent publications, including computation of inductive invariants [17,37,44], of symmetries and simulation relations of parameterised systems [33], of winning strategies of games [30,34], and of probabilistic bisimulations [24].

Several challenges remain. One bottleneck that has been identified in several of the studies is the *size of alphabets* necessary to model systems, to which the algorithms presented in Sect. 4 are very sensitive. This indicates that some analysis tasks require more compact or more expressive automata representations, for instance symbolic automata, and generalised learning methods; or abstraction to reduce the size of alphabets. Another less-than-satisfactory point is the handling of *well-foundedness* in the ESO framework. When restricting the class of considered systems to weakly finite systems, as done here, well-foundedness of relations can be replaced by acyclicity, which can be expressed easily in ESO (as shown in Sect. 3.3). It is not obvious, however, in which way ESO should be extended to also handle systems that are not weakly finite, without sacrificing the elegance of the approach.

Acknowledgment. First and foremost, we thank Bengt Jonsson for a source of inspiration for our research for many years, as well as for being the best colleague and friend one could wish for. We also thank our numerous collaborators in our work on regular model checking that led to this work, including Parosh Abdulla, Yu-Fang Chen, Lukas Holik, Chih-Duo Hong, Ondrej Lengal, Leonid Libkin, Rupak Majumdar, and Tomas Vojnar. This research was sponsored in part by the ERC Starting Grant 759969 (AV-SMP), Max-Planck Fellowship, the Swedish Research Council (VR) under grant 2018-04727, and by the Swedish Foundation for Strategic Research (SSF) under the project WebSec (Ref. RIT17-0011).

References

1. Abdulla, P.A., Bouajjani, A., Jonsson, B., Nilsson, M.: Handling global conditions in parametrized system verification. In: Halbwachs, N., Peled, D. (eds.) CAV 1999. LNCS, vol. 1633, pp. 134–145. Springer, Heidelberg (1999). https://doi.org/10.1007/3-540-48683-6_14
2. Abdulla, P.A., Jonsson, B., Mahata, P., d'Orso, J.: Regular tree model checking. In: Brinksma, E., Larsen, K.G. (eds.) CAV 2002. LNCS, vol. 2404, pp. 555–568. Springer, Heidelberg (2002). https://doi.org/10.1007/3-540-45657-0_47
3. Abdulla, P.A., Jonsson, B., Nilsson, M., Saksena, M.: A survey of regular model checking. In: Gardner, P., Yoshida, N. (eds.) CONCUR 2004. LNCS, vol. 3170, pp. 35–48. Springer, Heidelberg (2004). https://doi.org/10.1007/978-3-540-28644-8_3
4. Ahrendt, W., Beckert, B., Bubel, R., Hähnle, R., Schmitt, P.H., Ulbrich, M. (eds.): Deductive Software Verification - The KeY Book - From Theory to Practice. Lecture Notes in Computer Science., vol. 10001. Springer, Cham (2016). https://doi.org/10.1007/978-3-319-49812-6
5. Alur, R., et al.: Syntax-guided synthesis. In: Formal Methods in Computer-Aided Design, FMCAD 2013, Portland, OR, USA, 20–23 October 2013, pp. 1–8 (2013)
6. Angluin, D.: Learning regular sets from queries and counterexamples. Inf. Comput. **75**(2), 87–106 (1987)
7. Bardin, S., Finkel, A., Leroux, J., Schnoebelen, P.: Flat acceleration in symbolic model checking. In: Peled, D.A., Tsay, Y.-K. (eds.) ATVA 2005. LNCS, vol. 3707, pp. 474–488. Springer, Heidelberg (2005). https://doi.org/10.1007/11562948_35
8. Benedikt, M., Libkin, L., Schwentick, T., Segoufin, L.: Definable relations and first-order query languages over strings. J. ACM **50**(5), 694–751 (2003)
9. Blumensath, A., Grädel, E.: Automatic structures. In: Proceedings of the 15th Annual IEEE Symposium on Logic in Computer Science, pp. 51–62. IEEE (2000)
10. Blumensath, A., Grädel, E.: Finite presentations of infinite structures: automata and interpretations. Theory Comput. Syst. **37**(6), 641–674 (2004)
11. Bouajjani, A., Habermehl, P., Vojnar, T.: Abstract regular model checking. In: Alur, R., Peled, D.A. (eds.) CAV 2004. LNCS, vol. 3114, pp. 372–386. Springer, Heidelberg (2004). https://doi.org/10.1007/978-3-540-27813-9_29
12. Bouajjani, A., Jonsson, B., Nilsson, M., Touili, T.: Regular model checking. In: Emerson, E.A., Sistla, A.P. (eds.) CAV 2000. LNCS, vol. 1855, pp. 403–418. Springer, Heidelberg (2000). https://doi.org/10.1007/10722167_31
13. Bradley, A.R., Manna, Z.: The Calculus of Computation: Decision Procedures with Applications to Verification. Springer, Heidelberg (2007). https://doi.org/10.1007/978-3-540-74113-8
14. Brockschmidt, M., Cook, B., Ishtiaq, S., Khlaaf, H., Piterman, N.: T2: temporal property verification. In: Chechik, M., Raskin, J.-F. (eds.) TACAS 2016. LNCS, vol. 9636, pp. 387–393. Springer, Heidelberg (2016). https://doi.org/10.1007/978-3-662-49674-9_22

15. Bruyere, V., Hansel, G., Michaux, C., Villemaire, R.: Logic and p-recognizable sets of integers. Bull. Belg. Math. Soc. **1**, 191–238 (1994)
16. Chaum, D.: The dining cryptographers problem: unconditional sender and recipient untraceability. J. Cryptol. **1**(1), 65–75 (1988)
17. Chen, Y., Hong, C., Lin, A.W., Rümmer, P.: Learning to prove safety over parameterised concurrent systems. In: 2017 Formal Methods in Computer Aided Design, FMCAD 2017, Vienna, Austria, 2–6 October 2017, pp. 76–83 (2017)
18. Colcombet, T., Löding, C.: Transforming structures by set interpretations. Log. Methods Comput. Sci. **3**(2), (2007)
19. Esparza, J., Gaiser, A., Kiefer, S.: Proving termination of probabilistic programs using patterns. In: Madhusudan, P., Seshia, S.A. (eds.) CAV 2012. LNCS, vol. 7358, pp. 123–138. Springer, Heidelberg (2012). https://doi.org/10.1007/978-3-642-31424-7_14
20. Ferguson, T.S.: Game Theory. Online Book, 2nd edn (2014)
21. Giesl, J., Thiemann, R., Schneider-Kamp, P., Falke, S.: Automated termination proofs with AProVE. In: van Oostrom, V. (ed.) RTA 2004. LNCS, vol. 3091, pp. 210–220. Springer, Heidelberg (2004). https://doi.org/10.1007/978-3-540-25979-4_15
22. Grädel, E., Thomas, W., Wilke, T. (eds.): Automata, Logics, and Infinite Games: A Guide to Current Research. Lecture Notes in Computer Science, vol. 2500. Springer, Cham (2002). https://doi.org/10.1007/3-540-36387-4. Outcome of a Dagstuhl Seminar, February 2001
23. Hague, M., Lin, A.W., Ong, C.L.: Detecting redundant CSS rules in HTML5 applications: a tree rewriting approach. In: Proceedings of the 2015 ACM SIGPLAN International Conference on Object-Oriented Programming, Systems, Languages, and Applications, OOPSLA 2015, Part of SPLASH 2015, Pittsburgh, PA, USA, 25–30 October 2015, pp. 1–19 (2015)
24. Hong, C.-D., Lin, A.W., Majumdar, R., Rümmer, P.: Probabilistic bisimulation for parameterized systems. In: Dillig, I., Tasiran, S. (eds.) CAV 2019. LNCS, vol. 11561, pp. 455–474. Springer, Cham (2019). https://doi.org/10.1007/978-3-030-25540-4_27
25. Jonsson, B., Nilsson, M.: Transitive closures of regular relations for verifying infinite-state systems. In: Graf, S., Schwartzbach, M. (eds.) TACAS 2000. LNCS, vol. 1785, pp. 220–235. Springer, Heidelberg (2000). https://doi.org/10.1007/3-540-46419-0_16
26. Kearns, M.J., Vazirani, U.V.: An Introduction to Computational Learning Theory. MIT Press, Cambridge (1994)
27. Resten, Y., Maler, O., Marcus, M., Pnueli, A., Shahar, E.: Symbolic model checking with rich assertional languages. In: Grumberg, O. (ed.) CAV 1997. LNCS, vol. 1254, pp. 424–435. Springer, Heidelberg (1997). https://doi.org/10.1007/3-540-63166-6_41
28. Kroening, D., Strichman, O.: Decision Procedures: An Algorithmic Point of View, 1st edn. Springer, Heidelberg (2008). https://doi.org/10.1007/978-3-540-74105-3
29. Leino, K.R.M.: Dafny: an automatic program verifier for functional correctness. In: Clarke, E.M., Voronkov, A. (eds.) LPAR 2010. LNCS (LNAI), vol. 6355, pp. 348–370. Springer, Heidelberg (2010). https://doi.org/10.1007/978-3-642-17511-4_20
30. Lengál, O., Lin, A.W., Majumdar, R., Rümmer, P.: Fair termination for parameterized probabilistic concurrent systems. In: Legay, A., Margaria, T. (eds.) TACAS 2017. LNCS, vol. 10205, pp. 499–517. Springer, Heidelberg (2017). https://doi.org/10.1007/978-3-662-54577-5_29

31. Libkin, L.: Elements of Finite Model Theory. Springer, Heidelberg (2004). https://doi.org/10.1007/978-3-662-07003-1
32. Lin, A.W.: Accelerating tree-automatic relations. In: IARCS Annual Conference on Foundations of Software Technology and Theoretical Computer Science, FSTTCS 2012, Hyderabad, India, 15–17 December 2012, pp. 313–324 (2012)
33. Lin, A.W., Nguyen, T.K., Rümmer, P., Sun, J.: Regular symmetry patterns. In: Jobstmann, B., Leino, K.R.M. (eds.) VMCAI 2016. LNCS, vol. 9583, pp. 455–475. Springer, Heidelberg (2016). https://doi.org/10.1007/978-3-662-49122-5_22
34. Lin, A.W., Rümmer, P.: Liveness of randomised parameterised systems under arbitrary schedulers. In: Chaudhuri, S., Farzan, A. (eds.) CAV 2016. LNCS, vol. 9780, pp. 112–133. Springer, Cham (2016). https://doi.org/10.1007/978-3-319-41540-6_7
35. Löding, C., Spelten, A.: Transition graphs of rewriting systems over unranked trees. In: Kučera, L., Kučera, A. (eds.) MFCS 2007. LNCS, vol. 4708, pp. 67–77. Springer, Heidelberg (2007). https://doi.org/10.1007/978-3-540-74456-6_8
36. McMillan, K.L.: Symbolic Model Checking. Kluwer, Dordrecht (1993)
37. Neider, D., Jansen, N.: Regular model checking using solver technologies and automata learning. In: Brat, G., Rungta, N., Venet, A. (eds.) NFM 2013. LNCS, vol. 7871, pp. 16–31. Springer, Heidelberg (2013). https://doi.org/10.1007/978-3-642-38088-4_2
38. Neider, D., Topcu, U.: An automaton learning approach to solving safety games over infinite graphs. In: Chechik, M., Raskin, J.-F. (eds.) TACAS 2016. LNCS, vol. 9636, pp. 204–221. Springer, Heidelberg (2016). https://doi.org/10.1007/978-3-662-49674-9_12
39. Nilsson, M.: Regular model checking. Ph.D. thesis, Uppsala Universitet (2005)
40. Rivest, R.L., Schapire, R.E.: Inference of finite automata using homing sequences. Inf. Comput. **103**(2), 299–347 (1993)
41. Sipser, M.: Introduction to the Theory of Computation. PWS Publishing Company, Boston (1997)
42. To, A.W.: Model checking infinite-state systems: generic and specific approaches. Ph.D. thesis, School of Informatics, University of Edinburgh (2010)
43. To, A.W., Libkin, L.: Algorithmic metatheorems for decidable LTL model checking over infinite systems. In: Ong, L. (ed.) FoSSaCS 2010. LNCS, vol. 6014, pp. 221–236. Springer, Heidelberg (2010). https://doi.org/10.1007/978-3-642-12032-9_16
44. Vardhan, A., Sen, K., Viswanathan, M., Agha, G.: Learning to verify safety properties. In: Davies, J., Schulte, W., Barnett, M. (eds.) ICFEM 2004. LNCS, vol. 3308, pp. 274–289. Springer, Heidelberg (2004). https://doi.org/10.1007/978-3-540-30482-1_26
45. Vojnar, T.: Cut-offs and automata in formal verification of infinite-state systems. Habilitation thesis, Faculty of Information Technology, Brno University of Technology (2007)
46. Walkinshaw, N., Taylor, R., Derrick, J.: Inferring extended finite state machine models from software executions. Empir. Softw. Eng. **21**(3), 811–853 (2016)
47. Wolper, P., Boigelot, B.: Verifying systems with infinite but regular state spaces. In: Hu, A.J., Vardi, M.Y. (eds.) CAV 1998. LNCS, vol. 1427, pp. 88–97. Springer, Heidelberg (1998). https://doi.org/10.1007/BFb0028736

High-Level Representation of Benchmark Families for Petri Games

Manuel Gieseking(✉) and Ernst-Rüdiger Olderog(✉)

University of Oldenburg, Oldenburg, Germany
{gieseking,olderog}@informatik.uni-oldenburg.de

Abstract. Petri games have been introduced as a multi-player game model representing causal memory to address the synthesis of distributed systems. For Petri games with one environment player and an arbitrary bounded number of system players, deciding the existence of a safety strategy is EXPTIME-complete. This result forms the basis of the tool ADAMSYNT that implements an algorithm for the synthesis of distributed controllers from Petri games. To evaluate the tool, it has been checked on a series of parameterized benchmarks from manufacturing and workflow scenarios.

In this paper, we introduce a new possibility to represent benchmark families for the synthesis of distributed systems modeled with Petri games. It enables the user to specify an entire benchmark family as one parameterized high-level net. We describe example benchmark families as a high-level version of a Petri game and exhibit an instantiation yielding a concrete 1-bounded Petri game. We identify improvements either regarding the size or the functionality of the benchmark families by examining the high-level Petri games.

1 Introduction

Automatically creating a program from a formal specification without any human programming involved, is of great interest for the implementation of correct systems. A *synthesis* algorithm either automatically derives an implementation satisfying a given formal specification or states the non-existence of such an implementation [3]. For *reactive systems*, i.e., system which continuously interact with their environment, the synthesis problem is often described as a game between the environment and the system. In this game-theoretic approach the specification is given as a *winning condition* of the game and a correct implementation is a *strategy* for the system players which satisfies the given winning condition against all moves of the environment. The synthesis approach fundamentally simplifies the development of complex systems by defining only the possible actions of the system and specifying the winning condition over these actions. This puts the development process on a more abstract level and avoids the error-prone manual coding.

This work was supported by the German Research Foundation (DFG) through the grant Petri Games (No. 392735815).

E.-R. Olderog et al. (Eds.): Jonsson Festschrift, LNCS 13030, pp. 115–137, 2021.
https://doi.org/10.1007/978-3-030-91384-7_7

For the *monolithic synthesis*, where the system can be seen as one unit with a central controller as the strategy, there is a growing number of tools [1,2,4,19] solving nontrivial applications. However, for the synthesis of *distributed systems*, i.e., systems composed of multiple independent processes possibly distributed over wide distances, the tool support is restricted. This is mainly due to the high complexity of the solving algorithms or the undecidability results for the general problem. In the two well-established models, the *Pnueli/Rosner* model [25] and *Zielonka's asynchronous automata* [28], the complexity is in general nonelementary [14,15,22] or even undecidable [13,25]. For the class of Zielonka automata with acyclic communication architectures the control problem has been shown to be decidable, with nonelementary complexity in general and EXPTIME for the special case of architectures of depth 1 [23]. For *Petri games* [11,12], reasonable subclasses can be solved with affordable costs and suitable tool support [7–9].

This paper extends the work on Petri games and presents a model for representing benchmark families for the synthesis of distributed systems in a concise way. *Petri games* model the distributed synthesis problem as a game between two teams: the environment players, representing external influences (the *uncontrollable* behavior), and the system players, representing the processes (the *controllable* behavior). In Petri games each player is modeled as a token of an underlying place/transition Petri net. The places of the net are partitioned between the teams. All players remember their own *causal* past and communicate this knowledge to every player participating in a joint transition. An example can be seen in Fig. 1.

Benchmark families depend on parameters which define a set of problems with increasing complexity. The new representation is based on schemata of Colored Petri Nets [16,18] rather than place/transition Petri nets, to intuitively deal with the parameters and sets of problems. We use places with individual tokens ranging over predefined domains of parametric size, transitions labeled with conditions that guard their fireability, and arcs labeled with expressions stating the result of the firing. Conditions and expressions may have variables ranging over the predefined domains. This enables the user to specify the entire benchmark family as one parametric high-level net rather than introducing a set of instances of the family and descriptions how to generalize these Petri games. Generally, the individual elements of a benchmark family (e.g., robots, work pieces, tools, humans, etc.) can be modeled by parametric sets of individual tokens and are processed by the transitions according to the semantics. Figure 4 serves as an example for a set of alarm systems and locations of a burglary.

In this paper, we introduce a new parameterized high-level representation of Petri games based on high-level Petri nets for a concise and clear definition of benchmark families. We apply the new definition to some of the existing benchmark families and show the correspondence of the high-level version to an example instantiation. During the application we identified improvements (either in size or functionality) of these benchmark families.

The remainder of the paper is structured as follows. Section 2 recaps the ideas, results, and solving techniques of Petri games and informally motivates the new high-level representation by an example. The formal definition of the high-level representation is given in Sect. 3. In Sect. 4 we illustrate the new approach by presenting two examples from the manufacturing domain and depicting for each example both the high-level representation and an instantiation.

Dedication. Ernst-Rüdiger Olderog dedicates this paper to Bengt Jonsson in memory of scientific and social meetings in Kiel in the 1980s. During the period 1984–87 we discussed the research by Jay Misra and Mani Chandy on asynchronous networks that led to Bengt's first publication [20] and his PhD thesis [21]. While visiting Kiel in December 1984, Bengt surprised us with his many talents: speaking Russian he served as an interpreter for a newly arrived Ukrainian visitor of Hans Langmaack, and playing the piano he delighted us with pieces of Chopin in the home of Annemarie and Hans Langmaack. This made an unforgettably impression on all those who were present at these occasions.

2 Petri Games for the Synthesis of Distributed Systems

In this section a brief overview of Petri games [11,12] is given. We illustrate the model via an instantiation of the benchmark family of an distributed alarm system from [8] and motivate the new high-level representation for a concise and clear presentation of the family. Basic knowledge about *Petri nets* [24,26] is assumed. We fix the notation of a Petri net $\mathcal{N} = (\mathcal{P}, \mathcal{T}, \mathcal{F}, In)$, with places $\mathcal{P}$, transitions $\mathcal{T}$, a flow relation $\mathcal{F} \subseteq (\mathcal{P} \cup \mathcal{T}) \times (\mathcal{T} \cup \mathcal{P})$, and an initial marking $In \subseteq \mathcal{P}$.

2.1 Petri Games

A *Petri game* $\mathcal{G} = (\mathcal{P}_S, \mathcal{P}_E, \mathcal{T}, \mathcal{F}, In, \mathcal{B})$ models the distributed synthesis problem as a multi-player game where the tokens of an underlying Petri net $\mathcal{N}$ represent the players of the game. The players act in two teams: the uncontrollable players (*environment players*) are the token residing on environment places $\mathcal{P}_E$ (depicted as white circles) and controllable players (*system players*) are the token residing on the system places $\mathcal{P}_S$ (depicted as gray circles). Those sets are the disjoint union of the places of the underlying Petri net, i.e., $\mathcal{P} = \mathcal{P}_E \dot{\cup} \mathcal{P}_S$. The uncontrollable players are used for modeling external influences on the system, whereas the controllable ones represent its processes. Each player knows its own *causal past*, i.e., the places and transitions which had been used to reach the current place. This information is exchanged with all players participating at a joint transition. These intricate causal dependencies (and independencies) are naturally represented by the *unfolding* of the underlying Petri net [5,6]. An unfolding represents the behavior of a Petri net by unrolling each loop of the execution and introducing copies of a place $p \in \mathcal{P}$ for each join of transitions in p. Hence, each transition of the unfolding represents a unique instance of a transition $t \in \mathcal{T}$ during an execution. The system players have to cooperate to win the game, i.e., to avoid reaching certain *bad places* $p \in \mathcal{B}$ (depicted as

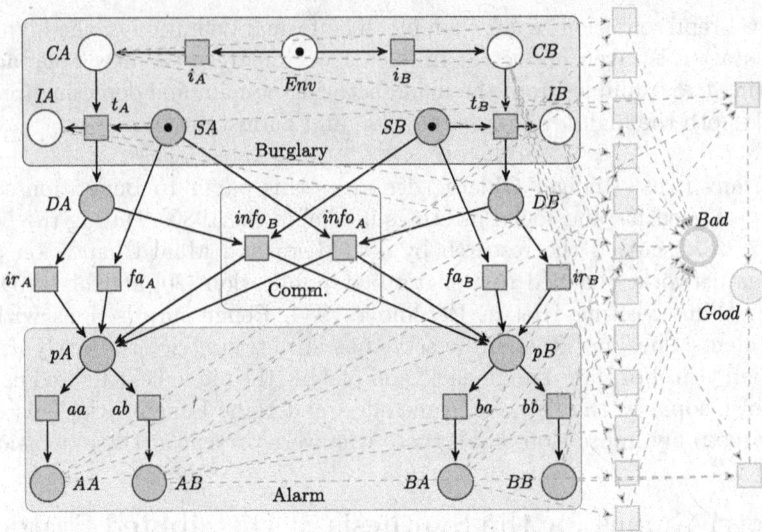

Fig. 1. Two distant locations A and B are secured by the alarm systems represented by the token initially residing in SA and SB. The alarm system in location X can state that there should be a burglary at location Y by putting a token at place XY (for $X, Y \in \{A, B\}$). The goal is that no system produces a false alarm, or, in case of an intrusion, indicates the wrong intrusion point.

double circled places). To satisfy this *safety objective*, the players can solely use their locally available information.

A *strategy* is a local controller for each system player which only decides on its current view and available information about the whole system. A strategy can be obtained by removing certain system controlled branches of the unfolding. That is, transitions and their complete future are removed which are considered as not be taken from the system. We search for *deterministic* strategies, where in every situation no two transition are enabled for a single system player, and *deadlock-avoiding* strategies, i.e., whenever the system can proceed in $\mathscr{G}$ there must also be a continuation in the corresponding situation in the strategy. Furthermore, no purely environment behavior is allowed to be restricted and whenever a system player *refuses* an instance of a transition $t \in \mathscr{T}$ in a place p of the strategy, all instances of t have to be refused in p. This means, in each state the system player can only allow or disallow *all* instances of a transition of the Petri game, because, due to its local knowledge, these instances are indistinguishable for the player.

We illustrate the model with an example of two system players and one environment player, modeling a distributed alarm system from [11], visualized in Fig. 1.

Example 1 (Distributed Alarm System for Two Locations). We consider an alarm system for two locations A and B distributed over two system components securing one location each. Location A is depicted in the left part and location B in the right part of Fig. 1. The system components are represented by the tokens in the system places called SA and SB. In case of a burglary at any of these locations, modeled by the environment in place Env putting its token via transition i_A into place CA (choose location A) or via i_B into CB (choose location B), each alarm system component should indicate the correct intruding point despite their distribution over different locations. That is, for an intrusion in location $Y \in \{A, B\}$ the token of each component $X \in \{A, B\}$ should eventually reach place XY.

Note that the environment can at any moment choose one of the transitions i_A or i_B leading to the places CA or CB, without participation of any of the two system players in SA and SB. While the token is in place CA or CB, the alarm system is not yet aware of the burglary. This is the case only after the synchronization transition t_A or t_B is taken, which puts one token in the system place DA (burglary in A detected) or DB (burglary in B detected) and a second token in the environment place IA or IB (recording that the intruder is in A or B, respectively).

Each alarm system component has also the possibility to trigger a *false alarm*, i.e., setting off an alarm without any detection of a burglary, or to give an *incomplete report*, i.e., indicating its own detection of the burglary without informing the other system component. These incorrect behaviors can occur by taking transition fa_X or ir_X for $X \in \{A, B\}$, respectively. The intended correct behavior is that each alarm system component SX for $X \in \{A, B\}$ waits until a burglary has been detected and then informs the other component Y (via transition $info_Y$), or waits for getting informed by the other component (via the synchronization transition $info_X$). Generally, the system should only take a decision (and the right one) when it is informed well enough.

The dashed, gray transitions to the places *Good* or *Bad* are enabled and taken when the alarm system behaved correctly or incorrectly, respectively. For example, tokens in the places CA and AA enable a transition to place *Bad* because the system raised an alarm without detecting the burglary in location A. Admittedly, the graphic representation of these transition is too crowded. It will become very clear in the high-level version of this Petri game shown in Fig. 4.

The *unfolding* of the Petri game is shown in Fig. 2, where we omit all instances of the places *Good* or *Bad* and the transitions leading to them in order to enhance the readability. This unfolding displays the causal history of every place in it. In particular, the place pA of the original Petri game is unfolded into four copies denoted by pA_1, pA_2, pA_3, and pA_4. Likewise, pB is unfolded into pB_1, pB_2, pB_3, and pB_4. The places pA_1 and pA_2 represent the knowledge that the alarm system component chose the erroneous transitions ir_A and fa_A, respectively. Place pA_3 represents the knowledge that the alarm system component in site A detected a burglary in location A and informed the other system component in site B via the synchronization transition $info_B$ of this burglary. Place pA_4 represents the knowledge that the alarm system component in site A has been informed

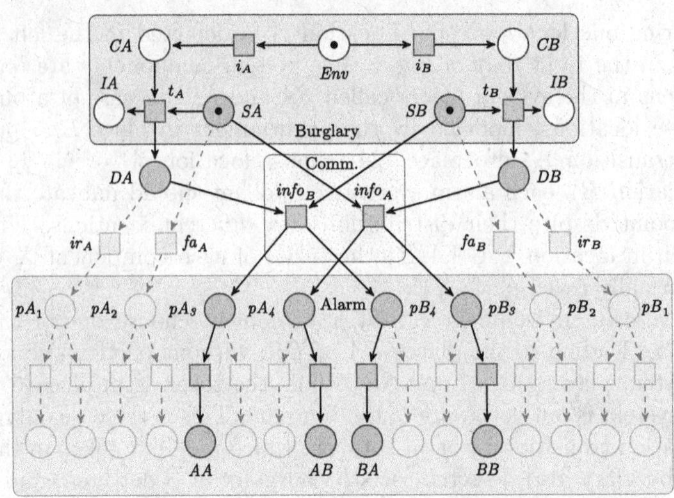

Fig. 2. Unfolding and winning strategy of the Petri game from Fig. 1. The places *Bad* and *Good* and the corresponding transitions are omitted for readability reasons. The winning strategy for the system players is visualized by the solid elements.

by the other system component via the synchronization transition $info_A$ that a burglary in location B has been detected.

The intended correct behavior of the alarm system is achieved by the *strategy* depicted as the part of the unfolding in Fig. 2 that is highlighted by solid elements. It is obtained from the unfolding by deleting system choices that lead to a bad place. Thus only the good system choices are kept in the strategy. For example, from place pA_3 the transition leading to place AA is chosen, representing the knowledge that location A knows that a burglary at location A has been detected. Correspondingly, from place pB_4 the alarm system at B chooses the transition leading to place BA, representing the knowledge that also location B knows (via the synchronization transition $info_B$) that a burglary at location A has been detected. This strategy is *winning* because it avoids reaching any bad place representing a wrong information of the burglary at location A or B. □

2.2 Solving Petri Games

There are four major results on finding winning strategies for Petri games with safety objectives. Firstly, deciding the question whether it exists a strategy for the system players for Petri games with one environment player and an arbitrary but bounded number of system players and a safety objective is EXPTIME-complete [12]. The strategy can be obtained in single-exponential time. Secondly, interchanging the players, meaning the setting of $n \in \mathbb{N}$ distributed environment players and one system player, yields the same complexity results [10]. Thirdly, for unbounded underlying Petri nets the question is undecidable [12]. Finally,

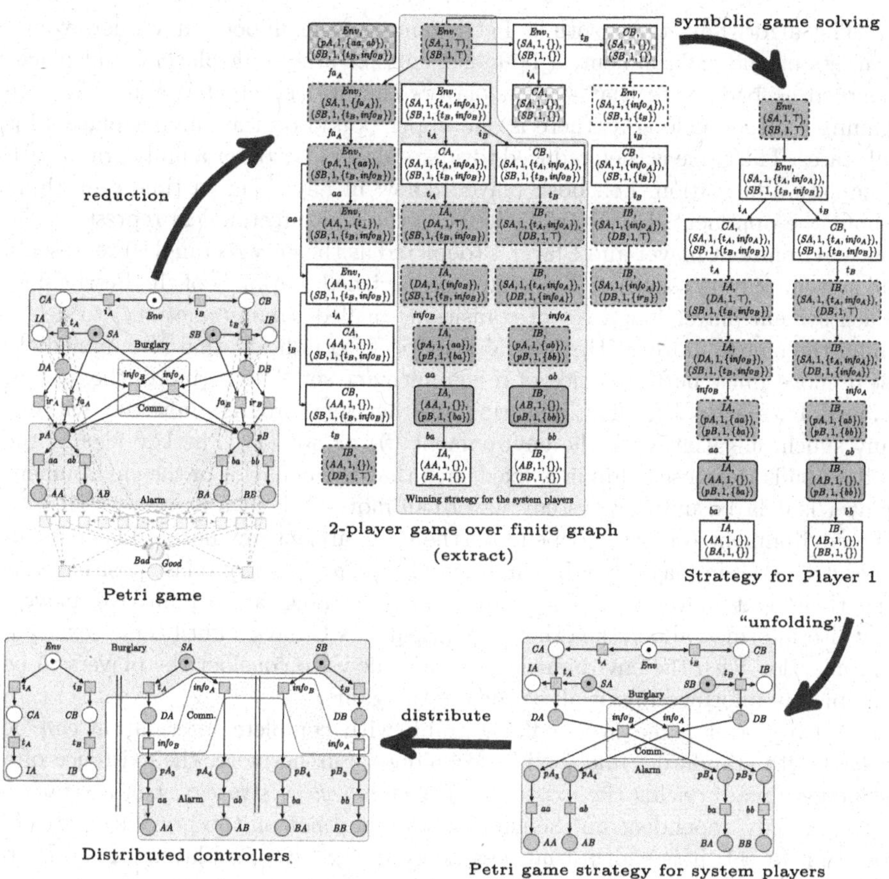

Fig. 3. A schematic overview of the symbolic game solving algorithm for Petri games with one environment and a bounded number of system players with a safety objective.

the paper [7] introduces a bounded synthesis approach which limits the size of the strategy. This constitutes a semi-decision procedure which is optimized in finding small implementations.

In the following we briefly recap the idea of the decision procedure for one environment player and $n \in \mathbb{N}$ system players on a Petri game with a safety objective. The algorithm consists of four major steps: Firstly, the input Petri game is reduced to a two-player game over a finite graph G with complete information. Secondly, the question of the existence of a strategy in G is answered with standard symbolic game solving algorithms and a strategy for G is constructed. Thirdly, the strategy of G is used to extract a common strategy for the system players of $\mathscr{G}$. Fourthly, this strategy is distributed into one local controller for each process. A schematic overview of the approach is visualized in Fig. 3.

The algorithm starts with a Petri game in the upper left corner, which consists of one environment, a bounded number of system players, and places denoted as bad. Note that system players can still be created and terminate infinitely often, as long as there is one upper bound on the number players for all states. The game is then reduced to a two-player game over a finite graph with complete information, i.e., both players know in any point in time everything about the opponent. Player 0 (depicted as the white rectangles) represents the one environment player and Player 1 (depicted as the gray rectangles) represents all system players together. The states are enriched markings of the Petri game. Each system player has a set of transitions (called *commitment set*) to determine their next move or the special symbol $\top$ to indicate that the immediate next move must be the choice of a commitment set. Furthermore, the system players have a Boolean flag indicating whether they progress infinitely without any synchronization with the environment (0) or not (1). The key idea of the reduction is that a scheduling is fixed such that the behavior of the environment player is delayed until no system player can move without any interaction with the environment (or never depend on the environment anymore). This ensures that each system player will be informed of the environment's last position during their next movement. Since deterministic strategies are built, the players are also informed about the other system player's behavior until their next synchronization with the environment. All this allows to consider the players to be completely informed about all actions in the game.

A two-player game over a finite graph with complete information can be solved with standard game solving techniques. Furthermore, the existence of a strategy already yields the existence of a *memoryless* strategy, i.e., a strategy which is only dependent on the current state and not on the previous states of the run. In [11] it is shown that a strategy for the system players of the Petri game exists if and only if a strategy for Player 1 exists in the two-player game. Thus, we achieve a memoryless strategy for the system players such that they can cooperatively play without encountering any bad behavior against all possible actions of an hostile environment. By traversing the winning strategy of the two-player game over the finite graph in breadth-first order, a finite Petri net can be constructed which is a winning strategy of the system players of the Petri game. Finkbeiner and Olderog [11] showed that for a *concurrency-preserving* strategy, i.e., the number of ingoing arcs is equal to the number of outgoing arcs for each transition, this common strategy of the system players can be distributed into local strategies. This yields one controller for each player.

In AdamSynt [8,9] this algorithm is implemented for *1-bounded* Petri games, i.e., in every situation of the underlying Petri net there is at most one player residing on each place, with a symbolic game solving algorithm utilizing BDDs for the representation of the state space.

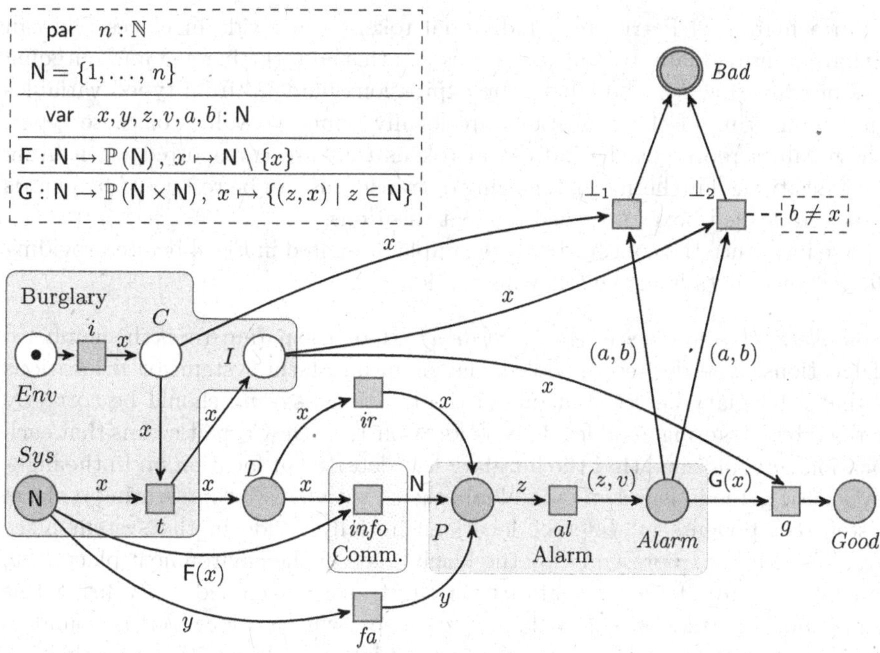

Fig. 4. Parameterized high-level Petri game for a benchmark family of an alarm system for n locations. The parameter is $n \in \mathbb{N}$. The low-level Petri game of Fig. 1 can be seen as an instantiation of the benchmark family with $n = 2$.

2.3 Motivating the High-Level Representation

The beauty of the high-level representation of Petri games, formally defined in the following section, stems from the conciseness and clarity of the illustration of the system's behavior. This can be seen in Fig. 4, where the Petri game of an alarm system for two locations of Example 1 is extended to a benchmark family of an alarm system for n locations.

All locations have to be informed about the burglary and trigger the alarm accordingly. This means that new intrusion points and new alarm system components are introduced by adding copies of the corresponding places and transitions. Using P/T Petri nets only, the exact description of a benchmark family requires a high amount of precise descriptive texts but nevertheless bears the risk of introducing misunderstandings. Also an instantiation, e.g., the one in Fig. 1, cannot show the details appropriately. For example, it does not clarify whether in this benchmark family the alarm system component at the burglarized location informs the other alarm system components synchronously or in any sequential order. But visualizing the family for three locations is already quite unwieldy, especially for the transitions leading into the bad place. By contrast, the high-level representation in Fig. 4 allows for a concise, parametric definition of the benchmark family.

In a high-level Petri game, individual tokens can reside in places and can be moved individually by the transitions. To this end, the ingoing and outgoing arcs of transitions can be labeled by expressions built up from typed variables that upon firing of the transitions are locally bound to values of these types. These values represent the individual tokens that are transported when firing the transitions. Furthermore, the firing of transitions can be restricted by guards shown in dashed boxes attached to the transitions.

We introduce the concept by the example presented in Fig. 4 before providing the technical details in the following section.

Example 2 (Parameterized Alarm System). Here, the parameter is the number n of locations. The desired "good" behavior of an alarm system for n locations is that a burglary detected at one of the locations, say m, should be correctly notified by triggering an alarm in each location $1, \ldots, n$. Correct means that each location gets informed that the burglary was detected at location m. In the high-level Petri game in Fig. 4, n individual tokens, with $n \in \mathbb{N}$, representing n alarm system components at different locations initially reside in the system place *Sys*. The burglar, represented by the black token in the environment place *Env*, can intrude any of the n locations via the transition named i. By firing this transition, any value $m \in \mathsf{N} = \{1, \ldots, n\}$ (representing a location) is bound to the variable x at the outgoing arc of i and put into the place C (location chosen).

Next, only the corresponding alarm system component at that location can detect the intrusion by transition t, because both ingoing arcs are labeled with the same variable x that needs to be bound to the same location, which is the value m residing in place C. By firing t, this location value is put into the places D (burglary detected) and I (intrusion recorded). In any case, every alarm system component can trigger a false alarm by transition *fa*. After detecting an intrusion, an alarm system component can synchronously inform all other components by firing transition *info* or do not report the intrusion at all by firing *ir*. Note that the ingoing arcs of transition *info* are labeled with x and $\mathsf{F}(x)$. Since place D stores the unique location m where the burglary has been detected, x is bound to this value m and thus $\mathsf{F}(x)$ evaluates to the set $\mathsf{N} \setminus \{m\}$ of all remaining locations. So transition *info* empties the place *Sys* and puts all location values into the place P.

Finally, the alarm system can decide by transition *al* which alarm to trigger. It is *bad* if one alarm system component z decides to trigger an alarm for location v, by putting (z, v) into *Alarm*, but another location has been intruded (transition $\bot_2$ leading to place *Bad*) or if some alarm is triggered, but no intrusion has ever been detected (transition $\bot_1$ leading to place *Bad*). If all alarm system components have detected the intruded location correctly, the place *Good* can be reached. □

By replacing the transition *info* according to Fig. 5, we can easily switch from a synchronously informing of the other systems to an arbitrary sequential order of information dissemination. Note that the strategy of each alarm system can decide which other system should be informed next. The last informed system

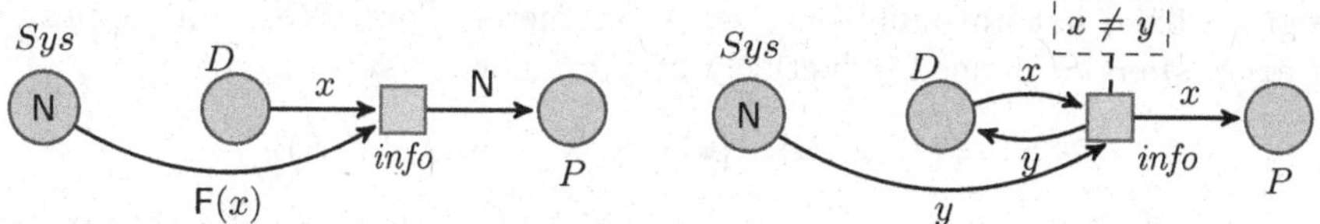

(a) Transition *info* of Fig. 4 for informing all other systems *synchronously*.

(b) A possible replacement for *info* to inform all other systems *sequentially*.

Fig. 5. The left figure shows the synchronously informing of the burglary of Fig. 4. The right one introduces a possible replacement of the transition *info*, such that after one system detected the intruding or got informed about the intrusion, it informs an arbitrary other system. Thus, the systems can inform one another in any arbitrary order.

can take transition *ir* because no other system has to be informed anymore. The guard $x \neq y$ has no effect on the behavior of the system but allows to omit the n dead transitions which otherwise would automatically be created (cp. Sect. 3.3). This yields $n \cdot (n-1)$ transitions in the low-level version one for each combination of x and y ranging over N, minus those satisfying $x = y$), in contrast to the n transitions in the synchronous case. Such differences are more complex to visualize in the low-level presentation because the difference can only be recognized for $n > 2$.

3 Parameterized High-Level Petri Games

In high-level Petri nets *values* may appear as individual tokens in places [27]. Such a value is also referred to as a "color", leading to the terminology of Coloured Petri Nets [18]. In high-level Petri nets, the ingoing and outgoing arcs of transitions are labeled by expressions that specify which of the individual tokens are withdrawn from the preset and which ones are added to the places in the postset of the transition. Additionally, Boolean expressions labeling the transitions serve as guards.

In this section, we use these concepts to introduce high-level Petri games. We constrain ourselves to high-level Petri games that have sets (rather than multisets) of individual tokens in their places. We consider parameterized high-level games where the size of the sets of individual tokens that may appear in the places depends on parameters.

3.1 Preliminaries

We consider *parameters*, with typical letters k, m, n, ranging over the set $\mathbb{N}$ of natural numbers and write $\mathsf{par}\ k, m, n : \mathbb{N}$ to declare that k, m, n are parameters. There may be a constraint added to the parameters like $m \leq n$. An *instantiation* assigns a fixed natural number to each parameter. Parameters may appear in *set expressions* S, defined inductively by the following syntax:

$$S ::= \{1,\ldots,n\} \mid \{\bullet\} \mid S_1 \times \cdots \times S_n \mid \mathbb{P}(S)$$

Here $\{1,\ldots,n\}$ is a finite set of parametric size n, the symbol $\bullet$ denotes the *black token* used in normal Petri nets, $\times$ denotes Cartesian product, and $\mathbb{P}$ the power set. Set expressions are used as (parametric) *types*. An instantiation of the parameters turns each set expression into a fixed set. *Constants*, with typical letters $\mathsf{K},\mathsf{M},\mathsf{N}$, are used as abbreviations for set expressions. We write $\mathsf{K} = S$ to declare that K abbreviates the set expression S.

We consider *variables*, with typical letters x, y, z, ranging over set expressions and write $\mathsf{var}\ x, y, z : S$ to declare that x, y, z are variables of type S. We write $ty(x)$ to denote the type of a variable x. We consider *function symbols*, with typical letters F,G, and write $\mathsf{F} : S_1 \longrightarrow S_2$ to declare that F is a symbol standing for a function from elements of S_1 to elements of S_2, for set expressions S_1, S_2.

Out of parameters, constants, variables, and function symbols we construct Boolean expressions and expressions of set type. We shall not define the syntax of these expressions in detail here, but give typical examples. Suppose $\mathsf{par}\ m, n : \mathbb{N}$ and $\mathsf{var}\ x, y, x', y' : S_1$ and $\mathsf{F} : S_1 \longrightarrow S_2$. Then $m < n$, $x \neq y$, and $x = x' \wedge y = y'$ are Boolean expressions, the pair (x, y) is an expression of type $S_1 \times S_1$ and the function application $\mathsf{F}(x)$ is an expression of type S_2. To define the function denoted by F we write a maplet $x \mapsto e$, where x is a variable of type S_1 and e is an expression of type S_2 containing x as a free variable. For a given instantiation, the maplet describes how F assigns to a given element d of type S_1 a value of type S_2 by evaluating e with d substituted for x in e.

3.2 High-Level Petri Games

In high-level Petri games *values* may appear as individual tokens in addition to the black tokens of normal Petri nets. Syntactically, a high-level Petri game is a structure

$$\mathcal{H} = (\mathcal{P}^H_S, \mathcal{P}^H_E, \mathcal{T}^H, \mathcal{F}^H, In^H, \mathcal{B}^H, ty, g, e, in),$$

where the following components are as in 1-bounded Petri games:

- $\mathcal{P}^H_S$ is a set of *system places*,
- $\mathcal{P}^H_E$ is a set of *environment places*,
- $\mathcal{P}^H$ is the set of all places: $\mathcal{P}^H = \mathcal{P}^H_S \cup \mathcal{P}^H_E$,
- $\mathcal{T}^H$ is a set of *transitions*,
- $\mathcal{F}^H \subseteq (\mathcal{P}^H \times \mathcal{T}^H) \cup (\mathcal{T}^H \times \mathcal{P}^H)$ is the *flow relation*,
- $In^H \subseteq \mathcal{P}^H$ is the set of *initially marked* places,
- $\mathcal{B}^H \subseteq \mathcal{P}^H$ is the set of *bad places*.

Additionally, the following components represent the high-level structure:

- ty is a mapping that assigns to each place $p \in \mathcal{P}^H$ a *type* $ty(p)$ in the form of a set expression, describing the set of individual tokens that may reside in p during the game,

- g is a mapping that assigns to each transition $t \in \mathcal{T}^H$ a Boolean expression $g(t)$ serving as a *guard* describing when t can fire,
- e is a mapping that assigns to each ingoing arc $(p, t) \in \mathcal{F}^H$ and each outgoing arc $(t, q) \in \mathcal{F}^H$ of a transition $t \in \mathcal{T}^H$ an expression $e(p, t)$ and $e(t, q)$ of set type, respectively, describing which tokens are withdrawn by t from p and which tokens are placed by t on q when t is fired,
- in is a mapping that assigns to each initially marked place $p \in In^H$ a non-empty subset of $in(p) \subseteq ty(p)$.

Guards and expressions will typically contain variables. For a transition $t \in \mathcal{T}^H$ let $\mathsf{var}(t)$ denote the set of free variables occurring in the guard $g(t)$ or in one of the expressions $e(p, t)$ and $e(t, q)$ for places p in t's *preset*, defined by $pre(t) = \{p \in \mathcal{P}^H \mid (p, t) \in \mathcal{F}^H\}$, or q in t's *postset*, defined by $post(t) = \{q \in \mathcal{P}^H \mid (t, q) \in \mathcal{F}^H\}$.

Graphically, a high-level Petri game $\mathcal{H}$ looks like a normal Petri game, except that guards $g(t)$ appear inside a dashed box connected to the transition t by a dashed line, expressions $e(p, t)$ and $e(t, q)$ appear as labels of the arcs (p, t) and (t, q), respectively, and types $ty(p)$ appear as labels of places p. To avoid clutter, guards equivalent to *true* are not shown. Also, if the type of a place p can be easily deduced from the context, the label $ty(p)$ is not shown. The declarations of parameters, constants, variables, and function symbols are listed in a dashed box near the graphics of the Petri game.

The *semantics* of a high-level Petri game $\mathcal{H}$ is given by its token game. To define it, we assume an instantiation of the parameters so that each set expression defines a fixed set. A *marking* M of $\mathcal{H}$ assigns to each place p a *set* $M(p) \subseteq ty(p)$. Unlike in [18], we do not admit multisets as markings because we aim at 1-bounded Petri games as low-level instantiations of high-level Petri games. The *initial marking* M_0 of $\mathcal{H}$ is the marking with $M_0(p) = in(p)$ for $p \in In^H$ and $M_0(p) = \emptyset$ otherwise.

A *valuation* v *of a transition* t assigns to each variable $x \in \mathsf{var}(t)$ a value $v(x) \in ty(x)$. By $Val(t)$ we denote the set of all valuations of t. Each valuation v of t is lifted inductively from the variables in $\mathsf{var}(t)$ to the expressions around t. For the guard $g(t)$ we denote by $v(t)$ the Boolean value assigned by v to $g(t)$. For an ingoing arc (p, t) we denote by $v(p, t)$ the value assigned by v to $e(p, t)$, and analogously for an outgoing arc (t, p).

A transition t is *enabled at a marking* M *under a valuation* v *of* t if $v(t) = true$ and $v(p, t) \subseteq M(p)$ for each arc (p, t). *Firing* (the enabled) transition t at M under v yields the marking M', where for each place p

$$M'(p) = (M(p) - v(p, t)) \cup v(t, p).$$

This is denoted by $M\,[t, v\rangle\, M'$. We assume here that $\cup$ is a disjoint union, which is satisfied if the Petri game is *contact-free*, i.e., if for all $t \in \mathcal{T}^H$ and all reachable markings M

$$pre(t) \subseteq \mathcal{P}(M) \Rightarrow post(t) \subseteq (\mathcal{P}^H - \mathcal{P}(M)) \cup pre(t),$$

where $\mathscr{P}(M) = \{p \in \mathscr{P}^H \mid M(p) \neq \emptyset\}$. The set of *reachable markings* of $\mathscr{H}$ is

$$\mathscr{R}(\mathscr{H}) = \{M \mid \exists\, n \geq 0\ \exists\, t_1, \ldots, t_n \in \mathscr{T}^H\ \exists\, v_1 \in Val(t_1) \ldots \exists\, v_n \in Val(t_n) : \\ M_0\ [t_1, v_1\rangle\ M_1\ [t_2, v_2\rangle \ldots [t_n, v_n\rangle\ M_n = M\}.$$

3.3 Instantiations of High-Level Petri Games

For fixed parameter values, a given high-level Petri game

$$\mathscr{H} = (\mathscr{P}_S^H, \mathscr{P}_E^H, \mathscr{T}^H, \mathscr{F}^H, In^H, \mathscr{B}^H, ty, g, e, in)$$

with $\mathscr{P}^H = \mathscr{P}_S^H \cup \mathscr{P}_E^H$ can be transformed into a safe Petri game

$$\mathscr{G} = (\mathscr{P}_S, \mathscr{P}_E, \mathscr{T}, \mathscr{F}, In, \mathscr{B}).$$

Let $\mathscr{D} = \bigcup_{p \in \mathscr{P}^H} ty(p)$ be the set of all possible values that individual tokens in places $p \in \mathscr{P}^H$ can take, and let *Val* be the set of valuations assigning values $d \in \mathscr{D}$ of the right type to each variable. The constituents of $\mathscr{G}$ are as follows:

- system places: $\mathscr{P}_S = \{(p, d) \in \mathscr{P}_S^H \times \mathscr{D} \mid d \in ty(p)\}$,
- environment places: $\mathscr{P}_E = \{(p, d) \in \mathscr{P}_E^H \times \mathscr{D} \mid d \in ty(p)\}$,
- transitions: $\mathscr{T} = \{(t^H, v) \mid t^H \in \mathscr{T}^H \wedge v \in Val(t^H) \wedge v(t^H) = true\}$,
- an arc from (p, d) to (t^H, v) occurs in $\mathscr{F}$ if $d \in v(p, t^H)$ holds in $\mathscr{H}$,
- an arc from (t^H, v) to (q, d) occurs in $\mathscr{F}$ if $d \in v(t^H, q)$ holds in $\mathscr{H}$,
- initial marking: $In = \{(p, d) \in In^H \times \mathscr{D} \mid d \in in(p)\}$,
- bad places: $\mathscr{B} = \{(p, d) \in \mathscr{B}^H \times \mathscr{D} \mid d \in ty(p)\}$.

The set of all places of $\mathscr{G}$ is thus given by

$$\mathscr{P} = \mathscr{P}_S \cup \mathscr{P}_E = \{(p, d) \in \mathscr{P}^H \times \mathscr{D} \mid d \in ty(p)\}.$$

Example 3. Figure 1 shows the instantiation of the alarm system for $n = 2$ locations of the high-level Petri game in Fig. 4.

3.4 Correspondence of High-Level and Low-Level Petri Games

We relate the firing behavior of the high-level Petri game $\mathscr{H}$ to that of the low-level Petri game $\mathscr{G}$ defined in Sect. 3.3. To this end, we define a mapping ρ from markings M^H in $\mathscr{H}$ to sets of places in $\mathscr{G}$ as follows:

$$\rho(M^H) = \{(p, d) \in \mathscr{P}^H \times \mathscr{D} \mid d \in M^H(p)\} \subseteq \mathscr{P}.$$

Note that for the initial markings M_0 of $\mathscr{H}$ and *In* of $\mathscr{G}$ we have $\rho(M_0) = In$. Then we can state the following correspondence that is essentially due to [18].

Theorem 1. *For all markings M_1^H and M_2^H of $\mathscr{H}$, all transitions $t^H \in \mathscr{T}^H$, and all valuations $v \in Val(t^H)$ the following properties hold:*

1. *The transition t^H is enabled at M_1^H under v in $\mathscr{H}$ if and only if the transition (t^H, v) is enabled at $\rho(M_1^H)$ in $\mathscr{G}$.*
2. *The firing of enabled transitions under v corresponds to each other:*

$$M_1^H\ [t^H, v\rangle\ M_2^H \iff \rho(M_1^H)\ [(t^H, v)\rangle\ \rho(M_2^H).$$

Proof. *Re 1*: Consider first the enabledness of the corresponding transitions:

$$\begin{aligned}
& t^H \in \mathscr{T}^H \text{ is enabled at } M_1^H \text{ under } v \text{ in } \mathscr{H} \\
\iff & t^H \in \mathscr{T}^H \text{ and } v(t^H) = \mathit{true} \text{ and } v(p, t^H) \subseteq M_1^H(p) \text{ for all } p \in \mathit{pre}(t^H) \\
\iff & (t^H, v) \in \mathscr{T} \text{ and } (p, d) \in \{(p, d) \mid d \in M_1^H(p)\} \\
& \qquad\qquad\qquad \text{for all } p \in \mathit{pre}(t^H) \text{ and } d \in v(p, t^H) \\
\iff & (t^H, v) \in \mathscr{T} \text{ and } \{(p, d) \mid p \in \mathscr{P}^H \wedge d \in v(p, t^H)\} \subseteq \rho(M_1^H) \\
\iff & (t^H, v) \in \mathscr{T} \text{ and } \mathit{pre}(t^H, v) \subseteq \rho(M_1^H) \\
\iff & (t^H, v) \in \mathscr{T} \text{ is enabled at } \rho(M_1^H) \text{ in } \mathscr{G}.
\end{aligned}$$

Re 2: Consider now the firing of the corresponding enabled transitions:

$$\begin{aligned}
& M_1^H\ [t^H, v\rangle\ M_2^H \\
\iff & M_2^H(p) = (M_1^H(p) - v(p, t^H)) \cup v(t^H, p) \text{ for all } p \in \mathscr{P}^H \\
\iff & \{(p, d) \mid p \in \mathscr{P}^H \wedge d \in M_2^H(p)\} = \\
& \quad (\{(p, d) \mid p \in \mathscr{P}^H \wedge d \in M_1^H(p)\} - \{(p, d) \mid p \in \mathscr{P}^H \wedge d \in v(p, t^H)\}) \\
& \quad \cup \{(p, d) \mid p \in \mathscr{P}^H \wedge d \in v(t^H, p)\} \\
\iff & \rho(M_2^H) = (\rho(M_1^H) - \mathit{pre}(t^H, v)) \cup \mathit{post}(t^H, v) \\
\iff & \rho(M_1^H)\ [(t^H, v)\rangle\ \rho(M_2^H).
\end{aligned}$$

This concludes the proof. □

4 Parametric Benchmark Families

Several benchmark families served to demonstrate the applicability of the algorithm for solving Petri games using the tool AdamSYNT [8,9]. These families define Petri games with natural numbers as parameters that stand for the size of certain patterns in the games, modeling persons, machines or phases of a real-world application. The parameters serve to check the scalability of the algorithms implemented in AdamSYNT. With parameterized high-level Petri games such benchmark families can now be represented concisely by one single formal object. We exemplify this for the benchmarks *Concurrent Machines* (**CM**) and *Self-Reconfiguring Robots* (**SR**). Due to the clarity of the high-level representation both families could be optimized (in the size of the game or the functionality, respectively) in comparison to the implemented versions of [8,9].

4.1 CM: Concurrent Machines

This benchmark family models n machines of which only $n - 1$ are working correctly. The environment decides nondeterministically which one is defective. The desired "good" behavior of the system is that each of the k orders is processed by one of the n machines that is not defective. Each machine should process only one order.

The high-level version of the benchmark family is depicted in Fig. 6. The parameters are the number n of machines and the number k of orders, with $k < n$. Each order can inform itself of the defective machine and decide, with or without this information, on which machine it would like to be processed. At the end, no order should decide for the defective or for an already used machine.

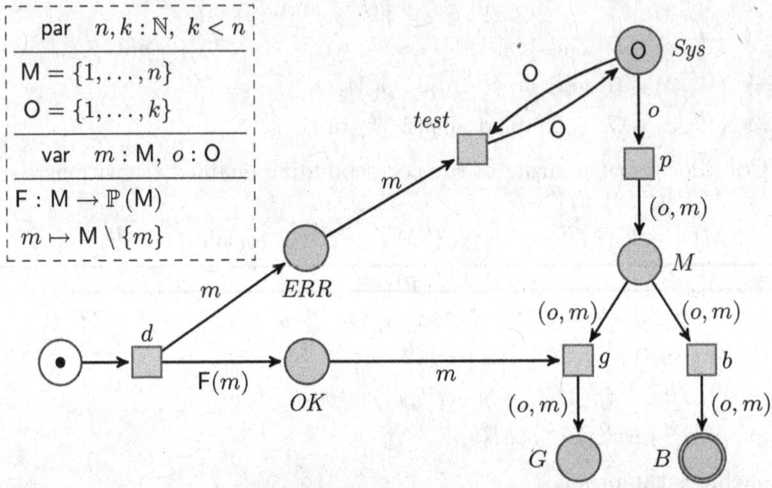

Fig. 6. Parameterized high-level Petri game for the benchmark family of concurrent machines. There are $k \in \mathbb{N}$ orders which can be processed on $n \in \mathbb{N}$ machines. Each machine should only process one order. A hostile environment decides on the functionality of the machines.

The n different machines of the family are identified by the individual tokens in the set $\mathsf{M} = \{1, \ldots, n\}$. The hostile environment decides to destroy one of them by putting it into place *ERR* and all other but this token into place *OK* via transition d. The k orders which should be processed by the machines are identified by the individual tokens in the set $\mathsf{O} = \{1, \ldots, k\}$, which initially reside in place *Sys*. The orders can decide to first test which machine is defective (via transition *test*) and decide afterwards on which machine they want to be processed, or choose a machine without any knowledge about the functionality of the machines (both via transition p). A tuple (o, m) residing in M, for $o \in \mathsf{O}$ and $m \in \mathsf{M}$, indicates that the order o should be processed by machine m. Since the place *OK* only contains one unique token for each intact machine, transition g can only fire at most $|\mathsf{M}| - 1$ times and takes one of those machine identifiers of *OK* each time. Hence, a token $(i, e) \in \mathsf{O} \times \mathsf{M}$ for orders i which decide on the defective machine e or a machine e which already processed another order, is not moved to G but stays in M. Since we are searching for deadlock-avoiding strategies, this token must eventually end up in the bad place B for every strategy.

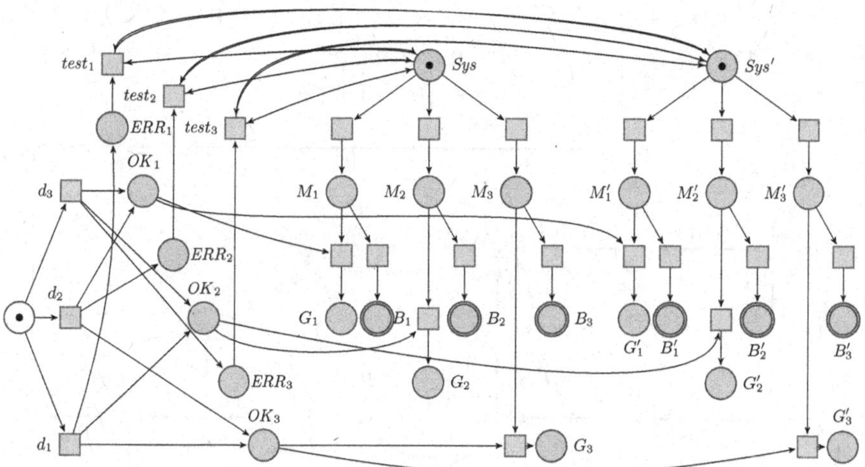

Fig. 7. Instantiation of the Petri game of Fig. 6 for $|\mathsf{M}| = 3$ and $|\mathsf{O}| = 2$. The $k = 2$ orders of this instantiation of the concurrent machines benchmark family are initially residing in Sys and Sys'. The $n = 3$ machines are represented by the six places: M_i for the first order and M'_i for the second order (for $i \in \{1, \ldots, 3\}$).

Figure 7 shows the instantiation of this benchmark family for three machines and two orders. The nondeterministic destruction of machines is visualized in the left-most part, whereas the possibilities of the two orders is depicted in the middle and the right-most part of the figure, respectively. Each of the three machines $m \in \{1, 2, 3\}$ can be functioning, i.e., a token resides in OK_i, or defective, i.e., a token resides in ERR_i. The place M collecting which order is processed on which machine of Fig. 6, as well as the corresponding good and bad place, is split into $|\mathsf{M} \times \mathsf{O}| = 6$ places each. The three undecorated copies of each of these places in the middle belong to the first and the decorated in the most-right part of Fig. 7 to the second order. This game can be won by the system players by first testing which of the three machines is defective, hence knowing which two are functioning, and afterwards unequally deciding on one of the two functioning machines.

4.2 SR: Self-reconfiguring Robots

This benchmark is inspired by [17] and deals with the following scenario. Each piece of material needs to be processed by n different tools. This is done by n robots, each one having all n tools to their disposal, but only one of which is

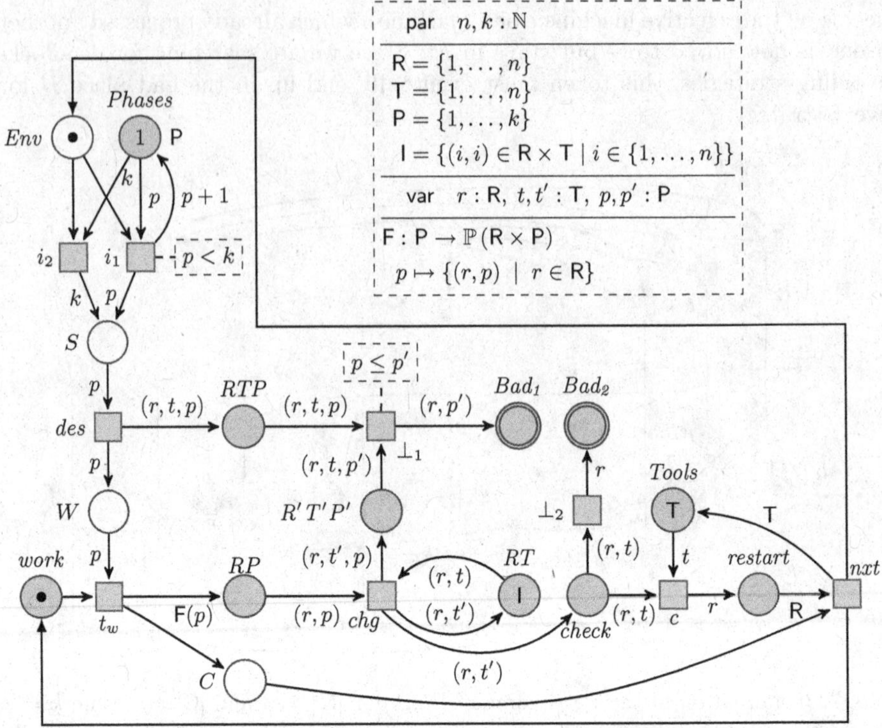

Fig. 8. Parameterized high-level Petri game for the benchmark family of self-reconfiguring robots. The n robots have n tools to their disposal of which nondeterministically k tools can be destroyed over time. In this smart factory each piece of material needs to be machined by every tool. Every robot can use one single tool at a time and can decide on a different one after the factory recognizes a defective tool on any of the robots.

currently used. The environment may destroy a tool on any robot r. Then all robots reconfigure themselves so that r uses another tool and the other robots adapt their usage of tools accordingly. Destructions can occur repeatedly in subsequent phases. The desired "good" behavior for this family of games is that the following two safety objectives are satisfied:

1. *No wrong tool assignment*, i.e., no robot uses a tool that is destroyed by the environment.
2. *Unique tool assignment*, i.e., each tool is assigned only to a single robot.

The high-level representation of this benchmark family is depicted in Fig. 8. It uses two parameters n, k of type $\mathbb{N}$, where n is both the number of robots in the set R and the number of tools in the set T on each robot and where k is the number of phases in the set P, in each of which one tool on one of the robots is destroyed. The game proceeds in phases, each one starting in the place *Phases* with type P. Initially, the game starts with phase 1 and for each but the last phase k (ensured by the predicate $p < k$) the transition i_1 puts the number of the next phase, $p + 1$, back into *Phases* and remembers the current phase p in place S. In the last phase the identifier k is directly put into S via transitions i_2 and no token resides in *Phases* anymore. Next the environment can destroy via the transition *des* on one robot r one tool t in this phase p by putting the information triple (r, t, p) into the system place RTP and the environment token into place W (for *working*). Now the system in place *work* gets active by firing transition t_w, which withdraws the system token from place *work* and puts the set of all robot identifiers equipped with the current phase p into the system place RP and the environment token into place C (for *completed*). Next the transition *chg* (for *change*) is enabled. In its preset are the places RP and RT of which the latter contains the current assignment of tools to robots. Here we assume w.l.o.g. that initially RT stores the assignment I where robot $i \in \mathsf{R}$ uses tool $i \in \mathsf{T}$. In general, transition *chg* takes one robot identity (r, p) of the current phase p from place RP and a tool assignment (r, t) out of place RT and replaces it by the (possibly new) assignment (r, t'). The idea is that t' is the tool that robot r should use from now on. The transition *chg* stores this new assignment by putting the triple (r, t', p) into place $R'T'P'$. If t is destroyed by the environment transition *des* in any prior phase $\widetilde{p}$ yielding $(r, t, \widetilde{p})$ in place RTP then a winning strategy for the system players should choose $t \neq t'$. Otherwise the transition $\bot_1$ is enabled and eventually has to fire, i.e., $\bot_1$ puts the *wrong tool assignment* (r, t) into the bad place Bad_1. Additionally, transition *chg* stores the new tool assignment (r, t') into place *check*. Here the *unique tool assignment* property, i.e., whether each tool is assigned only to a single robot, is checked. The place *Tools* contains one unique identifier $t \in \mathsf{T}$ for each tool. Every firing of transition c withdraws one of these tools. A robot r can only reach the place *restart* via transition c if it currently uses a tool t, i.e., the current tool assignment (r, t) resides in place *check*, which has not already been used by another robot already moved to *restart*. This means for two robots r_1 and r_2 using the same tool t, i.e., (r_1, t) and (r_2, t) residing in *check*, that one of these duplicate assignment remains in place *check*. Since every winning strategy has to be deadlock-avoiding, transition $\bot_2$ eventually fires and puts one of the robots with the duplicate tool assignment into the bad place Bad_2. When every robot uses a different tool, eventually all robots gather in place *restart* and the transition *nxt* can enable a new phase by putting a black token back into the environment place *Env*.

Figure 9 shows an instantiation of this high-level representation for two robots equipped with two tools each and two destruction phases. The first phase is presented in the left part of the figure, whereas the second part is depicted in the right one. The destruction of the tools is done in the upper part of the figure. Note that we simplified the unfolding of the high-level place Bad_1, for a clearer presentation. In the middle of the figure the changing of the tool for the first and below the changing for the second robot is depicted. The bottom of Fig. 9 shows the starting of the second phase.

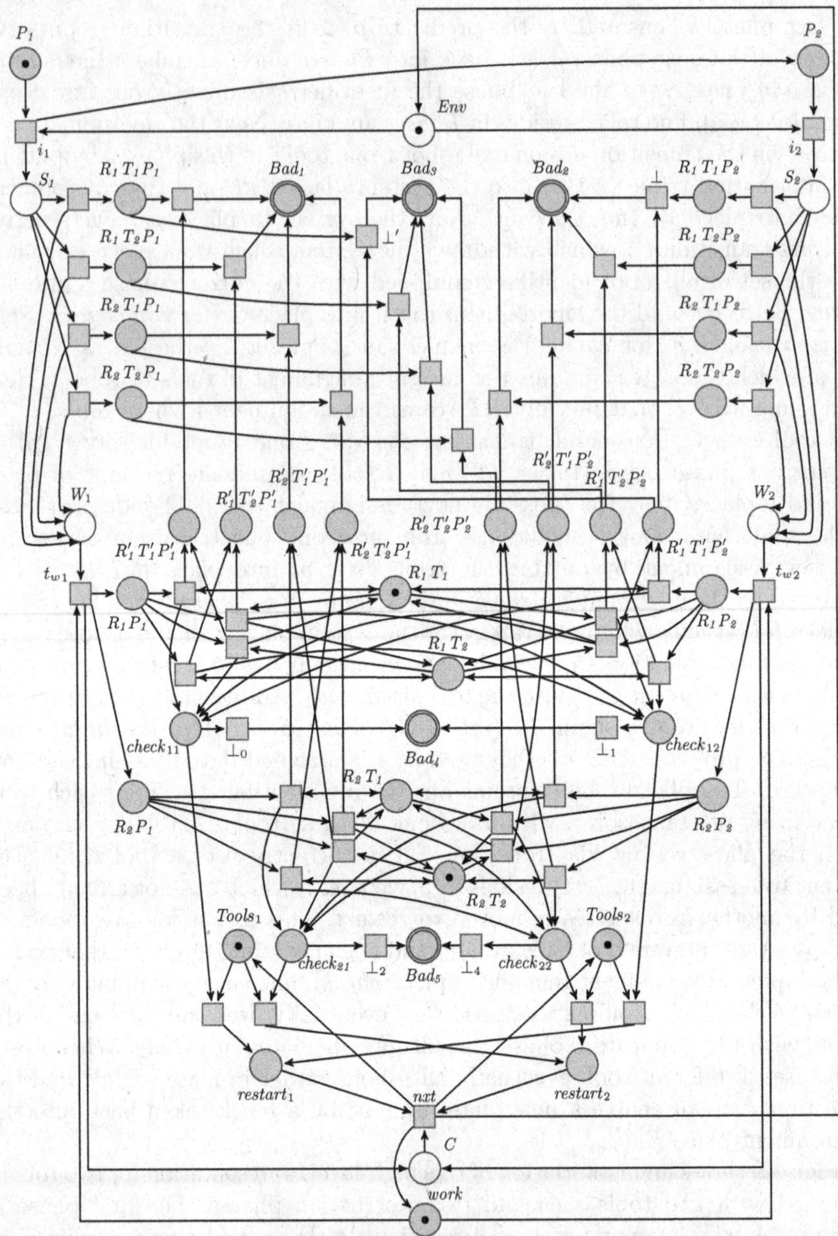

Fig. 9. Instantiation of the Petri game depicted in Fig. 8 for $|\mathsf{R}| = |\mathsf{T}| = |\mathsf{P}| = 2$. The $k = 2$ destruction phases are presented in the upper left and upper right part, respectively. The tool changing of the robots is depicted in the middle: in the upper left part for the first robot in the first phase, in the upper right part for the first robot in the second phase, in the lower left part for the second robot in the first phase, and in the lower right for the second robot in the second phase. The bottom of the figure presents the starting of the second phase.

This game cannot be won by the system players, because the environment can either decide to destroy both tools of one robot, say of robot $r = 1$, or decide to destroy the same tool, say the tool $t = 1$, on each robot. In the first case the robot has no other possibility than to chose an already destroyed tool, say the tool $t = 1$, in the second phase. This enables transition $\bot_1$ in the high-level version, which corresponds in the low-level version to the enabledness of either transition $\bot$ or $\bot'$, depending on the phase in which the tool t has been destroyed. In the second case, either one of the robots decides on an already destroyed tool (which leads us to the previous case), or both robots decide on taking tool $t' = 2$. This means transition c of the high-level version can only fire for one robot, because afterwards the place *Tools* only contains the tool 1. Thus, *nxt* cannot fire and therewith $\bot_2$ eventually has to put the other robot into Bad_2. For the low-level version both robots choosing tool 2 results in having a token in each of the places $check_{12}$ and $check_{22}$. Hence, only one of the transitions in the postset of $Tools_2$ can fire, resulting in firing eventually $\bot_1$ or $\bot_4$, respectively.

5 Conclusion

We have introduced a new representation of benchmark families for Petri games. Similarly to the advantages of high-level Petri nets versus place/transition Petri nets, the representation captivates by its concise and complete abilities of defining the families. The possibility to keep the expression sets parametric allows for a uniform representation of the entire family. We have presented an instantiation technique to obtain a low-level version as standard 1-bounded Petri game for each element of the benchmark family. Those Petri games can then be solved by the existing algorithms and tool. Furthermore, we have experienced that parameterized high-level representations of Petri games help to understand the key ideas of benchmark families even better. This has enabled us to improve each of the presented benchmark families compared to their original implementations regarding their size or functionality.

For this paper, the introduction of high-level Petri games was driven primarily by the desire to have a clear, concise, and unambiguous definition of the benchmark families used to show how our synthesis algorithms scale with increasing complexity. In future work we would like to investigate for which parameters such high-level Petri games have a solution and possibly even generate parameterized strategies. This means we aim for directly obtaining parameterized distributed controllers from parameterized high-level Petri games.

Acknowledgement. We thank Wolfgang Reisig for suggesting to use high-level Petri nets to represent families of benchmarks during a Dagstuhl Workshop. We also thank two anonymous reviewers for their helpful comments.

References

1. Bloem, R.P., Gamauf, H.J., Hofferek, G., Könighofer, B., Könighofer, R.: Synthesizing robust systems with RATSY. In: Peled, D.A., Schewe, S. (eds.) Proceedings of First Workshop on Synthesis (SYNT), EPTCS, vol. 84, pp. 47–53 (2012)

2. Bohy, A., Bruyère, V., Filiot, E., Jin, N., Raskin, J.-F.: Acacia+, a tool for LTL synthesis. In: Madhusudan, P., Seshia, S.A. (eds.) CAV 2012. LNCS, vol. 7358, pp. 652–657. Springer, Heidelberg (2012). https://doi.org/10.1007/978-3-642-31424-7_45
3. Church, A.: Applications of recursive arithmetic to the problem of circuit synthesis. In: Summaries of the Summer Institute of Symbolic Logic, vol. 1, pp. 3–50. Cornell University, Ithaca (1957)
4. Ehlers, R.: Unbeast: symbolic bounded synthesis. In: Abdulla, P.A., Leino, K.R.M. (eds.) TACAS 2011. LNCS, vol. 6605, pp. 272–275. Springer, Heidelberg (2011). https://doi.org/10.1007/978-3-642-19835-9_25
5. Engelfriet, J.: Branching processes of Petri nets. Acta Inf. **28**(6), 575–591 (1991)
6. Esparza, J., Heljanko, K.: Unfoldings - A Partial-Order Approach to Model Checking. Springer, Heidelberg (2008). https://doi.org/10.1007/978-3-540-77426-6
7. Finkbeiner, B.: Bounded synthesis for Petri games. In: Meyer, R., Platzer, A., Wehrheim, H. (eds.) Correct System Design. LNCS, vol. 9360, pp. 223–237. Springer, Cham (2015). https://doi.org/10.1007/978-3-319-23506-6_15
8. Finkbeiner, B., Gieseking, M., Hecking-Harbusch, J., Olderog, E.R.: Symbolic vs. bounded synthesis for Petri games. In: Fisman, D., Jacobs, S. (eds.) Proceedings of Sixth Workshop on Synthesis (SYNT), EPTCS, vol. 202, pp. 19–39 (2017)
9. Finkbeiner, B., Gieseking, M., Olderog, E.-R.: Adam: causality-based synthesis of distributed systems. In: Kroening, D., Păsăreanu, C.S. (eds.) CAV 2015. LNCS, vol. 9206, pp. 433–439. Springer, Cham (2015). https://doi.org/10.1007/978-3-319-21690-4_25
10. Finkbeiner, B., Gölz, P.: Synthesis in distributed environments. In: Lokam, S.V., Ramanujam, R. (eds.) Foundations of Software Technology and Theoretical Computer Science (FSTTCS), LIPIcs, vol. 93, pp. 28:1–28:14. Schloss Dagstuhl - Leibniz-Zentrum für Informatik (2017)
11. Finkbeiner, B., Olderog, E.R.: Petri games: synthesis of distributed systems with causal memory. In: Peron, A., Piazza, C. (eds.) Proceedings of Fifth International Symposium on Games, Automata, Logics and Formal Verification (GandALF), EPTCS, vol. 161, pp. 217–230 (2014). https://doi.org/10.4204/EPTCS.161.19
12. Finkbeiner, B., Olderog, E.R.: Petri games: synthesis of distributed systems with causal memory. Inf. Comput. **253**(Part 2), 181–203 (2017). https://doi.org/10.1016/j.ic.2016.07.006
13. Finkbeiner, B., Schewe, S.: Uniform distributed synthesis. In: Logic in Computer Science (LICS), pp. 321–330. IEEE (2005). https://doi.org/10.1109/LICS.2005.53
14. Gastin, P., Lerman, B., Zeitoun, M.: Distributed games with causal memory are decidable for series-parallel systems. In: Lodaya, K., Mahajan, M. (eds.) FSTTCS 2004. LNCS, vol. 3328, pp. 275–286. Springer, Heidelberg (2004). https://doi.org/10.1007/978-3-540-30538-5_23
15. Genest, B., Gimbert, H., Muscholl, A., Walukiewicz, I.: Asynchronous games over tree architectures. In: Fomin, F.V., Freivalds, R., Kwiatkowska, M., Peleg, D. (eds.) ICALP 2013. LNCS, vol. 7966, pp. 275–286. Springer, Heidelberg (2013). https://doi.org/10.1007/978-3-642-39212-2_26
16. Genrich, H.J., Lautenbach, K.: System modelling with high-level Petri nets. Theor. Comput. Sci. **13**, 109–136 (1981). https://doi.org/10.1016/0304-3975(81)90113-4
17. Güdemann, M., Ortmeier, F., Reif, W.: Formal modeling and verification of systems with self-x properties. In: Yang, L.T., Jin, H., Ma, J., Ungerer, T. (eds.) ATC 2006. LNCS, vol. 4158, pp. 38–47. Springer, Heidelberg (2006). https://doi.org/10.1007/11839569_4

18. Jensen, K.: Coloured Petri Nets: Basic Concepts, Analysis Methods and Practical Use, vol. 1. Springer, Heidelberg (1992). https://doi.org/10.1007/978-3-662-06289-0
19. Jobstmann, B., Galler, S., Weiglhofer, M., Bloem, R.: Anzu: a tool for property synthesis. In: Damm, W., Hermanns, H. (eds.) CAV 2007. LNCS, vol. 4590, pp. 258–262. Springer, Heidelberg (2007). https://doi.org/10.1007/978-3-540-73368-3_29
20. Jonsson, B.: A model and proof system for asynchronous networks. In: Malcolm, M.A., Strong, H.R. (eds.) Proceedings of Fourth Annual ACM Symposium on Principles of Distributed Computing (PODC), pp. 49–58. ACM (1985). https://doi.org/10.1145/323596.323601
21. Jonsson, B.: Compositional verification of distributed systems. Ph.D. thesis, Department of Computer Systems, Uppsala University, Sweden (1987)
22. Madhusudan, P., Thiagarajan, P.S., Yang, S.: The MSO theory of connectedly communicating processes. In: Sarukkai, S., Sen, S. (eds.) FSTTCS 2005. LNCS, vol. 3821, pp. 201–212. Springer, Heidelberg (2005). https://doi.org/10.1007/11590156_16
23. Muscholl, A., Walukiewicz, I.: Distributed synthesis for acyclic architectures. In: Foundations of Software Technology and Theoretical Computer Science (FSTTCS), LIPIcs, vol. 29, pp. 639–651. Schloss Dagstuhl - Leibniz-Zentrum für Informatik (2014). https://doi.org/10.4230/LIPIcs.FSTTCS.2014.639
24. Nielsen, M., Plotkin, G.D., Winskel, G.: Petri nets, event structures and domains, part I. Theor. Comput. Sci. **13**, 85–108 (1981)
25. Pnueli, A., Rosner, R.: Distributed reactive systems are hard to synthesize. In: Foundations of Computer Science (FOCS), pp. 746–757. IEEE (1990)
26. Reisig, W.: Petri Nets: An Introduction. Springer, Heidelberg (1985). https://doi.org/10.1007/978-3-642-69968-9
27. Reisig, W.: Understanding Petri Nets - Modeling Techniques, Analysis Methods, Case Studies. Springer, Heidelberg (2013). https://doi.org/10.1007/978-3-642-33278-4
28. Zielonka, W.: Notes on finite asynchronous automata. Theoret. Inform. Appli. (ITA) **21**(2), 99–135 (1987)

Towards Engineering Digital Twins by Active Behaviour Mining

Tiziana Margaria[1,2,3(✉)] and Alexander Schieweck[1,2,3(✉)]

[1] Department of Computer Science and Information Systems, University of Limerick, Limerick, Ireland
{tiziana.margaria,alexander.schieweck}@ul.ie

[2] Lero - The SFI Research Centre for Software, Limerick, Ireland

[3] Confirm - Smart Manufacturing SFI Research Centre, Limerick, Ireland

Abstract. In the context of Confirm, the Irish Research Centre on Smart Manufacturing, field demonstrators are used to show new techniques to industrial partners, various kinds of students, and the general public alike. Considering the robotics demonstrator for the Digital Thread concept used in Confirm, which is a small cyberphysical system based on the UR3 cobot and a web controller for it, we apply Active Automata Learning in order to obtain a Digital Twin for it. Behavior mining done in this fashion is nowadays uncommon, but it has various advantages over, e.g., models obtained with popular AI techniques in that the AAL models are accurate deterministic behavioural explanations for the system behaviour at the chosen level of abstraction, and they may be further amenable to formal verification, e.g., by model checking, in order to establish properties of interest.

This extension has the effect of showcasing the Digital Twin concept, the AAL technique, the use of model checking, and the importance of working with formal models that are amenable to these technologies. We then reflect on the nature of the models and their uses and meaning, from the point of view of the comments and questions we receive in the demonstrations. We also consider the use of a feature-based approach to modelling the systems and their interactions, which is a further aspect for which the demonstrator could be used, with a special attention to the aspects of this work, like AAL and the feature based and feature interaction research, that connect directly with the collaboration with and the research of Bengt Jonsson.

Keywords: Formal methods · Active automata learning · Model driven design · Digital twin · Digital thread · Industry 4.0 · Smart manufacturing

---

This work was supported, in part, by Science Foundation Ireland grant 16/RC/3918 to Confirm, the Smart Manufacturing SFI Research Centre (www.confirm.ie) and 13/RC/2094 to Lero - The SFI Research Centre for Software (www.lero.ie).

E.-R. Olderog et al. (Eds.): Jonsson Festschrift, LNCS 13030, pp. 138–163, 2021.
https://doi.org/10.1007/978-3-030-91384-7_8

1 Digital Twins and CPSs

Engineering adequate Digital Twins for Cyber-Physical Systems is a complex, multidimensional challenge. While there are many definitions of what is a digital twin, we choose to refer to the recent, quite realistic and encompassing definition is by Ashtari et al. [50]: "*The Digital Twin is a virtual representation of a physical asset in a Cyber-Physical Production System (CPPS), capable of mirroring its static and dynamic characteristics. It contains and maps various models of a physical asset, of which some are executable, called simulation models. But not all models are executable, therefore the Digital Twin is more than just a simulation of a physical asset. Within this context, an asset can be an entity that already exists in the real world or can be a representation of a future entity that will be constructed.*"

In 2019 the Gartner group [43] listed digital twins in the top 10 strategic technology trends, next to blockchain, artificial intelligence, empowered edge, privacy and ethics, quantum computing, immersive experiences, augmented analytics, and autonomous things. While some of these technologies are evergreens, like quantum computing and the rather generic "autonomous things", digital twins are a new entry, and they start to play a role, at least conceptually, well beyond the smart manufacturing domain from which they originate. For example, one starts to hear about initiatives to co-create digital twins for (cancer) patients [1]. The digital twins of the future will be patient-tailored models that:

- Can be used to evaluate potential preventative and/or therapeutic plans,
- Incorporate information across length and time scales,
- Continually integrate new data and knowledge,
- Help clinicians and patients understand the risks and benefits of a particular treatment plan that best meets the patient's objectives.

Digital Twins are used as well for and within supply chains [21], in particular in connection with supply chain disruption for manufacturing, as the last year has acutely manifested. Most of these Digital Twin variants concern simulation models that arise distinctly from the physical thing, or more realistically, the real-world system, they model.

Cast in new words, a digital twin is an instance-level model of an entity (physical or not), that, as IBM's Chris O'Connor puts it, is *"simple, but detailed"*[1]. A digital twin implies a strong notion of **adequacy for purpose** (otherwise it is not a "twin", lacking sufficient sameness), a **context-dependency** of the purpose (there can be different digital twins for the same entity if this entity serves different purposes, and these differences of purpose matter, inducing difference of context), and it is required to have an ability to **support and guide the design, build and operation** phases of the entity it represents. It is therefore descriptive (like a design model), behavioural (as it must encompass what the physical twin can do), and predictive: during operations it must be able to

[1] https://youtu.be/RaOejcczPas.

predict maintenance needs as well as out-of-order behaviours, and serve as a baseline to figure out their prevention and repair.

Most frequently we see digital twins of some physical entities, like manufacturing machines and products that are more generally abstracted as Cyber-Physical Systems (CPSs) models. Most recently they started to include also any kind of Internet of Things (IoT) and Industrial Internet of Things (IIoT) devices.

At design time, the digital twin models serve the main purpose of increasing the expected dependability of their physical counterpart. At build time they serve to assess and monitor the faithfulness of the production processes for the physical twin. During operation, once the physical twin has been produced and installed, they find use to monitor the dependability of the products, for each individual piece with its individual characteristics, aging, and anomalies.

However, many engineers still associate the concept of digital twin to a quantitative, mathematical simulation based model, that allows (mostly mechanical) engineers to ask what-if questions that inform design, usage, and evolution decisions for a mechanical object or mechanical forming process [12]. Statistical models, Finite Element Analysis (FEA) as the simulation of a physical phenomenon using a numerical mathematical technique referred to as the Finite Element Method (FEM) are the most frequent types of models, and in some application domains they are still nearly synonyms of Digital Twins. The awareness that software plays a role in the "fullness" of modern devices, that the behavior of the software may go beyond a pure controller of the physical part, that there is inherently a heterogeneity, and thus an integration problem with discrete, finite state machine-like models are still not obvious today.

The most modern intuitive connection is with models derived by Machine Learning (ML) from data acquired from the physical twin, retrofitting the device (a black box) with models that are based on statistics, and incomplete knowledge and descriptions. They are therefore at best approximations of the real behaviours, thus themselves a black box model, and a blurry one.

What we are trying to achieve, on the contrary, is the systematic, and possibly automatic, production of **behavioural models** for real devices, that describe precisely the observed behaviours and are congruent to such behaviours, thus can be used as faithful predictors, like a sosia, and are able to explain the predicted and the observed behaviour on an execution by execution basis, i.e., use case by use case, test run by test run.

The challenge towards this scenario is, how can one systematically enable the well-founded engineering of such digital twins for dependable CPSs?

We are going use the simple Confirm *Digital Thread* prototype consisting of 1) a commercial Universal Robots cobot and 2) a Web-based remote controller application as a small example for a concrete CPS of industrial relevance. This mini-system of systems case study includes a Cyber part (the web application), a Physical part (the robot), and a communication system, which is here the internet plus a TCP socket connection to the robot. Although simple, this system exhibits the essential traits of many CPSs, and it is simple and small enough (i.e., physically transportable) that it has been repeatedly used for many teaching and demonstration purposes.

We will show how already the simple Active Automata Learning for Mealy machines can be an effective technique to retrofit existing CPS systems with models that satisfy these characteristics. We then reflect on several aspects of the system, the model, the learning, and how the model, behavior and properties are expressed, that can be interesting from a research and practical point of view.

In the following, Sect. 2 presents the case study and Sect. 3 provides an overview of MDD and Active Automata Learning techniques. We then explain the setup for experiments of the Confirm Digital Thread prototype in conjunction with the robot simulator (Sect. 4), followed by a discussion of the learning results in Sect. 5 and an application of CTL model checking for property checking on the learned model in Sect. 1. In Sect. 7 we discuss the insights gained so far, the lessons learned and our reflections along various perspectives of past experience, collaboration with Bengt Jonsson and future work. Lastly, Sect. 8 concludes the paper.

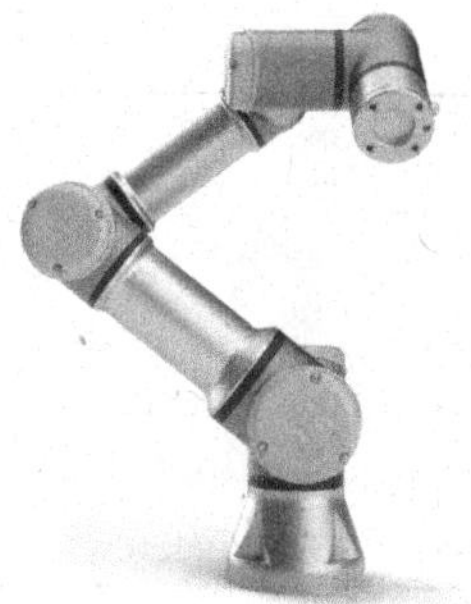

(a) Universal Robots' UR3

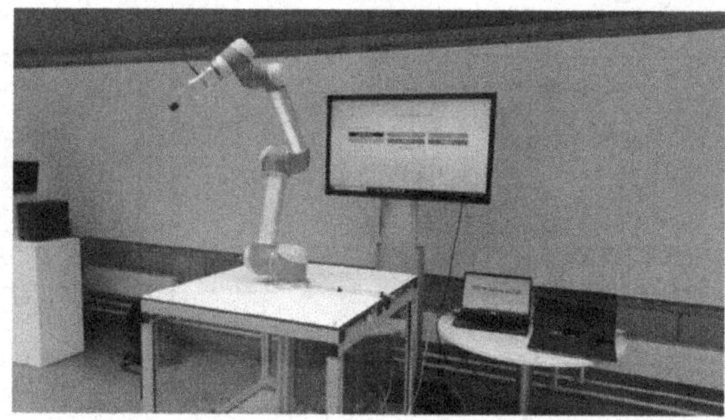

(b) Demonstrator Setup with UR 5

Fig. 1. The physical system

2 The Case Study: XMDD Steers a Cobot

The Confirm *Digital Thread* demonstrator, introduced in [32], showcases a MDD-based application in the smart manufacturing context. It is a handy example that brings together two worlds still culturally very distant and effectively disjoint: commercial collaborative robots and advanced Model Driven Development.

This portable demonstrator consists of a collaborative robot (cobot) produced by Universal Robots (UR) together with a web application designed to remotely control such cobots. In the world of robotics, this is a very small installation, easy to transport and set up for demonstration and outreach purposes. As shown in Fig. 1b, the UR5 is mounted on a portable rolling table, and the large display shows the Web Application, running on the laptop at the right.

The UR product line consists of flexible 7 joints robotic arms that can be equipped with a wide variety of mountable devices like a grip arm, a camera, and various sensors and actuators. It is widely customizable and retargetable for different applications with little effort and expense, by retooling and reprogramming. Cobots are particularly safe because they are equipped with special sensors to detect whether something is in their way. This ability allows them to operate without special work cages, opening the possibility of collaborative work with humans. UR, the first company to produce such robots, offers four models: UR3 (see Fig. 1a), UR5 (see Fig. 1b), UR10 and UR16. The number indicates the maximum payload in Kg of each model. The models grow in size and weight accordingly, but the core design and concepts, like the joints, degrees of freedom and skills, are very similar for all models. They use for example the same API, which allows custom programs to be interchangeable [32].

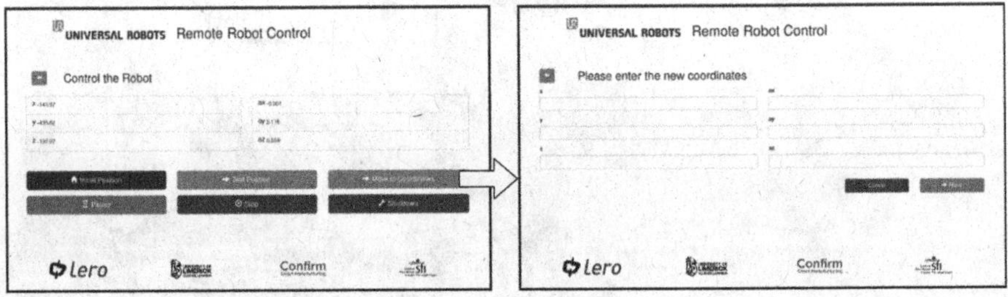

Fig. 2. The web application: The controller main page (left). Clicking the 'Move to Coordinates' button leads to the coordinates input page (right)

While this describes the Physical side of the CPS demonstrator, the user-level interactable view of the Cyber component is shown in Fig. 2. The main page of the controller offers a set of six predisposed operations: `Initial position` (dark blue button) `Pause` (yellow button), `Test position` and `Move to coordinates` (light blue buttons), `Stop` and `Shutdown` (red buttons). Each of them can be launched by clicking the corresponding GUI button. The `Initial position` and `Test position` skills are fully predefined: clicking the respective button brings the robot to a fixed position. For example, the `Initial position` button leads to the balanced vertical "zero" position shown in Fig. 3. The `Move to coordinates` button, however, allows a remote configuration of the robot: it

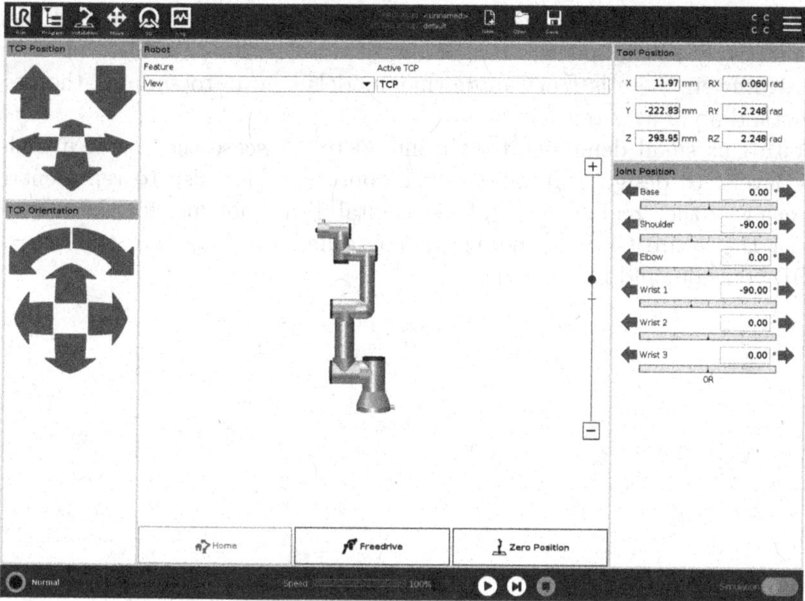

Fig. 3. Interactive simulator by universal robots

leads to a second web page (Fig. 2(right)), where a mask allows the user to input target coordinates of the tip of the arm. The choice of these skills is intentional: it is a minimum set of skills that covers the categories *Home*, *Move*, *Timing* and *Manage*, associated with the colour of the button as well as with a small symbol near the skill name on the button. This is, in effect, a minimal Domain Specific Language in the application domain of the robots, what we would call an A-DSL for Application-specific DSL. The colours and symbols associated to the individual skills expose the internal structure of the A-DSL, which has a taxonomic structure.

Traditionally, the controller is programmed and tested either on-site, using the tablet physically tethered to the machine, or by means of a simulator software that behaves like the UR equipment, so that the program tested on the simulator can be then uploaded with confidence to the cobot. The simulator provided by Universal Robots shown in Fig. 3 covers the entire family of cobots. It can be installed on a Linux system or used in a virtual machine via a provided virtual machine image. For the purpose of this paper we choose the latter option, as this adds a layer of separation between the now virtual robot and the rest of our technology stack, similar to how a real cobot would be separated from the other technologies. The simulator also offers the option to change timing parameters. This allows the simulated robot to move like a real machine, but at accelerated speed. This feature is going to be very useful during the automata learning campaign that leads to the Digital Twin of this system.

The simulator is seen by many in robotics and manufacturing as "the" model, and effectively as the in-silico reification, of the Digital Twin in terms of software. However, there is much more that models can do to support the deeper understanding of a system.

With this small demonstrator we intend to showcase the use of models at many levels: to design and validate the controller, but also to represent in a different way the "real essence" of the Digital Twin, not just for the robot but also for the entire CPS, including the controller. To do so, we will use some XMDD concepts and technologies.

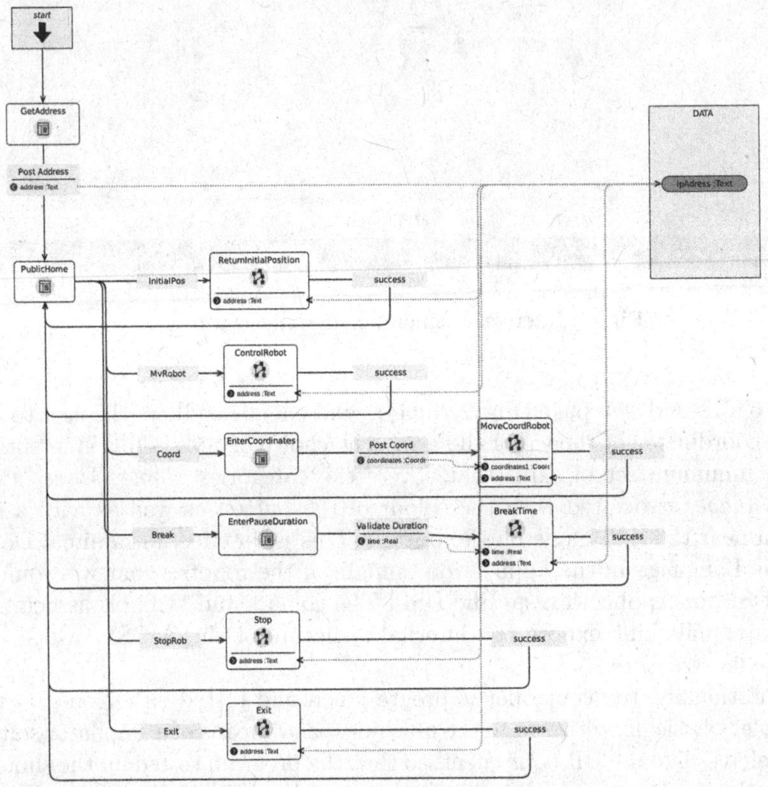

Fig. 4. Process model of the remote controller: App's main workflow in DIME

3 XMDD Concepts and Technologies

We adopt the eXtreme MDD paradigm of [33,34], and use the DIME [7] tool and platform first to model, and then to code-generate and deploy the Web application that controls the cobot. In this section we briefly introduce XMDD and provide a short introduction in Active Automata Learning, the approach we use to generate the Digital Twin. We assume that model checking is known.

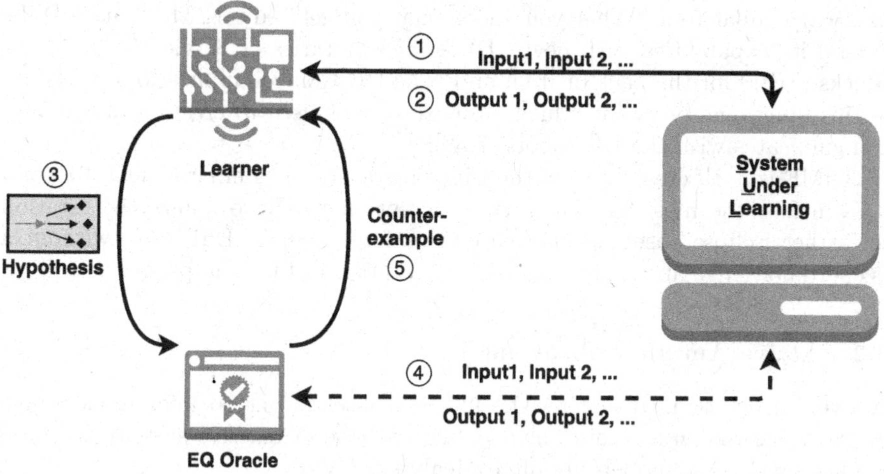

Fig. 5. Overview of the active automata learning loop

3.1 XMDD in DIME

The Model Driven Design (MDD) approach breaks with the paradigm that everything needs to be written in native code and puts instead models at the center of a software development project. Those models can be textual or graphical, they help the developer to describe what the software should be doing. Depending on the choice of models and modelling languages, they have different levels of expressiveness, automatic model analysis and transformation support. In most approaches, a key advantage is that they help delegate the worry about the "how" to a separate design granularity, and often to a separate professional profile [11,26–28].

From a generic MDD point of view, DIME is an Integrated Modelling Environment, i.e. a model driven design tool, specialized for the design, development and deployment of web applications. DIME is open source, provides flexibility, ease of extension, supports high-assurance software quality, agility, a service-oriented approach, and also containerization. For the specific low-code support, its model-driven approach is based on Domain Specific Languages (DSLs) at two levels:

- Language DSLs, as a mechanism to design and implement the application design environment itself, i.e., the Integrated Modeling Environment (IME),
- and a number of Application domain DSLs, at application design time. We want to use Native DSLs as the means to integrate and expose collections of capabilities offered by end devices and other sources of functionalities to the application designers, and Process DSLs (see Fig. 4) as the means to foster reuse of medium and large grained business logic across applications.

DIME's DSLs cover all layers of a modern web applications, e.g. the data model, the process models to describe the business logic, and the GUI front end in a way similar to a "What you see is what you get" editor. The Native DSLs extend its capabilities with new GDLSs: new libraries of Service Independent Blocks (SIBs) for the back or front end. The UR Control application makes use of this functionality by introducing robotics DSLs used to create a plugin that communicates with the UR robots [7,49].

DIME is itself created using the Cinco meta-modeling environment [37], and it is in fact the most sophisticated Cinco-product. Cinco allows the creation of further Eclipse based specialized editors for Language DSL tools without a deeper knowledge about the various Eclipse graphical tooling projects.

3.2 Active Automata Learning

Active Automata Learning (AAL) [2] uses observations to infer models of a system's internal states and behavior. In the case of reactive systems like web applications, those models are often Mealy machines.

Definition 1 (Mealy Machine).
A Mealy Machine is defined as a tuple $(Q, q_0, \Sigma, \Lambda, \delta, \lambda)$*, where* Q *is a finite set of states,* $q_0 \in Q$ *is the initial state,* Σ *is a finite set of input symbols, i.e. the input alphabet,* Λ *is a finite set of output symbols, i.e. the output alphabet,* $\delta : Q \times \Sigma \rightarrow Q$ *is the transition function, and* $\lambda : Q \times \Sigma \rightarrow \Lambda$ *is the output function.*

The core Active Automata Learning process is illustrated in Fig. 5. The learning algorithm, called the learner, interacts with the System Under Learning (SUL) via testing and observes its behavior. Those interactions are called Membership Queries. In a Membership Query, the learner sends inputs to the SUL, collects the corresponding observed outputs, and collects the resulting input/output behaviour traces, producing a hypothesis model of the internal states of the system. Once the learner reaches a point where it has seen enough behaviour, along a predefined notion of "enough", it passes the current hypothesis model to the Equivalence (EQ) Oracle. In an ideal world, the EQ Oracle would have perfect knowledge of the SUL and could decide this question directly. In the real world this is impossible: instead, the EQ Oracle applies another set of criteria to the model, and tells the learner whether the current hypothesis is correct, i.e. satisfies all those criteria, or not. If one or more counterexamples are found, they are passed back to the learner, which starts a new MQ campaign based on the new insights. This leads to successive evidence-based refinement cycles of the hypothesis model. When the deployed counter-example search strategies do not find any counter example anymore in reasonable time, the current hypothesis model is assumed to be correct and the learning process terminates with that learned model.

It is important to note that every membership and equivalence query needs to start with the same prerequisites, so a reset mechanism of the SUL to the same initial state is needed too.

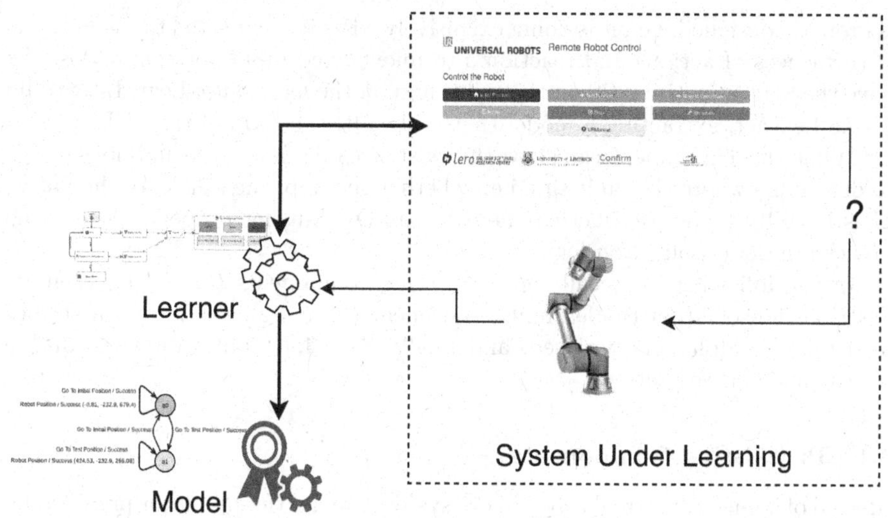

Fig. 6. The setup of the learning experiment: AAL with LearnLib Studio

LearnLib[2] [19,40] is a state of the art open source framework for AAL, which offers a wide set of algorithms, counter examples search strategies and infrastructure components in Java. Many tools have been designed to create customized learn experiments utilizing the LearnLib.

The Active Automata Learning Experience (ALEX) tool is built upon LearnLib and allows a no-code way to learn web applications and even to mix them with REST APIs. *ALEX* is itself a web application. It offers a comfortable GUI to describe the interactions with a web application or a RESTful API. The learning can be parameterized, but the overall learning process is fixed [19,40]. Because the UR robot itself does not offer a REST API, ALEX is unfortunately not applicable to this case. We use instead LearnLib Studio[3], a specialized *Cinco*-product for defining LearnLib experiments through a custom MDD editor.

4 Automata Learning Experiments: Set Up with Learnlib Studio

In our Digital Thread prototype, the UR Remote Control Web Application and the robot, here a UR simulator, constitute the SUL (see Fig. 6). We wish to automatically extract a Digital Twin of the SUL in order to find out whether the web application interacts with the robot in the expected way. Concretely, we wish to find out if the native SIB libraries of the UR DSL are used in the expected way, e.g. following the correct protocol, and if the controller application

[2] https://learnlib.de.

[3] https://github.com/learnlib/learnlib-studio.

is properly designed, i.e., it is doing exclusively what it is expected to do, in terms of sewuences of actions and reaction s to unexpected inputs or commands. We have the SUL as entire CPS on the right, and on the left we use LearnLib Studio as the Learner, extracting a model that is the Digital Twin of the SUL.

While this experiment can show the existence of a fault, it would not be able to determine where the fault sits, i.e., whether the implementation of the native SIBs is faulty (code) or whether the SIBs are OK but not properly used in the process model (application logic).

In the following we recall the preexisting components (Sect. 4.1), then we describe the set up of the learning experiment (Sect. 4.2). Section 4.3 describes in detail the alphabets we used, and finally Sect. 4.4 reports on performance issues and their resolution.

4.1 Preexisting Components

Instead of connecting a real robot to the system, we use the simulator provided by Universal Robots in a Virtual Box. As the robot is in reality also connected with an IP Address, the Virtual Box helps to create a realistic scenario. Within this setup, the simulator and the robot are interchangeable, as was confirmed through tests. We parameterized the simulator with the data and coordinates for the UR3 model, but the UR scripting language and the communication with the robot are identical for the whole UR family. To cover other models, which have different dimensions of the arm segments, the specific coordinates for predefined positions would need to be changed to those for the specific UR model. Using the simulator also allowed us to speed up the robot responsiveness, significantly reducing the overall time for our learning experiment. The robot is in fact mechanically quite slow. We used instead a simulator setting with a near immediate response to commands, preserving the execution traces but much faster than the real system. As we are not examining timed behaviour or performance, this difference did not impact the behaviour to be learned.

The UR Control Web Application, which is itself designed as a *DIME* application, once compiled and deployed runs in a Docker environment and it can be used independently of *DIME*. For the learning experiments, everything was thus executed on a single local machine.

4.2 The Learning Experiment Set up

The learning experiment was described graphically using *LearnLib Studio*'s models, as shown in Fig. 7. The left side of the *Learn Experiment Model* shows the definition of the experiment setup. It uses the TTT algorithm [18] and the Random Word Equivalence Oracle, which is a random word counterexample search parameterized with 20 random words with a length between 5 and 10 symbols. The right side of the model shows the graphical definition of the SUL in terms of the commands in its alphabet. The cycle between the TTT algorithm and the Random Word Equivalence Oracle represents the learn loop. Both these elements connect to the SUL via a query counter and a cache, which are filters defined

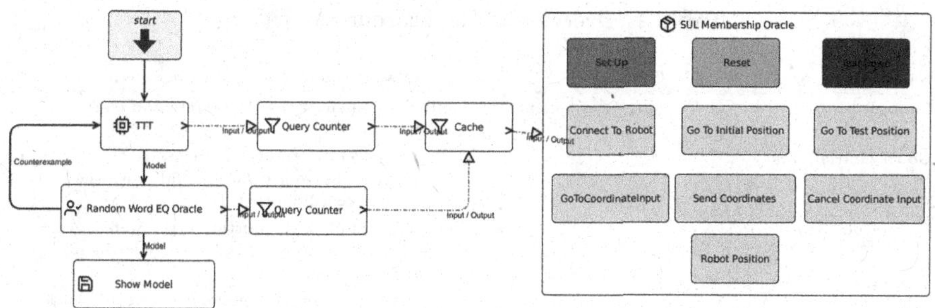

Fig. 7. Definition of the Learning Experiment as a *Learn Experiment Model*

as part of the LearnLib pipeline. While the query counter provides insights on the learning use of resources, the cache offers a potentially increased efficiency because it directly answers known queries instead of invoking the SUL anew. The SUL is represented as a set of 10 symbols: the learning alphabet consists of seven symbols, and the further three are special symbols which deal with the setup and tear down of the SUL and the connection to it.

4.3 The Learning Alphabet

The symbols defined for the learning experiment are described in Table 1. The seven symbols Connect to Robot, Go To Initial Position, Go to Test Position, Go to Coordinate Input, Send Coordinates, Cancel Coordinate Input and Robot Coordinates constitute the learning alphabet. Their names constitute the *input alphabet* to the algorithm. The *output alphabet* consists of their possible outputs: Success, Success (X, Y, Z) which includes the actual robot coordinates at time of calling, and the additional symbol ElementNotFound. The use of the robot coordinates in this set up allows to independently observe the robot coordinates in the learning process, and correlate them to interactions with the web application.

Beside the input and output symbols, the three helper symbols Set Up, Reset and Tear Down described in Table 2 help manage the experiment, for example to ensure a reliable reset.

These handling of the symbols is implemented in LearnLib Studio. It adopts a MDD approach with a Cinco GDSL similar to the process language of *DIME*, but modified to focus more on consistent outputs symbols. As an example, Fig. 8 shows the implementation of the *Go To Initial Position* symbol. This model is executed every time a learning component sends to the SUL a query containing this symbol. Starting from the *Start SIB*, a so-called WebDriver is needed to emulate the user behavior in a web browser. The *Start SIB* grabs it from a global context and passes it to the next SIB via the dotted data flow edge. As the *Start SIB* has only one control flow successor (the solid line), the *WaitForNode* is executed next. This SIB takes care of extra waiting time to ensure the page has properly loaded. Each SIB has input (blue, top) and output (orange, bottom) ports. Input ports can either be dynamic, i.e. they accept data flow from other

Table 1. Overview of the Learning Alphabet

Name	Outputs	Description
Connect To Robot	Success, ElementNotFound	Tries to enter the IP address and click 'Connect'
Go to {Initial, Test} Position		Tries to click the button {initial, test} position button, which should move the robot accordingly
Go to Coordinate Input		Tries to click the button in the web application to navigate to the coordinate input page
Send Coordinates		Tries to enter custom coordinates and click the move button on the coordinate input page
Cancel Coordinate Input		Tries to click the cancel button on the coordinate input page
Robot Coordinates	Success (X, Y, Z)	Connects to the robot and receives the current robot coordinates, which are part of the output

Table 2. Overview of the helper symbols

Name	Description
Set Up	Starts the web browser It is called only once at the beginning of the learn experiment
Reset	Opens the web app in a fresh environment Moves the robot to the initial position Called before every query
Tear down	Closes the web browser It is only called once at the end of the learning experiment

SIBs, or static, i.e. the value is fixed and predefined when modeling the symbol. The next action in this symbol's workflow, the *Click SIB*, actually clicks the button, and then the symbol execution terminates with its *End SIB*, which in this case is the *Success* output. This *End SIB* also updates the *WebDriver* in the global context. Should any of those two execution SIBs fail, e.g., if the *WaitForNode* reaches a timeout while waiting for the button in, or if the *Click SIB* is unable to click the button, the alternative error path indicated by the red dotted lines is taken. These error paths lead to the *End SIB ElementNotFound*, which signals to the learn experiment that the button is missing.

The collections of symbols in Tables 1 and 2 are defined in this way. They use a newly created custom SIB library to interact with the web application, see Fig. 9. It is part of the example experiments included with *LearnLib Studio* and deals with buttons, numeric fields, and other interactable GUI elements of web application.

Another SIB library was used to interact with the robot directly.

4.4 Performance Issues

During the first learning experiment there were speed management issues with the network socket of the robot: even the sped-up robot in the simulator, much

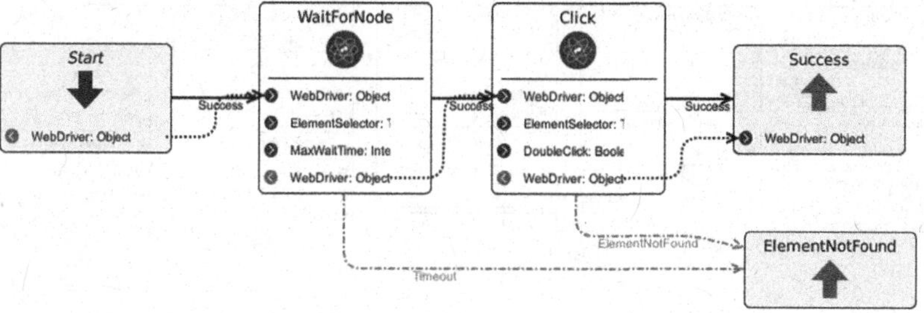

Fig. 8. Symbol definition in LearnLib studio for the click on the *Go to Initial Position* Button

faster to respond than the real robot, could not keep up with the amount of different commands automatically sent to it by the learning algorithm. The adopted solution was to introduce an artificial wait time of ten seconds before querying the coordinates from the robot, the SIB *WaitForNode*, even though this slowed down the overall learning process.

A different approach would have been to poll the robot multiple times until the reported coordinates stop changing, indicating that the robot has reached its final position, or alternatively to instruct the robot call back once the movement is finished. Both approaches would have requested multiple interactions and a more complex logic, so we preferred to opt for the simpler wait solution.

5 Results: The Learned Digital Twin

The Mealy machine shown in Fig. 10 is the behavioral Digital Twin of the UR Controller Web Application as learned through the AAL experiment. It has seven states, based on the seven input symbols introduced with the learning alphabet, the corresponding output symbols, i.e. *Success*, *ElementNotFound* and the different coordinates.

The state q_0 on the top left, shaded in green, is the initial state. The very first page of the web application asks for the IP address of the robot and is otherwise only reachable by reloading the application. This behavior is evident in the Digital Twin model's state q_0: it is the initial state and it only allows to move ahead with the Connect To Robot action.

Upon closer inspection, one notices that the final model is a product of the possible states of the web application, i.e. main 'button' page and coordinate input page, and the three possible robot positions from the app, i.e. initial position, test position, and custom coordinates. In the three states q_0, q_1 and q_3 (in the dashed oval) the robot is in the initial position. The states q_2 and q_5 (solid oval) represent the robot in the test position. And in states q_4 and q_6 (dotted oval) the robot is in the custom coordinates position. Between those areas there are only the Go to Initial Position, Go to Test Position and Send Coordinates transitions, and they lead always successfully to the according target state.

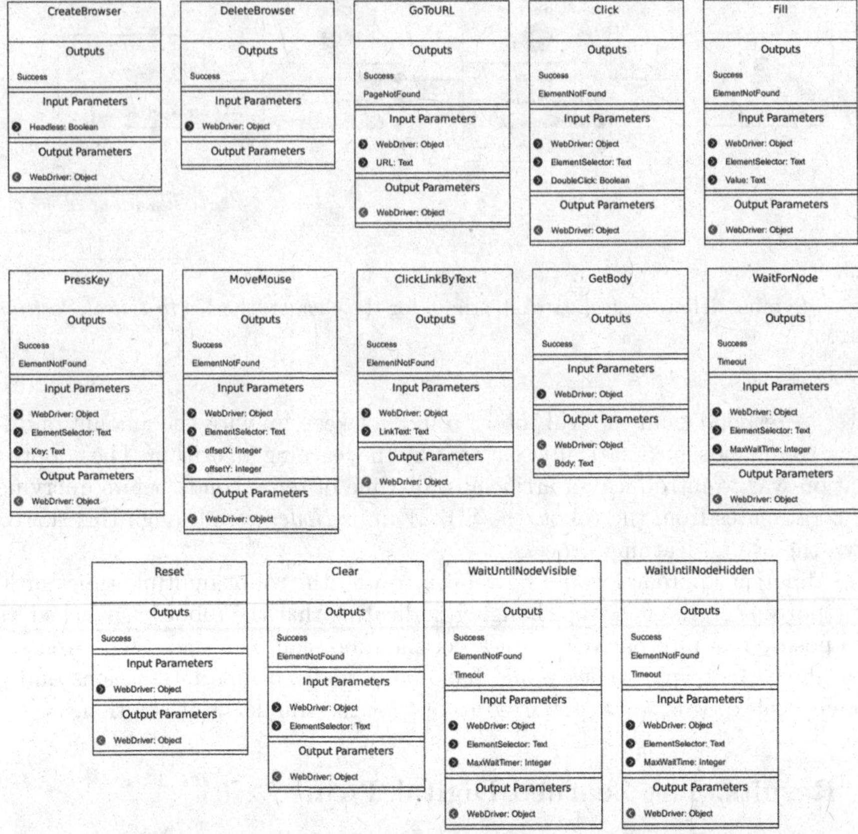

Fig. 9. Selenium SIB library for interactions with web applications.

In each robot position, one state represents the main button page of the website: $q1$, $q2$ and $q4$, highlighted by blue squares. Furthermore, these position-related areas of the model include the states $q3$, $q5$ and $q6$ (highlighted by orange triangles) representing the coordinate input page. Between pairs of those states there are only transitions with Go to Coordinate Input and Cancel Coordinate Input: these transitions are present and successful. The only exception is the Send Coordinates transition between $q6$ and $q4$, which can be easily explained as it is the reflexive edge within the robot position area.

Overall, the final model that emerged is structured as a product between the states of the web application and the three chosen robot positions, with a network of correct transitions according to the *good machine* behaviour we expected.

The learning experiment was run on a Dell XPS 15 9560 (Intel Core i7-7700HQ, 32 GB RAM, Manjaro Linux) and took 80 min of execution time. Its production took four iterations of the learning loop, with algorithmic search and

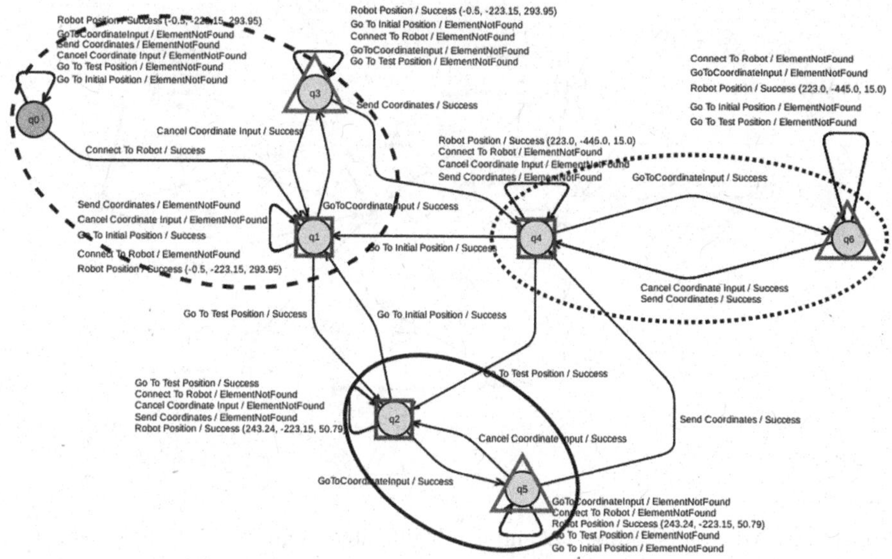

Fig. 10. The final model: the digital twin obtained by AAL

counterexample. The learner asked 218 Membership Queries and 34 Equivalence Queries were posed by the counter example strategy.

6 Property Checking on the Digital Twin

The Digital Twin extraction is interesting per se, but, as we see, its interpretation requires manual analysis and a good understanding of how the system under learning functions: its architecture, its components, both individually and in their communication patterns. This can be done for a small model. However, as soon as systems and models grow, for example in our case when adding a camera that observes from outside the real robot behaviour and steers adjustments to coordinates based on precise measurements, e.g., to limit the movements within a 'virtual cage', the model size grows as well, the interactions become more intricate, and a different method of analysis is needed in order to properly evaluate the model and its meaning. Property checking on the Digital Twin is a useful technique.

We use here CTL model checking, specifically model checking with the GEAR [3,4] tool, in order to a) express behavioural properties of the system that can be assessed on the model, and b) automatically check them on the produced Digital Twin model. The four properties we checked are:

Property 1: *If the* Go to Initial *button is clickable, clicking it leads to the robot being positioned in the initial position.*

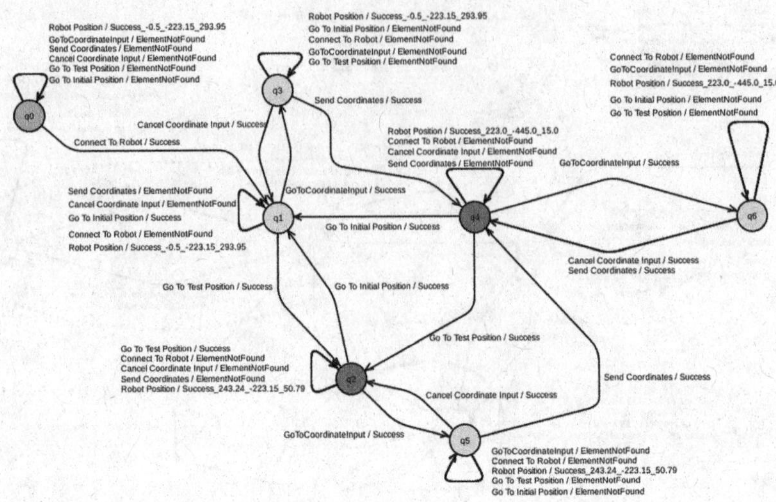

Fig. 11. GEAR results: States Q2 and Q4, highlighted in green, fulfill the constraint.

```
    (["Go_To_Initial_Position/Success"]
        "Robot_Position/Success (-0.5,_-223.15, 293.95)")
OR
    "Go_To_Initial_Position/Element_Not_Found"
```

Property 2: *If the* Go to Test *button is clickable, clicking it leads to the robot being positioned in the test position.*

```
    (["Go_To_Test_Position/Success"]
        "Robot_Position/Success (243.24, -223.15, 50.79)")
OR
    "Go_To_Test_Position/Element_Not_Found"
```

Property 3: *If the* Go to Coordinate Input *button is clickable, clicking it does not change the position of the robot.*

```
(
    ("Robot Position/Success (-0.5, -223.15, 293.95)"
     ["Go To Coordinate Input/Success"]
        "Robot Position/Success (-0.5, -223.15, 293.95)"
    )
 AND
    ("Robot Position/Success (243.24, -223.15, 50.79)"
     ["Go To Coordinate Input/Success"]
        "Robot Position/Success (243.24, -223.15, 50.79)"
    )
 AND
    ("Robot Position/Success (223.0, -445.0, 15.0)"
     ["Go To Coordinate Input/Success"]
        "Robot Position/Success (223.0, -445.0, 15.0)"
```

```
    )
  )
OR
    "Go To Coordinate Input/Element Not Found"
```

Property 4: *If the* Cancel Coordinate Input *button is clickable, clicking it does not change the position of the robot.*

```
 (
     ("Robot Position/Success (-0.5, -223.15, 293.95)"
      ["Cancel Coordinate Input/Success"]
           "Robot Position/Success (-0.5, -223.15, 293.95)"
     )
   AND
     ("Robot Position/Success (243.24, -223.15, 50.79)"
      ["Cancel Coordinate Input/Success"]
            "Robot Position/Success (243.24, -223.15, 50.79)"
     )
   AND
     ("Robot Position/Success (223.0, -445.0, 15.0)"
      ["Cancel Coordinate Input/Success"]
           "Robot Position/Success (223.0, -445.0, 15.0)"
     )
 )
OR
    "Cancel Coordinate Input/Element Not Found"
```

As we see from the GEAR screenshot in Fig. 11, the model checker highlights the states satisfying a property, providing good visual feedback to the user. All these properties are fulfilled by this model. Property checking on the digital twin can be a useful way to validate the model, making sure that it captures those phenomena that are known to the designers.

7 Reflections and Lessons Learned

Several considerations come upon reflection on this even simple case study, especially in the context of our conversations with people interested in Digital Twins for Cyberphysical Systems that are not computer scientists themselves. In this group fall the recurring questions about the role of AI (Sect. 7.1), and the fact that there are many different kinds of software models, like design models and behavioral models (Sect. 7.2). We follow then with some reflections on two lines of work that are central to Bengt's and Tiziana's connection: the genesis and evolution of the specific AAL technology we used here (Sect. 7.3), and their work on features and feature interactions (Sect 7.4).

7.1 AAL vs. AI

When using AAL to extract digital twins of (software) systems, we are frequently asked:

Can't you use AI instead?

Resorting to AI as the all-encompassing solution to any unknown seems to become a reflex response to any question concerning systems and their analysis. There are at least two fundamental differences between the models produced by AAL and those produced in AI:

- Many popular AI techniques essentially retrofit (mostly) numerical and/or probabilistic models based on a data set interpreted as an input/output relation, without necessarily a relation with the real system. Even Grammatical Evolution [44], which is based on a BNF-style description of a system's potential actions, essentially tries to match an I/O behaviour provided in a file by first guessing and then recombining populations of alternative "programs" that approximate the real system.
  Instead, AAL systematically explores the real system (or the part of the system one decides to observe, as this is steered through the Learning Alphabet) and provides the minimal model that reflects faithfully all the observations. In this sense, there is an aspect of tightness to the system that the AAL approach has and the AI one does not.
- AI models that replicate systems are themselves mostly black boxes, and even the typical tools used for Explainable AI, like SHAP [25], provide percentages of correlation between certain inputs and certain outputs, but do not provide an analyzable, even enactable model of the system itself like the model in Fig. 10. The value of this Mealy machine as an explanation model, for any What-If analysis, is in a totally different class of confidence and evidence.

7.2 Design Models vs. Behavioural Models

Other frequent questions are:

Isn't the software the model itself?
Isn't the process diagram the model?
Why do you need a digital twin of software?

There is still a widespread belief that software does not need models, that software "is" per se modelling (because it is inherently immaterial, in contrast to the tangible things in manufacturing and production, or even communications, as communication tools come with apparati like transmitters, receivers, etc. In some circles, software is met in the form of simulators, and the simulation software is then identified itself as "the model". The fundamental distinctions between the simulation tool, the simulation run, the data, and the aggregated model from many runs are more or less unconsciously blurred.

In the same line of thought:

If the software is not the model, then the diagrams "are" the model, right?

The graphical presentation of process models and workflows induces some to see them as fundamentally different from code, and thus from software. A recipe like a DIME or BPMN process model is then taken as "being the model", which is true in a behaviour design sense, but not in the sense of exposing the semantic effects of the execution.

The difference between design-time models of behaviour and semantic and runtime or execution models in this guise was showcased and discussed in [38], on the case study concerning a prior version of the Online Conference System (OCS) published as part of the FMICS Working Group state of the art book [10]. There, we used the AAL technologies described in [15] in order to extract by learning the behaviour of a Web application that implements a conference management system. In that case, AAL was applied to a purely cyber system, i.e., not physical at all, and used to show that various properties that were requirements at design time were indeed satisfied by the implemented and deployed system.

This brings us to the specific learning technology used, then and now, in our work. This also brings us to the connection and collaboration with Bengt.

7.3 Learning Technology

We use here a new version of the LearnLib Studio which is now a specialized Cinco-product for defining LearnLib experiments through a custom MDD editor. We specifically used the TTT algorithm of [18]. However, the AAL technology has a long history and it has benefited greatly from Bengt Jonsson's research and work. The original LearnLib [40] was greatly enhanced in collaboration with Bengt and his group during the Connect EU project [41], leading to the first applications within FMICS [31] and to dynamic testing [42]. It was then followed by the Next Generation LearnLib (NGLL) [36], with full details described in [46], and more recently by the Open Source Learn Lib of [19]. This LearnLib has made school, becoming one of the most downloaded and widely used tools for Automata Learning, with the ALEX tool and others like LearnLib Studio as further derivatives. The LearnLib materialized in a very successful tool set the first observations about knowledge based relevance filtering for an efficient use of testing in order to save order of magnitudes of tests when we started to explore model extraction based on systematic execution as a way to extract compact models from deployed systems [17,29,30].

Specifically in AAL, or regular inferences, Bengt and his group contributed greatly to the development of algorithms and optimizations, e.g. exploring the connection between the connection between conformance testing and regular inference [5] back in 2005, then working on the inferring semantic interfaces for data structures [13] and on learning canonical register automata [16], and here most recently combining black-box and white-box techniques [14], until the more recent works on active learning for extended finite state machines [9], in the quest to solve the CONNECT challenges [20] and more.

7.4 Features and Feature Interaction

Also without addressing the topic of humans in the loop and human-machine collaboration that cobots address, it is clear that manufacturing systems deal with system interactions. In the language of coordination models, some of these interactions can be orchestrated, i.e. the interactions are designed in their entirety and can be to a good extent linearized to workflow-deterministic projections onto the individual actors, but this is not always the case. Already two UR3 that collaborate, e.g., to hold and weld a piece could give rise to more diverse interactions if they are considered independent systems that happen to cooperate. This is the realm of choreographies, akin to collections of independent (state) machines that only loosely coordinate. Sometimes one even observes emergent behaviours, that, from the point of view of the modelling, appear spontaneous. In this context, it is frequent to observe so called feature interactions, where independent behaviours that are individually correct and consistent become inconsistent and face ambiguous choices if they have to coexist. In a sense, coupling due by the fact that these behaviours are brought in the same context, often being one the context of the other, exposes inconsistencies for which there is often no good decision policy.

The phenomenon is observed in the robotics domain, where collisions happen because the individual rules and policies driving one of the moving components clash with the others. Early discovery of such interactions is one of the uses of digital twins, ideally with the ability to identify whether such situations are possible, and even better with the ability to reduce the model to a small or even minimal model that models precisely and only the interference potential.

Here, the ability to produce faithful digital twins though AAL, together with the ability to analyze the models by means of model checking is a real asset. Having fully fledged formal models like the Mealy Machine of our case or richer models, like the register automata, may for example help identify certain language elements of the learning alphabet as irrelevant, and produce, either by re-learning or by model abstraction, smaller versions that still correctly characterize the problem. This is difficult and expensive to achieve both by traditional testing and by AI. Some reinforcement learning approaches start to bear fruits, and it is noteworthy in this context that the principle of RL, with an omniscient teacher (mostly simulated by annotations) is similar to AAL's oracle, with its implementations by query-answering mechanisms.

The feature interaction problem was first discovered in the late1990 s in the telecommunications domain. Also here we can look back at joint contributions with Bengt and some of his students. Started with their modular specification of telephone services within first-order linear-time temporal logic [6] and their formalization of Service Independent Building Blocks [39] in that style, this line of work brought us to an intense collaboration in 1998–2001, leading to a sabbatical semester in Uppsala. The approach for incremental requirement specification for evolving systems [22] based on that modular modelling style [23]. Since 1994 we were already working on projects with Siemens concerning the use of formal models for Intelligent Network services. They included model hierarchy [47] and constraint techniques to specify service properties . In particular we produced what today would be called a DSL-based, model driven and generative design environment for the agile development of IN Services [48]. Soon later we added an automated service evolution technology based on constraint-driven modification of the business logic [8], so that at the time of the cooperation with Bengt in Uppsala both groups happened to have independent yet fully aligned modelling styles and technology stacks. This made the collaboration possible, easier, and productive. Eight years later, at the onset of service oriented computing, an overview paper cheekily stated that we had 10 year experience in a field that was 3 years old [35], a claim substantiated by all this experience in research and industrial products with real impact.

Thinking in features has played a significant role in two other contexts: when modelling, then learning and analyzing the Online Conference System already mentioned [24], and later in the approach to constraint-based variability modeling framework [45]. This framework has a much wider applicability than the original feature models, as it targets generic (software and systems) product lines. Families of artifacts are first described in terms of collection of features, then composed, selected and analaysed in terms of their behavioral properties specified as temporal logic constraints. It is this last evolution of our feature-oriented thinking that is closest to the approach we intend to adopt and apply to both the digital twins, in terms of behavioural models, and to the digital thread in terms of end-to-end integration and composition of software and systems.

8 Conclusion and Outlook

In this paper we applied active automata learning experiments to a scenario in remote robotics control, based on the UR family of collaborative robots. While this is a small example, the capability to retrofit Digital Twin models to the behaviour of cyberphysical systems can potentially pave the way to capturing the behaviour of legacy (control) applications in smart manufacturing by means of models amenable to formal analysis and model based testing. We used here the LearnLib Studio for the Automata learning, and the GEAR model checker to verify a few properties of the Mealy machine obtained in the learning phase.

We are currently extending the functionality of the case study by connecting the robot also via ROS, the Robot Operating System popular in the education and research community for CPS, with the goal to provide many versions of the demonstrator and to be able to profile the various technologies involved, sometimes as alternatives like ROS vs. TCP socket. Thinking in features and dealing with feature interaction when having more than one independent subsystem is a further direction of research.

We also reflected on many dimensions of modelling and technology choice stemming from the two contexts in which we see us immersed: the Confirm Research Centre on Smart Manufacturing, with its challenges as a multicultural, multidisciplinary and multisectoral community of research and practice, and the personal history and experience. The Confirm context, in particular the conversation with excellent partners with very different background, lead us to have to rethink, explicitly formulate, and many times tangibly demonstrate rather than explain assumptions and facts that are not common knowledge nor obviously accepted outside of computer science. Here we count the omnipresence of AI as the go-to solution, with the need to justify why one is adopting a different approach, and the understanding of software, its facets and its role in a wider context of production floors. On the personal experience, having worked with many industry sectors and with many collaborators turns out to be a great asset. Beside the familiarity with automata learning, particularly the experience in modelling of telecommunication systems and reasoning about feature interactions has proven useful in recent collaborations also in Confirm, and is a nice benefit that we now draw, stemming from the pleasant and productive collaboration with Bengt and his group in the past 23 years. It is nice to see that there is a long term effect also for collaborations in a research that seemed to be a niche topic at some point.

References

1. Nci-doe collaboration 2020 ideas lab: Toward building a cancer patient "digital twin." an ideas lab to shape the future of predictive modeling across scales from biology to clinical care. Information Age (2020). https://www.imagwiki.nibib.nih.gov/news-events/relevant-meetings/nci-doe-collaboration-2020-ideas-lab-toward-building-cancer-patient
2. Angluin, D.: Learning regular sets from queries and counterexamples. Inf. Comput. **75**(2), 87–106 (1987)
3. Bakera, M., Margaria, T., Renner, C., Steffen, B.: Verification, diagnosis and adaptation: tool-supported enhancement of the model-driven verification process. In: Revue des Nouvelles Technologies de l'Information (RNTI-SM-1), pp. 85–98, December 2007
4. Bakera, M., Margaria, T., Renner, C., Steffen, B.: Tool-supported enhancement of diagnosis in model-driven verification. Innovations Syst. Softw. Eng. **5**, 211–228 (2009). https://doi.org/10.1007/s11334-009-0091-6
5. Berg, T., Grinchtein, O., Jonsson, B., Leucker, M., Raffelt, H., Steffen, B.: On the correspondence between conformance testing and regular inference. In: Cerioli, M. (ed.) Fundamental Approaches to Software Engineering, FASE 2005. LNCS, vol. 3442, pp. 175–189. Springer, Heidelberg (2005). https://doi.org/10.1007/978-3-540-31984-9_14
6. Blom, J., Jonsson, B., Kempe, L.: Using temporal logic for modular specification of telephone services. In: In Feature Interactions in Telecommunications Systems, pp. 197–216. IOS Press (1994)
7. Boßelmann, S., et al.: DIME: a programming-less modeling environment for web applications. In: Margaria, T., Steffen, B. (eds.) Leveraging Applications of Formal Methods, Verification and Validation: Discussion, Dissemination, Applications, ISoLA 2016. LNCS, vol. 9953, pp. 809–832. Springer, Cham (2016). https://doi.org/10.1007/978-3-319-47169-3_60
8. Braun, V., Margaria, T., Steffen, B., Yoo, H., Rychly, T.: Safe service customization. In: Intelligent Network Workshop, 1997. IN 1997. IEEE, vol. 2, p. 4, May 1997. https://doi.org/10.1109/INW.1997.601576

9. Cassel, S., Howar, F., Jonsson, B., Steffen, B.: Active learning for extended finite state machines. Formal Aspects Comput. **28**(2), 233–263 (2016)
10. Gnesi, S., Margaria, T.: Formal Methods for Industrial Critical Systems: a Survey of Applications. Wiley, Hoboken (2013). http://eu.wiley.com/WileyCDA/WileyTitle/productCd-0470876182.html
11. Graf, S.: Building correct Cyber-Physical Systems - can we improve current practice? In: Proceedings of the 23rd International Conference on Formal Methods in Industrial Critical Systems (FMICS 2018). LNCS, vol. 11119 (2018)
12. Hinchy, E., Carcagno, C., O'Dowd, N., McCarthy, C.: Using finite element analysis to develop a digital twin of a manufacturing bending operation. Procedia CIRP **93**, 568–574 (2020)
13. Howar, F., Isberner, M., Steffen, B., Bauer, O., Jonsson, B.: Inferring semantic interfaces of data structures. In: Margaria, T., Steffen, B. (eds.) Leveraging Applications of Formal Methods, Verification and Validation. Technologies for Mastering Change, ISoLA 2012. LNCS, vol. 7609, pp. 554–571. Springer, Heidelberg (2012). https://doi.org/10.1007/978-3-642-34026-0_41
14. Howar, F., Jonsson, B., Vaandrager, F.: Combining black-box and white-box techniques for learning register automata. In: Steffen, B., Woeginger, G. (eds.) Computing and Software Science. LNCS, vol. 10000, pp. 563–588. Springer, Cham (2019). https://doi.org/10.1007/978-3-319-91908-9_26
15. Howar, F., Merten, M., Steffen, B., Margaria, T.: Practical Aspects of Active Automata Learning, chap. 11, pp. 235–267. Wiley, Hoboken (2012). https://doi.org/10.1002/9781118459898.ch11
16. Howar, F., Steffen, B., Jonsson, B., Cassel, S.: Inferring canonical register automata. In: Kuncak, V., Rybalchenko, A. (eds.) Verification, Model Checking, and Abstract Interpretation, VMCAI 2012. LNCS, vol. 7148, pp. 251–266. Springer, Heidelberg (2012). https://doi.org/10.1007/978-3-642-27940-9_17
17. Hungar, H., Margaria, T., Steffen, B.: Test-based model generation for legacy systems. In: Test Conference 2003 Proceedings ITC 2003, International, vol. 1, pp. 971–980, October 2003. https://doi.org/10.1109/TEST.2003.1271205
18. Isberner, M., Howar, F., Steffen, B.: The TTT algorithm: a redundancy-free approach to active automata learning. In: Bonakdarpour, B., Smolka, S.A. (eds.) Runtime Verification, RV 2014. LNCS, vol. 8734, pp. 307–322. Springer, Cham (2014). https://doi.org/10.1007/978-3-319-11164-3_26
19. Isberner, M., Howar, F., Steffen, B.: The Open-Source LearnLib. In: Kroening, D., Păsăreanu, C.S. (eds.) Computer Aided Verification, CAV 2015. LNCS, vol. 9206, pp. 487–495. Springer, Cham (2015). https://doi.org/10.1007/978-3-319-21690-4_32
20. Issarny, V., et al.: CONNECT challenges: towards emergent connectors for eternal networked systems. In: ICECCS, pp. 154–161. IEEE Computer Society, June 2009
21. Ivanov, D., Dolgui, A.: A digital supply chain twin for managing the disruption risks and resilience in the era of industry 4.0. Prod. Planning Control **32**(9), 775–788 (2021). https://doi.org/10.1080/09537287.2020.1768450
22. Jonsson, B., Margaria, T., Naeser, G., Nyström, J., Steffen, B.: Incremental requirement specification for evolving systems. Nordic J. of Computing **8**, 65–87 (2001). http://dl.acm.org/citation.cfm?id=774194.774199
23. Jonsson, B., Margaria, T., Naeser, G., Nyström, J., Steffen, B.: On modelling feature interactions in telecommunications. In: Proceedings of Nordic Workshop on Programming Theory 1999–008. http://www.it.uu.se/research/publications/reports/1999-008/nwpt99/proceedings/

24. Karusseit, M., Margaria, T.: Feature-based Modelling of a Complex, Online-Reconfigurable Decision Support Service. ENTCS (2), 101–118. https://doi.org/10.1016/j.entcs.2005.12.049
25. Lundberg, S.M., Lee, S.I.: A unified approach to interpreting model predictions. In: Proceedings of the 31st International Conference on Neural Information Processing Systems, pp. 4768–4777. NIPS 2017, Curran Associates Inc., Red Hook, NY, USA (2017)
26. Margaria, T.: Knowledge management for inclusive system evolution. In: Steffen, B. (ed.) Transactions on Foundations for Mastering Change I. LNCS, vol. 9960, pp. 7–21. Springer, Cham (2016). https://doi.org/10.1007/978-3-319-46508-1_2
27. Margaria, T.: Generative model driven design for agile system design and evolution: a tale of two worlds. In: Howar, F., Barnat, J. (eds.) FMICS 2018. LNCS, vol. 11119, pp. 3–18. Springer, Cham (2018). https://doi.org/10.1007/978-3-030-00244-2_1
28. Margaria, T.: Making sense of complex applications: constructive design, features, and questions. In: Margaria, T., Graf, S., Larsen, K.G. (eds.) Models, Mindsets, Meta: The What, The How, and The Why Not? LNCS, vol. 11200, pp. 129–148. Springer, Cham (2019). https://doi.org/10.1007/978-3-030-22348-9_9
29. Margaria, T., Niese, O., Raffelt, H., Steffen, B.: Efficient test-based model generation for legacy reactive systems. In: HLDVT 2004: Proceedings of the High-Level Design Validation and Test Workshop, 2004. Ninth IEEE International, pp. 95–100. IEEE Computer Society, Washington, DC, USA (2004). https://doi.org/10.1109/HLDVT.2004.1431246
30. Margaria, T., Raffelt, H., Steffen, B.: Knowledge-based relevance filtering for efficient system-level test-based model generation. Innovations Syst. Softw. Eng. **1**(2), 147–156 (2005)
31. Margaria, T., Raffelt, H., Steffen, B., Leucker, M.: The LearnLib in FMICS-jETI. In: ICECCS 2007: Proceedings of the 12th IEEE International Conference on Engineering Complex Computer Systems, pp. 340–352. IEEE Computer Society, Washington, DC, USA (2007). https://doi.org/10.1109/ICECCS.2007.43
32. Margaria, T., Schieweck, A.: The digital thread in industry 4.0. In: Ahrendt, W., Tapia Tarifa, S.L. (eds.) Integrated Formal Methods, IFM 2019. LNCS, vol. 11918, pp. 3–24. Springer, Cham (2019). https://doi.org/10.1007/978-3-030-34968-4_1
33. Margaria, T., Steffen, B.: Service-Orientation: Conquering Complexity with XMDD. In: Hinchey, M., Coyle, L. (eds.) Conquering Complexity, pp. 217–236. Springer, London (2012). https://doi.org/10.1007/978-1-4471-2297-5_10
34. Margaria, T., Steffen, B.: eXtreme Model-Driven Development (XMDD) Technologies as a Hands-On Approach to Software Development Without Coding, pp. 1–19. Springer International Publishing, Cham (2020). https://doi.org/10.1007/978-3-319-60013-0_208-1
35. Margaria, T., Steffen, B., Reitenspieß, M.: Service-oriented design: the roots. In: Benatallah, B., Casati, F., Traverso, P. (eds.) Service-Oriented Computing - ICSOC 2005, ICSOC 2005. LNCS, vol. 3826, pp. 450–464. Springer, Heidelberg (2005). https://doi.org/10.1007/11596141_34
36. Merten, M., Steffen, B., Howar, F., Margaria, T.: Next generation LearnLib. In: Abdulla, P.A., Leino, K.R.M. (eds.) Tools and Algorithms for the Construction and Analysis of Systems, TACAS 2011. LNCS, vol. 6605, pp. 220–223. Springer, Heidelberg (2011). https://doi.org/10.1007/978-3-642-19835-9_18
37. Naujokat, S., Lybecait, M., Kopetzki, D., Steffen, B.: CINCO: a simplicity-driven approach to full generation of domain-specific graphical modeling tools. Int. J. Softw. Tools Technol. Transf. **20**(3), 327–354 (2017). https://doi.org/10.1007/s10009-017-0453-66

38. Neubauer, J., Margaria, T., Steffen, B.: Design for verifiability: the OCS Case Study. In: Formal Methods for Industrial Critical Systems: A Survey of Applications, chap. 8, pp. 153–178. Wiley-IEEE Computer Society Press (2013)
39. Nyström, J., Jonsson, B.: A formalization of service independent building blocks. In: Proceedings of the International Workshop on Advanced Intelligen Networks, pp. 1–14 (1996)
40. Raffelt, H., Steffen, B.: LearnLib: a library for automata learning and experimentation. In: Baresi, L., Heckel, R. (eds.) Fundamental Approaches to Software Engineering, FASE 2006. LNCS, vol. 3922, pp. 377–380. Springer, Heidelberg (2006). https://doi.org/10.1007/11693017_28
41. Raffelt, H., Steffen, B., Berg, T., Margaria, T.: LearnLib: a framework for extrapolating behavioral models. Int. J. Softw. Tools Technolo. Transf. (STTT) **11**(5), 393–407 (2009). https://doi.org/10.1007/s10009-009-0111-8
42. Raffelt, H., Steffen, B., Margaria, T.: Dynamic testing via automata learning. In: Yorav, K. (ed.) Hardware and Software: Verification and Testing, HVC 2007. LNCS, vol. 4899, pp. 136–152. Springer, Heidelberg (2008). https://doi.org/10.1007/978-3-540-77966-7_13
43. Ross, A.: The top 10 strategic technology trends for 2019, according to gartner. Information Age (2019). https://www.information-age.com/strategic-technology-trends-123475549/
44. Ryan, C., O'Neill, M., Collins, J.J.: Introduction to 20 years of grammatical evolution. In: Ryan, C., O'Neill, M., Collins, J.J. (eds.) Handbook of Grammatical Evolution, pp. 1–21. Springer, Cham (2018). https://doi.org/10.1007/978-3-319-78717-6_1
45. Schaefer, I., Lamprecht, A.L., Margaria, T.: Constraint-oriented Variability Modeling. In: Rash, J., Rouff, C. (eds.) 34th Annual IEEE Software Engineering Workshop (SEW-34), pp. 77–83. IEEE CS Press (2011). https://doi.org/10.1109/SEW.2011.17
46. Steffen, B., Howar, F., Isberner, M.: Active automata learning: from DFAs to interface programs and beyond. J. Mach. Learn. Res.-Proc. Track, **21**, 195–209 (2012)
47. Steffen, B., Margaria, T., Braun, V., Kalt, N.: Hierarchical service definition. Ann. Rev. Commun. ACM **51**, 847–856 (1997)
48. Steffen, B., Margaria, T., Claßen, A., Braun, V., Nisius, R., Reitenspieß, M.: A Constraint-oriented service creation environment. In: TACAS, pp. 418–421 (1996)
49. Steffen, B., Margaria, T., Nagel, R., Jörges, S., Kubczak, C.: Model-driven development with the jABC. In: Bin, E., Ziv, A., Ur, S. (eds.) HVC 2006. LNCS, vol. 4383, pp. 92–108. Springer, Heidelberg (2007). https://doi.org/10.1007/978-3-540-70889-6_7
50. Talkhestani, B.A., Jung, T., Lindemann, B., et al.: An architecture of an intelligent digital twin in a cyber-physical production system. Automatisierungstechnik, **67**(9), 762–782 (2019). https://doi.org/10.1515/auto-2019-0039

Never-Stop Context-Free Learning

Markus Frohme(✉) and Bernhard Steffen(✉)

Chair of Programming Systems, TU Dortmund, Dortmund, Germany
{markus.frohme,steffen}@cs.tu-dortmund.de

Abstract. In this paper, we revisit the concept of *never-stop learning*, a combination of active automata learning and runtime monitoring. Published research focuses on regular systems and became practical with the development of the TTT algorithm and its redundancy-free approach of storing information. With the recent development of our active learning algorithm for systems of procedural automata (SPAs), we can infer instrumented context-free/procedural systems via a simultaneous inference of individual (regular) procedures. In this paper, we combine these two concepts to lift the concept of never-stop (or life-long) learning to the level of context-free/procedural systems. In an empirical evaluation we show that using the TTT algorithm for procedural learning allows us to tackle internal (procedural) redundancy whereas the inherent compositional structure and instrumentation of our SPA approach allows us to tackle external (global) redundancy. A comparison with the alternative formalism of visibly pushdown automata (VPAs) shows that our approach performs better by multiple orders of magnitude, making it a valuable choice for *practical* never-stop context-free learning.

Keywords: Active automata learning · Never-stop learning · Procedural systems · Context-free languages · Runtime verification

1 Introduction

What first touched me (Bernhard), and what I will never forget, was Bengt playing Chopin at my supervisor's home back in 1985. Our scientific connection built up much later, when I came to Uppsala for sabbatical in 1999 and served on the ASTEC[1] advisory board in the beginning of this millennium. A few years later, Bengt joined our work on active automata learning [6–8,27,33] pushing towards more expressive representation languages, in particular, for capturing data. Together with, in particular, Falk Howar, who recently came back to our university as associate professor, we extended automata learning to register automata, a variant of automata capable of expressing dataflow [15,16,20,26–28,36]. This turned out to be a major breakthrough, paving the way towards capturing even more expressive automata (programming language-like) formalisms with the help of SMT solving [17–19]. Learning recursive structures, so-called

[1] The Swedish ....

E.-R. Olderog et al. (Eds.): Jonsson Festschrift, LNCS 13030, pp. 164–185, 2021.
https://doi.org/10.1007/978-3-030-91384-7_9

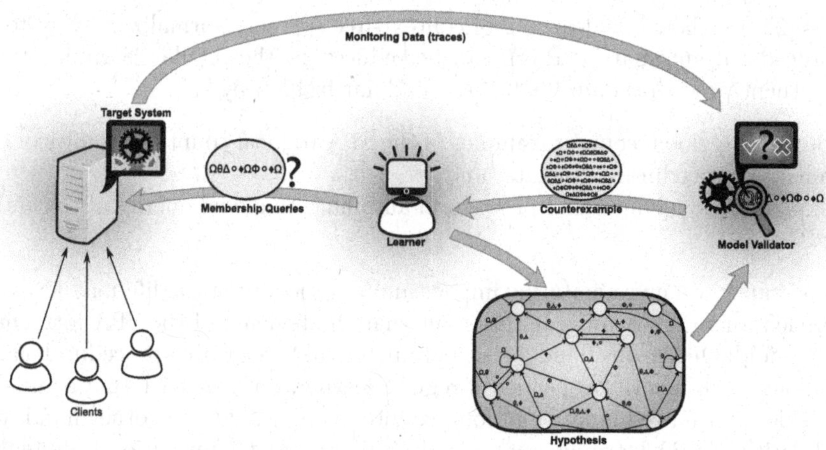

Fig. 1. Never-stop learning approach, proposed by Bertolino et al. [9] (source: [31])

procedural automata [12–14,21,22], is another research direction towards the goal of learning program-like structures [30,40].

In this paper, we revisit active automata learning (AAL) of recursive structures [22] under the perspective of never-stop or life-long learning (cf. Fig. 1) which is a paradigm jointly developed with Bengt in the CONNECT project [1,5,9,10,27,33]. The main idea behind never-stop or life-long learning is to instrument the (potentially in-production) system with a monitoring mechanism that observes and controls its runs on the basis of previously learned hypothesis models. Whenever the monitor recognizes a discrepancy between the current hypothesis model and the system (a so-called counterexample), we have detected either an error in the system or (the focus of this paper) an error in the hypothesis model in which case the monitored trace can be fed to the learner in order to refine the model and monitor. After hypothesis refinement the life-long learning process then continues with the next monitoring phase. This approach, which is characterized by its never-stopping, user-driven counterexample search, has shown promising results in a number of software projects in the past [9,33,38,41].

Life-long learning comes with a challenge: counterexamples may be excessively long as they typically arise as unexpected continuations of days-long normal operating. "Classical" AAL algorithms are not able to deal with this characteristic as their complexity depends (a least) linearly on the length of counterexamples. The TTT algorithm [31] has been specifically designed to address this problem. Its redundancy-free way of storing only relevant information throughout the learning process reduces the dependency on the length of counterexamples to a logarithmic factor, which turns life-long (never-stop) learning into a practical approach.

In [22] we show how learning of context-free systems, formalized by systems of procedural automata (SPAs), can be reduced to the regular learning of the constituent procedural automata in a modular fashion by

- projecting global counterexamples of the SPA to local counterexamples of the affected procedural automata, and
- expanding local queries of procedural automata to global queries of the entire SPA.

In this paper, we investigate the impact and practicality of the life-long learning approach for SPA learning. It turns out that the benefits of the SPA formalism are two-fold: On the one hand, being parameterizable regarding procedural learners allows us to inherit properties of regular learners such as TTT that enable us to tackle internal redundancy in long counterexamples. On the other hand, the modularity of SPA learning can be exploited to extract information from global counterexamples to dynamically optimize internal datastructures on-the-fly and tackle external redundancy.

Our evaluation further compares the performance of SPA learning with learning of visibly pushdown automata (VPAs) [2,3,29,35]. The difference is enormous. Admittedly, VPA learning is technically more general than SPA learning. On the other hand, we consider SPAs more practical, not only because of the mentioned performance difference, but also because they are much easier to comprehend and to work with.[2]

Outline. Sections 2 and 3 summarize the main definitions and concepts of [22]: Systems of procedural automata (SPAs) and the approach to infer these context-free systems by means of simultaneous inference of the individual (regular) procedures. In Sect. 4 we present the empirical evaluation of our approach and compare it with competing algorithms in this field of research. Section 5 concludes the paper and gives an outlook on possible future work.

2 Preliminaries

In this chapter we introduce the preliminary definitions and concepts for our procedural learning algorithm.

Active automata learning describes the inference of an unknown formal language by means of interacting with some form of teacher. In practice, one often associates a word of the language, i.e. a sequence of symbols, with a run of a system, i.e. a sequence of interactions, so that the inferred *language* of a system describes all successful executions of the system. Many AAL algorithms follow the *minimally adequate teacher* (MAT) framework introduced by Angluin [4], which operates in two alternating phases:

---

[2] See https://github.com/LearnLib/learnlib-spa for examples.

1. Exploration: The learning algorithm (or simply *learner*) poses *membership queries* (words over a predefined alphabet) to a membership oracle to test if a word is a member of the unknown language. They are often answered by testing/executing the word on the software-*system under learning* (SUL). The responses to these queries are then used by the learner to construct a hypothesis of the SUL.
2. Verification: Once a hypothesis is constructed, an *equivalence query* is posed to an *equivalence oracle* to decide whether or not the constructed hypothesis is equivalent to the SUL. If it is, the learning process terminates. If it is not, the equivalence query returns a *counterexample* (again, a word over an alphabet) which can be used to refine the previous hypothesis and start a new exploration phase.

While there have been plenty of success stories for AAL in the past, the process itself is neither correct nor complete because the black-box equivalence problem is in general undecidable [37]. Thus finding good approximations for equivalence oracles is of high importance for the practicality of AAL. Prominent are heuristics known from model-based testing [6,11]. An alternative is the life-long learning approach discussed in this paper.

The formal foundation of our SPAs are context-free grammars [24, Chapter 5]. For a context-free grammar, we interpret terminal symbols as atomic system actions and non-terminal symbols as invocations of procedures because the expansion process of a non-terminal effectively resembles the "execution" of a procedure. Key to our learning algorithm is an instrumentation that makes the start and the end of procedures observable. Formally, this can be achieved by enhancing the production rules of the context-free grammar (instrumenting the SUL) with new observable symbols at the start and end of each production rule. An example of this instrumentation is given in Fig. 2.

```
F  -> a |
      a F a |
      b |
      b F b |
      G |
      ε
G  -> c |
      c G c |
      F
```

```
F' -> F a R |
      F a F' a R |
      F b R |
      F b F' b R |
      F G' R |
      F R
G' -> G c R |
      G c G' c R |
      G F' R
```

Fig. 2. Left: production rules of an exemplary context-free grammar for palindromes over the three terminal symbols a, b, c, using two non-terminal symbols F and G. Right: production rules of the instrumented system, using the procedures F and G as observable *call* symbols and introducing an observable *return* symbol R.

To better distinguish between the different kinds of symbols and their respective roles, we introduce the notion of an *SPA alphabet*:

Definition 1 (SPA alphabet). *An* SPA alphabet $\Sigma = \Sigma_{call} \uplus \Sigma_{int} \uplus \{r\}$ *is the disjoint union of three finite sets, where* Σ_{call} *denotes the* call *alphabet,* Σ_{int} *denotes the* internal *alphabet and* r *denotes the* return *symbol.*

The SPA alphabet for the palindrome example in Fig. 2 is given by $\Sigma = \{F, G\} \uplus \{a, b, c\} \uplus \{R\}$ and we write $w \in \Sigma^*$ to denote words over an SPA alphabet. In the following, we differentiate between global words of an (instrumented) system and procedural words, where we use $\widehat{\ }$ to denote the procedural context. By adding (or removing) $\widehat{\ }$ from symbols and words, we switch between the two contexts. Given an SPA alphabet, we define (systems of) procedural automata as follows:

Definition 2 (Procedural automaton). *Let* Σ *be an SPA alphabet and* $c \in \Sigma_{call}$ *denote a procedure. A procedural automaton for procedure* c *over* Σ *is a deterministic finite automaton* $P^c = (Q^c, q_0^c, \delta^c, Q_F^c)$, *where*

- Q^c *denotes the finite, non-empty set of states,*
- $q_0^c \in Q^c$ *denotes the initial state,*
- $\delta^c \colon Q^c \times (\widehat{\Sigma}_{call} \uplus \widehat{\Sigma}_{int}) \rightarrow Q^c$ *denotes the transition function, and*
- $Q_F^c \subseteq Q^c$ *denotes the set of accepting states.*

We define $L(P^c)$ *as the language of* P^c, *i.e. the set of all accepted words of* P^c.

Definition 3 (System of procedural automata). *Let* Σ *be an SPA alphabet with* $\Sigma_{call} = \{c_1, \ldots, c_q\}$. *A* system *of procedural automata* S *over* Σ *is given by the tuple of procedural automata* $(P^{c_1}, \ldots, P^{c_q})$ *such that for each call symbol there exists a corresponding procedural automaton. The* initial *procedure of* S *is denoted as* $c_0 \in \Sigma_{call}$. *We define* $L(S)$ *as the language of* S, *i.e., the set of all words generated by the instrumented grammar induced by* $P^{c_1}, \ldots, P^{c_q}$ *and* c_0.

In essence, a procedural automaton resembles a deterministic finite automaton (DFA) that accepts the language of right-hand sides of (non-instrumented) production-rules for a specific non-terminal, where call symbols represent the corresponding non-terminals. Consequently, an SPA aggregates several production-rules that in total resemble an automaton-based representation of a context-free grammar (CFG). An SPA representation of the context-free grammar of Fig. 2 (left) is shown in Fig. 3.

Our proposed instrumentation allows us to deal with the different levels of observability of procedural invocations: In the DFA interpretation, the (non-terminal) call symbols need to be observable, whereas as in the CFG interpretation they are not. Therefore, we define the language of an SPA via its *instrumented* grammar interpretation (cf. Fig. 2, right) that allows us to observe procedural information that can be projected to an observable representation of the original production rule (cf. Sect. 3.2). Our projection exploits that any instrumented word of an SPA S is always *well-matched*, i.e. every (instrumented) call-symbol is at some point followed by its matching return symbol and vice versa.

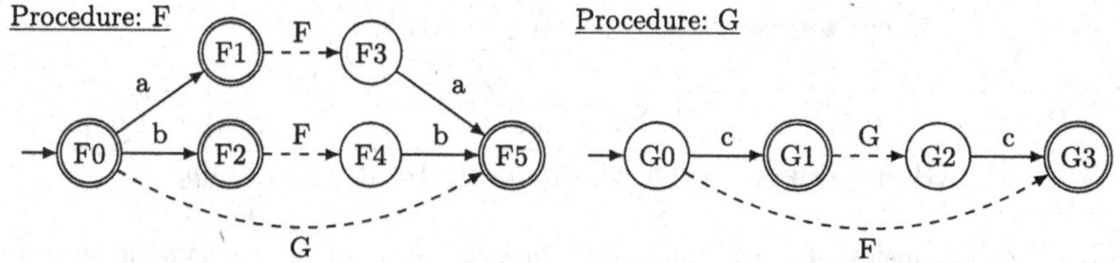

Fig. 3. An SPA representation of the context-free grammar of Fig. 2 with initial procedure F. Sink states and the corresponding transitions have been omitted for readability.

3 Compositional Learning

This chapter briefly summarizes from [22] the main concepts of our SPA learning algorithm. By construction, an SPA is characterized by its individual procedures. Therefore, the main task of inferring an SPA is to infer each of the individual procedural automata, which on its own is a regular inference problem. Our SPA learner coordinates individual regular learning algorithms (one for each procedure) and transforms information between the local procedural learners and the global (instrumented) context-free SUL.

Our instrumentation allows us for every procedural invocation p occurring in a successful run of the instrumented SUL to extract three fragments:

- an *access sequence* $as[p]$ (the prefix of the run reaching the call symbol of p)
- a *terminating sequence* $ts[p]$ (the subsequence of the run between the call symbol of p and its matching return symbol), and
- a *return sequence* $rs[p]$ (the suffix of the run starting from the matching return symbol).

Using these sequences we can switch between the local view of a procedural learner and the global view comprising the entire SUL via *membership query expansion* and *counterexample projection*.

3.1 Membership Query Expansion

During the local exploration phases, each regular learning algorithm poses membership queries which need to be answered by the SUL. However, each local learner only operates on a local view of a single procedure and not the actual global context-free system at hand. We solve this issue by translating *local queries* to *global queries*: We scan a (local) query and replace every single call symbol with a guaranteed successful run of the corresponding procedure, which can be constructed by using its terminating sequence. In order to embed the query itself in the correct context, we prepend the access sequence and append the return sequence of the procedure whose learner is posing the query. The translated query can then be posed to the global system and the response to the query is simply returned to the local learner. An example of this expansion step is shown in Fig. 4.

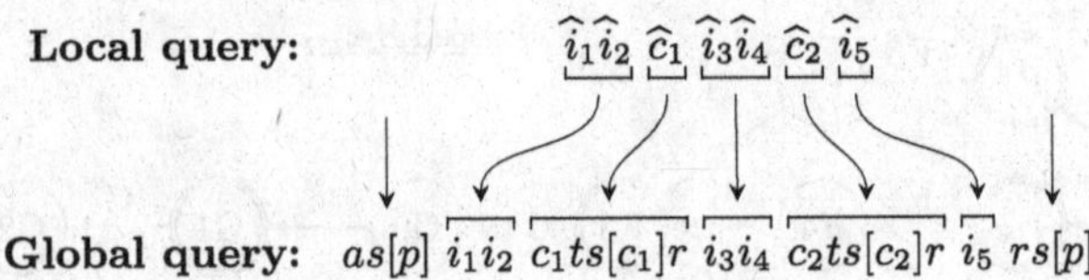

Fig. 4. The expansion of a local query of a procedural automaton p to a global query of the instrumented SUL.

3.2 Counterexample Projection

Upon hypothesis stabilization, the hypothesis SPA is checked for equivalence against the SUL, which may yield a global counterexample exposing in-equivalent behavior. The global counterexample can be analyzed to pinpoint a single procedure of the hypothesis SPA that behaves differently from its counterpart in the SUL. In order to refine the identified procedure, the concerned procedural sub-sequence of the global counterexample needs to be projected to a local context because it may contain nested procedural invocations which the local learner cannot process properly. This projection replaces every instrumented, well-matched occurrence of a procedural invocation with a single corresponding (non-instrumented) call symbol. This allows us to transfer information from the global context to the local context of the procedure and to construct a valid, local counterexample. An example of this projection step is shown in Fig. 5:

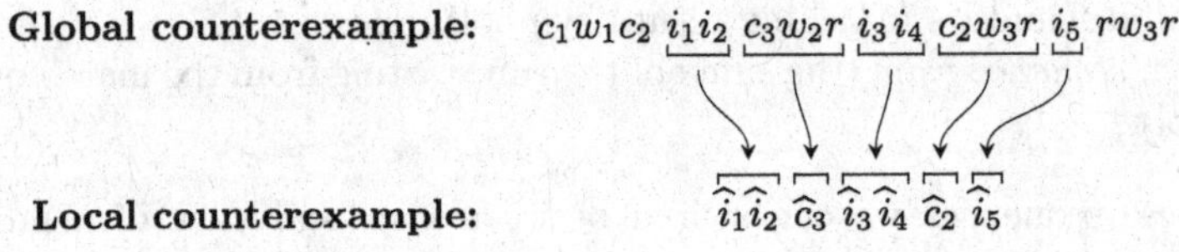

Fig. 5. The projection of a global counterexample in which c_2 has been identified as the violating procedure to a local counterexample for the concerned procedural automaton.

3.3 Sequence Optimizations

An integral property of our approach is that the projection step does not depend on a particular instance of an access, terminating or return sequence. They can be replaced on-the-fly throughout the learning process. This enables us to use two major optimization techniques that allow us to tackle the redundancy related problems encountered in the never-stop learning setting:

- Whenever we observe a shorter terminating sequence or a pair of shorter access and return sequences, we can replace the currently used ones and continue using the shortest found so far for future query expansion steps.

– Since we are inferring context-*free* systems, every occurrence of a nested, procedural invocation in any of the three sequences can be replaced by any valid terminating sequence without impacting the validity of the three sequences. By regularly replacing nested invocations with shortest terminating sequences, we can construct even shorter access, terminating and return sequences than we could originally extract from counterexamples.

As we show in Sect. 4.2, this translation has the potential to eliminate a majority of the external redundancy introduced in the never-stop learning scenario. Together with using TTT as a procedural learner to tackle the redundancy within local counterexamples, we can successfully tackle the problems of long counterexamples in the never-stop learning context and allow a practical application of this concept for context-free systems.

4 Experimental Evaluation

In this section we present our experimental setup and obtained results. For our experimental evaluation we looked at three different setups:

– Section 4.1 illustrates the effect of *internal redundancy* by comparing the performance of different regular learners for inferring the individual procedural automata in the context of global SPA learning.
– Section 4.2 illustrates the impact of *external redundancy* when using the best regular learning algorithm, i.e. the impact of excessive lengths of counterexample prefixes until an error is observed.
– Section 4.3 compares our approach with the formalism of visibly pushdown automata (VPAs) by Alur et al. [2,3], to our knowledge the only comparable formalism for which active automata learning algorithms have also been developed in the past [29,35].

For running the experiments, we used the open-source AAL library *LearnLib* [32] (version 0.13.1).

4.1 Inference Performance with High Internal Redundancy

For analyzing the performance of different SPA configurations, we conducted a series of 10 independent experiments and present in the following the averaged results of our observed data. Each experiment is characterized by a randomly generated SUL (see below) and an equivalence oracle that returns (local) counterexamples with a minimum length $lcel \in \{0, 25, \ldots, 1000\}$ to simulate internal redundancy. For each of the possible values of $lcel$, we investigated five different algorithms as local learners: L*, the algorithm by Angluin [4]; KV, the L* variant of Kearns and Vazirani [34]; RS, the L* variant using the counterexample analysis of Rivest and Schapire [39]; DT, the discrimination tree algorithm[3] by Howar [25] and TTT, the algorithm by Isberner et al. [31].

[3] Sometimes also called “Observation Pack” algorithm.

System Under Learning. For each experiment, we constructed an SPA alphabet with 10 call symbols, 25 internal symbols and the single return symbol. With this alphabet, we generated 10 random procedural automata (one for each call symbol) with 50 states each and selected an initial start procedure by randomly sampling a procedure from the call alphabet. From these components we constructed our random SPA-SUL which, in summary, had the following properties: $|\Sigma| = 36$ ($|\Sigma_{call}| = 10$, $|\Sigma_{int}| = 25$, $|\{r\}| = 1$) and $|S| = 500$ ($|P^c| = 50 \; \forall c \in \Sigma_{call}$).

During the construction of the SPA-SUL we also made sure that each procedural automaton was reachable from the chosen start procedure and each procedural automaton had a finite terminating sequence, so that our generated SUL represented a valid procedural system.

Counterexample Generation. For constructing local counterexamples of a specific length, we took the previously generated SPA-SUL as ground truth and compared this system in each verification step to the hypotheses returned by the learners. We randomly chose a procedural automaton of the SPA hypothesis which was not yet equivalent to the corresponding SUL procedure and constructed a *counterexample automaton.*[4] To generate a counterexample, we randomly sampled words of the required length (or longer if no exact counterexample existed) that were accepted by this automaton. These (local) counterexamples were then expanded to global counterexamples according to our expansion step (cf. Fig. 4) to constitute a proper global counterexample. To minimize the bias introduced by the expansion step and focus on the local redundancy aspect, we used shortest access, terminating and return sequences for this expansion.

Measurements. We investigated the following properties:

- **GCEL/LCEL ratio**: The *global counterexample length* (GCEL) to *local counterexample length* (LCEL) ratio to gauge if and how much the different configurations were affected by the expansion step during counterexample generation, which could potentially bias the results.
- **PCEL** The average *projected counterexample length*, i.e. the length of counterexamples that were forwarded to the local learning algorithms to measure any deviation from the *lcel* value.
- **Queries** [#]: The average combined number of membership queries posed by the SPA learner instance during (global) counterexample analysis and by the local learners during (local) hypotheses construction.
- **Symbols** [#]: The average accumulated number of symbols of each posed membership query.

[4] The product-automaton of the selected hypothesis procedure and its corresponding SUL procedure with symmetric difference (i.e., XOR) as acceptance criterion.

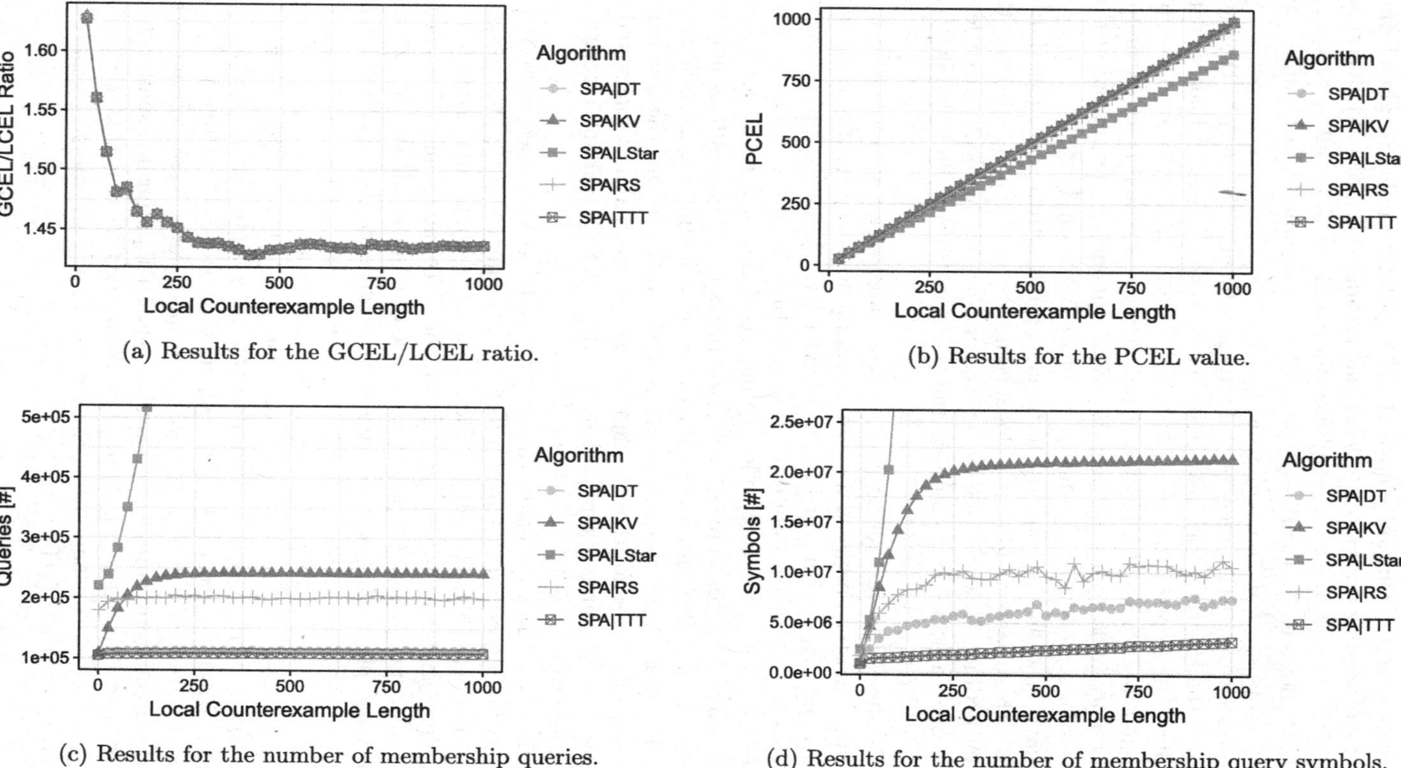

(a) Results for the GCEL/LCEL ratio.

(b) Results for the PCEL value.

(c) Results for the number of membership queries.

(d) Results for the number of membership query symbols.

Fig. 6. Results for the internal redundancy benchmark.

Results. Figure 6 shows our collected data. In Fig. 6a, we can see that for most *lcel* values the expansion step of local counterexamples to global ones added a symbol overhead of about 42% to each counterexample. What is more important is the fact that the overhead was almost identical for all local learner variants. This allows us to accurately compare the remaining data because each configuration was affected to a similar degree.

Figure 6b shows that the intended redundancy directly transfers to the local learners since the length of the projected counterexamples scales linearly with the *lcel* value. The slope of the averaged PCEL value is slightly below the value of 1 (most notably for the L* configuration) because a global counterexample may additionally expose in-equivalent behavior outside of the procedure that was selected for exposing in-equality (e.g. in its access and return sequence). Since we have used shortest access, terminating and return sequences during construction, these cases yield shorter local counterexamples and thus lower the average PCEL value. However, the overall redundancy at the local learner level still allows one to accurately compare the performance of the different local learning algorithms.

Figure 6c shows the number of queries each configuration posed. The classic L* algorithm uses every prefix of a counterexample for constructing subsequent procedural hypotheses. Consequently, the longer the counterexamples are, the more prefixes are added to its internal datastructure, resulting in more queries being posed as the counterexample length increased. The other learners extract from every valid counterexample only a single prefix or suffix, resulting in either a single new column in the observation table or in a single new node in the discrimination tree. As a result, after a short saturation phase the number of total membership queries for these configurations remained almost unaffected by the increase of local counterexample length. Of the four remaining algorithms, KV performed worst and TTT performed best.

Figure 6d shows the accumulated number of symbols of all posed membership queries. For each algorithm we can see, that with the increase of counterexample length, the number of posed symbols also increased. A slight increase was to be expected, since analyzing longer (global and local) counterexamples results in longer queries being posed. The drastic increase of L* comes from the fact that this learner also posed significantly more queries with increasing counterexample length. For the remaining learners we can see, that for *lcel* values greater than 250, the increase stabilized and longer counterexamples no longer affected the number of posed symbols unexpectedly. For the TTT algorithm, we can see that the impact of redundancy introduced by the counterexamples was tackled much earlier compared to the other algorithms, since the increase of posed symbols in the range of $0 \leq lcel \leq 250$ was much lower than for any other algorithm. For counterexamples of greater length, TTT performed similar to the other algorithms. This results in the best performance throughout all counterexample lengths, with less than 50% of the amount of posed symbols compared to the next best algorithm (DT).

Overall, the different configurations showed characteristics similar to their regular versions. This was to be expected since the inference process of an SPA is decomposed into a simultaneous inference of the regular procedures. With regard to dealing with internal redundancy, the data supports the notion of "inheritance" of the characteristics of the regular learning algorithms to the context-free case. In particular, TTT allows one to successfully tackle the problem of internal redundancy in context-free systems and therefore makes it a promising candidate to further investigate its performance in the context of external redundancy.

4.2 Inference Performance with High External Redundancy

In this series, we scaled the amount of input symbols before a counterexample for a procedure was observed (see below) to better simulate the structure of counterexamples in a monitor-like environment. We investigated four fixed configurations of the TTT learner ($lcel \in \{250, 500, 750, 1000\}$) to inspect the correlation between local and global redundancy and scaled the *external redundancy length* ($erl \in \{10^2, 10^3, \ldots, 10^6\}$) of the (local) counterexample. Again, we conducted 10 independent experiments and present in the following the averaged results.

System Under Learning. For the system under learning we used the same SPA-SULs from Sect. 4.1.

Counterexample Generation. For constructing counterexamples with a certain (global) overhead until an observable error occurred, we first generated a random successful run of the main procedure, with a fixed minimum length of 25 symbols and containing at least one call symbol (henceforth *expansion point*). For each expansion point in the run, we repeated this step (now generating a random successful run for the corresponding procedure of the expansion point) and replaced the expansion point with the generated run. We continued these generation/replacement steps recursively. Once the global trace reached the required minimal length, we expanded the currently processed expansion point with a valid counterexample trace (cf. Sect. 4.1) and replaced each pending expansion point with a terminating sequence (also with minimal length 25) containing only internal symbols to stop the recursion process.

Measurements. We investigated the following properties:

- **GCEL/ERL ratio**: The *global counterexample length* (GCEL) to *external redundancy length* (ERL) ratio to measure the overhead of our expansion step.
- **PCEL** The average *projected counterexample length*, i.e. the length of counterexamples that were forwarded to the local learning algorithms to measure how external redundancy impacts the counterexample length of the local learners.

- **Counterexamples [#] (pos./neg.)**: The average number of generated (global) counterexamples until the inference process terminated, split into positive and negative ones.
- **Queries [#] (normalized)**: The average number of posed queries throughout the learning process. Here, we differentiate between the combined (cf. Sect. 4.1) and the *normalized* number of posed queries, which only includes queries posed by the local learning algorithms and excludes queries from the global counterexample analysis.
- **Symbols [#] (normalized)**: The average accumulated number of symbols each posed membership query contained, also split between combined/normalized queries.

Results. Figures 7 and 8 show our collected data. In Fig. 7a we see that especially for small *erl* values, our expansion step significantly impacted the global counterexample length. This was to be expected, since a single expansion (25 symbols) already constitutes a quarter of the external redundancy length. However, with ongoing increments of the *erl* value this overhead became proportionally smaller, eventually stagnating around a value of 6 for *erl* values greater than 10^3. Most importantly, the expansion step again impacts every configuration to a similar degree, which allows us to adequately compare the remaining data.

With the increasing amount of the *erl* value we can see in Fig. 7b that the average length of the projected counterexamples decreased and converged to a value of approximately 25. Recall that after the redundancy threshold has been met, the counterexample generation inserted the (procedural) counterexample and replaced the pending expansion points with procedural invocations ranging over 25 symbols. Here, we can see the potential of our SPA approach to extract and utilize additional information available in a counterexample: While the original counterexample was embedded in local redundancy ($lcel \in \{250, \ldots, 1000\}$), the more global information was available, the more procedural information (invocations ranging over 25 symbols) could be used for individual procedural refinements. We can further see the impact of this additional information in the number of global counterexamples required.

In Figs. 7c and 7d we can see that with increasing *erl* values (and consequently increasing counterexample length) the counterexamples held more information as fewer were required for refining the hypotheses. This trend culminated in *erl* values of 10^5 and 10^6 for which only a single positive counterexample was sufficient for inferring the complete SPA-SUL in all configurations. An interesting characteristic in this experimental series is that for all *erl* values only positive counterexamples have been found. We will see this impacting the global query performance below.

In Figs. 8a and 8b we see the number of normalized queries and the number of symbols therein, i.e. the number of queries and symbols that the local, regular learning algorithms posed. For growing *erl* values this value slightly decreased which corresponds to the observations of Fig. 7b: The shorter the average projected counterexamples are, the fewer queries are required for their analysis. The

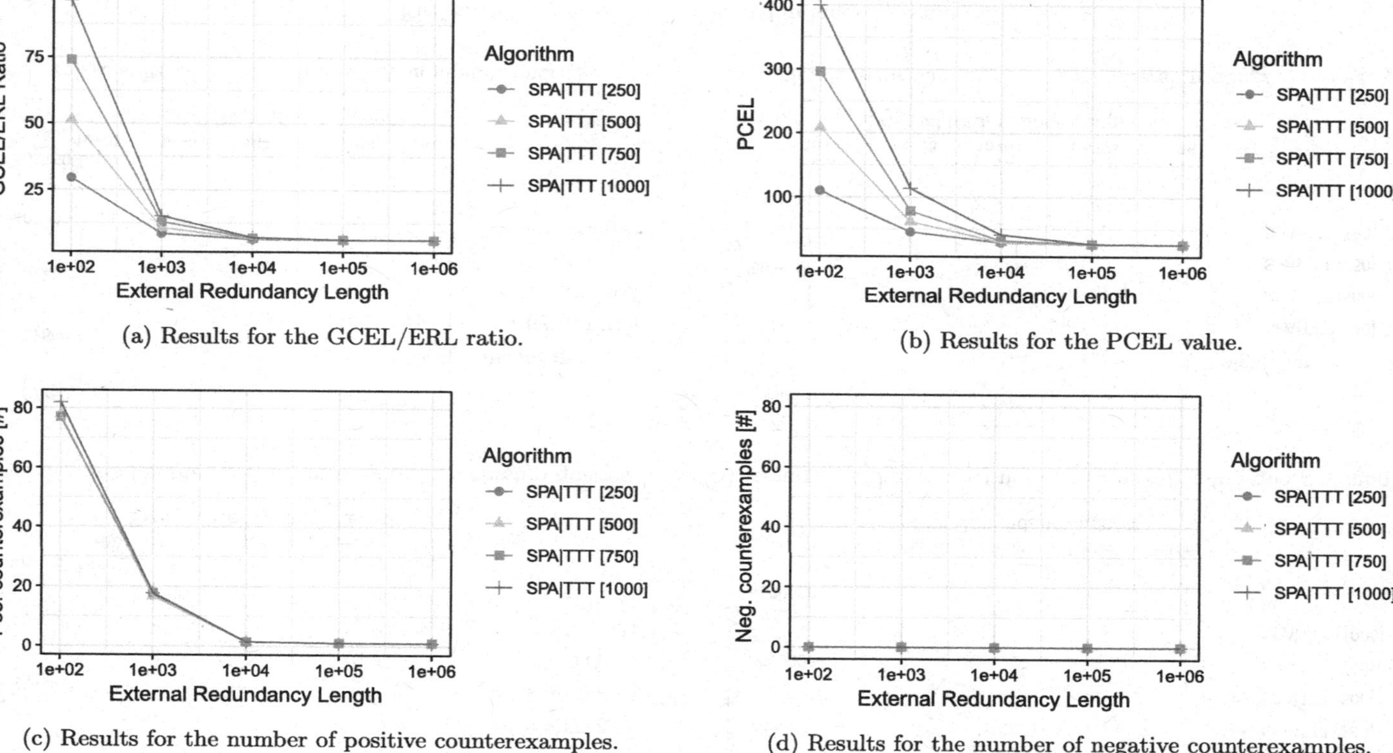

(a) Results for the GCEL/ERL ratio.

(b) Results for the PCEL value.

(c) Results for the number of positive counterexamples.

(d) Results for the number of negative counterexamples.

Fig. 7. Results for the external redundancy benchmark.

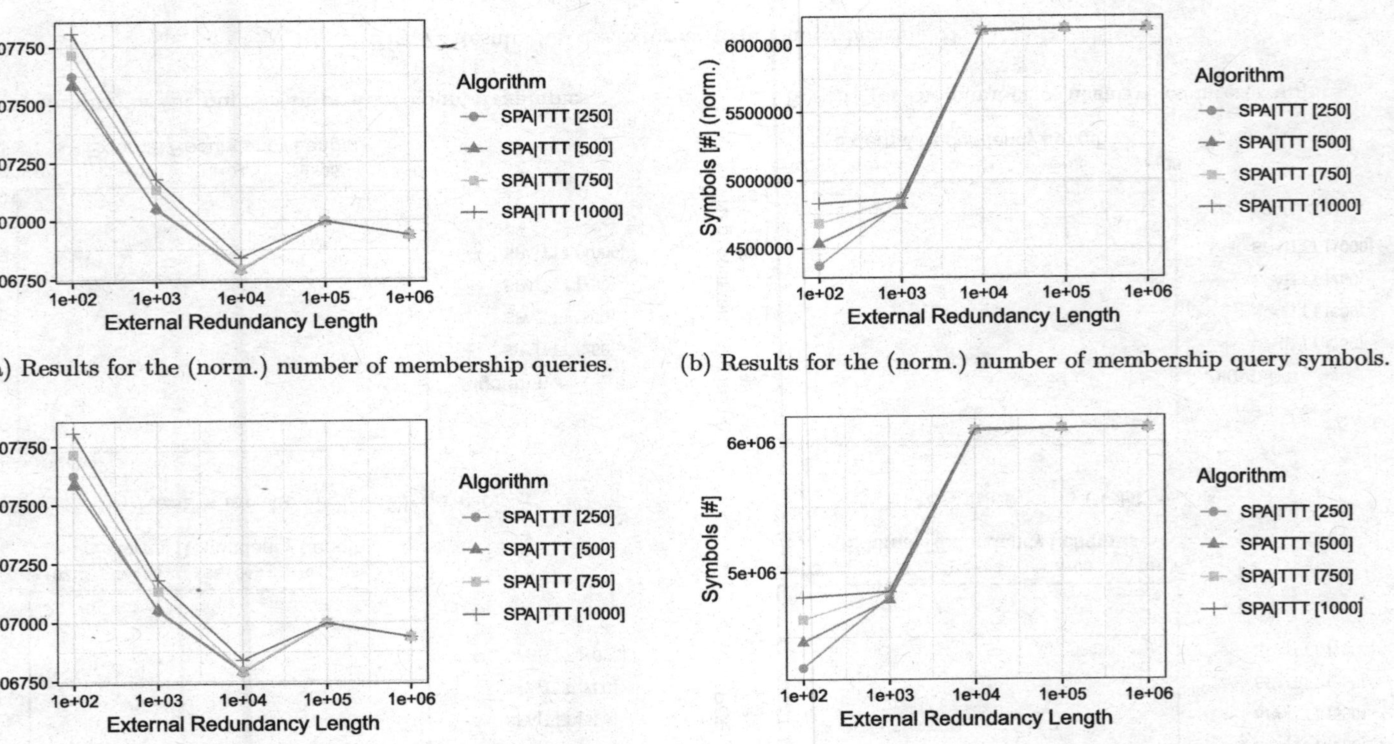

(a) Results for the (norm.) number of membership queries.

(b) Results for the (norm.) number of membership query symbols.

(c) Results for the number of membership queries.

(d) Results for the number of membership query symbols.

Fig. 8. Results for the external redundancy benchmark.

slight variance is explained by the random nature of the systems as well as the random counterexample generation.

The number of symbols correlates to the number of counterexamples (cf. Fig. 7c): The fewer counterexamples were encountered throughout the inference process, the less information was available for potentially improving access, terminating or return sequences. In its most extreme form, having only a single counterexample left the learner with exactly these information for embedding local queries into a global context. The constant performance for *erl* values greater than 10^3 further shows that, once the essential information about accessing, terminating and returning from a procedure was known to our approach, any additional redundancy did not affect its (local) inference performance.

Important to note here is that the number of (normalized) queries and symbols almost matches the data of Figs. 6c and 6d. Compared to the previous setup (cf. Sect. 4.1) the local learners required a nearly identical amount of queries which consisted of about twice the amount of symbols. Our concept of projection and expansion allows the local learning algorithms to nearly ignore all of the external redundancy.

In Figs. 8c and 8d we see that the query performance and symbol performance of the global learning algorithm is identical to the normalized case. This is because our SPA learner is able to analyze positive counterexamples without posing any additional queries to the SUL. As one can see this is a highly useful property in the never-stop learning setting where counterexamples with such high external redundancy are encountered regularly.

We want to emphasize the fact that, even with a single counterexample containing over a million symbols, the core inference process (cf. Figures 8a and 8b) almost matched the performance of a perfect environment (cf. Figures 6c and 6d): The idea of sequence optimization (cf. Sect. 3.3) almost eliminated any impact of external redundancy introduced in this experimental setup. To demonstrate the impact of our translation layer, we have run the same benchmark with a non-optimizing version of our algorithm which simply used the first access, terminating and return sequences encountered during the learning process. The results are shown in Fig. 9[5]. These results are highly promising for *never-stop learning* in the context-free scenario.

Admittedly, only encountering positive counterexamples benefited the (global) performance of our SPA learner. Our learner analyzes negative counterexamples in a binary-search fashion which adds a logarithmic overhead regarding query complexity. While this makes our approach competitive for this scenario as well, we are currently also investigating techniques (especially from the field of runtime monitoring) to further optimize its performance in this regard.

4.3 A Comparison to Visibly Pushdown Automata

This section compares our approach with the formalism of visibly pushdown automata by Alur et al. [2,3]. To our knowledge this is the only comparable for-

[5] The identical query performance is skipped.

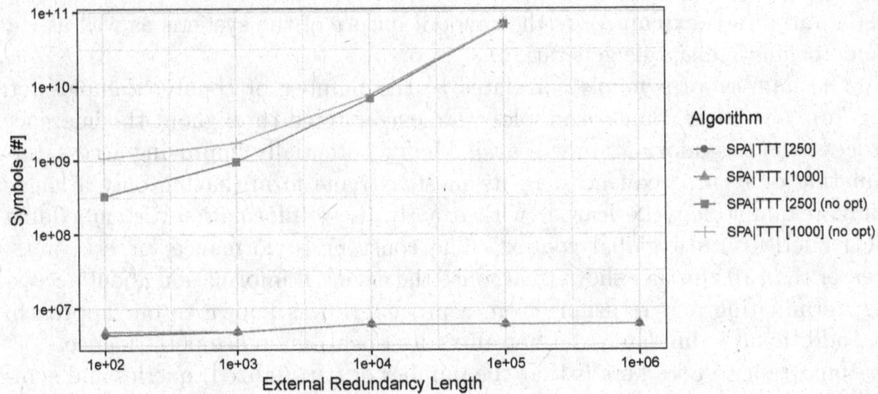

Fig. 9. Comparison of the optimizing and non-optimizing version of our approach for the external redundancy benchmark.

malism for which active automata learning algorithms have also been developed in the past [29,35].

In order to construct an experimental setup similar to Sects. 4.1 and 4.2, we would first have to transform our SPA to a corresponding VPA representation. This was unfeasible, due to a potential state explosion in the order of 50^{10} states. To avoid this state explosion, we chose to generate a *procedural characterization set* from the SPAs (see below). The VPAs learned on this basis are only guaranteed to approximate the full SPA behavior, but the results are clearly sufficient to make our point: The – admittedly slightly less general – SPA approach is by far more efficient than the VPA approach. As before, we conducted 10 independent experiments, for which we present the averaged data.

System Under Learning. We used the method of Sect. 4.1 to construct our SULs. However, due to runtime and memory constraints, we only generated procedural automata with 10 states, so that the final dimensions of our SPA-SUL in this setup were: $|\Sigma| = 36$ and $|S| = 100$.

Counterexample Generation. For constructing counterexamples, we took the previously generated SPA-SUL as ground truth and computed a *procedural characterizing set* (PCS): For each procedural automaton, we computed a local characterizing set (via the Wp method [23]) and used the concept of query expansion (cf. Fig. 4) to transform the local characterizing words to global ones. For this transformation, we used shortest access, terminating and return sequences. The PCS was then constructed by the union of all the (expanded) local characterizing sets. For finding counterexamples during the verification phase, we checked each word in the PCS, compared the expected output with the hypothesis output and returned the currently inspected word whenever there was a mismatch in outputs. For gauging the impact of counterexample length, we checked the traces of the PCS from shortest to longest (*ShoLo* variant) and from longest to shortest (*LoSho* variant).

Measurements. We investigated the following properties:

- **Hypothesis size**: For SPAs, this is the sum of number of states of the procedural automata. For VPAs this is the number of locations of the visibly pushdown automaton.
- **GCEL**: The average global counterexample length.
- **Queries** [#]: The combined number of queries, including counterexample analysis and hypothesis exploration
- **Symbols** [#]: The combined number of symbols the membership queries contained.

Results. The results are presented in Table 1. For the hypothesis sizes of the different algorithms, one can already see interesting properties of the learning algorithms:

- We can see that all hypotheses returned by the SPA-based learning algorithms were of the exact size of the originally generated SPA-SUL and further examination showed, they were in fact equivalent to the SPA-SUL. As such, the information contained in the PCS sufficed to characterize the global procedural system.
- The number of locations for the VPA highly exceeded the number of procedural states of the SPA. This in itself is an interesting observation, because previously [22] we have observed the opposite: For smaller and more structured systems, VPAs usually represented a system with fewer locations.
- The hypothesis size differed between the two VPA learners. This can be explained by the thorough counterexample analysis of the TTT variant, which – by posing more queries – also observes more system behavior. An interesting observation is that the *LoSho* variant, which checked (and returned) the longer PCS traces first, resulted in generally larger hypotheses of the identical SPA-SUL. We have yet to find a reasonable explanation for this.

In summary, these results show that the PCS is not complete for the formalism of VPAs, as both VPA learners returned a hypothesis conforming to the PCS but still not equivalent to the SUL-SPA (as the differences between the *ShoLo* and *LoSho* variant showed). So a truly equivalent model will have even more states and therefore have an even worse query performance (see below).

Regarding counterexample length we can see that in both configurations the counterexample length was about the size of a single procedural automaton. For the VPA learners it is interesting to see, that in both variants the average counterexample length was almost identical. It appears that there is a lot of variability in the VPA hypotheses because every trace of the PCS appeared to hold relevant information for this formalism: In the *ShoLo* variant the later,

Table 1. Averaged benchmark data for comparing the SPA and VPA approach. Top: *ShoLo* variant; Bottom: *LoSho* variant.

Algorithm	Hyp. Size	GCEL	Queries [#]	Symbols [#]
SPA—DT	100.0	7.29	13015.8	100975.6
SPA—KV	100.0	7.29	12917.9	100544.8
SPA—L*	100.0	6.75	25464.8	220237.8
SPA—RS	100.0	6.78	19686.7	160927.8
SPA—TTT	100.0	7.27	13470.7	99906.4
VPA—DT	1833.3	10.24	384486832.4	5621996712.8
VPA—TTT	2287.1	10.57	649920703.0	9647036650.7
Algorithm	Hyp. Size	GCEL	Queries [#]	Symbols [#]
SPA—DT	100.0	13.46	13014.7	176878.5
SPA—KV	100.0	13.44	13118.0	173778.4
SPA—L*	100.0	13.90	26547.6	346012.2
SPA—RS	100.0	13.78	19880.3	232591.6
SPA—TTT	100.0	13.53	13483.8	157626.8
VPA—DT	2234.4	10.78	542051650.0	10922349881.9
VPA—TTT	2597.8	11.91	648607182.2	11173838769.0

longer counterexample traces raised the average GCEL value whereas in the *LoSho* variant the later, shorter counterexamples lowered the GCEL value.

For the query complexity (both the number of queries and the number of symbols therein), we can see that our SPA approach drastically outperformed the VPA approach. The differences in the order of counterexamples (*ShoLo* vs. *LoSho*) mainly affected the number of symbols, although for the VPA—DT learner, the total number of queries was also affected. It is clear to see that in both variants the number of the queries and consequently the number of symbols posed by the VPA learners exceeded those of the SPA learners by multiple orders of magnitude.

5 Conclusion and Future Work

Motivated by the *never-stop/life-long learning* approach of Bertolino et al. [9] and the promising results of the TTT algorithm [31], we have analyzed the performance of our SPA learning algorithm for context-free systems in environments with high internal and external redundancy. Our empirical evaluation shows that using the TTT algorithm allows us to tackle internal (procedural) redundancy, whereas the inherent compositional structure and instrumentation of our SPA approach allows us to tackle external (global) redundancy. In fact, our observations suggest that the structure of procedural systems may be advantageous for learning scenarios with excessively long counterexamples like they arise in the monitoring-based life-long learning approach. Especially positive counterexamples which allow us to skip any work on (global) counterexample analysis turned out to have a huge beneficial impact on our benchmark performance.

Looking forward, we plan on further investigating the aspect of counterexamples for procedural/context-free systems. This not only covers AAL-related concepts such as the efficient analysis of (especially negative) counterexamples, but also counterexample generation. We believe that our formalism of SPAs is not only limited to AAL but may also be fruitful for fields such as (context-free) runtime monitoring and (context-free) runtime verification. We are looking forward to combine concepts from these fields to provide a practical formalism/framework for context-free runtime verification.

References

1. Aarts, F., et al.: Establishing basis for learning algorithms. Technical report, CCSd/HAL: e-articles server (based on gBUS) [http://hal.ccsd.cnrs.fr/oai/oai.php] (France), February 2010. http://hal.archives-ouvertes.fr/inria-00464671/en/
2. Alur, R., Kumar, V., Madhusudan, P., Viswanathan, M.: Congruences for visibly pushdown languages. In: Caires, L., Italiano, G.F., Monteiro, L., Palamidessi, C., Yung, M. (eds.) ICALP 2005. LNCS, vol. 3580, pp. 1102–1114. Springer, Heidelberg (2005). https://doi.org/10.1007/11523468_89
3. Alur, R., Madhusudan, P.: Visibly pushdown languages. In: Proceedings of the 36th annual ACM Symposium on Theory of computing, pp. 202–211. ACM (2004)
4. Angluin, D.: Learning regular sets from queries and counterexamples. Inf. Comput. **75**(2), 87–106 (1987)
5. Bennaceur, A., et al.: Machine learning for emergent middleware. In: Moschitti, A., Plank, B. (eds.) EternalS 2012. CCIS, vol. 379, pp. 16–29. Springer, Heidelberg (2013). https://doi.org/10.1007/978-3-642-45260-4_2
6. Berg, T., Grinchtein, O., Jonsson, B., Leucker, M., Raffelt, H., Steffen, B.: On the correspondence between conformance testing and regular inference. In: Cerioli, M. (ed.) FASE 2005. LNCS, vol. 3442, pp. 175–189. Springer, Heidelberg (2005). https://doi.org/10.1007/978-3-540-31984-9_14
7. Berg, T., Jonsson, B., Raffelt, H.: Regular inference for state machines with parameters. In: Baresi, L., Heckel, R. (eds.) FASE 2006. LNCS, vol. 3922, pp. 107–121. Springer, Heidelberg (2006). https://doi.org/10.1007/11693017_10
8. Berg, T., Jonsson, B., Raffelt, H.: Regular inference for state machines using domains with equality tests. In: Fiadeiro, J.L., Inverardi, P. (eds.) FASE 2008. LNCS, vol. 4961, pp. 317–331. Springer, Heidelberg (2008). https://doi.org/10.1007/978-3-540-78743-3_24
9. Bertolino, A., Calabrò, A., Merten, M., Steffen, B.: Never-stop learning: continuous validation of learned models for evolving systems through monitoring. ERCIM News **2012**(88), 28–29 (2012)
10. Bertolino, A., et al.:. Further development of learning techniques. Research report, February 2011
11. Broy, M., Jonsson, B., Katoen, J.-P., Leucker, M., Pretschner, A.: Model-Based Testing of Reactive Systems. LNCS, vol. 3472. Springer, New York (2005). https://doi.org/10.1007/b137241

12. Burkart, O., Caucal, D., Steffen, B.: An elementary bisimulation decision procedure for arbitrary context-free processes. In: Wiedermann, J., Hájek, P. (eds.) MFCS 1995. LNCS, vol. 969, pp. 423–433. Springer, Heidelberg (1995). https://doi.org/10.1007/3-540-60246-1_148
13. Burkart, O., Steffen, B.: Model checking for context-free processes. In: Cleaveland, W.R. (ed.) CONCUR 1992. LNCS, vol. 630, pp. 123–137. Springer, Heidelberg (1992). https://doi.org/10.1007/BFb0084787
14. Burkart, O., Steffen, B.: Composition, decomposition and model checking of pushdown processes. Nordic J. Comput. **2**(2), 89–125 (1995)
15. Cassel, S., Howar, F., Jonsson, B.: RALib: a LearnLib extension for inferring EFSMs. DIFTS, p. 5 (2015)
16. Cassel, S., Howar, F., Jonsson, B., Merten, M., Steffen, B.: A succinct canonical register automaton model. In: Bultan, T., Hsiung, P.-A. (eds.) ATVA 2011. LNCS, vol. 6996, pp. 366–380. Springer, Heidelberg (2011). https://doi.org/10.1007/978-3-642-24372-1_26
17. Cassel, S., Howar, F., Jonsson, B., Steffen, B.: Learning extended finite state machines. In: Giannakopoulou, D., Salaün, G. (eds.) SEFM 2014. LNCS, vol. 8702, pp. 250–264. Springer, Cham (2014). https://doi.org/10.1007/978-3-319-10431-7_18
18. Cassel, S., Howar, F., Jonsson, B., Steffen, B.: Active learning for extended finite state machines. Formal Aspects Comput. **28**(2), 233–263 (2016). https://doi.org/10.1007/s00165-016-0355-5
19. Cassel, S., Howar, F., Jonsson, B., Steffen, B.: Extending automata learning to extended finite state machines. In: Bennaceur, A., Hähnle, R., Meinke, K. (eds.) Machine Learning for Dynamic Software Analysis: Potentials and Limits. LNCS, vol. 11026, pp. 149–177. Springer, Cham (2018). https://doi.org/10.1007/978-3-319-96562-8_6
20. Cassel, S., Jonsson, B., Howar, F., Steffen, B.: A succinct canonical register automaton model for data domains with binary relations. In: Chakraborty, S., Mukund, M. (eds.) ATVA 2012. LNCS, pp. 57–71. Springer, Heidelberg (2012). https://doi.org/10.1007/978-3-642-33386-6_6
21. Frohme, M., Steffen, B.: Active mining of document type definitions. In: Howar, F., Barnat, J. (eds.) FMICS 2018. LNCS, vol. 11119, pp. 147–161. Springer, Cham (2018). https://doi.org/10.1007/978-3-030-00244-2_10
22. Frohme, M., Steffen, B.: Compositional learning of mutually recursive procedural systems. Int. J. Softw. Tools Technol. Transfer. **23**, 521–543 (2021). https://doi.org/10.1007/s10009-021-00634-y
23. Fujiwara, S., von Bochmann, G., Khendek, F., Amalou, M., Ghedamsi, A.: Test selection based on finite state models. IEEE Trans. Softw. Eng. **17**(6), 591–603 (1991)
24. Hopcroft, J.E., Motwani, R., Ullman, J.D.: Introduction to Automata Theory, Languages, and Computation. Addison-Wesley series in computer science, 2nd edn. Addison-Wesley-Longman, Boston (2001)
25. Howar, F.: Active learning of interface programs. Ph.D. thesis, TU Dortmund University (2012)
26. Howar, F., Isberner, M., Steffen, B., Bauer, O., Jonsson, B.: Inferring semantic interfaces of data structures. In: Margaria, T., Steffen, B. (eds.) ISoLA 2012. LNCS, vol. 7609, pp. 554–571. Springer, Heidelberg (2012). https://doi.org/10.1007/978-3-642-34026-0_41

27. Howar, F., Jonsson, B., Merten, M., Steffen, B., Cassel, S.: On handling data in automata learning - Considerations from the CONNECT perspective. In: Margaria, T., Steffen, B. (eds.) ISoLA 2010. LNCS, vol. 6416, pp. 221–235. Springer, Heidelberg (2010). https://doi.org/10.1007/978-3-642-16561-0_24
28. Howar, F., Steffen, B., Jonsson, B., Cassel, S.: Inferring canonical register automata. In: Kuncak, V., Rybalchenko, A. (eds.) VMCAI 2012. LNCS, vol. 7148, pp. 251–266. Springer, Heidelberg (2012). https://doi.org/10.1007/978-3-642-27940-9_17
29. Isberner, M.: Foundations of active automata learning: an algorithmic perspective. Ph.D. thesis, Technical University Dortmund, Germany (2015)
30. Isberner, M., Howar, F., Steffen, B.: Learning register automata: from languages to program structures. Mach. Learn. **96**(1), 65–98 (2014). https://doi.org/10.1007/s10994-013-5419-7
31. Isberner, M., Howar, F., Steffen, B.: The TTT algorithm: a redundancy-free approach to active automata learning. In: Bonakdarpour, B., Smolka, S.A. (eds.) RV 2014. LNCS, vol. 8734, pp. 307–322. Springer, Cham (2014). https://doi.org/10.1007/978-3-319-11164-3_26
32. Isberner, M., Howar, F., Steffen, B.: The Open-source LearnLib - A framework for active automata learning. In: Kroening, D., Păsăreanu, C.S. (eds.) CAV 2015. LNCS, vol. 9206, pp. 487–495. Springer, Cham (2015). https://doi.org/10.1007/978-3-319-21690-4_32
33. Issarny, V., et al.: CONNECT challenges: towards emergent connectors for eternal networked systems. In: ICECCS, pp. 154–161. IEEE Computer Society, June 2009
34. Kearns, M.J., Vazirani, U.V.: An Introduction to Computational Learning Theory. MIT Press, Cambridge (1994)
35. Kumar, V., Madhusudan, P., Viswanathan, M.: Minimization, learning, and conformance testing of Boolean programs. In: Baier, C., Hermanns, H. (eds.) CONCUR 2006. LNCS, vol. 4137, pp. 203–217. Springer, Heidelberg (2006). https://doi.org/10.1007/11817949_14
36. Merten, M., Howar, F., Steffen, B., Cassel, S., Jonsson, B.: Demonstrating learning of register automata. In: Flanagan, C., König, B. (eds.) TACAS 2012. LNCS, vol. 7214, pp. 466–471. Springer, Heidelberg (2012). https://doi.org/10.1007/978-3-642-28756-5_32
37. Moore, E.F.: Gedanken-experiments on sequential machines. Ann. Math. Stud. **34**, 129–153 (1956)
38. Neubauer, J., Windmüller, S., Steffen, B.: Risk-based testing via active continuous quality control. Int. J. Softw. Tools Technol. Transfer **16**(5), 569–591 (2014). https://doi.org/10.1007/s10009-014-0321-6
39. Rivest, R.L., Schapire, R.E.: Inference of finite automata using homing sequences. Inf. Comput. **103**(2), 299–347 (1993)
40. Steffen, B., Howar, F., Isberner, M.: Active automata learning: from DFAs to interface programs and beyond. J. Mach. Learn. Res.-Proc. Track **21**, 195–209 (2012)
41. Windmüller, S., Neubauer, J., Steffen, B., Howar, F., Bauer, O.: Active continuous quality control. In: 16th International ACM SIGSOFT Symposium on Component-Based Software Engineering, CBSE '13, pp. 111–120. ACM SIGSOFT, New York (2013)

A Taxonomy and Reductions for Common Register Automata Formalisms

Simon Dierl(✉) and Falk Howar(✉)

Department of Computer Science, TU Dortmund University, Dortmund, Germany
{simon.dierl,falk.howar}@cs.tu-dortmund.de

Abstract. Register automata model languages over infinite alphabets. A number of publications define different register automata formalisms. Equal expressiveness has been conjectured for many formalisms but a formal analysis is still open. In this paper on the occasion of the 63rd birthday of Bengt Jonsson we examine if these formalisms are equally expressive. We define a taxonomy to describe the different formalisms. By combining small-step reductions, we demonstrate that all models have equal expressiveness. We link these to model-specific complexity results for the NonEmptiness problem and decide which taxonomy features determine the complexity of NonEmptiness. The taxonomy enables formal classification of future models. The reductions permit transfer of formalism-specific results to other formalisms.

Keywords: Register automata · Non-emptiness · Decidability · Expressiveness

1 Introduction

Finite state machines are a common tool for modeling languages over finite alphabets and are amenable to algorithmic analysis. In recent years, the study of automata operating on *infinite* alphabets has gained some attention, e.g., in the field of automata learning [12]. The first extension of finite state machines to infinite alphabets was proposed by Kaminski and Francez [15]. An example of such a *register automaton* that can recognize strings in which a single character is repeated is given in Fig. 1. Subsequently, register automata have been extensively studied in literature. Many publications choose to use their own register automaton models, or variants of existing models. These models are more amenable to proofs or can express real-world concerns more succinctly. The succinct canonical register automaton [5,6] in Fig. 2, for example, expresses a fragment of the XMPP instant messaging protocol [21] in a way that is concise, easily understood, and can be inferred algorithmically [13] from tests.

While occasionally, the expressiveness of such formalisms has been noted to at least capture finite-memory automata (e.g., in [11]), no formal study of the different models' expressiveness has been conducted. Babari et al. provide a

E.-R. Olderog et al. (Eds.): Jonsson Festschrift, LNCS 13030, pp. 186–218, 2021.
https://doi.org/10.1007/978-3-030-91384-7_10

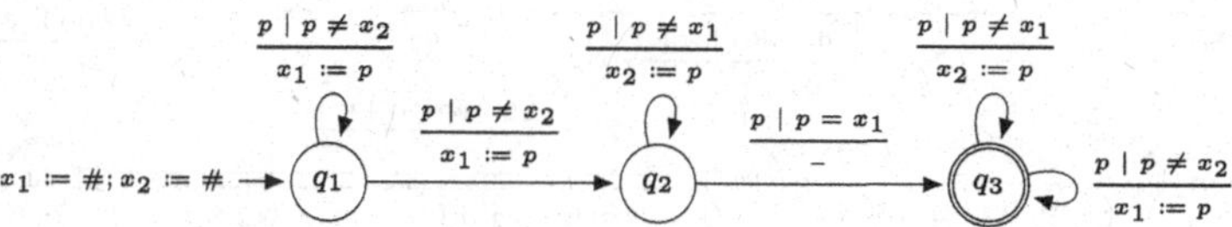

Fig. 1. Nondeterministic finite-memory automaton recognizing inputs in which at least one symbol occurs twice [15, Figure 1]. In the initial state q_1 the automaton reads and stores input until the duplicated symbol occurs. The symbol is recognized nondeterministically and state q_2 is entered. Input is read and stored until the saved symbol reoccurs. Then, the accepting state q_3 is reached.

taxonomy for extensions to the model of Kaminsky and Francez [1]. The complexity of NONEMPTINESS for different models of register interaction ("register disciplines") was examined by Murawski et al. in [17,18]. Cassel et al. [6] show that for some variants of their register automata that mimic restrictions imposed by other register automata formalisms the size of the automaton representation can blow up exponentially while expressiveness is not affected by the restrictions. Correspondingly, different complexity results have been proven for NONEMPTINESS: for Kaminsky and Francez's finite memory automata [15], the problem is NP-complete [22], for Murawski et al.'s more restricted model, it is NL-complete [17,18] and for Demri and Lazić's automata, it is PSPACE-complete [11]. A formal relation of different types of register automata would not only further our understanding of automata over infinite alphabets as a whole but could also serve as a basis for implementing and porting existing algorithms, e.g., in libraries for automata learning algorithms like LEARNLIB [14] or RALIB [4]. Learning algorithms have already been extended from register automata to some classes of more expressive extended finite state machines [7]. A formal analysis of the differences in expressiveness of different automata models (or lack thereof) may serve as a basis for further extensions and help understanding limits of expressivity.

In this paper on the occasion of the 63rd birthday of Bengt Jonsson, we provide a four-feature-taxonomy describing the most common types of register automata. For each feature, we define variants describing the types and individual reductions between variants to prove their equal expressiveness. We also present upper and lower bounds on the complexity of these reductions. Together with results from the literature on the complexity of deciding NONEMPTINESS in several register automaton models, we obtain a detailed characterization of the subtle differences between automata models as well as their expressiveness in relation to their size.

Outline. Section 2 will introduce data languages and provide a definition of generic register automata that encompasses all definitions found in the literature. Next, we will introduce a taxonomy of reductions in Sect. 3 and the taxonomy of register automata in Sect. 4, which will be applied to register automata definitions from the literature. Section 5 describes small-step reductions between the

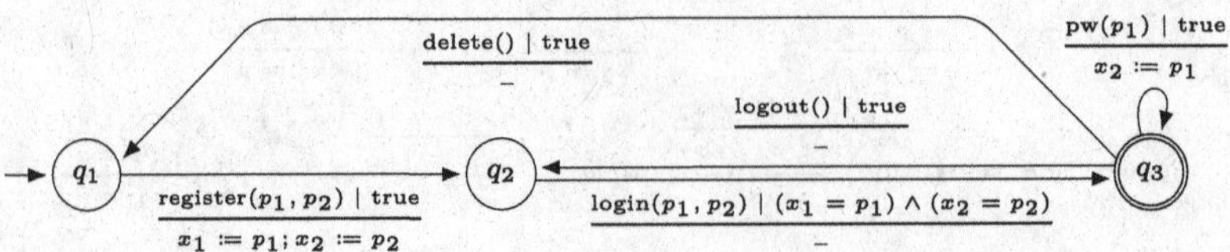

Fig. 2. Succinct Canonical Register Automaton that recognizes successful XMPP registrations and logins for a single user [5, Figure 1]. In the initial state q_1, no user is registered. By registering an account, state q_2 is entered and the credentials stored. A login with matching credentials enters state q_3. The logged-in user can update their password, log out or delete the account altogether.

taxonomy elements, including some lower complexity bounds; Sect. 6 combines these to construct reductions and lower bounds between the existing models. Section 7 summarizes our findings and describes possible extensions.

2 Preliminaries

We start by defining notation for some fundamental concepts.

Definition 1 (Power Set). *Given a set* S, $\mathfrak{P}(S) = \{S' \mid S' \subseteq S\}$ *is the* power set *of* S.

Definition 2 (Image). *Given a function* $f : A \to B$, $\mathfrak{I}(f) = \{f(a) \mid a \in A\}$ *denotes the* image *of* f.

Register automata operate on a combination of a finite and an infinite alphabet. The finite alphabet defines labels that are then combined with values from the infinite alphabet. We now formally define these combinations.

Definition 3 (Data Universe, Symbol, Word, Language). *A* data universe *is a tuple* $\mathcal{D} = (\Lambda, D, \mathfrak{a})$ *with a finite set* Λ *of* labels, *an infinite set* D *of* (data) values, *and an* arity *function* $\mathfrak{a} : \Lambda \to \mathbb{Z}_{\geq 0}$. *For a given label* λ, *the vector of* formal parameters *is* $P^\lambda = (p_1, \ldots, p_{\mathfrak{a}(\lambda)})$. *A* data symbol *is a tuple* $(\lambda, \vec{d})$ *with* $\lambda \in \Lambda$ *and a vector of data values* $\vec{d}$ *with* $|\vec{d}| = \mathfrak{a}(\lambda)$. *We usually write a symbol as* $\lambda(d_1, \ldots, d_{\mathfrak{a}(\lambda)})$. *A* data word *is a sequence of data symbols. A set of data words from the same data universe is a* data language.

Now, we provide a definition for register automata with equality and inequality comparisons. While in the literature, similar automata with more operations (e.g., less-than comparisons) have been studied, their expressiveness and theoretical properties are different from classic register automata. Our definition is designed to subsume all equality-based models present in the literature. These will later be represented as constraints for the following definitions.

Definition 4 (Register Automaton). *A* register automaton (RA) *is a tuple* $\mathcal{A} = (\mathcal{D}, Q, q_0, Q^+, X, X_Q, \chi_0, \Gamma)$, *defining*

- *a data universe* $\mathcal{D} = (\Lambda, D, \mathfrak{a})$,
- *a finite set of* states Q,
- *an* initial state $q_0 \in Q$,
- accepting states $Q^+ \subseteq Q$,
- *a finite set of* registers X *that can store data values,*
- *a* visibility function $X_Q : Q \to \mathfrak{P}(X)$,
- *an* initial valuation $\chi_0 : X \to D \cup \{\#\}$ *such that* $\# \notin D$ *is the* empty value *and for all* $x \notin X_Q(q_0)$, $\chi_0(x) = \#$, *and*
- *a set* Γ *of* transitions $\langle q, q', \lambda, g, u\rangle$, *each defining*
  - *a* source state $q \in Q$,
  - *a* target state $q' \in Q$,
  - *a label* $\lambda \in \Lambda$,
  - *a* guard g, *i.e. a propositional logic formula with an equality relation over free variables from* $X_Q(q) \cup P^\lambda$, *and*
  - *an* update $u : X_Q(q') \to (X_Q(q) \cup P^\lambda)$ *that selects new values for the registers visible in the target state, i.e.,* $u(x) = v$ *if the value of register or parameter* v *is copied to* x.

A transition $\langle q, q', \lambda, g, u\rangle$ is always written as

$$\frac{\lambda(p_1, \ldots, p_{|\mathfrak{a}(\lambda)|}) \mid g}{u},$$

where $p_1, \ldots, p_{|\mathfrak{a}(\lambda)|}$ are the formal parameters, g is the guard and u is a set of parallel updates $x_i := v$ with $v \in X_Q(q) \cup P^\lambda$. If no explicit assignment to a register $x_i \in X_Q(q) \cap X_Q(q')$ is given, the assignment $x_i := x_i$ is implicitly assumed.

Definition 5 (Deterministic Register Automaton). *A register automaton is* deterministic *if for each pair of transitions* $\langle q, q_1', \lambda, g_1, u_1\rangle$ *and* $\langle q, q_2', \lambda, g_2, u_2\rangle$ *with identical source state and label,* $(g_1 \wedge g_2)$ *is unsatisfiable.*

Note that our definition does not demand that a valid transition exists (i.e., the disjunction of all guards is a tautology), while e.g. [15, Definition 2] does. This can be rectified by adding a trap state and "missing" transitions. Now, we define how a register automaton processes words.

Definition 6 (State Transition). *For a register automaton* $(\mathcal{D}, Q, q_0, Q^+, X, X_Q, \chi_0, \Gamma)$ *with a transition* $\gamma = \langle q, q', \lambda, g, u\rangle \in \Gamma$, *a* state transition $\mathcal{T} = \langle q, \chi, \lambda(d_1, \ldots, d_{\mathfrak{a}(\lambda)}), q', \chi'\rangle$ *is a tuple of*

- source *and* target state q, q',
- *a data symbol* $\lambda(d_1, \ldots, d_{\mathfrak{a}(\lambda)}) \in \mathbb{D}_{\mathcal{D}}$,
- *a source valuation* $\chi : X_Q(q) \to D \cup \{\#\}$ *such that* g *is satisfied by the valuation* $\nu : X_Q(q) \cup P^\lambda \to D \cup \{\#\}$ *defined as*

$$\nu(v) := \begin{cases} \chi(v) & \text{if } v \in X_Q(q) \\ d_i & \text{if } v = p_i, \text{ and} \end{cases}$$

– a target valuation $\chi' : X_Q(q') \to D \cup \{\#\}$ *such that* $\chi'(x) = \nu(u(x))$.

Intuitively speaking, an RA automaton accepts a data word if there exists a sequence of state transitions from the initial to an accepting state using the word's symbols.

Definition 7 (Acceptance Behavior). *A register automaton* $A = (\mathcal{D}, Q, q_0, Q^+, X, X_Q, \chi_0, \Gamma)$ accepts *or* rejects *data words from its data universe. A data word* $\lambda_1(\vec{d_1}) \ldots \lambda_k(\vec{d_k})$ *is* accepted *if a sequence of state transitions* $\mathcal{T}_1, \ldots, \mathcal{T}_k$ *exists such that*

- *the source state of* $\mathcal{T}_1$ *is* q_0*,*
- *the source valuation of* $\mathcal{T}_1$ *is* χ_0*,*
- *the target state of* $\mathcal{T}_k$ *is in* Q^+*,*
- *for* $1 \leq i < k$*, the target state and valuation of* $\mathcal{T}_i$ *are the source state and valuation of* $\mathcal{T}_{i+1}$*, and*
- *for* $1 \leq i \leq k$*, the data symbol of* $\mathcal{T}_i$ *is* $\lambda_i(\vec{d_i})$*.*

A data word that is not accepted is rejected*. The language of words accepted by the automaton is* $L(A)$*.*

3 Reductions

In the previous section, we described a generic automaton model. Register automata with additional, disparate constraints have been studied in the literature. We call a set of automata with identical constraints a *class (of automata)*. To transfer decidability and complexity results between classes, we define reductions between classes. If the specific type of reduction is apparent from the context, we denote reducibility with the $\preceq$ operator.

Definition 8 (NonEmptiness-Turing Reduction). *Given two classes* C_1 *and* C_2 *of register automata,* C_1 *is* NonEmptiness-Turing reducible (NETR) *to* C_2 *if there exists an algorithm* $\mathcal{A}$ *that determines* NonEmptiness *for any* C_1*-automaton if* $\mathcal{A}$ *has access to an oracle that decides* NonEmptiness *for any* C_2*-automaton.*

Definition 9 (Membership-Turing Reduction). *Given two classes* C_1 *and* C_2 *of register automata,* C_1 *is* Membership-Turing reducible (MTR) *to* C_2 *if there exists an algorithm* $\mathcal{A}$ *that determines acceptance for any* C_1*-automaton and data word in its data universe if* $\mathcal{A}$ *has access to an oracle that decides* Membership *for any* C_2*-automaton and word from its data universe.*

We also define a reduction's complexity as the complexity of the underlying algorithm:

Definition 10 (Reduction Complexity). *Let* $\mathfrak{R}$ *be a type of reduction. Given a reduction of type* $\mathfrak{R}$ *such that the algorithm a is computable with complexity* T*, the reduction is a* T*-*$\mathfrak{R}$*.*

Definition 11 (Turing Reduction). *Given two classes C_1 and C_2 of register automata, C_1 is* Turing reducible (TR) *to C_2 if it is both* NONEMPTINESS- *and* MEMBERSHIP-*Turing reducible to C_2. If it is T*-NONEMPTINESS- *and T*-MEMBERSHIP-*Turing reducible for any complexity T, it is* T-Turing-reducible (T-TR).

These reductions are useful to prove lower bounds. We define a more constrained type of reduction as a transformation between automata and inputs analogously to Post [20]. Since the input-modifying function of this model is dependent on both automata's data universes, it is defined as a family of functions.

Definition 12 (Many-One Reduction). *Given two classes C_1 and C_2 of register automata, a* many-one reduction (M1R) *from C_1 to C_2 is a tuple $(f_A, f_{\mathbb{D}^\star}^{\mathcal{D},\mathcal{E}})$, where*

- *$\mathcal{D}$ and $\mathcal{E}$ are variables for data universes,*
- *$f_A : C_1 \to C_2$ is the* automaton reduction,
- *$f_{\mathbb{D}^\star}^{\mathcal{D},\mathcal{E}} : C_1 \times \mathbb{D}_\mathcal{D}^\star \to \mathbb{D}_\mathcal{E}^\star$ is a family of* data reductions,
- *given $A \in C_1$ with data universe $\mathcal{D}$ such that $f_A(A)$ has data universe $\mathcal{E}$,*

$$w \in L(A) \iff f_{\mathbb{D}^\star}^{\mathcal{D},\mathcal{E}}(A, w) \in L(f_A(A)), \text{ and}$$

- *$L(A) = \emptyset \iff L(f_A(A)) = \emptyset$.*

We will make this generic definition more specific, since the resulting automaton does not need to resemble the original automaton and, given enough computation time, it is possible to "solve" the original automaton during the reduction and create a trivial reduced instance. We define a more constrained reduction type that requires all modifications to the input to be computationally inexpensive. A linear time bound ensures that each symbol can be examined, but that no non-trivial computation can be performed on it. Additionally, all changes to the input must be independent of the source automaton and the surrounding symbols. Automaton- or word-specific information can only be added to the word as a prefix.

Definition 13 (Linear-Local Reduction). *Given two classes C_1 and C_2 of register automata, a* linear-local reduction (LLR) *from C_1 to C_2 is a tuple $(f_A, f_D^{\mathcal{D},\mathcal{E}}, f_{PA}^{\mathcal{E}}, f_{PD}^{\mathcal{D},\mathcal{E}})$, where*

- *$\mathcal{D}$ and $\mathcal{E}$ are variables for data universes,*
- *$f_A : C_1 \to C_2$ is the* automaton reduction,
- *$f_D^{\mathcal{D},\mathcal{E}} : \mathbb{D}_\mathcal{D} \to \mathbb{D}_\mathcal{E}^\star$ is a family of linear time computable* data reductions,
- *$f_{PA}^{\mathcal{E}} : C_1 \to \mathbb{D}_\mathcal{E}^\star$ is a family of linear time computable* automaton prefix-generating reductions, *and*
- *$f_{PD}^{\mathcal{D},\mathcal{E}} : \mathbb{D}_\mathcal{D}^\star \to \mathbb{D}_\mathcal{E}^\star$ is a family of linear time computable* data prefix-generating reductions

such that $(f_A, f_{\mathbb{D}^\star}^{\mathcal{D},\mathcal{E}})$ *with*

$$f_{\mathbb{D}^\star}^{\mathcal{D},\mathcal{E}}(A, w) = f_{PA}^{\mathcal{E}}(A) f_{PD}^{\mathcal{D},\mathcal{E}}(w) f_D^{\mathcal{D},\mathcal{E}}(w_1) \ldots f_D^{\mathcal{D},\mathcal{E}}(w_{|w|})$$

is a many-one reduction.

In some cases, we can omit the reduction functions to obtain an even simpler reduction.

Definition 14 (Prefix Free). *Given two classes* C_1 *and* C_2 *of register automata, a* prefix free reduction (PFR) *from* C_1 *to* C_2 *is a tuple* $(f_A, f_D^{\mathcal{D},\mathcal{E}})$*, where*

- $\mathcal{D}$ *and* $\mathcal{E}$ *are variables for data universes,*
- $f_A : C_1 \to C_2$ *is the* automaton reduction, *and*
- $f_D^{\mathcal{D},\mathcal{E}} : \mathbb{D}_{\mathcal{D}} \to \mathbb{D}_{\mathcal{E}}^\star$ *is a family of linear-time-computable* data reductions

such that $(f_A, f_D^{\mathcal{D},\mathcal{E}}, f_{PA}^\epsilon, f_{PD}^\epsilon)$ *with*

$$f_{PA}^\epsilon(A) = \epsilon \textit{ for all } A \in C_1 \textit{ and } f_{PD}^\epsilon(w) = \epsilon \textit{ for all } w \in \mathbb{D}_{\mathcal{D}}^\star$$

is a linear-local reduction.

Independently of the presence or absence of prefixes, some reductions do not modify the input word itself, e.g., when constants are transformed into a prefix, but the word is unchanged. We also formalize this property.

Definition 15 (Data Stable). *Given two classes* C_1 *and* C_2 *of register automata, a* data stable reduction (DSR) *from* C_1 *to* C_2 *is a tuple* $(f_A, f_{PA}^{\mathcal{D}}, f_{PD}^{\mathcal{D},\mathcal{D}})$*, where*

- $\mathcal{D}$ *is a variable for a data universe,*
- $f_A : C_1 \to C_2$ *is the* automaton reduction,
- $f_{PA}^{\mathcal{D}} : C_1 \to \mathbb{D}_{\mathcal{D}}^\star$ *is a family of linear-time-computable* automaton prefix-generating reductions, *and*
- $f_{PD}^{\mathcal{D},\mathcal{D}} : \mathbb{D}_{\mathcal{D}}^\star \to \mathbb{D}_{\mathcal{D}}^\star$ *is a family of linear-time-computable* data prefix-generating reductions

such that $(f_A, f_D^{\mathrm{id}}, f_{PA}^{\mathcal{D}}, f_{PD}^{\mathcal{D},\mathcal{D}})$ *with*

$$f_D^{\mathrm{id}}(d) = d \textit{ for all } d \in \mathbb{D}_{\mathcal{D}}$$

is a linear-local reduction.

Some reductions satisfy both properties, i.e., only the automaton structure is modified.

Definition 16 (Automaton-Only Reduction). *Given two classes* C_1 *and* C_2 *of register automata, a* automaton-only reduction (AOR) *from* C_1 *to* C_2 *is a function* $f_A : C_1 \to C_2$ *such that* $(f_A, f_D^{\mathrm{id}}, f_{PA}^\epsilon, f_{PD}^\epsilon)$ *is a linear-local reduction.*

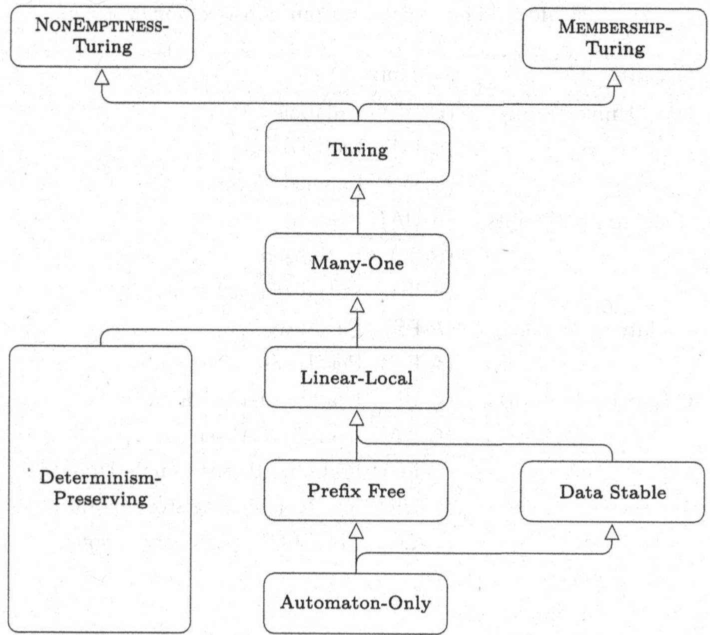

Fig. 3. The different types of reduction. Arrows indicate an is-a relation. If types are horizontally adjacent, a reduction can be a member of any subset of them.

The complexity of the Membership problem is lower for deterministic register automata, so we distinguish reductions that preserve the automaton's determinism.

Definition 17 (Determinism-Preserving). *A many-one reduction* $(f_A, f_{\mathbb{D}^*}^{\mathcal{D},\mathcal{E}})$ *is* determinism-preserving (DP) *iff for a deterministic register automaton* A*,* $f_A(A)$ *is deterministic.*

All types of reduction introduced in this section and their relations are outlined in Fig. 3.

4 Taxonomy for Register Automata Formalisms

This section describes the proposed taxonomy for RA models and applies it to existing models from the literature.

4.1 Proposed Taxonomy

In the literature, more restricted models of register automata than that described in Definition 4 have been studied. Each model adds constraints to certain aspects of the automaton. To describe these classes of register automata, we introduce

Table 1. The register automaton taxonomy.

Feature	Variants	
Data Universe Type	(U-UL)	Unlabeled
	(U-LU)	Labeled Unary
	(U-LV)	Labeled Variadic
Register Availability	(R-UA)	Update-Activated
	(R-IN)	Initialized
	(R-IE)	Initialized or Empty
Update Granularity	(A-PS)	Per State
	(A-PT)	Per Transition
Guard-Update Model	(G-UP)	Update-or-Present
	(G-UA)	Update-if-Absent
	(G-FG)	Full Guard with Single Update
	(G-NR)	No Register-Register Operations
	(G-CC)	Conjunction of Comparisons

a taxonomy using four features. It is outlined in Table 1. A class of automata with a common feature variant is described by its variant label, e.g., (G-CC). An intersection of feature variants is denoted with a plus, e.g., (A-PT)+(G-CC). If each automaton in a class is automatically member of another, this is denoted by the $\sqsubseteq$ operator, e.g., (G-NR) $\sqsubseteq$ (G-CC).

For each variant, deterministic and non-deterministic automata can be constructed. Since these are known to differ in expressiveness, we do not include determinism in this taxonomy. The taxonomy is therefore "orthogonal" to the question of determinism.

Data Universe Type. The first feature is the automaton's type of data universe, i.e., the number of labels and their arities. The variants are:

Unlabeled (U-UL). The data universe has a single label λ with arity $\mathfrak{a}(\lambda) = 1$. For brevity, the label is usually omitted.

Labeled Unary (U-LU). The universe contains an arbitrary number of labels, each with arity one.

Labeled Variadic (U-LV). The universe has an arbitrary number of labels, each with arbitrary arity.

By definition, (U-UL) $\sqsubseteq$ (U-LU) $\sqsubseteq$ (U-LV).

Register Availability. The second feature are the semantics of register availability, i.e., if registers are visible in every state and if initial values are provided for the registers. Three models are described in the literature:

Update-Activated (R-UA). Under this model, no registers are visible in the initial state. Therefore, $X_Q(q_0) = \emptyset$ and $\chi_0(x) = \#$ for all $x \in X$. All registers must be activated by an update operation before becoming visible. Since this will overwrite the register's contents, the empty values are effectively invisible to the automaton.

Initialized (R-IN). Registers are initialized to a non-empty value and all registers are visible in every state, so $X_Q(q) = X$ for all $q \in Q$ and $\chi_0(x) \neq \#$ for all $x \in X$.

Initialized or Empty (R-IE). Registers are initialized to a data value or # and are visible in every state. This is the only type of automaton that can encounter the empty value during a guard evaluation.

By definition, (R-IN) $\sqsubseteq$ (R-IE).

Update Granularity. The third feature describes the scope of update rules. Two models are present in the literature:

Per State (A-PS). For each state, there exists a single canonical update function. Each outgoing transition must either use the source state's canonical update function or keep all registers unchanged. As a result, all outgoing transitions must discard their parameter or write to the same register.

Per Transition (A-PT). Each transition's update can be arbitrarily defined.

By definition, (A-PS) $\sqsubseteq$ (A-PT).

Guard-Update Model. The fourth feature describes the form of guards and updates. Five models are prevalent in the literature:

Update-or-Present (G-UP). This model ensures that no duplicate values (except for #) can be present in the registers. Initial values – if present – must be distinct as well. All data symbols must have arity one. This invariant is maintained by the following transition semantics:

1. First, the update operation is executed. Four scenarios can occur:
   (a) The value is not assigned to a register.
   (b) The value v is assigned to a register x_i, but there exists a register $x_j \neq x_i$ with valuation $\chi(x_j) = v$. The assignment is then ignored.
   (c) The value v is assigned to a register x_i and $\chi(x_i) = v$. The assignment has no observable effect.
   (d) The value v is assigned to a register x_i and $\chi(x) \neq v$ for all $x \in X$. The update then stores the value in x_i.
2. Afterwards, the parameter is tested for equality with a single register, i.e., contrary to our definition, the guard takes the update operation into account. It can thereby check if a write operation was successful under the no-duplicates rule outlined above.

Under this model, two types of transitions can be expressed. They can be transformed to use guard-before-update semantics as follows:

1. The parameter p is assigned to x_i, then x_i is tested for equality with p. This test succeeds if either p was not stored in any register and the assignment was executed or if x_i contained p previously. The previous value of x_i is therefore irrelevant. Using a source state q, this yields following transition:

$$\frac{\lambda(p) \mid \bigwedge_{x \in X_Q(q) \setminus \{x_i\}} (p \neq x)}{x_i := p}$$

2. The parameter p is either not assigned or assigned to a register x_j with $j \neq i$, then x_i is tested for equality with p. This can only be

the case if the value of p was already present in that register. If p was assigned to x_j, the assignment can therefore have had no effect. Therefore, both cases yield the transition:

$$\frac{\lambda(p) \mid p = x_i}{-}$$

Update-if-Absent (G-UA). This model also does not allow duplicate values and all data symbols must have arity one. This invariant is maintained by allowing two classes of transition:

1. The parameter is tested for equality with a single register. The definition allows for multiple tests, but since no duplicates are present, multiple comparisons cannot succeed:

$$\frac{\lambda(p) \mid p = x_i}{-}.$$

2. Alternatively, an update operation is executed if the value is present in no register. Two scenarios can occur:
   (a) The value v is assigned to a register x_i, but there exists a register $x \in X$ (including $x = x_i$) with valuation $\chi(x) = v$. The transition fails.
   (b) The value v is assigned to a register x_i and $\chi(x) \neq v$ for all $x \in X$. The update then stores the value in x_i.

   Again, the definition allows multiple assignment, but only one attempt can succeed. This can be expressed as:

$$\frac{\lambda(p) \mid \bigwedge_{x \in X_Q(q)} (p \neq x)}{x_i := p}.$$

Full Guard with Single Update (G-FG). Duplicate values in registers are permitted. The parameter must be compared (using $=$ or $\neq$) to every visible register. The update may then write the parameter to a single register; no register-to-register assignments aside from the implicit self-assignments are permitted. For example, if $X = \{x_1, x_2, x_3\}$, the following transition satisfies these constraints:

$$\frac{\lambda(p) \mid (x_1 = p) \wedge (x_2 \neq p) \wedge (x_3 \neq p)}{x_2 := p}.$$

No Register-Register Operations (G-NR). Guards are a conjunction of comparisons between the parameter and registers. The parameter does not need to be compared to every register. The update may copy the parameter to multiple registers. For example, the following transition satisfies these constraints:

$$\frac{\lambda(p) \mid (x_1 = p) \wedge (x_3 \neq p)}{x_2 := p; x_3 := p}.$$

Conjunction of Comparisons (G-CC). Guards are a conjunction of parameter-to-parameter, parameter-to-register, and register-to-register comparisons. Updates may copy data from parameters and registers. For example, the following transition satisfies these constraints:

$$\frac{\lambda(p) \mid (x_1 = p) \wedge (x_2 = x_3) \wedge (x_3 \neq p)}{x_2 := p; x_3 := p}.$$

By definition, (G-UP) $\sqsubseteq$ (G-NR), (G-UA) $\sqsubseteq$ (G-NR), (G-FG) $\sqsubseteq$ (G-NR), and (G-NR) $\sqsubseteq$ (G-CC). (G-UP), (G-UA), and (G-FG) are not contained in one another.

We do not allow several combinations of (U-LV) that are difficult to define and are not present in the literature:

- (A-PS)+(U-LV) would require all outgoing updates to be identical. Given transitions on $\lambda(p_1)$ and $\mu(p_1, p_2)$, p_2 could not be assigned, since this update would not match the formal parameters of λ.
- (U-LV)+(G-NR) would permit circumventing the lack of register-to-register-comparisons by introducing "witness" parameters and using guards $(x_1 = p) \wedge (x_2 = p)$ to imply equality. Consequently, we also disallow (U-LV)+(G-UP), (U-LV)+(G-UA), and (U-LV)+(G-FG).

When discussing reductions between automata classes, a reduction might only be defined for a variant of a secondary feature and its supervariants. For example, a reduction might reduce (A-PT) to (A-PS), but will only be defined for automata that are at least (G-CC). A (A-PT)+(G-NR) automaton will be reduced to a (A-PS)+(G-NR) one, while a (A-PT)+(G-CC) automaton will yield a (A-PS)+(G-CC) one. We denote a reduction that requires a secondary feature and preserves it in the transformed automaton, as (A-PT)+(G-NR)$^{\sqsubseteq}$ to (A-PS)+(G-NR)$^{\sqsubseteq}$.

4.2 Classification of Some Existing Models

This taxonomy can now be applied to models from the literature. The descriptions are summarized in Table 2. For some of these models, complexity results are present in the literature and are recapped below.

Finite-Memory Automata. Kaminsky and Francez were the first to define a register automaton model [15]. They defined update-or-present semantics, enforced identical updates per state and initialization with empty registers and did not use labels. Bojańczyk et al. previously proved these automata to be equivalent in expressiveness to G-automata [3]. The model is characterized as (A-PS)+(U-UL)+(R-IE)+(G-UP).

Figure 4b shows a sample finite-memory automaton accepting the language D (i.e., all single-symbol words). Note that the transition from q_1 to q_2 is unusable since x_1 always has value # in q_1.

Table 2. Taxonomy of automata models.

Automaton model		Variant
Initialized finite-memory automata	[17,18]	(A-PS)+(U-UL)+(R-IN)+(G-UP)
Finite-memory automata	[15]	(A-PS)+(U-UL)+(R-IE)+(G-UP)
Neven-Schwentick-Vianu automata	[19]	(A-PT)+(U-UL)+(R-IE)+(G-UA)
Segoufin automata	[23]	(A-PT)+(U-LU)+(R-IN)+(G-FG)
Demri-Lazić automata	[11]	(A-PT)+(U-LU)+(R-IN)+(G-NR)
Succinct canonical register automata	[5,6]	(A-PT)+(U-LV)+(R-UA)+(G-CC)

Lemma 1 ([22, Theorem 1])**.** MEMBERSHIP *of words in deterministic finite-memory automata is* P*-complete.*

Lemma 2 ([22, Theorem 2])**.** MEMBERSHIP *of words in finite-memory automata is* NP*-complete.*

Lemma 3 ([22, Theorem 4])**.** NONEMPTINESS *of finite-memory automata is* NP*-complete.*

Initialized Finite-Memory Automata. Murawski et al. remarked on a variant of finite-memory automata [17,18] in which all registers are initialized with data values (i.e., no empty value # is used). The model is characterized as (A-PS)+(U-UL)+(R-IN)+(G-UP).

Figure 4a shows a sample initialized finite-memory automaton accepting the language

$$(D \setminus \{\mathtt{a}\}) \cup \{\mathtt{ba}\}.$$

In contrast to the automaton in Fig. 4b, all transitions are usable.

Lemma 4 ([17, Footnote 5])**.** NONEMPTINESS *of initialized finite-memory automata is* NL*-complete.*

Neven-Schwentick-Vianu Automata. Neven et al. presented a slight modification of finite-memory automata [19]. Their model additionally permits ε-transitions, i.e., transitions that do not consume input values. Additionally, it requires every input word to start with a designated start symbol. We propose this theorem, the proof of which is outside the scope of this paper:

Proposition 1. *Every automaton satisfying the model by Neven et al. can be transformed into a equivalent* (A-PT)+(U-UL)+(R-IE)+(G-UA) *automaton using our notation.*

Figure 4c shows a sample (transformed) Neven-Schwentick-Vianu automaton accepting the language

$$(D \setminus \{\mathtt{b}\}) \cup \{dd \mid d \in D \setminus \{\mathtt{b}\}\}.$$

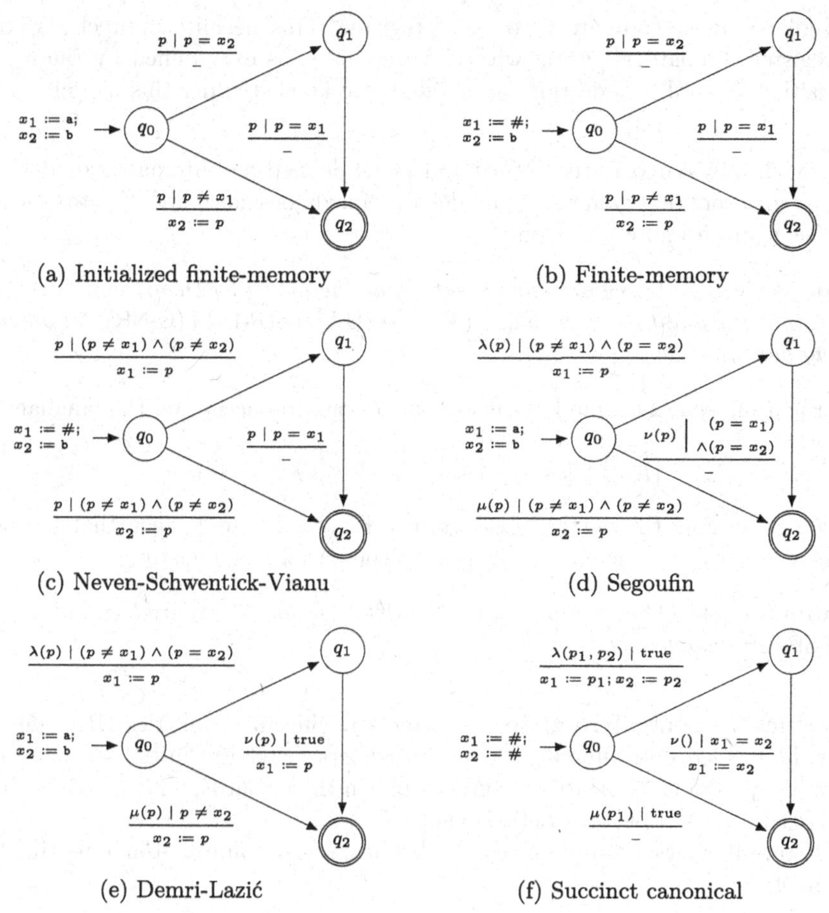

(a) Initialized finite-memory (b) Finite-memory

(c) Neven-Schwentick-Vianu (d) Segoufin

(e) Demri-Lazić (f) Succinct canonical

Fig. 4. Sample automata demonstrating the expressiveness of existing models.

In comparison with Fig. 4b's automaton, different assignment targets for transitions with the same origin are permitted and guards for assignments must compare the value to the target register.

Segoufin Automata. Segoufin's automaton model [23] extends finite-memory automata with per-transition updates and labels, does forbid empty registers and defines single update with full test semantics. The model is characterized as (A-PT)+(U-LU)+(R-IN)+(G-FG).

Figure 4d shows a sample Segoufin automaton accepting the language

$$\{\mu(d) \mid d \in D \setminus \{\mathsf{a}, \mathsf{b}\}\} \cup \{\lambda(\mathsf{b})\nu(\mathsf{b})\}.$$

In contrast to the automaton shown in Fig. 4c, #-intialized registers are not permitted. Guards and assignments can be used in arbitrary combinations, but guards must compare p to every register. This permits indirect register-to-register comparisons using witness parameters, as exemplified by the q_1-q_2-transition's guard. In addition, data values are labeled under this model.

Demri-Lazić Automata. Demri and Lazić defined an automaton model [11] for use in acceptance games. The model as-defined does not match this taxonomy, but we again propose a theorem:

Proposition 2. *Every automaton satisfying the model by Demri and Lazić can be transformed into a equivalent* (A-PT)+(U-LU)+(R-IN)+(G-NR) *automaton using our notation.*

Figure 4e shows a sample Demri-Lazić automaton accepting the language

$$\{\mu(d) \mid d \in D \setminus \{\mathsf{b}\}\} \cup \{\lambda(\mathsf{b})\nu(d) \mid d \in D\}.$$

When comparing this to the automaton in Fig. 4d, it can be seen that the permissible guard statements do not need to compare every register.

Lemma 5 ([11, Theorem 5.1(a)]). NONEMPTINESS *of Demri-Lazić automata is* PSPACE*-complete.*

Succinct Canonical Register Automata. Succinct canonical RAs [5] use variadic labeled data, update-activated registers instead of initialized ones and allow conjunctions of arbitrary comparisons in their guards. This model is characterized as (A-PT)+(U-LV)+(R-UA)+(G-CC).

Figure 4f shows a sample succinct canonical register automaton accepting the language

$$\{\mu(d) \mid d \in D \setminus \{\mathsf{b}\}\} \cup \{\lambda(d,d)\nu() \mid d \in D\}.$$

Note that in contrast to the other models such as the automaton in Fig. 4e, guards can compare registers, i.e., the availability of the q_1-q_2 transition depends on the values of p_1 and p_2 in the q_0-q_1-transition. Additionally, registers can be #-initialized, but must be written to before reading. Data values can have arbitrary arity, including arity zero.

5 Reductions Between Variants

In this section, we will examine reductions between the RA variants. While all variants have equal expressiveness, two lower complexity bounds for reductions as well as the non-existence of a specific reduction type are proven, outlining differences between the variants. This section considers each automaton feature in turn.

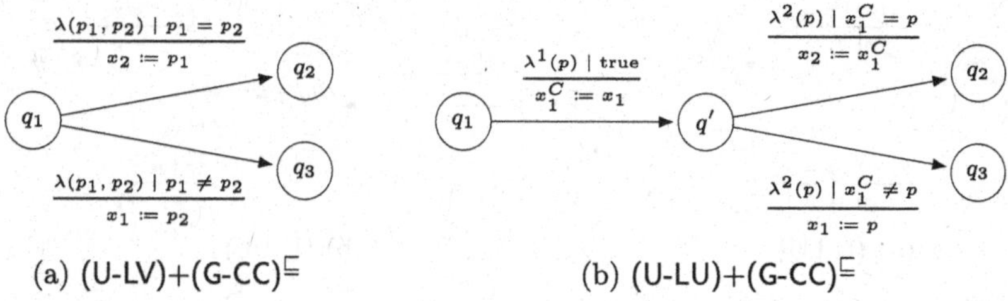

(a) (U-LV)+(G-CC)$^{\sqsubseteq}$ (b) (U-LU)+(G-CC)$^{\sqsubseteq}$

Fig. 5. Sample transformation from two (U-LV)+(G-CC)$^{\sqsubseteq}$ transitions to multiple (U-LU)+(G-CC)$^{\sqsubseteq}$ transitions.

5.1 Data Universe Type

Theorem 1. *There exists a determinism-preserving* P*-prefix free reduction from* (U-LV)+(G-CC)$^{\sqsubseteq}$ *to* (U-LU)+(G-CC)$^{\sqsubseteq}$.

Note that (U-LV)+(G-CC)$^{\sqsubseteq}$ = (U-LV), since (U-LV) is only defined for (G-CC). Intuitively, this reduction replaces each symbol of arity k with k symbols of arity one and modifies the automaton accordingly.

Proof Sketch. We construct a new input language in which we replace every label λ with $\mathfrak{a}(\lambda)$ labels $\lambda^1, \ldots, \lambda^{\mathfrak{a}(\lambda)}$. The data reduction then replaces every instance of $\lambda(\vec{d})$ with $\lambda^1(d_1)\ldots\lambda^{\mathfrak{a}(\lambda)}(d_{\mathfrak{a}(\lambda)})$. The automaton reduction modifies each state's outgoing transitions. For every label present, $\mathfrak{a}(\lambda)$ transitions to intermediate states are created. Since guards and updates can only be safely evaluated in the last transition, these transition only store their parameters in *cache registers.* The automaton requires a total of $\max_{\lambda\in\Lambda}\mathfrak{a}(\lambda)-1$ cache registers X^C. For each transition, a final step from the last intermediate state to the target state is generated during which guards and updates are evaluated, substituting cached values for the parameters.

For each word

$$\lambda_1(d_1,\ldots,d_{\mathfrak{a}(\lambda_1)})\ldots\lambda_k(d_1,\ldots,d_{\mathfrak{a}(\lambda_k)}) \tag{LV}$$

accepted by the original, the word

$$\lambda_1^1(d_1)\ldots\lambda_1^{\mathfrak{a}(\lambda_1)}(d_{\mathfrak{a}(\lambda_1)})\ldots\lambda_k^1(d_1)\ldots\lambda_l^{\mathfrak{a}(\lambda_k)}(d_{\mathfrak{a}(\lambda_k)}) \tag{LU}$$

is accepted by the newly created automaton. The construction ensures that each word accepted by the new automaton is of form LU, i.e., for each original label, all partial labels are present in the word in correct order. Such words can be reassembled into an input of form LV accepted by the original automaton, preserving acceptance behavior. □

The process is exemplified in Fig. 5. Note that in the example, the intermediate state q' is shared between transitions to preserve determinism.

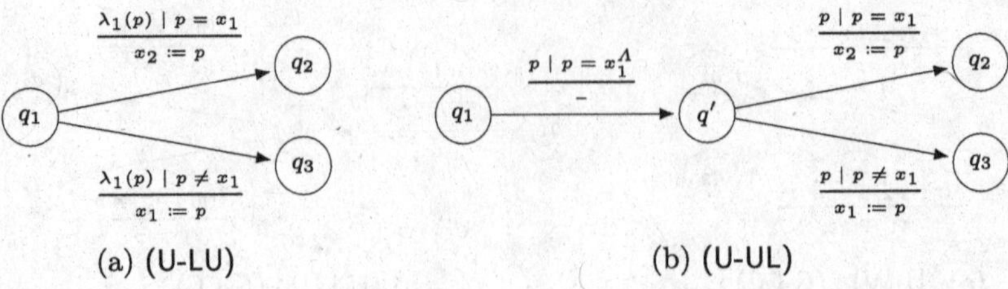

Fig. 6. Sample transformation from two (U-LU) transitions to multiple (U-UL) transitions.

Theorem 2. *There exists a determinism-preserving* P*-many-one reduction from* (U-LU) *to* (U-UL).

Proof Sketch. The reduction designates data values as proxies for labels and alternatingly reads a proxy and a "real" value. We require $|\Lambda|$ data symbols as *label proxies.* These proxies are stored in additional registers X^{Λ}, with λ_i being replaced by x_i^{Λ}. The input word $\lambda_1(d)\lambda_2(e)$ would then be replaced with $x_1^{\Lambda}dx_2^{\Lambda}e$. The proxy values are then added as a prefix and are assigned to the registers during an initialization before the first original transition. They must be selected to differ from any value in the input so that (G-UP) and (G-UA) semantics are retained, requiring access to both input and automaton.

For each label Λ_i present on a state's outgoing transitions, the automaton reduction creates a transition with guard $p = x_i^{\Lambda}$ and no assignment to an intermediate state similar to Theorem 1. For each original transition, a second transition from the matching intermediate state is created that uses the original guard, update, and target. □

If the automaton permits duplicate values in registers ((G-FG) and above), the proxies can be chosen at random instead, yielding a narrower reduction type.

Corollary 1. *There exists a determinism-preserving* P*-linear-local reduction from* (U-LU)+(G-FG)$^{\sqsubseteq}$ *to* (U-UL)+(G-FG)$^{\sqsubseteq}$.

An example of the transformation is shown in Fig. 6. As with the last example, the intermediate state q' is shared between transitions to preserve determinism.

All results presented in this section are outlined in Fig. 11a.

5.2 Register Availability

Theorem 3. *There exists a determinism-preserving* LIN*-automaton-only reduction from* (R-UA) *to* (R-IN).

Proof Sketch. The automaton-only reduction sets $X_Q(q) := X$ for all $q \in Q$, i.e., all registers are always visible. All updates are extended to assign the newly visible registers to themselves and the initial valuation is set to random values. Since these values are guaranteed to be overwritten before being accessed by a guard, this does not change the automaton's semantics. □

Theorem 4. *There exists a determinism-preserving* LIN*-data stable reduction from* (R-IE)+(G-FG)$^{\sqsubseteq}$ *to* (R-IN)+(G-FG)$^{\sqsubseteq}$.

Proof Sketch. We employ the proxy value technique presented in Theorem 2. The automaton reduction inserts an initial transition that reads a proxy value for # that is distinct from all non-# initial values and stores it in every #-initialized register and a new register, $x^{\#}$. If the proxy value is encountered in the input, the automaton's semantics could change. To preserve NONEMPTINESS, we ensure that every such input is rejected by modifying every guard g to $g \wedge (p_1 \neq x^{\#}) \wedge \cdots \wedge (p_{\mathfrak{a}(\lambda)} \neq x^{\#})$. The data prefix-generating reduction selects a proxy value from the data value set that does not occur in the remaining input. □

We can demonstrate that under common assumptions about complexity classes, more space-efficient reductions do not exist.

Theorem 5. *If* NL $\neq$ NP, *there exists no* NL-NONEMPTINESS-*Turing reduction from* (R-IE) *to* (R-IN).

Proof. We demonstrate that the existence of such a reduction permits the creation of an NL algorithm for an NP-complete problem. Assume that an NL-Turing reduction from (R-IE) to (R-IN) exists. Since NONEMPTINESS of initialized finite-memory automata can be decided in NL, we obtain an $\mathsf{NL}^{\mathsf{NL}}$ algorithm for NONEMPTINESS of finite-memory automata. Since the original problem is NP-complete and $\mathsf{NL}^{\mathsf{NL}} = \mathsf{NL}$ due to NL = coNL, NL = NP. □

Theorem 6. *There exists a determinism-preserving* LIN*-data stable reduction from* (R-IN) *to* (R-UA).

Proof Sketch. Again, we employ a proxy value technique to substitute values for the initialization. We then use an existing result to demonstrate the automaton's emptiness is unchanged. The automaton reduction inserts initial steps that reads $|X|$ *proxy values* and assigns them to the correct registers, ensuring that values that were equal in the initial valuation remain so. The automaton prefix-generating reduction can write the original initialization to maintain the original behavior.

We demonstrate that this reduction preserves NONEMPTINESS. For each word accepted by the original automaton, the proxy values can be set to the original initialization to create an accepting input. For the inverse direction, consider a word accepted by the new automaton. It consists of a prefix of length $|X|$ that is used to initialize the registers and a remaining input word. We define an automorphism on data values that maps the prefix's values to the source automaton's initialization. Since a register automaton's language is closed under automorphisms on the data value set [15, Proposition 2], the new automaton will accept the resulting word. By definition, this word must also have been accepted by the original automaton. □

All results presented in this section are outlined in Fig. 11b.

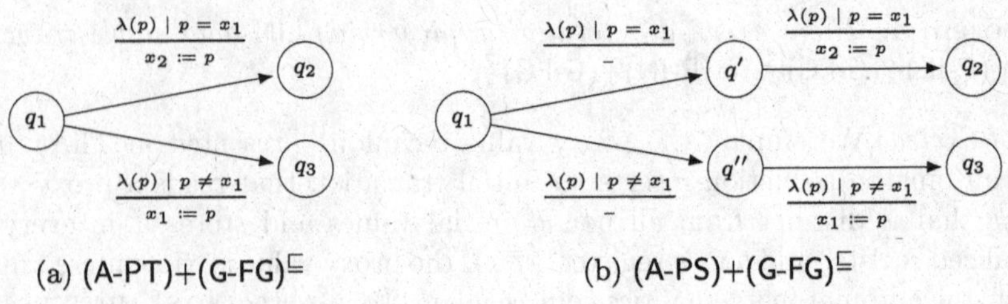

(a) (A-PT)+(G-FG)$^{\sqsubseteq}$ (b) (A-PS)+(G-FG)$^{\sqsubseteq}$

Fig. 7. Sample transformation from two (A-PT)+(G-FG)$^{\sqsubseteq}$ transitions to multiple (A-PS)+(G-FG)$^{\sqsubseteq}$ transitions.

5.3 Update Granularity

Theorem 7. *There exists a determinism-preserving* LIN*-prefix free reduction from* (A-PT)+(G-FG)$^{\sqsubseteq}$ *to* (A-PS)+(G-FG)$^{\sqsubseteq}$.

Proof Sketch. This reduction requires duplication of every input symbol. The first instance is used to make a transition to an intermediate state, while the second is used in the assignment.

The automaton reduction modifies all transitions. Given a transition

$$\frac{\lambda(p_1,\ldots,p_{\mathfrak{a}(\lambda)}) \mid g}{a},$$

it introduces an intermediate state. The transition from intermediate to target state is identical to the original and the transition from source to intermediate state is

$$\frac{\lambda(p_1,\ldots,p_{\mathfrak{a}(\lambda)}) \mid g}{-}.$$

Since all guards remain identical, determinism is preserved.

The data reduction duplicates every data symbol in the input word. Due to the structure of the new automaton, an accepted word can be transformed to an accepting word for the original by removing all symbols in odd positions, preserving emptiness. □

An example is shown in Fig. 7. For other guard-update models, the reduction needs to be modified slightly.

Theorem 8. *There exists a determinism-preserving* LIN*-prefix free reduction from* (A-PT)+(G-UP) *to* (A-PS)+(G-UP) *and from* (A-PT)+(G-UA) *to* (A-PS)+(G-UA).

Proof Sketch. Due to the limited types of transitions available, the technique used in the last proof needs to be adapted to these classes.

We alter the automaton by adding $|\Lambda|$ additional *scratch registers* X^{Λ} to the automaton and initializing it to data values D^{Λ} not present in the input. The

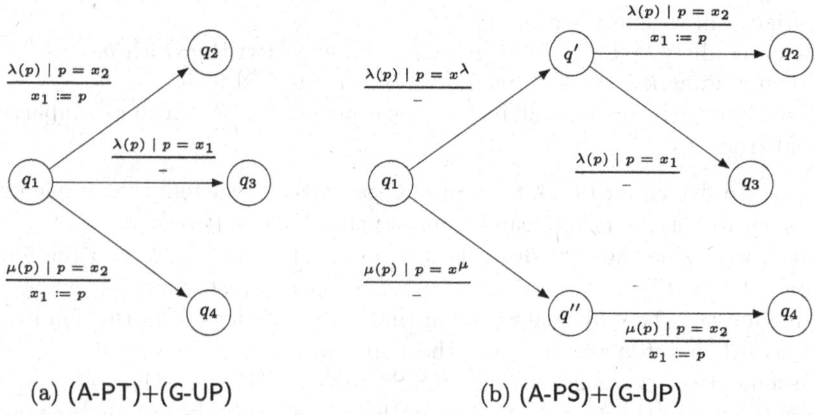

Fig. 8. Sample transformation from two (A-PT)+(G-UP) transitions to multiple (A-PS)+(G-UP) transitions. The transitions to q_2 and q_3 both used label λ and now share the intermediate state q'. The transition to q_4 was labeled μ and is reached over a separate state q''.

reduction then introduces intermediate states similar to the proof of Theorem 7. However, we use the transition

$$\frac{\lambda(p) \mid p = x^\lambda}{-}$$

to transit from source to intermediate state. Since these transitions are mutually exclusive and transitions from the intermediate to the target state are copied as-is, determinism is preserved.

The data reduction inserts d_s before every data symbol in the input word. Again, an accepted word can be transformed to an accepting word for the original by removing all symbols in odd positions, preserving emptiness. □

An example for this variant (using (G-UP) semantics) is given in Fig. 8. Duplication or insertion of dummy symbols is required to efficiently perform the reduction. If the data language is untouched, no efficient algorithm exists:

Theorem 9. *There exists no determinism-preserving data stable reduction from* (A-PT) *to* (A-PS).

Proof Sketch. Intuitively, a (A-PT)+(G-NR) automaton can store information by selecting an assignment's target register. A (A-PS)+(G-NR) automaton is forced to store the same information by transitioning to different states. This results in a superpolynomial amount of required states for certain languages.

We provide a (U-LU) language that can be recognized by a (A-PT) automaton of size k. Then, we prove by contradiction that a (A-PS) automaton must have $k!$ states to recognize the same language. The language uses labels $\lambda_1, \ldots, \lambda_\ell, \kappa_1, \ldots, \kappa_\ell$ to simulate an *ℓ-memory cell* storage as follows:

- Initially, all registers are empty.
- When reading $\lambda_k(p)$, the k-th memory cell is overwritten with p.
- When reading κ_k, the k-th memory cell is compared to p.
- The language is the set of all instruction sequences for which all κ-comparisons hold true.

A two-state deterministic (A-PT) automaton with k registers that implements memory cells using registers can be constructed for this language.

Now, we define the permutations $\pi : \{1, \ldots, k\} \rightarrow \{1, \ldots, k\}$ and the family of input strings $S^\pi := \lambda_{\pi(1)}(p_1)\lambda_{\pi(2)}(p_2) \ldots \lambda_{\pi(k)}(p_k)$ for distinct $p_0, \ldots, p_k$. We now inductively show by contradiction that no two strings from this family can cause a (A-PS) automaton to enter the same state.

Assume that two such strings $S^\pi, S^{\pi'}$ exist, $\pi(1) \neq \pi'(1)$ and that the automaton enters the same state after both strings. Since the automaton started in the same state, p_1 must have been written to the same register x_1 and must not have been overwritten on any path (otherwise, $\kappa_{\pi(1)}$ and $\kappa_{\pi'(1)}$ cannot be handled).

Now, assume the automaton reads $\kappa_{\pi(1)}(p_1)$. It will accept after the input S^π and reject after $S^{\pi'}$. However, in that state, the guard

$$p = x_1 \wedge \left(\bigwedge_{x \in X_Q(q) \setminus \{x_1\}} p \neq x \right)$$

and all more general guards will be satisfied after both inputs, while all other (G-NR) guards will not be satisfied. Therefore, it must either accept or reject after both S^π and $S^{\pi'}$.

If we set $\pi(1) = \pi'(1)$, the argument can be repeated for the second input symbol. By induction, $\pi = \pi'$, i.e., no two different paths can merge. Since there are $k!$ permutations, we require at least as many states. □

All results presented in this section are outlined in Fig. 11c.

5.4 Guard-Update Model

Theorem 10. *There exists a determinism-preserving* LIN*-automaton-only reduction from* (G-UP) *to* (G-UA).

Proof Sketch. The reduction splits all transitions of form

$$\frac{\lambda(p) \mid \bigwedge_{x \in X_Q(q) \setminus \{x_i\}} (p \neq x)}{x_i := p}$$

into two transitions with the same source and target states:

$$\frac{\lambda(p) \mid \bigwedge_{x \in X_Q(q)} (p \neq x)}{x_i := p} \text{ and } \frac{\lambda(p) \mid p = x_i}{-},$$

which are equivalent to the original and compatible with (G-UA). Since the transitions are mutually exclusive, the reduction preserves determinism. □

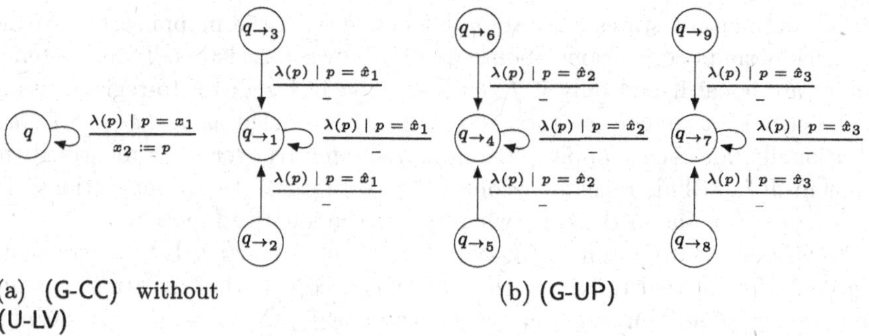

(a) (G-CC) without (U-LV)

(b) (G-UP)

Fig. 9. Sample transformation from a (G-CC) without (U-LV) transition to (G-UP) transitions. For this example, the set of mapping functions are defined as $\rightarrow_i := \langle x_1 = \hat{x}_j, q_2 = \hat{x}_k \mid j = (i \bmod 3) + 1, k = \lfloor \frac{i-1}{3} \rfloor + 1 \rangle$.

Theorem 11. *There exists a determinism-preserving* P*-automaton-only reduction from* (G-UA) *to* (G-FG).

Proof Sketch. The automaton reduction extends all guards to add the missing comparisons to registers. While this would normally result in an exponential number of transitions to describe all possible comparisons of parameters and registers, (G-UA) guarantees that a parameter can be equal to at most one register. A transition

$$\frac{\lambda(p) \mid \bigwedge_{x \in X_Q(q)} (p \neq x)}{a}$$

already satisfies (G-FG), while one of form

$$\frac{\lambda(p) \mid p = x_i}{-}$$

is equivalent to

$$\frac{\lambda(p) \mid p = x_i \wedge \bigwedge_{x \in X_Q(q) \setminus \{x_i\}} (p \neq x)}{-}.$$

□

Theorem 12. *There exists a determinism-preserving* EXP*-automaton-only reduction from* (G-CC) *without* (U-LV) *to* (G-UP).

Proof Sketch. The construction circumvents the lack of register-to-register operations by virtualizing the automaton's registers. Each state of the resulting automaton is associated with a register mapping, making register-to-register operations essentially "free".

To prepare the transformation, we add an additional register to the automaton, resulting in the register set $\hat{X}$ and define a family of functions $f_\rightarrow : X \rightarrow \hat{X}$ that defines the register mapping. There is a maximum of $|X|^{|X|+1}$ such functions, resulting in an exponential blow-up. For each function $f_\rightarrow$, we create a copy of the automaton's states. A state q associated with the mapping $f_{\rightarrow}$ is called $q_{\rightarrow}$. This permits conclusions about equality between registers. Two registers x_i and x_j are equal if and only if $f_{\rightarrow}(x_i) = f_{\rightarrow}(x_j)$. A register-to-register assignment becomes a change in storage: $x_i := x_j$ is modeled as $f_{\rightarrow}(x_i) := f_{\rightarrow}(x_j)$. Additionally, for each mapping function, a *scratch register* $\hat{x}_s$ is identified that is not in $\mathfrak{I}(f_{\rightarrow})$. This register becomes the sole target of write operations. The initial state remains in the copy where $f_{\rightarrow}$ is the identity function.

Each source automaton's transition $\langle q, q', \lambda, g, u\rangle$ now needs to be translated to account for the register virtualization. First, a copy of the transition is created for each copy of its source, i.e., for every mapping $f_{\rightarrow}$. Next, we extend the guard clause for each resulting copy, to ensure that the parameter p is compared to every register in the original automaton. We refer to the registers that p is not compared to as $\bar{X}$. Now, we generate guards

$$(g \wedge p = \bar{x}_1 \wedge p = \bar{x}_2 \wedge \cdots \wedge p = \bar{x}_{|\bar{X}|}), (g \wedge p \neq \bar{x}_1 \wedge p = \bar{x}_2 \wedge \cdots \wedge p = \bar{x}_{|\bar{X}|}),$$
$$(g \wedge p = \bar{x}_1 \wedge p \neq \bar{x}_2 \wedge \cdots \wedge p = \bar{x}_{|\bar{X}|}), (g \wedge p \neq \bar{x}_1 \wedge p \neq \bar{x}_2 \wedge \cdots \wedge p = \bar{x}_{|\bar{X}|}),$$
$$\ldots, (g \wedge p \neq \bar{x}_1 \wedge p \neq \bar{x}_2 \wedge \cdots \wedge p \neq \bar{x}_{|\bar{X}|})$$

and create a copy of the transition for each guard variant. We can now use the knowledge that $x_i = x_j \iff f_{\rightarrow}(x_i) = f_{\rightarrow}(x_j)$ to check if register-to-register comparisons are satisfied in the source state. If not, the transition copy is discarded. Otherwise, redundant comparisons can be omitted, resulting in either a single comparison $p = x_i$ or $\wedge_{x \in X}(p \neq x_i)$.

In the first case, we can generate transitions

$$\frac{\lambda(p) \mid p = f_{\rightarrow}(x_i)}{-}. \tag{EQ1}$$

In the second case, the guard is always satisfiable in the original automaton, but the value of p might still be stored in any register not $\in \mathfrak{I}(f_{\rightarrow})$ from a previous write operation. For each register $\bar{x} \notin \mathfrak{I}(f_{\rightarrow}) \cup \{\hat{x}_s\}$, we create a transition

$$\frac{\lambda(p) \mid p = \bar{x}_i}{-}. \tag{EQ2}$$

Finally, for the scratch register $\hat{x}_s$, we add the transition

$$\frac{\lambda(p) \mid \bigwedge_{\hat{x} \in \hat{X} \setminus \hat{x}_s} (p \neq \hat{x})}{\hat{x}_s := p}. \tag{NEQ}$$

Since the generated transitions are mutually exclusive, the resulting automaton will be deterministic if the original automaton was.

Finally, the update is transformed into a new register mapping $f_{\rightarrow'}$. The transition's target is then set to $q'_{\rightarrow'}$.

- For all registers that are not explicitly written to by the update, $f_{\rightarrow'}$ behaves identically to $f_{\rightarrow}$.

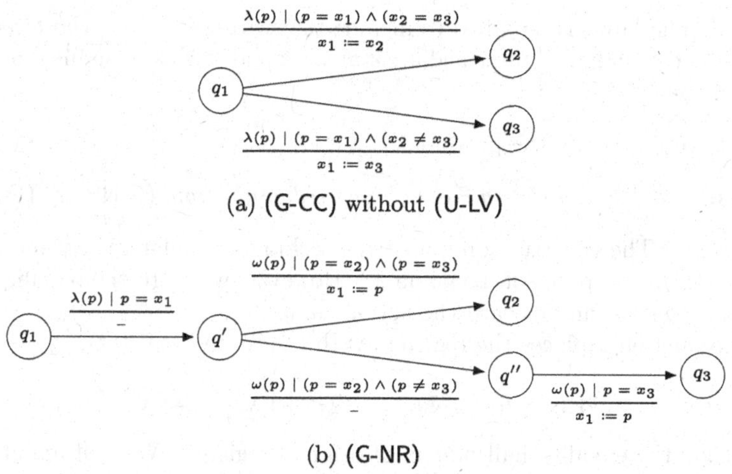

(a) (G-CC) without (U-LV)

(b) (G-NR)

Fig. 10. Sample transformation from two (G-CC) without (U-LV) transitions to multiple (G-NR) transitions.

- For each register that is assigned another register's values using $x_j := x_i$, the mapping function is modified such that $f_{\rightarrow'}(x_j) := f_{\rightarrow}(x_i)$.
- Each register that is assigned a parameter using $x_j := p$ must be handled differently for the three types of transitions. For EQ1-transitions, we can exploit that $p = x_i$, yielding $f_{\rightarrow'}(x_j) := f_{\rightarrow}(x_i)$. For EQ2-transitions, we obtain $f_{\rightarrow'}(x_j) := \bar{x}_i$. NEQ-transitions result in $f_{\rightarrow'}(x_j) := \hat{x}_s$. □

A small example for the transformation of a transition with an equality test is given in Fig. 9. Note that the illustration assumes only two registers, for more, an even larger blow-up would result.

Theorem 13. *There exists a determinism-preserving* P*-many-one reduction from* (G-CC) *without* (U-LV) *to* (G-NR).

Proof Sketch. For each transition, the reduction introduces up to $|X|^2$ "witness" values into the input to replace register-register operations, making the data reduction automaton dependent.

Given a transition with k register-to-register comparisons and ℓ register-to-register assignments, $k+\ell$ intermediate states are created. The original transition is stripped of all register-register operations. For each comparison $x_i = x_j$, an additional transition

$$\frac{\omega(p) \mid (p = x_i) \wedge (p = x_j)}{-}$$

is inserted and for each assignment $x_i := x_j$, a transition

$$\frac{\omega(p) \mid p = x_j}{x_i := p}$$

is created. The input is modified to include the "witness" values where required. To preserve determinism, intermediate states with identical incoming transitions can be merged. □

Figure 10 illustrates the process.

Theorem 14. *There exists a* P*-many-one reduction from* (G-NR) *to* (G-FG).

Proof Sketch. The construction employs a technique similar to register virtualization used in the proof of Theorem 12. However, we store the equality information in registers and discard the actual values.

The reduction replaces the registers with $|X|^2 - |X|$ registers

$$x_{1,2}, \bar{x}_{1,2}, x_{1,3}, \bar{x}_{1,3}, \ldots, x_{|X|-1,X}, \bar{x}_{|X|-1,X}$$

that encode the equality half-matrix of original registers. We will maintain the following invariants:

1. if in the original automaton for $i < j$, $x_i = x_j$, then $x_{i,j} = \bar{x}_{i,j}$,
2. if in the original automaton for $i < j$, $x_i \neq x_j$, then $x_{i,j} \neq \bar{x}_{i,j}$,
3. and for $i < j$ and i', j' with $i \neq i'$ or $j \neq j'$, $\{x_{i,j}, \bar{x}_{i,j}\} \cap \{x_{i',j'}, \bar{x}_{i',j'}\} = \emptyset$.

To avoid unnecessary concern for register order, we will also refer to $x_{i,j}$ as $x_{j,i}$. Using these registers, we can compare $x_i = x_j$ by using

$$\frac{\lambda(p) \mid (p = x_{i,j}) \wedge (p = \bar{x}_{i,j}) \wedge \bigwedge_{x \in X_Q(q) \setminus \{x_{i,j}, \bar{x}_{i,j}\}} (p \neq x)}{-}$$

and $x_i \neq x_j$ by using

$$\frac{\lambda(p) \mid (p = x_{i,j}) \wedge \bigwedge_{x \in X_Q(q) \setminus \{x_{i,j}\}} (p \neq x)}{-}.$$

Storing equalities needs to take into account the previous state. We store $x_i = x_j$ using two parallel transitions:

$$\frac{\lambda(p) \mid (p = x_{i,j}) \wedge (p = \bar{x}_{i,j}) \wedge \bigwedge_{x \in X_Q(q) \setminus \{x_{i,j}, \bar{x}_{i,j}\}} (p \neq x)}{-}$$

is used if the registers were previously equal and

$$\frac{\lambda(p) \mid (p = x_{i,j}) \wedge \bigwedge_{x \in X_Q(q) \setminus \{x_{i,j}\}} (p \neq x)}{\bar{x}_{i,j} := p}$$

is used if they were not. Storing an inequality $x_i \neq x_j$ is possible in one transition:

$$\frac{\lambda(p) \mid \bigwedge_{x \in X_Q(q) \setminus \{x_{i,j}\}} (p \neq x)}{\bar{x}_{i,j} := p}.$$

Now, all transitions need to be transformed. We distinguish two types of transitions, those that guarantee the equality of the parameter and a register (e.g., $p = x_i$) and those that do not. In the first case, all other instances of p in the guard can be replaced with x_i. Since $p = x_i$ is always satisfiable, the guard can be replaced with test of equalities between registers. Each such comparison is done in a separate transition. The assignment is then done by updating all relevant equalities.

If p is only compared negatively to some registers, the guard is always satisfiable and can be removed. However, it is unknown if p is equal to registers it was not compared to. For each group of equal registers p might be equal to, we non-deterministically select either equality or inequality and write the corresponding information to the half-matrix. □

We now demonstrate that under widely-held assumptions about complexity classes, no efficient reduction between (G-NR) and (G-UP) can exist.

Theorem 15. *If* NP $\neq$ PSPACE, *there exists no* P*-many-one reduction from* (G-FG) *to* (G-UP).

A similar result for deterministic (U-LV) automata has been proven by Cassel et al. [6]. Here, we demonstrate that such a reduction would allow us to construct an NP algorithm for a PSPACE-complete problem.

Proof. Assume that an NP-many-one reduction from (G-FG) to (G-UP) exists ($\star$). We can now construct an NP-algorithm for NonEmptiness of deterministic Demri-Lazić automata.

The following sequence of reductions reduces the Demri-Lazić automaton to a finite-memory automaton:

$$\begin{aligned}
& \text{(A-PT)+(U-LU)+(R-IN)+(G-NR): Demri-Lazić automaton} \\
\overset{\text{Thm. 2}}{\preceq}\ & \text{(A-PT)+(U-UL)+(R-IN)+(G-NR)} \\
\overset{\text{Thm. 14}}{\preceq}\ & \text{(A-PT)+(U-UL)+(R-IN)+(G-FG)} \\
\overset{(\star)}{\preceq}\ & \text{(A-PT)+(U-UL)+(R-IN)+(G-UP)} \\
\sqsubseteq\ & \text{(A-PT)+(U-UL)+(R-IE)+(G-UP)} \\
\overset{\text{Thm. 8}}{\preceq}\ & \text{(A-PS)+(U-UL)+(R-IE)+(G-UP): finite-memory automaton}
\end{aligned}$$

The finite-memory automaton's emptiness can be decided in NP; the result holds for the original automaton. Since the original problem is PSPACE-complete, NP = PSPACE. □

By using Turing reductions in the proof, permitting multiple oracle queries, we obtain statements conditional on the collapse of the polynomial hierarchy. These corollaries can be extended to arbitrary hierarchy levels.

Corollary 2. *If the polynomial hierarchy does not collapse, there exists no* PH-NonEmptiness*-Turing reduction from* (G-FG) *to* (G-UP).

Theorem 16. *There exists a* LIN*-automaton-only reduction from* (G-UA) *to* (G-UP).

Proof Sketch. For all transitions that store the parameter (e.g., using $x_i := p$), the reduction removes $(p \neq x_i)$ from the guard, yielding a (G-UP) automaton. This operation can remove determinism from the automaton. To demonstrate that this does preserve NONEMPTINESS, consider an input that does "overwrite" a register with its value. This would not be permissible in the original automaton. We demonstrate that an accepted input must exist that does not overwrite a value.

Let the register valuation prior to overwriting be χ, the previous state be q and the overwritten value be $\bar{d}$. Consider a modification of the register automaton in which χ is the initial valuation and q the initial state. This register automaton's language is closed under automorphisms on the data value set [15, Proposition 2]. Let $\bar{d}'$ be a value not occurring in the remaining input and $\sigma : D \to D$ be the automorphism defined by

$$\sigma(d) = \begin{cases} \bar{d}' & \text{if } d = \bar{d} \\ \bar{d} & \text{if } d = \bar{d}' \\ d & \text{otherwise.} \end{cases}$$

If σ is applied to the remaining input, it is still accepted, but no overwriting occurs. This process can be repeated for each instance of overwriting. The resulting input is accepted by both the original and the newly created automaton. □

All results presented in this section are outlined in Fig. 11d.

6 Application to Existing Models

We now employ the feature-wise reductions from Sect. 5 to define reductions between the existing models from Sect. 4.2.

Theorem 17. *Every initialized finite-memory automaton is a valid finite-memory automaton.*

Theorem 18. *There exists a determinism-preserving* LIN*-automaton-only reduction from finite-memory to Neven-Schwentick-Vianu automata.*

Proof. We apply the following sequence of reductions:

(A-PS)+(U-UL)+(R-IE)+(G-UP): finite-memory automaton
$\sqsubseteq$ (A-PT)+(U-UL)+(R-IE)+(G-UP)
$\preceq_{\text{Thm. 10}}$ (A-PT)+(U-UL)+(R-IE)+(G-UA): Neven-Schwentick-Vianu automaton

□

Theorem 19. *There exists a determinism-preserving* P*-data stable reduction from Neven-Schwentick-Vianu to Segoufin automata.*

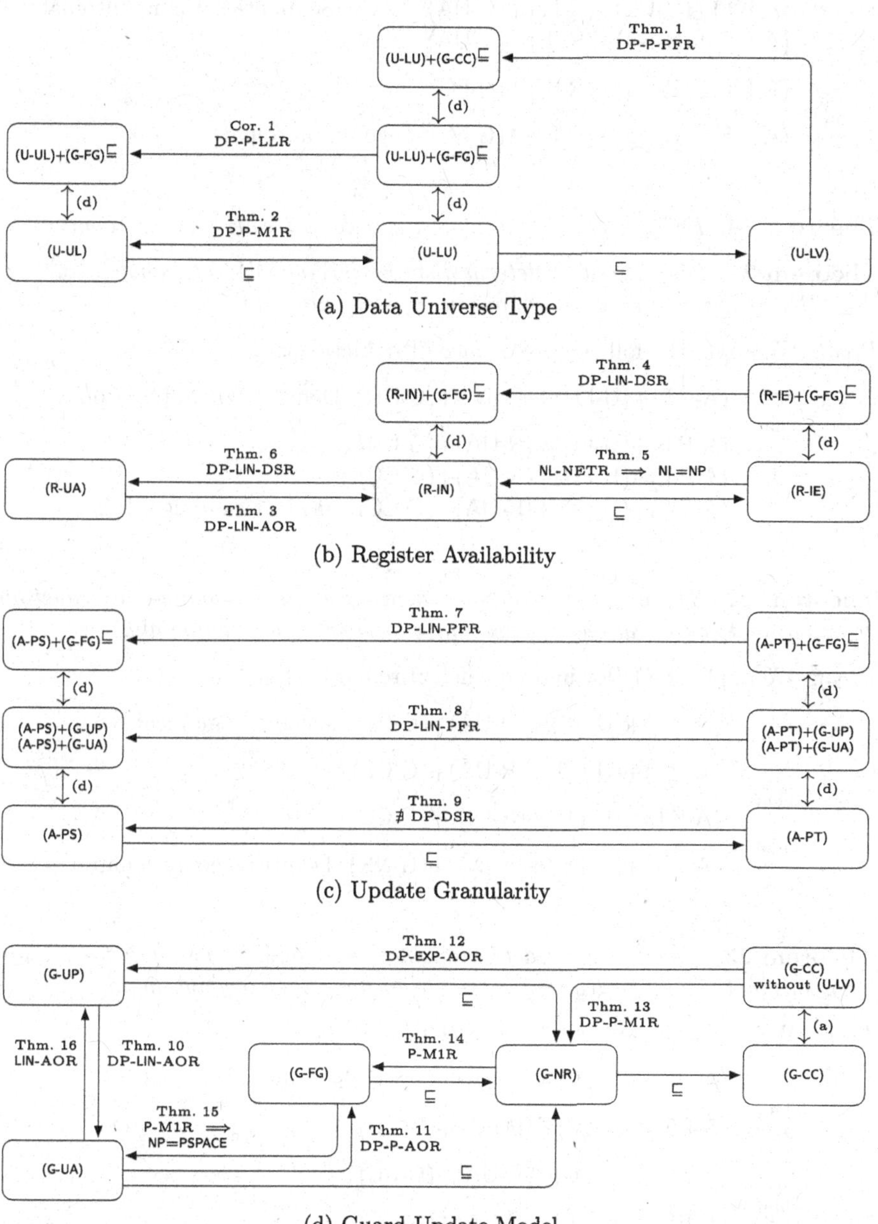

Fig. 11. Inequalities, reductions, and lower reduction complexity bounds between variants.

Proof. We apply the following sequence of reductions:

$$\begin{aligned}
& \textsf{(A-PT)+(U-UL)+(R-IE)+(G-UA)}\text{: Neven-Schwentick-Vianu automaton} \\
\sqsubseteq\ & \textsf{(A-PT)+(U-LU)+(R-IE)+(G-UA)} \\
\overset{\text{Thm. 11}}{\preceq}\ & \textsf{(A-PT)+(U-LU)+(R-IE)+(G-FG)} \\
\overset{\text{Thm. 4}}{\preceq}\ & \textsf{(A-PT)+(U-LU)+(R-IN)+(G-FG)}\text{: Segoufin automaton}
\end{aligned}$$

□

Theorem 20. *Every Segoufin automaton is a valid Demri-Lazić automaton.*

Theorem 21. *There exists a determinism-preserving* LIN*-data stable reduction from Demri-Lazić to succinct canonical register automata.*

Proof. We apply the following sequence of reductions:

$$\begin{aligned}
& \textsf{(A-PT)+(U-LU)+(R-IN)+(G-NR)}\text{: Demri-Lazić automaton} \\
\overset{\text{Thm. 6}}{\preceq}\ & \textsf{(A-PT)+(U-LU)+(R-UA)+(G-NR)} \\
\sqsubseteq\ & \textsf{(A-PT)+(U-LU)+(R-UA)+(G-CC)} \\
\sqsubseteq\ & \textsf{(A-PT)+(U-LV)+(R-UA)+(G-CC)}\text{: succinct canonical RA}
\end{aligned}$$

□

Theorem 22. *There exists a determinism-preserving* P*-many-one reduction from succinct canonical register automata to Demri-Lazić automata.*

Proof. We apply the following sequence of reductions:

$$\begin{aligned}
& \textsf{(A-PT)+(U-LV)+(R-UA)+(G-CC)}\text{: succinct canonical RA} \\
\overset{\text{Thm. 1}}{\preceq}\ & \textsf{(A-PT)+(U-LU)+(R-UA)+(G-CC)} \\
\overset{\text{Thm. 3}}{\preceq}\ & \textsf{(A-PT)+(U-LU)+(R-IN)+(G-CC)} \\
\overset{\text{Thm. 13}}{\preceq}\ & \textsf{(A-PT)+(U-LU)+(R-IN)+(G-NR)}\text{: Demri-Lazić automaton}
\end{aligned}$$

□

Theorem 23. *There exists a determinism-preserving* EXP*-many-one reduction from succinct canonical register automata to finite-memory automata.*

Proof. We apply the following sequence of reductions:

$$\begin{aligned}
& \textsf{(A-PT)+(U-LV)+(R-UA)+(G-CC)}\text{: succinct canonical RA} \\
\overset{\text{Thm. 7}}{\preceq}\ & \textsf{(A-PS)+(U-LV)+(R-UA)+(G-CC)} \\
\overset{\text{Thm. 1}}{\preceq}\ & \textsf{(A-PS)+(U-LU)+(R-UA)+(G-CC)} \\
\overset{\text{Thm. 2}}{\preceq}\ & \textsf{(A-PS)+(U-UL)+(R-UA)+(G-CC)} \\
\overset{\text{Thm. 3}}{\preceq}\ & \textsf{(A-PS)+(U-UL)+(R-IN)+(G-CC)} \\
\sqsubseteq\ & \textsf{(A-PS)+(U-UL)+(R-IE)+(G-CC)} \\
\overset{\text{Thm. 12}}{\preceq}\ & \textsf{(A-PS)+(U-UL)+(R-IE)+(G-UP)}\text{: finite-memory automaton}
\end{aligned}$$

□

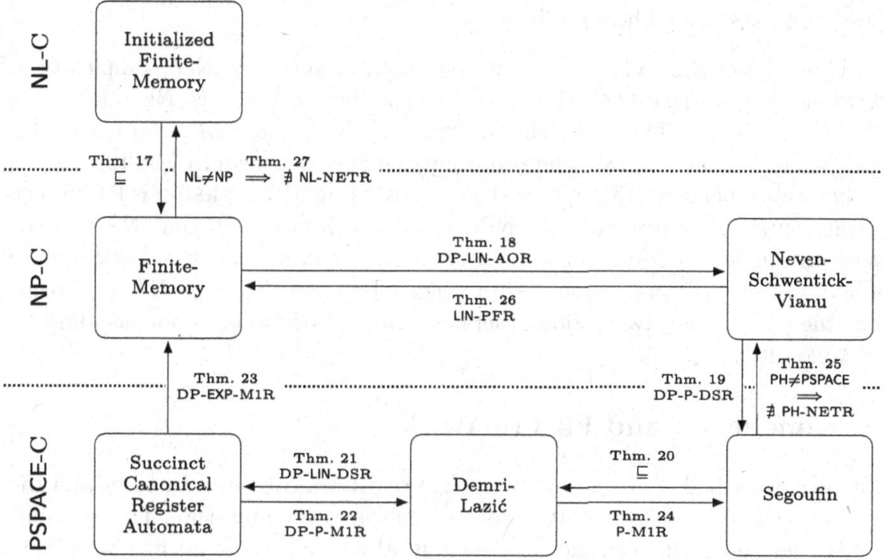

Fig. 12. Reductions between models and the complexity of NONEMPTINESS.

Theorem 24. *There exists a* P*-many-one reduction from Demri-Lazić to Segoufin automata.*

Proof. Follows from Theorem 14.

Theorem 25. *If the polynomial hierarchy does not collapse, there exists no* PH-NONEMPTINESS-*Turing reduction from Segoufin to Neven-Schwentick-Vianu automata.*

Proof. Follows from Corollary 2.

Theorem 26. *There exists a* LIN*-prefix free reduction from Neven-Schwentick-Vianu to finite-memory automata.*

Proof. We apply the following sequence of reductions:

$$\begin{aligned} &\text{(A-PT)+(U-UL)+(R-IE)+(G-UA): Neven-Schwentick-Vianu automaton} \\ \overset{\text{Thm. 8}}{\preceq}\ &\text{(A-PS)+(U-UL)+(R-IE)+(G-UA)} \\ \overset{\text{Thm. 16}}{\preceq}\ &\text{(A-PS)+(U-UL)+(R-IE)+(G-UP)} \\ &\text{(A-PS)+(U-UL)+(R-IE)+(G-UP): finite-memory automaton} \end{aligned}$$

□

Theorem 27. *If* NL $\neq$ NP, *there exists no* NL-NONEMPTINESS-*Turing reduction from finite-memory to initialized finite-memory automata.*

Proof. Follows from Theorem 5.

Three categories of model can be distinguished by the complexity of deciding NonEmptiness: those for which the problem is NL-, NP-, and PSPACE-complete. These match the "register disciplines" SF, $S\#_0$, and MF by Murawski et al. [17,18]. The resulting structure is shown in Fig. 12.

For finite-memory automata and above, deciding Membership is P-complete for deterministic automata and NP-complete otherwise. P- and NP-hardness were proven for finite-memory automata. For every model, the Membership of a word can – depending on determinism – be verified in P or NP by "executing" the automaton. Reductions therefore are of little interest for deciding the Membership problem.

7 Conclusion and Future Work

We have described a taxonomy for several register automaton features and successfully applied it to several types of automaton in the literature. The examined feature variants have been shown to be mutually reducible, as outlined in Fig. 11. This shows that all variants have identical expressiveness. We also charted the complexity of the NonEmptiness problem for different features and identified three categories of automaton, those for which it is NL-, NP-, and PSPACE-complete. The possibility of transition guards to be unsatisfiable for certain register valuations defines the difference between the first two, while the ability to store the same value in multiple registers defining the difference between the latter[1]. This implies that the size of automaton required to recognize a language varies between models, i.e., automata with PSPACE-complete NonEmptiness require less size to recognize a language.

Some register automaton formalisms, such as M-automata [15] and the automata defined by Benedikt et al. [2] cannot be described using our taxonomy. The former bears more similarity to pebble automata [19], while the latter's use of states is dissimilar to any other model's. In future work, our taxonomy could be extended to capture these formalisms.

Semantic extensions that strictly increase expressiveness such as register pushdown automata [9], fresh-register automata [24], register automata with non-deterministic reassignment [16] or with linear arithmetic [8] and symbolic register automata [10] have been proposed as extensions to the classical register automaton model studied by us. Again, these extensions could be taxonomized to permit the transfer of applicable results.

References

1. Babari, P., Droste, M., Perevoshchikov, V.: Weighted register automata and weighted logic on data words. In: Sampaio, A., Wang, F. (eds.) ICTAC 2016. LNCS, vol. 9965, pp. 370–384. Springer, Cham (2016). https://doi.org/10.1007/978-3-319-46750-4_21

[1] Segoufin mistakenly attributes this to the presence of labels in [23].

2. Benedikt, M., Ley, C., Puppis, G.: What you must remember when processing data words. In: Laender, A.H.F., Lakshmanan, L.V.S. (eds.) Proceedings of the 4th Alberto Mendelzon International Workshop on Foundations of Data Management. CEUR Workshop Proceedings, vol. 619, pp. 11.1–11.8. CEUR-WS.org, Aachen (2010). http://ceur-ws.org/Vol-619/paper11.pdf
3. Bojańczyk, M., Klin, B., Lasota, S.: Automata theory in nominal sets. Log. Methods Comput. Sci. **10**(4), 1–44 (2014). https://doi.org/10.2168/LMCS-10(3:4)2014
4. Cassel, S., Howar, F., Jonsson, B.: RALib: a LearnLib extension for inferring EFSMs. In: Proceedings of the 4th International Workshop on Design and Implementation of Formal Tools and Systems (2015). https://www.faculty.ece.vt.edu/chaowang/difts2015/papers/paper_5.pdf
5. Cassel, S., Howar, F., Jonsson, B., Merten, M., Steffen, B.: A succinct canonical register automaton model. In: Bultan, T., Hsiung, P.-A. (eds.) ATVA 2011. LNCS, vol. 6996, pp. 366–380. Springer, Heidelberg (2011). https://doi.org/10.1007/978-3-642-24372-1_26
6. Cassel, S., Howar, F., Jonsson, B., Merten, M., Steffen, B.: A succinct canonical register automaton model. J. Log. Algebr. Methods Program. **84**(1), 54–66 (2015). https://doi.org/10.1016/j.jlamp.2014.07.004
7. Cassel, S., Howar, F., Jonsson, B., Steffen, B.: Active learning for extended finite state machines. Formal Aspects Comput. **28**(2), 233–263 (2016). https://doi.org/10.1007/s00165-016-0355-5
8. Chen, Y.F., Lengál, O., Tan, T., Wu, Z.: Register automata with linear arithmetic. In: 2017 32nd Annual ACM/IEEE Symposium on Logic in Computer Science (LICS), pp. 1–12. IEEE, June 2017. https://doi.org/10.1109/LICS.2017.8005111
9. Cheng, E.Y.C., Kaminski, M.: Context-free languages over infinite alphabets. Acta Inform. **35**(3), 245–267 (1998). https://doi.org/10.1007/s002360050120
10. D'Antoni, L., Ferreira, T., Sammartino, M., Silva, A.: Symbolic register automata. In: Dillig, I., Tasiran, S. (eds.) CAV 2019. LNCS, vol. 11561, pp. 3–21. Springer, Cham (2019). https://doi.org/10.1007/978-3-030-25540-4_1
11. Demri, S., Lazić, R.: LTL with the freeze quantifier and register automata. ACM Trans. Comput. Log. **10**(3), 16:1-16:30 (2009). https://doi.org/10.1145/1507244.1507246
12. Howar, F.: Active learning of interface programs. Ph.D. thesis, Technische Universität Dortmund, June 2012. https://doi.org/10.17877/DE290R-4817
13. Isberner, M., Howar, F., Steffen, B.: Learning register automata: from languages to program structures. Mach. Learn. **96**(2), 65–98 (2013). https://doi.org/10.1007/s10994-013-5419-7
14. Isberner, M., Howar, F., Steffen, B.: The open-source LearnLib. In: Kroening, D., Păsăreanu, C.S. (eds.) CAV 2015. LNCS, vol. 9206, pp. 487–495. Springer, Cham (2015). https://doi.org/10.1007/978-3-319-21690-4_32
15. Kaminski, M., Francez, N.: Finite-memory automata. Theor. Comput. Sci. **134**(2), 329–363 (1994). https://doi.org/10.1016/0304-3975(94)90242-9
16. Kaminski, M., Zeitlin, D.: Finite-memory automata with non-deterministic reassignment. Int. J. Found. Comput. Sci. **21**(05), 741–760 (2010). https://doi.org/10.1142/S0129054110007532
17. Murawski, A.S., Ramsay, S.J., Tzevelekos, N.: Reachability in pushdown register automata. In: Csuhaj-Varjú, E., Dietzfelbinger, M., Ésik, Z. (eds.) MFCS 2014. LNCS, vol. 8634, pp. 464–473. Springer, Heidelberg (2014). https://doi.org/10.1007/978-3-662-44522-8_39

18. Murawski, A.S., Ramsay, S.J., Tzevelekos, N.: Reachability in pushdown register automata. J. Comput. Syst. Sci **87**, 58–83 (2017). https://doi.org/10.1016/j.jcss.2017.02.008
19. Neven, F., Schwentick, T., Vianu, V.: Finite state machines for strings over infinite alphabets. ACM Trans. Comput. Logic **5**(3), 403–435 (2004). https://doi.org/10.1145/1013560.1013562
20. Post, E.L.: Recursively enumerable sets of positive integers and their decision problems. Bull. Am. Math. Soc. **50**(5), 284–316 (1944). https://doi.org/10.1090/S0002-9904-1944-08111-1
21. Saint-Andre, P.: Extensible messaging and presence protocol (XMPP): Core. RFC 6120, RFC Editor, March 2011. https://doi.org/10.17487/RFC6120
22. Sakamoto, H., Ikeda, D.: Intractability of decision problems for finite-memory automata. Theor. Comput. Sci. **231**(2), 297–308 (2000). https://doi.org/10.1016/S0304-3975(99)00105-X
23. Segoufin, L.: Automata and logics for words and trees over an infinite alphabet. In: Ésik, Z. (ed.) CSL 2006. LNCS, vol. 4207, pp. 41–57. Springer, Heidelberg (2006). https://doi.org/10.1007/11874683_3
24. Tzevelekos, N.: Fresh-register automata. In: Proceedings of the 38th Annual ACM SIGPLAN-SIGACT Symposium on Principles of Programming Languages, pp. 295–306. ACM, New York (2011). https://doi.org/10.1145/1926385.1926420

Author Index

Printed in the United States
by Baker & Taylor Publisher Services